May Sinclair

May Sinclair

A Modern Victorian

SUZANNE RAITT

CLARENDON PRESS · OXFORD

OXFORD
UNIVERSITY PRESS

Great Clarendon Street, Oxford OX2 6DP

Oxford University Press is a department of the University of Oxford.
It furthers the University's objective of excellence in research, scholarship,
and education by publishing worldwide in

Oxford New York

Athens Auckland Bangkok Bogotá Buenos Aires Calcutta
Cape Town Chennai Dar es Salaam Delhi Florence Hong Kong Istanbul
Karachi Kuala Lumpur Madrid Melbourne Mexico City Mumbai
Nairobi Paris São Paulo Singapore Taipei Tokyo Toronto Warsaw

and associated companies in Berlin Ibadan

Oxford is a registered trade mark of Oxford University Press
in the UK and in certain other countries

Published in the United States
by Oxford University Press Inc., New York

British Library Cataloguing in Publication Data

Data available

Library of Congress Cataloging in Publication Data

Raitt, Suzanne.
May Sinclair : a modern Victorian / Suzanne Raitt.
p. cm.
Includes bibliographical references and index.
1. Sinclair, May. 2. Feminism and literature—England—History—20th century. 3.
Women and literature—England—History—20th century. 4. Novelists, English—20th
century—Biography. 5. Feminists—Great Britain—Biography. 6. Modernism
(Literature)—England. I. Title.
PR6037.I73 Z84 2000   823'.912—dc21   99-055119   [B]

ISBN 0-19-812298-5

1 3 5 7 9 10 8 6 4 2

Typeset in Fournier
by Jayvee, Trivandrum, India
Printed in Great Britain
on acid-free paper by
Biddles Ltd.,
Guildford and King's Lynn

For my father,
the first biographer I ever met

ACKNOWLEDGEMENTS

—

I owe a great debt of gratitude to May Sinclair's literary executors, her great-nephews Frank and Peter, and her great-niece the late Naomi Assinder, for allowing me unlimited access to the papers and photographs in their collection, for reading the final manuscript, and for permission to quote from May Sinclair's published and unpublished work. Thanks too to Jamie Fergusson for helping me find the Assinders.

Many individuals and institutions on both sides of the Atlantic have given me help, support, and advice throughout the long gestation of this project. I am grateful to Queen Mary and Westfield College, University of London, and to the University of Michigan for research leaves and funding that allowed me to work on the manuscript. The British Academy, the English Department at Queen Mary and Westfield College, and the Institute for Research on Women and Gender at the University of Michigan all gave me small personal research grants that enabled me to travel to vital archives. In 1998–9 I was lucky enough to be awarded a National Endowment for the Humanities Fellowship at the National Humanities Center, where I completed the book. I am grateful to all the staff at the Center for their unfailing cheerfulness and efficiency, and I want particularly to thank the librarians, Alan Tuttle, Jean Houston, and especially Eliza Robertson, who spent hours poring through databases and downloading bibliographical aides for me.

Many people read and commented on earlier drafts of part or all of this book. I am grateful to Nicola Beisel, Hermione Lee, Ruthie Petrie, Jacqueline Rose, P. A. Skantze, Trudi Tate, David Thomas, David Trotter, and Patricia Yaeger, for all their help and advice. The Biography Group at the National Humanities Center was an ideal environment in which to work through many of the difficulties I encountered during the final stages of the writing, and I wish to thank Janet Beizer, Jon Bush, Ed Friedman, R. W. B. Lewis, Elizabeth McHenry, Wilfrid Prest, Bert and Anne Wyatt-Brown, and especially Rochelle Gurstein, Marilynn Richtarik, and Ashraf Rushdy, who literally read pages as they tumbled out of the printer. Thanks to Tony La Vopa for always knowing, and improving on, what I wanted to say, and for teaching me so much about biography, philosophy, and the pleasures of intellectual exchange. Liz Barnes patiently read every word of this manuscript, and many more that did not make the final version. Her influence and insight are apparent on every page. Thanks too to the following people for advice, references, and practical help: Nathalie Blondel, Simon Buxton, Helen Carr, Elizabeth Crawford, Jane Hiddleston, Donna K. Johnston, Matthew Kibble, Michael Millgate, Alex Owen, Morag Shiach, and Peter Slee. I am grateful to Maggie Funderburg, and Jack and Jackie Gregory for their kindness during my stay in Philadelphia, to Anne Treisman and Daniel Kahneman for their hospitality and generosity in Manhattan, and to Irene Rosenfeld for making my stay in Chapel Hill such a happy one. Thanks also to Jason Freeman, Sophie Goldsworthy, Frances Whistler, and especially Kim Scott Walwyn at Oxford University Press, for all their help and advice.

I am grateful to audiences at the following places for their comments, criticism, and advice: the English Department, Stanford University; the Gender, Society and Culture Seminar, Birkbeck College, University of London; the Graduate Research Seminar, University of Glasgow; Twentieth-Century Graduate Seminar, University of Cambridge (especially Maud Ellmann and Heather Glen); the Modernism Research Seminar, University of North London (especially Claire Buck, Carolyn Burdett, and Lyndsey Stonebridge); Cardiff Critical Theory Seminar, University of Wales; Seminar on Culture and Psychoanalysis, King's College Research Centre, University of Cambridge; the Narrative Conference, Northwestern University; the Legacy of the Brontës Conference, University of Leeds; the Orlando Project's Women and History Conference, University of Alberta, Edmonton; the Cultural Contexts of Modernism Conference, Centre for European Studies, University of London; Romance Revisited, Women's Studies Network Conference, University of Lancaster.

I am also indebted to staff at the following libraries and archives, who have given me invaluable assistance in locating and in many cases xeroxing published and unpublished material: the Annenberg Rare Book and Manuscript Library, Van Pelt-Dietrich Library Center, University of Pennsylvania, especially Nancy Shawcross and Daniel Traister; the British Library; Senate House Library, University of London; Queen Mary and Westfield College Library; the London Library; Harlan Hatcher Library, University of Michigan; the Earl G. Swem Library, College of William and Mary; the Davis Library, University of North Carolina at Chapel Hill, especially

Tom Nixon; the Fawcett Library; the Bodleian Library, Oxford; the Berg Collection, New York Public Library; the John Rylands Library, University of Manchester, especially Janet Wallwork; Cheltenham Ladies' College Archive Department, especially Janet Johnstone; the Thomas Hardy Memorial Collection, Dorset County Museum, especially Richard de Peyer; Division of Rare and Manuscript Collections, Cornell University Library; The Brotherton Collection, Leeds University Library; the Archives, Emmanuel College, University of Cambridge, especially Janet Morris and Frank Stubbings; Harry Ransom Humanities Research Center, the University of Texas at Austin; the Macmillan Archive, University of Reading; the Rare Book and Manuscript Library, Columbia University; the Charles Deering McCormick Library of Special Collections, Northwestern University Library; the Houghton Library, Harvard University; the Huntington Library, San Marino, California; University of Illinois Library at Urbana-Champaign; the Library of University College London; the Beinecke Rare Book and Manuscript Library; the Special Collections Department, University of Virginia Library; Trinity College, University of Cambridge; the Archive Department at King's School, Canterbury; the Bertrand Russell Archives, Mills Memorial Library, McMaster University; the Bancroft Library, University of California at Berkeley; the Picture Library, National Portrait Gallery, London; the Bentley Library, University of Michigan.

Thank you to the following people for their support, love, and help during the writing of this book: my family, Janet Hiddleston, Alan Raitt, Jim Hiddleston, Lia Raitt, Claire Raitt, Anna and Jane Hiddleston, Nicky Mooney, and Alain Galloni; Sarah Ahmed, Caroline Ash, Phillip Blumberg, Matthew Fink, Elizabeth Gregory, Rebecca Hall, Stephen Heath, Mandy Hetherton, Diana Hinds, Caroline Kay, Arlene Keizer, Vasant Kumar, Brenda K. Marshall, Elizabeth Maslen, Amanda Mitchison, Anita Norich, Yopie Prins, P. A. Skantze, Simonette Strachey, Gill Thomas, Valerie Traub, Emma Whitlock, and Patsy Yaeger. Thanks are inadequate to Liz Barnes for her companionship, her generosity, her *joie de vivre*, and for coming with me to the wrong Salcombe.

*

Unpublished material is reproduced by kind permission of the curators of the following collections: for letters to Sinclair from a range of correspondents, and for unpublished manuscripts, the May Sinclair Papers, Rare Book and Manuscript Library, University of Pennsylvania; for letters from May Sinclair to Dorothea Beale, the Archive Department, Cheltenham Ladies' College; for letters from Sinclair to Thomas Hardy, the Thomas Hardy

Memorial Collection, Dorset County Museum; for letters from Sinclair to Evelyn Sharp, Linda Villari, and Gilbert Murray, the Bodleian Library, Oxford; for a letter from Sinclair to Violet Hunt, the Division of Rare and Manuscript Collections, Cornell University Library; for a letter from Sinclair to Clement Shorter, the Brotherton Collection, Leeds University Library; for letters from Sinclair to Lucy and Henry Melvill Gwatkin, and Henry Melvill Gwatkin to Sinclair, the Master and Fellows of Emmanuel College, Cambridge; letters from Sinclair to Violet Hunt, Charlotte Mew, J. B. Pinker, and Ford Madox Hueffer, the Berg Collection of English and American Literature, the New York Public Library, Astor, Lenox and Tilden Foundations; for letters from Sinclair to Richard Gilder, Edward Garnett, E. Duneka, Professor Macdonald, Marie Belloc Lowndes, and Curtis Brown, Harry Ransom Humanities Research Center, the University of Texas at Austin; for letters from Sinclair to Katharine Tynan Hinkson, the Tynan/Hinkson Collection, John Rylands University Library of Manchester; for letters from Sinclair to Macmillan, the Macmillan Archive, University of Reading; for a letter from Sinclair to Louis N. Parker, the Louis Napoleon Parker Papers, Rare Book and Manuscript Library, Columbia University; for letters from Sinclair to Otto Kyllmann, the Charles Deering McCormick Library of Special Collections, Northwestern University Library; for letters from Sinclair to Witter Bynner, Sarah Orne Jewett, and William Rothenstein, and a letter from Bynner to Sinclair, the Houghton Library, Harvard University; for letters from Sinclair to Annie Fields, the Huntington Library, San Marino, California; for letters from Sinclair to H. G. Wells, University of Illinois Library at Urbana-Champaign. Unpublished letters from Ezra Pound to May Sinclair are copyright © 2000 by Mary de Rachewiltz and Omar Pound, and are used by permission of New Directions Publishing Corporation. Every effort has been made to trace copyright holders. The author and publisher would be grateful for information on those that we have not been able to trace.

*

Photographs are reproduced by kind permission of the following: cover photograph and Plates 1, 2, 3, 5, 8, 9, 12, 20, 21, and 24, the Rare Book and Manuscript Library, University of Pennsylvania; Plate 4, the Archive Department, the Cheltenham Ladies' College; Plate 7, the Master and Fellows of Emmanuel College, Cambridge; Plate 14, the British Library, from *Temple Magazine*, 2 (1897–8), 867, shelf mark P. P. 6004.gmt; Plates 15, 16, 17, and 18, the National Portrait Gallery, London; Plates 11, 19, 22, and 23, Frank, Peter, and the late Naomi Assinder; Plate 25, the Tynan/Hinkson Collection, John Rylands University Library of Manchester. Plate

6 is from Anthony C. Deane, *Time Remembered* (London: Faber and Faber, 1945); Plate 10 is from *Bookman* (London), 14 (Sept. 1898), 151; and Plate 13 is illustration no. 1, by Arthur I. Keller, from May Sinclair, *The Creators* (New York: Holt, 1910), also published with the first instalment of *The Creators, Century Illustrated Monthly Magazine*, 79 (Nov. 1909), 100–16.

CONTENTS

=

LIST OF PLATES

—

LIST OF ABBREVIATIONS

—

TEXTS BY MAY SINCLAIR

I have used the first American edition of May Sinclair's texts for citations, apart from the early volumes of poetry, which never appeared in the USA.

AC   *Audrey Craven* (1897; 1st American edn. New York: Holt, 1906)
AS   *Anne Severn and the Fieldings* (New York: Macmillan, 1922)
C   *The Creators: A Comedy* (New York: Century, 1910)
DF   *The Divine Fire* (New York: Holt, 1904)
EV   *Essays in Verse* (London: Kegan Paul, Trench, Trübner & Co., 1891)
H   *The Helpmate* (New York: Holt, 1907)
HF   *Life and Death of Harriett Frean* (New York: Macmillan, 1922)
I   'The Intercessor', in *The Intercessor and Other Stories* (New York: Macmillan, 1932)
JI   *A Journal of Impressions in Belgium* (New York: Macmillan, 1915)
KT   *Kitty Tailleur* [American title *The Immortal Moment: The Story of Kitty Tailleur*] (New York: Doubleday, Page & Co., 1908)
MO   *Mary Olivier: A Life* (New York: Macmillan, 1919)
N   *Nakiketas, and Other Poems* [published under the name 'Julian Sinclair'] (London: Kegan Paul, Trench & Co., 1886)
R   *The Romantic* (New York: Macmillan, 1920)
TB   *The Three Brontës* (Boston and New York: Houghton Mifflin, 1912)
TH   *The Tree of Heaven* (New York: Macmillan, 1917)
TS   *The Three Sisters* (New York: Macmillan, 1914)

ARCHIVES

EC   Emmanuel College, Cambridge
HA   Berg Collection of English and American Literature, The New York Public Library, Astor, Lenox and Tilden Foundations
HL   The Houghton Library, Harvard University

HR Harry Ransom Humanities Research Center, the University of Texas at Austin

JR John Rylands University Library of Manchester

UP May Sinclair Papers, Rare Book and Manuscript Library, University of Pennsylvania

SINCLAIR FAMILY TREE

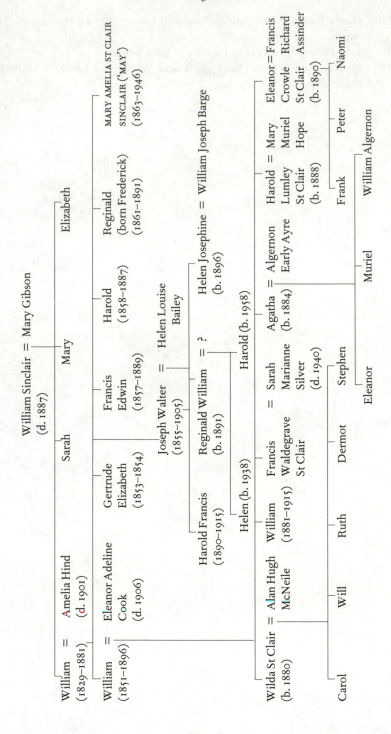

Introduction

===

IN 1912, May Sinclair wrote of one of her favourite authors, Charlotte Brontë, that she had

an outer life where no great and moving event ever came, saving only death (Charlotte's marriage hardly counts beside it); an outer life of a strange and almost oppressive simplicity and silence; and an inner life, tumultuous and profound in suffering, a life to all appearances frustrate, where all nourishment of the emotions was reduced to the barest allowance a woman's heart can depend on and yet live. (TB, 192)

Sinclair's description of the meagreness of Brontë's life is full of a peculiarly imaginative sympathy. Although Sinclair was born in 1863, eight years after Brontë's death, there were many similarities between her life and that of her illustrious predecessor. Like Brontë, Sinclair became famous as a novelist relatively late in life; like Brontë, she wrote vividly about the frustrating and unfulfilling conditions of women's lives; and like Brontë's, her life was punctuated by a mournful series of deaths (both women outlived all their five siblings). As Sinclair's friend Janet Hogarth noted, 'there are aspects of Miss Sinclair's work which almost suggest a Brontë incarnation'.[1]

But Sinclair's life was in some respects even lonelier. Instinctively a radical and a modernizer, she grew up fighting her mother for the right to think for herself. Amelia Sinclair wanted a daughter who was quiet and demure, and who did not presume to challenge the opinions of others. Torn between her own rebellious instincts and her desire to please her mother by keeping herself in check, Sinclair came to see intimacy as the enemy of freedom. Her isolation bore silent witness to the peculiar difficulties that faced intellectual women of her generation, as the world around them struggled to come to terms with challenges to religious, political, and literary orthodoxies, and widespread demands for equality between the sexes.

---

[1] Janet E. Courtney [née Hogarth], *The Women of My Time* (London: Lovat Dickson, 1934), 53. See Ch. 4 for a full discussion of the resemblances between Sinclair and Charlotte Brontë.

Although Sinclair was a well-known and respected public figure in the early years of the twentieth century, she spent most of her time alone. She died childless and unmarried; she was reticent and withdrawn; she passed her days working diligently on novels that, even when they seemed to court scandal (like *The Helpmate* in 1907, which opened with a conversation between a honeymooning couple lying in their bed), extolled the virtues of sexual pleasure only when it was an expression of deep spiritual communion. She was a marginal figure in the lives of countless famous writers (Thomas Hardy, Henry James, Edith Wharton, Ezra Pound, H.D., Katherine Mansfield, Virginia Woolf, Ford Madox Ford) but she was central to no one's. Many people knew her slightly, or even fairly well, but very few responded strongly to her. From the outside she seemed to be living a life, like Brontë's, of 'a strange and almost oppressive simplicity and silence', a silence which nobody, apparently, cared to penetrate.

But no one's life is silent to themselves. Like Charlotte Brontë, Sinclair was preoccupied with the storms of the 'inner life'. Her memories of childhood and her adult reading fed her imagination as she wrote novel after novel about women's struggles with their sexual desires, the demands of creativity, and the friction of family relationships. When she discovered psychoanalysis in the years before the First World War, she embraced it immediately as a language for the busy intensity of even the most unassuming existence. From time to time the ferocity of her unexpressed emotions resulted in awkward intrusions into the public world: her foray with an ambulance unit out to the front lines during the first weeks of the war, for example. Episodes such as her adolescent refusal to give up philosophy, or her defence of imagism in the face of widespread critical opposition, revealed the existence of an intellectual integrity and stubbornness nourished by a strong and anguished sense of her self.

Her allegiances were complex and contradictory. We remember her now, if we remember her at all, as the author of the 1918 review of the first volumes of Dorothy Richardson's novel *Pilgrimage* in which the phrase 'stream of consciousness' was applied for the first time to literature.[2] She has often been included among the pioneers of literary modernism, both as a critic and as a novelist. In *Mary Olivier: A Life* (1919) and *Life and Death of Harriett Frean* (1922) (both revived by Virago Press in 1980) she experimented with recreating the crowded interior of the mind in the same sort of fragmentary prose

---

[2] See May Sinclair, 'The Novels of Dorothy Richardson', *Egoist*, 5 (Apr. 1918), 57–9; repr. *Little Review*, 4 (Apr. 1918), 3–11, as 'Introduction' to Dorothy Richardson, *Pointed Roofs* (New York: Knopf, 1919), and in Bonnie Kime Scott (ed.), *The Gender of Modernism: A Critical Anthology* (Bloomington, Ind.: Indiana University Press, 1990), 442–8 [the edn. I cite in this book].

that Richardson was using in *Pilgrimage*, Katherine Mansfield in short stories such as 'Prelude' (1918), or Virginia Woolf in *Jacob's Room* (1922).[3] But, although Sinclair identified with what her radical contemporaries were trying to do, she was also something of an anomaly. Older by a generation than Dorothy Richardson, Ezra Pound, H.D., Rebecca West, Katherine Mansfield, and Virginia Woolf, she was already a best-selling author when modernism began to gather force in the years during and after the First World War. The novel that made her famous, *The Divine Fire* (1904), was a lengthy exposé of the commercialization of the book trade along the lines of George Gissing's *New Grub Street* (1891). In order to be counted among the earliest proponents of literary modernism, Sinclair had to reconstruct herself and her aspirations as a novelist. She was acutely sensitive to cultural change, and eager to be regarded as one of the pioneers of literary innovation.

But Sinclair's intellectual adventurousness often had the awkwardly schematic abruptness of a new and frightened convert. After all, Sinclair's emotional and epistemological roots extended far back into the nineteenth century, and throughout her life she remained preoccupied with issues such as heredity and evolution, concerns that to many of her younger friends seemed outdated. People were struck by her 'primly virginal' demeanour and her adherence to the formal social customs of her childhood.[4] When Dorothy Richardson and her husband Alan Odle attended a dinner party at Sinclair's, they were amused by Sinclair's discomfiture when her guests refused to leave the table and adjourn to another room for coffee.[5] She was ill-suited to the informal lifestyles of her literary associates, even if intellectually and philosophically she was fully in sympathy with what they were trying to do. Caught in the contradictions of her historical moment, she found it hard to find a form of companionship that made both intellectual and psychological sense. She approached friendships with both enthusiasm and suspicion. For her they were awkward negotiations of the conflict between her need for reassurance and her desire to defend herself against misunderstanding, and unwanted demands.

Sinclair's anxiety to protect her own privacy meant that her few dealings with biographers were uncomfortable and antagonistic. Several months

---

[3] Virago also published *The Three Sisters* in 1982. At the time of writing only *Life and Death of Harriett Frean* remains in print in the UK, and none of Sinclair's novels are in print in the USA (*The Three Brontës*, 1912, *Tales Told by Simpson*, 1930, and *The Intercessor and Other Stories*, UK 1931, USA 1932, are currently available through the reprint service).

[4] See Arnold Bennett, *The Journal of Arnold Bennett* (Garden City, NY: Doubleday, 1932), 410–11: 'I rather liked this prim virgin. Great sense.'

[5] See Dorothy Richardson to Bryher, 4 Oct. 1936: 'I still see the face of her maid at the door—Am I to bring coffee in 'ere, Miss? And May's helpless "I suppose so" ' (*Windows on Modernism: Selected Letters of Dorothy Richardson*, ed. Glora Fromm, Athens, Ga.: University of Georgia Press, 1995, 320).

after the publication of *The Divine Fire*, an American journalist, Witter Bynner, wrote asking her for some biographical details for an article he was writing about her. At first Sinclair, newly famous, was flattered. She answered Bynner at length, listing the various places where she had lived, and telling him about her creative process and her past publications. But she also sounded a note of caution: 'you may make use of the few notes I am giving you for the article . . . I cannot give you anything more personal, because I object strongly to the personal note, & in any case it bores me to write about myself.'[6] When she arrived in New York in the autumn of 1905 for a celebrity tour, she invited Bynner to tea and they had a pleasant and fairly intimate chat.[7] But when Sinclair finally received a draft of his article in December in Boston, she was horrified, and sent him a telegram saying: 'Publication of paper impossible entire or in part am writing'.[8] And write she did, telling him:

you promised me that you wd. write nothing of a personal nature, & what you <u>have</u> written is, if you will believe me, not only an insult to me, but an outrage on all the courtesies & decencies wh. make us acceptable to one another. You admit that you have repeated some things told you in confidence! I assure you that if you had intended deliberately to hurt me you cd. not have succeeded better.[9]

Bynner was taken aback and apologetic, or, as he put it, 'dismayed and dis-heartened'.[10] Sinclair accused him of misleading her as to the nature of their teatime conversation in New York: 'I only met you either as yr. guest or as your fellow-guest; you assured me that your first call was <u>not</u> an interview', but Bynner countered: 'I am confident that I told you there was to be in your case no interview of which you would be conscious;—so that you might edit as you should choose what I might remember, and the general effect would be more natural and characteristic.'[11] Sinclair was genuinely hurt and puz-zled by what she saw as, if not a deception, at least a betrayal, telling Bynner: 'You see, all of us, even the wisest, say foolish things in unguarded moments when we feel secure. These things do not matter in themselves, but it wd. be horrible if they were noted down & printed for the benefit of the public. Wh. is what you proposed to do with <u>my</u> conversational imbecilities!'[12] What really upset her in Bynner's article was that he had recorded her comments

---

[6] Sinclair to Witter Bynner, 29 Aug. 1905, HL, bMS Am 1891 (766).

[7] Sinclair to Bynner, 10 Nov. 1905, HL, bMS Am 1891 (766).

[8] Sinclair to Bynner, 11 Dec. 1905, HL, bMS Am 1891 (766).   [9] Ibid.

[10] Bynner to Sinclair, 1 [misdated for 11?] Dec. 1905, HL [copy], bMS Am 1891.1 (1119).

[11] Sinclair to Bynner, 11 Dec. 1905, HL, bMS Am 1891 (766); Bynner to Sinclair, 1 [misdated for 11?] Dec. 1905, HL, bMS Am 1891.1 (1119).

[12] Sinclair to Bynner, 21 Dec. 1905, HL, bMS Am 1891 (766).

about other people. If speaking indiscreetly about herself was unfortunate, speaking indiscreetly about others was simply immoral. Sinclair forbade Bynner to publish any article at all, and the piece was dropped.

Sinclair's experience with Witter Bynner confirmed all her worst fears about biographical writing. From then on, she saw it as a dangerously invasive form which could easily elude its subject's—and even its writer's—control. When in 1920 her close friend Catherine Dawson Scott drafted an essay about her, she was once again indignant, telling Arthur Adcock, editor of the *Bookman*, the magazine for which the article was intended: 'I'm afraid I do object, strongly, to much of the personal part of it, & I must beg of you to omit the passages I've erased.'[13] In a short story written in the same year about a biographer's search for his subject's lost letters, and the subsequent publication of an indiscreet 'unofficial' biography by another author, the original biographer regrets ever starting his research: 'The awful thing, he said, was that if only we had left Chamberlin to his obscurity we should never have known these things about him. And now everybody knew them. Nobody would forget them until *he* was forgotten.'[14] Even when Sinclair was asked to write her autobiography she refused, and the only autobiographical writing she ever published, *A Journal of Impressions in Belgium* (1915), was carefully edited to remove all compromising material.[15] Biography, for Sinclair, was a way of overwhelming people with the evidence of their own indiscretions. She had no difficulty discussing her intellectual development as a philosopher and as a novelist. *Mary Olivier*, as she freely acknowledged, is the story of her own mental development, and she happily gave interviews in which she discussed her books and her creative processes.[16] But throughout her life Sinclair was remarkably reserved about every aspect of her early years except for her intellectual experiences, and she never spoke in public about her private life or her feelings for people.

Sinclair was also very careful about the records she left behind her. We know from her book *The Three Brontës* (1912) that Sinclair was opposed not only to the publication of private letters but even, in certain cases, to their

---

[13] Sinclair to Arthur Adcock, 9 Aug. 1920, UP, Box 1, fo. 1.

[14] Sinclair, 'Fame', *Pictorial Review*, 21 (May 1920), 10; repr. as a limited edn. (London: Elkin Matthews and Marrot, 1929), 40.

[15] She wrote to Adcock on 7 Sept. 1925 that she was sorry she was unable to write the article he suggested: 'I'm no good at that sort of autobiographical stunt' (UP, Box 1, fo. 1).

[16] Sinclair wrote to Marc Logé, translator of *Mary Olivier*: 'all this description of the *inner life* is autobiographically as accurate as I can make it' (quoted in Theophilus E. M. Boll, *Miss May Sinclair: Novelist: A Biographical and Critical Introduction*, Cranbury, NJ: Associated University Presses, 1973, 244). Her interviews include 'People in the Foreground', *Current Literature*, 38 (Mar. 1905), 223; Willis Steell, 'Miss Sinclair Tells Why She Isn't a Poet', *Literary Digest International Book Review*, 2 (June 1924), 513, 559, and the citations in n. 18, below.

preservation.[17] The personal papers that were found in her house after her death had clearly been meticulously sorted, presumably by her, since she had no children to worry about her reputation. She left no diary or journal, and the earliest surviving letter to her dates from 1893, when she was already 30 years old. Some of the extant letters actually have small sections carefully cut out of them, as if whoever was preparing her correspondence for posterity was on the lookout for references to events or feelings which needed to be excised. I have been unable to locate any letters written by her earlier than 1897, when she was 34. Even Sinclair's personal demeanour was calculated to conceal her emotions: more than one journalist commented in the 1920s on her inscrutability and the 'impersonal' scrutiny of her black eyes.[18] She was determined to give nothing away.

It might be tempting to speculate that she was especially concerned to cover her tracks because she had something significant to hide. After all, in *Mary Olivier*, Mary, who is committed, like Sinclair, to the care of her ageing mother, has an affair with a celebrated London novelist, and Sinclair wrote sympathetically in novels such as *Anne Severn and the Fieldings* (1922) and *The Allinghams* (1927) about women who have lovers—and even babies—outside marriage. Her contemporaries certainly gossiped about her, and there were vague rumours in Sinclair's family that she might have given birth to an illegitimate baby at some point (perhaps after she went into seclusion with her mother and brother in Salcombe Regis in 1890).[19] The erotic intensity of Sinclair's interest in babies and breastfeeding in many of

---

[17] In *The Three Brontës* Sinclair writes of letters written by Branwell about his love for a married woman: 'It is inconceivable that such letters should have been kept' (TB, 44).

[18] See e.g. Burton Rascoe, 'Contemporary Reminiscences: Two Important English Visitors—May Sinclair and Bertrand Russell', *Arts and Decoration*, 21 (July 1924), 25–6: at 26: 'She dominates any gathering less heterogeneous than a noisy banquet, by her Buddha-like calm and inscrutable charm.' See also Walter Tittle, 'Personal Portraits—May Sinclair', *Illustrated London News*, 166 (27 June 1925), 1280: 'my greeting was met with a scrutiny from her black eyes that was at once so intense and impersonal that it kindled curiosity within me as to its possible meaning'.

[19] Brigit Patmore wrote to Sinclair's friend, the poet H.D. in 1923: 'I met Violet Hunt round about here. Says V. "I'm just going round to tea at the Heads (a noted brain specialist) to hear five points in May Sinclair's book which prove she is a virgin." We almost sank onto the pavement with laughter—as Cole says. "Nobody gives the poor woman the credit of anything" . . . Lunching with Florian I told him the little gem & he said: "That's amusing for Violet, since in 1884 she surprised May Sinclair in bed with Oswald Crawfurd in their (V's and O's) private little flat." ' (Patmore to H.D., 9 Dec. 1923, Beinecke Rare Book and Manuscript Library, Yale Collection of American Literature 24, Box 13, fo. 446.) However, the details of this story do not add up: although Violet Hunt and Oswald Crawfurd did have a long affair, they did not meet until 1890, and there is no mention of any incident with May Sinclair in Hunt's diaries of her relationship with Crawfurd, or in their correspondence. Hunt found out in 1898–9 that Crawfurd had been writing passionate letters to a friend of hers, May Bateman: it may be this episode that was distorted into Patmore's story (see Barbara Belford, *Violet: The Story of the Irrepressible Violet Hunt and Her Circle of Lovers and Friends—Ford Madox Ford, H. G. Wells, Somerset Maugham, and Henry James*, New York: Simon and Schuster, 1990, for further discussion of the Hunt–Crawfurd affair). I am grateful to Helen Carr for this reference.

the novels could imply that Sinclair had a tantalizing taste of the pleasures of motherhood before her baby was abruptly taken away. Other scraps of evidence here and there suggest that there may have been some romantic interest or scandal, quickly hushed up: the letter from Gwendoline Keats at the time of Sinclair's mother's death, for example (I discuss this in Chapter 3), or Alida Monro's contention that Charlotte Mew was obliged to end her friendship with Sinclair because of something Mew 'heard about' her.[20]

But none of these tiny clues *necessarily* point to an affair or a baby. Keats's letter and Mew's alienation could be interpreted in a number of different ways, and Sinclair could have had an intense imaginative connection to children without ever having given birth to one of her own. Perhaps at the end of the twentieth century we find it difficult to believe in the existence of a woman like Sinclair who lived so fiercely the life of the mind, and who could empathize so passionately with romantic or sexual love without ever having experienced it herself, but of course she was by no means the only woman of her time to turn her back on sexual intimacy and family life. In 1908 she told Louis N. Parker, a professor at Columbia University: 'I have done all my work in an almost incredible isolation, & ideas simply refuse to visit me unless they find me alone.'[21] Sinclair was often uncomfortable in the company of others, she hated being interrupted while she was working, she had a strong sense of privacy, and she had an aversion to drawing attention to herself. An affair would simply have been too risky, and her experience of family life had made her wary of the blandishments of men.

Given the amount of biographical and critical attention that has been lavished on other inhabitants of Sinclair's world (Pound, Woolf, Mansfield, H.D.), surprisingly little has been written about May Sinclair herself.[22] When she died in 1946 she was the author of twenty-one novels, a novel in verse, scores of short stories, two books on idealist philosophy, a book on the Brontës, and a personal account of her time in Belgium during the first months of the First World War. But she wrote and published nothing after 1927, living out her last two decades in a village in the Buckinghamshire countryside, crippled by Parkinson's disease and with only her housekeeper for company. Most of her friends assumed that she was dead. This extended

---

[20] See Gwendoline Keats to Sinclair, 23 Aug. 1900, UP, Box 2, fos. 50–5, and Alida Monro, 'Charlotte Mew—A Memoir', in *Collected Poems of Charlotte Mew*, ed. Alida Monro (London: Duckworth, 1953), pp. vii–xx: at p. xv.

[21] Sinclair to Louis N. Parker, 3 Oct. [1908?], Louis Napoleon Parker Papers, Rare Book and Manuscript Library, Columbia University.

[22] See Theophilus E. M. Boll, 'On the May Sinclair Collection', *Library Chronicle of the University of Pennsylvania*, 27 (Winter 1961), 1–15: at 1–3; and Corrine Yvonne Taylor, 'A Study of May Sinclair—Woman and Writer, 1863–1946—with an Annotated Bibliography', Ph.D. thesis (Washington State University, 1969), 1–3, for lists of the brief and scattered references to May Sinclair in criticism before 1970.

period in limbo may well have contributed to the waning of public interest in her work. There was an awkwardness about commemorating her as one of the great writers of the past while she was still alive, and yet the public was no longer reminded of her by the regular publication of novel after novel. She also damaged her reputation by overextending herself in the mid-1920s when she was already ill and running out of energy. As her reviewers pointed out, her last six novels—all published between 1924 and 1927—are thin and repetitive, showing little of the gift for poignant understatement that was so apparent in her last major novel, *Life and Death of Harriett Frean*.[23]

Her solitude also contributed to her neglect. As well as the fact that she destroyed so much (she left no multi-volume diary like Virginia Woolf's, for example, and she did not keep carbon copies of her letters), she wrote far fewer letters than she might have done. She had no intimate companion to whom she sent daily news and reflections, as Katherine Mansfield and Vita Sackville-West did. She had no widower preparing edition after edition of posthumous works, as Middleton Murry had done for Katherine Mansfield, and no children to gather her scattered papers, as Sara Coleridge did for her father. Many of her correspondents (or their descendants) apparently threw her letters away. Presumably by the 1940s she was so thoroughly forgotten that there seemed no point in keeping them. She was in danger of sinking virtually without trace.

But there was one person who mourned Sinclair bitterly and cherished the carefully sorted collection of letters and manuscripts she had left behind her: her companion in her final years, Florence Bartrop. When in 1959 Theophilus E. M. Boll, a professor at the University of Pennsylvania, stumbled across Sinclair's novels and went to England to explore the possibilities for a biography, he was directed first to Sinclair's nephew Harold, and then, by him, to Bartrop and her trunk full of papers.[24] Harold Sinclair agreed to let Boll take the papers back to Philadelphia with him, and they were later deposited in the Rare Book and Manuscript Library at the University of Pennsylvania, together with all Boll's related correspondence. Boll's biography, a diligent compilation of all the sources he found at Bartrop's house, appeared in 1973, and was followed in 1976 by Hrisey D. Zegger's

---

[23] Naomi Royde-Smith noted that with *The Allinghams* (1927) 'for the first time in her accomplished work [MS] has produced a book which it will be almost easy to forget' ('New Novels', *New Statesman*, 24, 23 Apr. 1927, 44–5: at 44); the *Booklist* called *Far End* (1926) 'disappointing' (23 Nov. 1926, 84); and the anonymous reviewer of *A Cure of Souls* (1924) in the *Dial* described Sinclair as 'an excellent example of a really good writer whose very brilliant facility causes her on more than one occasion to write too much and hence to write herself down' ('Briefer Mention', *Dial*, 76, June 1924, 560).

[24] See Boll, 'On the May Sinclair Collection', for an account of the genesis of his biography.

May Sinclair, a critical assessment of her major prose works. To date these are the only book-length studies of Sinclair's life and career.

Writing a biography of someone who was determined to protect herself against exactly that eventuality presents a peculiar kind of challenge. Without Boll's determined research in the 1960s, it would have been impossible. Anyone working on May Sinclair is enormously in his debt. I have relied on the archive he put together, and on other collections of letters and other materials, both in the USA and the UK, that have come to light in the years since Boll published his book. My focus is on Sinclair's intellectual development, the one aspect of her life that she was willing to discuss—and to have discussed—freely. Her resistance to biography did not mean that she did not care whether or not she was forgotten: quite the reverse. Her anxiety was that if too much was known about her private life, however uneventful it was, she would be remembered not as a writer, but as a woman. She was indignant that critics devoted so much time to the question of whether or not Charlotte Brontë was in love with Paul Héger, the teacher with whom she worked in Brussels. Sinclair declared in *The Three Brontës* that 'when a woman's talent baffles you, your course is plain, *cherchez l'homme*' (TB, 82). In Sinclair's view, this strategy was a subtle way of suggesting that Brontë's 'genius was, after all, only a superior kind of talent' (TB, 82). Sinclair was determined that her own creative gift should not be similarly belittled. When she went through her papers in an attempt to control the terms in which she was remembered, it was her intimate life that was excised: she kept letters from other writers and public figures.

This biography is first and foremost a reconstruction of Sinclair as a writer and an intellectual. But in order fully to explore the context and the significance of what she wrote, I have made many decisions of which she would not have approved. I deal as fully as possible, for example, with her father's bankruptcy and alcoholism, events which she was at pains to conceal throughout her life, but which played a definitive role in shaping her attitude to the world and to her self. I have also allowed myself to speculate about her romantic life. In the late 1990s a biography which simply drew a veil over feelings or occurrences which to a contemporary sensibility no longer seem shameful or humiliating would not do justice to its subject. It is crucial to our understanding of our culture's transition into modernity that we acknowledge the emotional cost of such significant changes to women like May Sinclair who were courageous enough to confront them head on. But in order to explain, it is necessary to reveal and discuss.

Although this volume traces Sinclair's evolution as a writer and as a thinker, it is not an exhaustive survey of every piece of writing she produced.

I concentrate on Sinclair's literary output, rather than her philosophical work, since, remarkable as it was in its time, it has limited significance for philosophers nowadays. I have sought to draw attention to novels and stories which have been unjustly neglected and which—if they were better known—would continue to grip and move readers today. Sinclair still has her devotees (like journalist Katha Pollitt, who in a recent issue of the *Nation* mentions 'the once-celebrated, now totally forgotten novels of May Sinclair, which I love'), but they have to rummage in second-hand bookshops and the recesses of libraries in order to indulge their passion.[25] I have commented on almost all of Sinclair's publications somewhere in this book, but I have focused on those which represented a crucial moment of progress in her thinking, which attracted significant attention in her time, or which were important commentaries on controversial issues of the day. Some of her novels, especially the later ones, but also a few of the earlier ones, do not stand up well to rereading. It was as if on occasion she wrote simply to mark time, or, more prosaically, to make money. Those who are interested in finding out more about the texts I do not discuss in detail should refer to Boll's *Miss May Sinclair*, which summarizes everything Sinclair wrote.

In some ways, then, this May Sinclair biography is more selective than its predecessor, even though I have had access to archival materials that neither Boll nor Zegger ever saw. But I have also broadened the contexts in which Sinclair's work has been discussed. Boll makes little attempt to move beyond the scope of Sinclair's own life and preoccupations to consider her role in remaking British culture in the early twentieth century. Sinclair's few scholarly critics have by and large identified her with high modernism and the work of her later years. But her writing career confounds many of our standard categorizations (we cannot, for example, unproblematically call her a 'modernist'), and exposes both the continuities and the ruptures between late Victorian and high modernist art. Many of the crucial issues of the late nineteenth and early twentieth centuries were played out in the various episodes of Sinclair's life: her agonized questioning of the Christian faith, her turn to Kantian and then to Hegelian idealism, her transition to experimental literary techniques during the First World War, her lifelong fear of the constraints of heredity. She was an active participant in many of the most significant movements and events of her day: the 'commercialization' of the book trade, as one eminent publisher called it, the suffrage movement, the

---

[25] Katha Pollitt, 'Masterpiece Theatre: Subject to Debate', *Nation*, 267 (24/31 Aug. 1998), 9. I am grateful to P. A. Skantze for this reference.

coming of psychoanalysis to Britain, the First World War.[26] I believe that her biography still has much to tell us about the emotional fate of women of her generation who came of age in the late Victorian period but instinctively identified with the rebellious mores and artistic aspirations of their much younger counterparts. We may have known her until now as a helpful footnote to the lives of her more famous friends but, of course, it is often out of footnotes that the most complex and revealing stories emerge. This book moves Sinclair from the bottom to the centre of the page.

[26] The term 'commercialization' is used by American publisher Henry Holt, in 'The Commercialization of Literature: A Summing Up', *Putnam's Monthly* (Feb. 1907), 563–75.

1863–1897

I

Learning Philosophy

═

ONE DAY in the early 1870s, in a house in Ilford, East London, near the gloomy City of London cemetery, a lonely, studious little girl, the only sister of five older boys, sat down to read a book. Decades later the girl, now a well-known and wealthy novelist, recalled that day:

Years and years ago, when I was a child, hunting forlornly in my father's bookshelves, I came upon a small shabby volume, bound in yellow linen. The title-page was adorned with one bad wood-cut that showed a grim, plain house standing obliquely to a churchyard packed with tombstones, tombstones upright and flat, and slanting at all angles. . . . Tombstones always fascinated me in those days, because I was mortally afraid of them; and I opened that book and read it through.

I could not, in fact, put it down. For the first time I was in the grip of a reality more poignant than any I had yet known, of a tragedy that I could hardly bear. (TB, 276–7)

The impressionable, frightened little girl was May Sinclair, and the volume was Elizabeth Gaskell's *Life of Charlotte Brontë* (1857). This image of a silent child, head bent over a book that told of lives even more restricted than her own, anticipates the adult Sinclair's ambivalent fascination with the Victorian morbidity that saturated her formative years. Even as, in her fifties and sixties, she defended experimental fiction such as Dorothy Richardson's *Pilgrimage*, and in 1919 published her own unconventional novel, *Mary Olivier: A Life*, she continued to return to the years of her childhood as if in search of an answer to the questions raised by her own development.[1]

All her life Sinclair relied on books for instruction and solace. Paradoxically for someone whose novels reveal such an intensely sensuous imagination, her conscious life was dominated by her passion for intellectual enquiry

---

[1] Sinclair's review of the first three volumes of *Pilgrimage*, 'The Novels of Dorothy Richardson', was published in the *Egoist*, 5 (Apr. 1918), 57–9.

and for writing. The sombre, preoccupied little girl in her father's library developed into a woman whose habits were formed by the pleasures and the dangers of the imagination and the inner life. As she found herself increasingly at odds, especially in matters of religious belief, with the mother whose approval she craved, she retreated more and more into philosophical enquiry in an attempt to understand and master her own doubts. Her journey into the twentieth century began with a characteristically Victorian crisis of faith.

There was little in Sinclair's background to indicate that she would grow into such a solitary, studious woman. Her parents were not intellectuals, although her father, William Sinclair, was interested in books and had a fairly substantial library in which young Mary (she did not become May until 1891) browsed freely.[2] William was part-owner of a shipping business in Liverpool, while Sinclair's mother, born Amelia Hind, was the daughter of a Northern Irish Protestant, whose commercial interests allowed him to settle some money on Amelia. Thus Sinclair's family was not especially privileged in class terms: they came from the mercantile middle class, involved in trade and commerce, aspiring to a comfortable and cultured life. After their marriage in Belfast on 26 September 1850, William and Amelia Sinclair settled in Cheshire at New Ferry, Lower Bebington, near Liverpool. Those early years were prosperous. Amelia was preoccupied with raising her growing family; William seemed to be making a reasonable success of the shipping company. Their eldest son, William, was born about a year after they married, on 18 October 1851. A daughter, Gertrude Elizabeth, came next, born on 7 July 1853, but she survived only just over a year, dying of scarlet fever on 24 September 1854. A year after Gertrude's death, on 29 July 1855, a third child was born, Joseph Walter, and a fourth, Francis Edwin, followed on 11 March 1857. After Francis's birth the family's prospects had improved enough to allow them to move from the little village of Lower Bebington to a house at the much more desirable address of Thorncote, Rock Park, Higher Bebington, a purpose-built development with secluded lanes, and large, ostentatious houses. The development was designed for the families of businessmen who, like William Sinclair, worked in Liverpool, and one of its attractions was that it was close to the Mersey ferry, which departed regularly for the city. In later life Sinclair described it as 'by no means a romantic spot, a sort of suburb of Birkenhead & Liverpool'.[3] Here,

---

[2] Mary Sinclair did not adopt the name 'May' until she was 28, in the signature to her second published volume of poetry, *Essays in Verse* (London: Kegan Paul, Trench, Trübner & Co., 1891, pub. Jan. 1892). Her nieces and nephews knew her as 'Mary May' (see Wilda McNeile to T. E. M. Boll, 16 June 1959, UP, Box 48, fo. 529).

[3] Sinclair to Witter Bynner, 29 Aug. 1905, HL, bMS Am 1891 (766).

on 12 September 1858, the fourth Sinclair boy, Harold, was born, and another boy, Frederick Amelius St Clair (later called Reginald), followed on 23 January 1861. Mary Amelia St Clair, born on 24 August 1863, was the last of the Sinclairs' six children, all boys apart from her.

In later life, Sinclair was unusually reticent about her childhood and adolescence. As Catherine Dawson Scott and Witter Bynner discovered to their cost, she resisted all attempts to publish biographical pieces about her.[4] But, all the same, she did occasionally break her silence, in interviews, in little vignettes like the one of her childhood reading of *The Life of Charlotte Brontë* with which I started, or, more extensively, in her account of her weeks with an ambulance unit at the beginning of the First World War, *A Journal of Impressions in Belgium* (1915).

She was slightly less guarded in her fiction, where she could disguise or distort the events of her life so that their autobiographical origins were more ambiguous. In many of her novels she returned obliquely to certain crucial scenes and events—her childhood in Liverpool, her father's bankruptcy and alcoholism, her brothers' deaths from mitral valve disease—as if her imagination could never quite break free of them. As autobiographical fiction (especially the female *Bildungsroman*, or novel of development) became increasingly common and popular after the First World War (Dorothy Richardson's *Pilgrimage* from 1915 onwards, Katherine Mansfield's 'Prelude' in 1918, Virginia Woolf's *To the Lighthouse* in 1927), Sinclair grew bolder. The lives of the protagonists of two of her later novels, *Mary Olivier: A Life* (1919) and *Arnold Waterlow: A Life* (1924), follow her own biography closely enough that it is clear that she conceived them as semi-autobiographical, and drew closely on her own experiences as she wrote them. Indeed Sinclair admitted to Marc Logé, who translated *Mary Olivier*, that *Mary Olivier* was the story of her own life (although she explicitly dissociated herself from Mary's love affairs) and she referred to *Arnold Waterlow* as 'a male "Mary Olivier" '.[5] Her creativity fed off the childhood and adolescence she kept well hidden from critics and friends alike. The lonely

---

[4] See the Introduction, above, for a more extended discussion of Sinclair's attitude to biography.

[5] Sinclair's first biographer, T. E. M. Boll, notes that in a letter to Logé Sinclair listed the numerous sections of *Mary Olivier* which were autobiographically accurate, and also reports that Florence Bartrop, Sinclair's companion for the last thirty years of her life, told him that Sinclair had told her that *Mary Olivier* was substantially her own life-story, 'excepting only the love episodes' (Boll, *Miss May Sinclair*, 244). Hrisey D. Zegger also calls the novel 'almost entirely autobiographical' (*May Sinclair*, Boston: Twayne, 1976, 15). Sinclair compared *Arnold Waterlow* and *Mary Olivier* in Steell, 'May Sinclair Tells Why She Isn't a Poet', 559. Arnold, like Sinclair, is born in a big house in East Ferry on the Wirral, and his father's shipping business fails. Sinclair's niece Agatha Ayre, and her niece-by-marriage Muriel Sinclair, told Boll that there was a general belief in their family that *Mary Olivier* was the story of Sinclair's own life (see Muriel Sinclair to Boll, 1 Aug. 1967, UP, Box 48, fo. 533).

little girl in her father's library grew into a woman whose primary mode of self-exploration and self-expression was through her fiction.

Little Mary Sinclair grew up in an atmosphere dominated by the boisterous activities of her elder brothers. She recalled in a 1912 review of Cicely Hamilton's *Man* that 'Until I was twenty-seven (but for a few inconsiderable terms at school) I spent the greater part of my life with men, sharing largely in that open air life which shows my sex what is best in theirs, besides being mixed up even more in those critical and intimate family relations which most infallibly reveal the worst in it.'[6] Even in middle age Sinclair remained physically active and fearless, riding, cycling, walking, skating, sailing, and swimming. An article based on an interview in 1905, when she was 42, noted that Sinclair liked 'cycling [and] . . . most things that can be done actively and in the open air'.[7] Ten years later her enthusiasm was still just as strong: in October 1915 she told H. G. Wells: 'I love life—the very feeling of my feet on the ground is an exquisite pleasure, & out-of-door games & hard exercise, all the robust side of it.'[8] The foundations of this love of exertion were laid during long afternoons in the large garden at Thorncote, when young Mary ran after her brothers, desperate to join in their games. Years later she would use that childhood experience of exclusion to describe her feelings during the two weeks she spent in Belgium at the start of the First World War:

It is with the game of war as it was with the game of football I used to play with my big brothers in the garden. The women may play it if they're fit enough, up to a certain point, very much as I played football in the garden. The big brothers let their little sister kick off; they let her run away with the ball; they stood back and let her make goal after goal; but when it came to the scrimmage they took hold of her and gently but firmly moved her to one side. If she persisted she became an infernal nuisance. (JI, 105–6)

Sinclair never forgot what it felt like to be admitted to the company of males only on sufferance, and decades later, in spite of her fear of drawing attention to herself, she ventured out with a collecting-box in support of the women's suffrage movement.[9] But as a child she was not yet sensitive to

---

[6] Sinclair, 'A Defence of Men', *English Review*, 11 (July 1912), 556–66: at 557 (also pub. in *Forum*, 48 Oct. 1912, 409–20).

[7] 'People in the Foreground', 223. Sinclair learned to ride in 1880, at the age of 17, and to swim in 1886, when she was 23. See the unpublished typescript 'The Way of Sublimation' (1916), 98, UP, Box 23, fos. 436–8.

[8] Sinclair to H. G. Wells, 16 Oct. 1915, University of Illinois Library at Urbana-Champaign.

[9] In Mar. 1908, as their contribution to Mrs Pethick Lawrence's 'week of self-denial', Sinclair and Violet Hunt rattled collection boxes outside Kensington High Street tube station. Hunt described the experience as one of public humiliation: 'I fancy [May] felt as I did—as if we had suddenly been stripped

masculine injustice, and was overjoyed to be allowed to join in at all. Her favourite brother, Frank, was the leader of the younger group of children (Frank, Harold, Reginald, and Mary), who all played noisily together while William and Joseph formed their own alliance. Frank and Mary had a special affection for one another: they would jump brooks together, and sometimes Mary would climb the stairs and fling herself into the air, confident that her strong, handsome elder brother would be there to catch her.[10] Sinclair never forgot the excitement and the security of sibling attachments, describing them over and over again in her novels. In *Anne Severn and the Fieldings* (1922), Anne even ends up becoming her adoptive brother's mistress.

But the carefree pleasure of Mary Sinclair's outdoor life was not matched by the life she led indoors. Her mother was an unimaginative and inflexible woman who took no pains to hide either her preference for her sons, especially Frank, or her disappointment with her husband. Her austere Northern Irish Protestantism dominated the household. In later years Sinclair described it as a 'cold, bitter, narrow tyranny'.[11] William seems to have been jealous and resentful of the attention his wife gave to her sons, particularly Frank; and Amelia in turn grew irritable in their defence. Family occasions were formal and chilly with tension. In 1915 Sinclair wrote that her youth was 'spoiled with too many ceremonies . . . ceremonies that lacked all beauty and sincerity and dignity' (JI, 32). In this emotionally charged atmosphere Mary Sinclair was largely left to fend for herself: she barely saw her father, who was always either at the office, or sailing in his yacht the *Windward*.[12] As a little girl in the 1860s her love of tomboyish games was frowned on. She spent hours sitting with her mother learning to sew and to play the piano. However hard she tried, it was difficult for her to act like the demure and obedient shadow-self her mother wanted her to be. The early chapters of *Mary Olivier* show Mary in constant competition with her brothers for her mother's attention. Mary Sinclair too must have felt rivalry with these older boys whose opportunities and achievements were always so far ahead of anything she could hope for.

But Amelia Sinclair's early lack of interest in her daughter belied the intensity and the ambivalence of the relationship that developed between them as Mary grew older. In spite of her resentment of her mother, Mary

---

naked, with a cross-sensation of being drowned in a tank and gasping for breath.' See Violet Hunt, *The Flurried Years* (London: Hurst and Blackett, 1926), 42.

[10] This game is authenticated in a letter from G. B. Stern to Sinclair, 15 June 1919, UP, Box 3, fo. 89.

[11] Sinclair to Katharine Hinkson, 14 Apr. 1912, JR.

[12] In 'The Way of Sublimation' Sinclair includes herself among those who 'had so little to do with [their fathers] in infancy that [they] were to all intents and purposes not known to them' (typescript, 95, UP, Box 23, fos. 436–8).

longed for her approval and for some token of affection. Although her elder sister Gertrude's life and death pre-dated Mary's birth by about a decade, it is hard, from the evidence of Sinclair's fiction, not to feel that her imagination was haunted by the spectral presence of her sister. Dead children appear in almost every story she ever wrote: 'The Intercessor' (1911), *Mary Olivier*, and *Life and Death of Harriett Frean* (1922), to name but a few examples. The evidence of these texts suggests that Sinclair was dogged by the fear that her mother compared her unfavourably to the daughter she had lost. In *Arnold Waterlow* young Arnold comes upon his mother caressing photographs and locks of hair, one set belonging to her favourite son Richard, and the other to an unknown child. She tells Arnold that he had another brother who died three days before Arnold was born. Arnold is horrified:

He didn't know what was the matter with him. He couldn't put into words what he felt about the little dead brother whose likeness should have been his and wasn't. It was as if he had looked into his mother's heart and had found no place for himself there. But her eyes made him frightened and ashamed.[13]

His mother has no photograph of Arnold, and no lock of his hair, and in her embarrassment tells him he must never mention his dead brother again. If Mary Sinclair grew up under a similar injunction, it is no surprise that dead children appear obsessively in her fiction. In 'The Intercessor' the ghost of an elder daughter even takes the place of her younger sibling who has died at birth.[14] It was perhaps because of this consciousness of a bereavement in which she felt in some way implicated that Sinclair reacted with such fascinated horror to the frontispiece in her father's edition of Gaskell's *Life of Charlotte Brontë*. She continued to be afraid of graveyards all her life.

The circumstances of Mary Sinclair's life became even more difficult when she was 7. Until then, however fraught her inner world, she had at least enjoyed the luxuries of affluent middle-class life in a large and well-appointed home, with an extensive garden lovingly supervised by her mother. But in the late 1860s her father's business began to fail; one by one things and people started to disappear: first the yacht went, then the parlour-maid, the kitchenmaid, and the gardener. *Arnold Waterlow* describes the changes that came over Arnold's house when his father, like Sinclair's, was no longer bringing in enough money to support the household:

The dandelions and daisies and ladies' slippers spread higher up the lawn, and in the wild places the peacock's legs were hidden in the long grass . . . Then Miss Rodick

[13] Sinclair, *Arnold Waterlow: A Life* (New York: Macmillan, 1924), 89–90.
[14] I discuss this story at length in Ch. 4, below.

[the governess] went. And the same day Richard [Arnold's brother] left off going to Miss Peppercorn's. Holidays began the first week in May.

You would have thought that summer would have been a happy summer, but it wasn't; because whoever went away or didn't go Papa was always at home. There had been a time when he was hardly ever there at all. That time, Richard said, was too good to last.[15]

As Sinclair told Willis Steell fifty-four years later, her 'family had lost everything'.[16] Eventually Mary was sent to stay with her uncle in Liverpool and, when she returned home, it was not to the house at Rock Ferry, but to another, much smaller one.

The movements of the family after the failure of the shipping business are very hard to trace. Sinclair remained extremely reticent about her family's sudden descent into genteel poverty: the comment she made to Steell during the 1924 interview is the only recorded public reference she ever made to their financial difficulties. But they must have been acute: William Sinclair seems never to have worked again, and some at least of the Sinclair boys took office jobs to supplement what remained of their mother's income. Sinclair told Steell that the family were financially dependent on relatives for quite some time. We can be fairly sure that they left the Liverpool area soon after the disaster: in 1870 there are records of a William Sinclair living briefly in Brentwood, Essex, where the Waterlow family in *Arnold Waterlow* also goes immediately after their business fails.[17] In 1872 the Sinclairs left Brentwood for Ilford, in those days a village just east of London, and ten years later, they moved again, still in the same area, to Forest Gate. Their living conditions were cramped and unhappy. They held on to as much of their furniture as they could, but that meant that the rooms were crowded with inappropriately large sofas and beds. The pathos of such households is carefully recorded in many of Sinclair's novels. The bedroom in the house Mary Olivier's family move to after Emilius Olivier's shipping insurance business fails is 'nearly filled with the yellow birchwood wardrobe and bed' (MO, 162), and Juliana Quincy and her aunt, in their small house in the suburb of Camden, in 'Superseded' (1901), 'crowded themselves out with relics of their past, a pathetic salvage, dragged hap-hazard from the wreck in the first frenzy of preservation'.[18] Some of Mary's brothers were no longer around to

[15] Sinclair, *Arnold Waterlow*, 42–3.

[16] Steell, 'May Sinclair Tells Why She Isn't a Poet', 513.

[17] Boll, *Miss May Sinclair*, 25, notes that the Essex Court Directory for 1870 lists William Sinclair's address as Warley Road, Brentford (presumably a misprint for Brentwood). Boll also includes details of other directory entries for the family.

[18] Sinclair, 'Superseded', in *Two Sides of a Question* (New York: J. F. Taylor, 1901), 214. When the Waterlows first move to Brentwood, Arnold wakes to find that the room he is sharing with his sister and his

lighten the gloom of the claustrophobic Ilford house: in 1874 Frank entered the Royal Military Academy in Woolwich, and three years later left the country to serve with the army in India. Mary's mother, already angry and depressed at the downturn in her family's fortunes, become even more demanding after Frank's departure. In the mid-1870s Mary's brother William started work in an office in the City, and then, in 1879, married Eleanor Adeline Cook and settled in Hull, where he worked for Finningley & Co., a firm of provision merchants. With two of her sons gone Amelia Sinclair felt even more abandoned and humiliated. It was Mary's task to stay home with her and keep her entertained.

Boll and Zegger both assume that at some point during the 1870s William and Amelia separated.[19] Certainly much of the documentary evidence points in that direction: William's death in 1881 was registered by someone called Martha Mitchell, and not by any member of his family, and his address on the death certificate (and in a directory for 1879) is not the Ilford address where the family seem to have been living, but one in Fairford, a small town about twenty miles south-east of Cheltenham. Sinclair herself was evasive and contradictory about the family's movements during these years. In 1905 she told an anonymous interviewer for *Outlook* magazine that she had 'lived a very quiet life in the country' until she moved to London in 1896, and she wrote to critic Witter Bynner that she 'did not settle in town till '96'.[20] During the 1920s, when she had a writing retreat at Stow-on-the-Wold, about twenty miles from Fairford, visitors would regularly be taken there to see the church and the house where she claimed to have lived.[21] All these comments suggest that the whole family went into retreat together in an attempt to conceal William's growing dependence on alcohol. However, Sinclair was not above falsifying—or at least repressing—the uncomfortable details of her own past. In direct contradiction to the story she had told other people, she said to Steell in 1924 that she had never lived outside London, commenting that after her father's financial failure, 'We were living all over—that is, we were constantly moving, of course in London, where I have lived since I was five years old. I was not born in London, but have no

nurse is 'so small that Martha's bed almost filled it, and the rest of the furniture out of Martha's room at East Ferry was piled high in the recesses of the chimney' (Sinclair, *Arnold Waterlow*, 46). The drawing-room furniture is in storage in the charwoman's cottage 'as if [it] had all struggled and squeezed into Mrs. Kite's cottage in a headlong flight before disaster' (ibid. 51).

[19] See Boll, *Miss May Sinclair*, 25, 27, 29, 39; Zegger, *May Sinclair*, 15.

[20] 'The Author of "The Divine Fire" ', *Outlook*, 131 (25 Nov. 1905), 727–9: at 728; Sinclair to Bynner, 29 Aug. 1905, HL, bMS 1891 (766). She also told Bynner: 'My people were rather given to migrating, so that I've lived in many places & many counties—Essex, Gloucestershire, Denbighshire, Devonshire for the most part.'

[21] See Dorothy Hyde, 'Miss May Sinclair', 2, UP, Box 48, fo. 525.

recollection of any other home'.[22] She was clearly concerned to cover her tracks. On balance, it seems likely that the family did not, in fact, separate, and that even if they did break up for a brief time, with William moving to Fairford and Amelia and the children staying in London, Mary and her brothers stayed in close touch with their father. (Her mother, on the other hand, finally severed all ties: she and her husband were not even buried together.)

Whatever her living situation, Mary was forced to witness, and to try to conceal, her father's, and possibly one or more of her brothers', episodes of drunkenness. The detailed descriptions of alcoholism in her fiction suggest that Sinclair had first-hand experience of sharing a house with someone whose drinking was out of control. In *Mary Olivier* Mary's brother Roddy steers his father home from the pub every night, 'and Papa would stiffen and draw himself up, trying to look dignified and sober' (MO, 180), while his wife refuses to acknowledge that anything is amiss. Arnold Waterlow's father has 'floppy moods': 'Mr. Waterlow carried himself very straight and stiff, balancing himself affectedly and putting his feet down with exaggerated care. When Arnold spoke to him he didn't answer and his face had a queer, uneasy look, as though he were holding liquid in his mouth'.[23] Matty's son in *The Rector of Wyck* (1925) even vomits on the threshold of his father's church.[24] Literary critic Frank Swinnerton commented that in 1904, after reading *The Divine Fire*: 'the most intelligent and sophisticated man known to me then shook his head over May Sinclair's knowledge of what a man felt like when he was drunk. My friend said, gravely: "She knows too much." '[25] Disgusted by all that she had seen, Sinclair herself remained a teetotaller for the rest of her life. Her father's death on 19 November 1881 at the age of 52 from cirrhosis of the liver and kidney disease only reinforced her sense of alcohol's danger. In *Mary Olivier* Sinclair described the death of Mary's alcoholic father in chilling detail. He has been given an emetic:

The basin kept on slipping from the bed. She could see its pattern—reddish flowers and green leaves and curlykews—under the splashings of mustard and water. . . . The curtains were drawn back, holding the sour smell of sickness in their fluted folds. . . . Papa's head was thrown stiffly back on the high pillows; it sank in, weighted with the blood that flushed his face. Around it on the white linen there was a spatter and splash of mustard and water. His beard clung to his chin, soaked in the yellowish stain. He breathed with a loud, grating and groaning noise. (MO, 188)

[22] Steell, 'May Sinclair Tells Why She Isn't a Poet', 513   [23] Sinclair, *Arnold Waterlow*, 107.
[24] Sinclair, *The Rector of Wyck* (New York: Macmillan, 1925), 166.
[25] Frank Swinnerton, *The Georgian Literary Scene: A Panorama* (London: Hutchinson, 1935), 401.

Mary Olivier watches with a feeling of hysterical pity—as perhaps Mary Sinclair had done—as the father for whom she has had less and less respect finally spews out his last breath.

But by the time her father died, Mary Sinclair had a place of refuge. She had met the deprivations and the loneliness of her teens with a characteristic-ally intense determination. Struggling against her mother's constant disap-proval and resentment, envious of her brothers' education, and increasingly unsure of her belief in Christian orthodoxy, she put as much energy as she could manage into educating herself in languages, the classics, and philoso-phy, partly as a way of trying to resolve her questions about religion. By 1881 Mary had taught herself German, Greek, and French, and read works by Shakespeare, Milton, Macaulay, Plutarch, Locke, Homer, Aeschylus, Sophocles, Aristophanes, Euripides, Shelley, Plato, Hume, and Kant.[26] It became increasingly clear both to Mary herself and, more ominously, to her mother, that she was developing not only a defensively solitary tempera-ment, but also a remarkably agile and enquiring mind. She retreated from the frictions and the petty frustrations of her everyday life into an unusually strict and demanding regime of thought and study.[27]

In the autumn of 1881, when Mary was 18, her scholarly dedication was rewarded: she was sent for a year to Cheltenham Ladies' College where, many years earlier, her mother had once been a pupil. The College was founded in 1853 and, by 1881, under the extraordinary leadership of Dorothea Beale, it was flourishing and widely recognized, along with the North London Collegiate School founded by Frances Buss in 1850, as a land-mark educational institution for girls and women.[28] Mary Sinclair's year at school was the first time that she had been exposed to the exclusive company of her own sex for any sustained period of time, and it was the first time, too, that she had had formal intellectual guidance from trained and experienced teachers. After years of strain at home, with her father's alcoholism and her mother's dissatisfaction dominating the household, Sinclair found herself suddenly responsible to no one but herself. She was not studying for any for-mal examination, and she was free to live a life centred around intellectual

---

[26] See Boll, *Miss May Sinclair*, 29, for a full list of Sinclair's reading during her teenage years.

[27] In later years Sinclair continued to have a tendency to overwork. She wrote to Violet Hunt e.g. some-time early in 1918: 'I want to be in Yorkshire, all alone, writing my novel. But I'm very, very tired, & I don't know how I'm going to do it' [n.d.], HA.

[28] For detailed accounts of the history of the Cheltenham Ladies' College, see Dorothea Beale, *History of the Cheltenham Ladies' College 1853–1904* (Cheltenham: Looker-On Printing Works, 1904); Elizabeth Raikes, *Dorothea Beale of Cheltenham* (1908; 2nd edn. London: Constable, 1910); Josephine Kamm, *How Different from Us: A Biography of Miss Buss and Miss Beale* (London: Bodley Head, 1958); and Elizabeth H. Shillito, *Dorothea Beale* (London: Society for the Propagation of Christian Knowledge, 1920).

enquiry and philosophical speculation. Sinclair derived enormous benefit from her time at the college, brief as it was. She enjoyed the rigorous academic discipline of lessons every morning, in a range of subjects including scripture, history, literature, English language, geography, arithmetic, geometry, algebra, natural science, physics, physiology, chemistry, French, German, Latin, and Greek. As one of the older girls at the school she was also permitted to undertake, as Beale recommended, 'some systematic reading regarding the history and foundations of philosophy in general and Christian philosophy in particular'.[29] Much of this reading (Beale assigned Plato, for example) was, of course, already familiar to Sinclair.[30]

Mary Sinclair soon came to Dorothea Beale's attention. Their relationship began with a conflict: Sinclair refused to write an essay that Beale had assigned on God.[31] In spite of her fear and mistrust of agnosticism (in the late 1870s she had herself been traumatized by religious doubt), Beale was impressed by Mary Sinclair's insistence on her right to think for herself. Sinclair's obituary in the *Cheltenham Ladies' College Magazine* notes that Beale was struck most of all by her strength of mind: 'Whilst still at College May Sinclair showed conspicuous qualities of independence, originality and intellectual integrity which gained her the special interest of Miss Beale who encouraged her to write.'[32] Beale's concern with women's place in the world, her passionate but troubled Christian faith, and her enthusiasm for philosophical speculation, made her an ideal intellectual guide for Mary Sinclair. Janet Hogarth (later Courtney), who taught philosophy at Cheltenham in the late 1880s, wrote that 'though inclined . . . to be pontifical', Beale could also be 'extremely human', with 'a wonderful instinct for dealing with girls'.[33] Unlike Sinclair's mother, Beale was willing to listen to her religious doubts without simply dismissing them as infantile or wicked. She encouraged and guided Sinclair's study of Western and Eastern philosophies in an attempt simultaneously to acknowledge her anxieties, and to strengthen her wavering faith (Hogarth noted that Beale herself 'yearned to complete the link between Greek thought and Christian mystical interpretation').[34] Like her cousin, Caroline Cornwallis, anonymous author of a series of pamphlets on philosophical and other matters, Beale had no fear that the

[29] Dorothea Beale, 'Philosophy and Religion', in Dorothea Beale, Lucy H. M. Soulsby, and Jane Frances Dove, *Work and Play in Girls' Schools* (New York and Bombay: Longman, Green and Co., 1898), 211.

[30] Ibid. 211–12.

[31] Wilda McNeile to Boll, 16 June 1959, UP, Box 48, fo. 529. *Mary Olivier* also describes a conflict over religion between the headmistress and the young Mary (140), but their relationship survives, and is even strengthened by, their frank disagreement.

[32] See Sinclair's obituary in the *Cheltenham Ladies' College Magazine* (Autumn 1946), 36.

[33] Janet E. Courtney, *Recollected in Tranquillity* (London: William Heinemann, 1926), 113.

[34] Ibid. 116.

study of philosophy would weaken religious belief, and echoing Corn-wallis's own phrase, she believed that philosophy was necessarily the explor-ation of 'the grounds of a rational faith'.[35] For Beale the object of education was to understand the world's, and the child's, relation to God, and the development of an enquiring mind was to her an article of faith. Schools linked the material and the immaterial worlds, as well as helping pupils make their own links and transitions: 'The school is the link between infancy and mature life, between the home and the world, the secular and the spiritual'.[36] The intertwining of the secular and the spiritual, though, could only be experienced if the life of the mind were taken seriously, if girls and women were encouraged to develop their own intellectual autonomy. For a belief to be convincing, it must recognize both 'liberty and obedience': the liberty to ask questions and the obedience to abide by their answers.[37] As editor and founder (in 1880) of the *Cheltenham Ladies' College Magazine* Beale encour-aged Sinclair to think of herself first and foremost as a independent-minded philosopher, and the *Magazine* published a number of Sinclair's early essays and poems on philosophical topics.[38] When in 1895 Sinclair began to publish short stories Beale admonished her: 'You really must not let yourself be diverted altogether from philosophy. You have not thought and suffered so much for nothing, and though your philosophy will come out in most things, even in stories, you *must* give it us sometimes "neat".'[39] Although she could not afford to stop publishing pieces that would earn money, Sinclair, perhaps mindful of Beale's advice, continued to write philosophical books alongside her fiction almost until the end of her career. Beale consolidated her emer-ging sense of herself as a thinker, a woman of ideas, who had the right to challenge even the beliefs which her mother held most dear.

[35]   Beale, 'Philosophy and Religion', 213. Caroline Cornwallis was the anonymous author of most of the books in the series *Small Books on Great Subjects*, which included histories of philosophy, books on gram-mar, a history of the 'ragged schools', and a book on geology. Cornwallis was, to her delight, repeatedly assumed to be a man (see Caroline Frances Cornwallis, 'Preface', *Selections from the Letters of Caroline Frances Cornwallis*, London: Trübner and Co., 1864, p. iii). Cornwallis insisted that she 'would not believe anything which would not *accord* with reason' (Cornwallis to Mrs Atkins, mid-1830s, in Cornwallis, *Selections from the Letters*, 157).

[36]   Beale, 'Philosophy and Religion', 202.

[37]   Beale, *A Few Words to Those Who Are Leaving* (London: George Bell, 1881), 4.

[38]   Sinclair's publications in the *Cheltenham Ladies' College Magazine* include an account of a lecture on 'Descartes', no. 5 (Spring 1882), 95–8; a poem 'A Custance of To-day', no. 20 (Autumn 1889), 207–9; a long narrative poem 'A Study from the Life of Goethe', no. 24 (Autumn 1891), 188–95, later repr. in May Sinclair, *Essays in Verse* (London: Kegan Paul, Trench and Trübner, 1891); *Studies in Plato*. I: 'Was Plato a "Dual-ist"?', no. 27 (Spring 1893), 40–8; 'Sonnets—Professor Jowett', no. 29 (Spring 1894), 48; 'The Platonic Sociology', no. 29 (Spring 1894), 49–53; 'The Philosopher-King', no. 32 (Autumn 1895), 20–6; 'The Things Which Belong Unto the Truth: A Translation of the Fragment . . . from the poem of Parmenides on *Nature*', no. 33 (Spring 1896), 1–6; 'Sonnet', no. 36 (Autumn 1897), 248; 'A Fable', no. 38 (Autumn 1898), 257–8.

[39]   Beale to Sinclair, n.d., in Raikes, *Dorothea Beale of Cheltenham*, 393.

Sinclair did, however, have some doubts about some of Beale's methods. Beale insisted that women, however domestic their habits, should devote as much time as they could to academic study and learning. In her testimony to the Schools' Enquiry Commission of 1864, she stressed the ill effects of intellectual idleness: 'For one girl in the higher middle classes who suffers from overwork, there are, I believe, hundreds whose health suffers from the . . . irritability produced by idleness and frivolity and discontent.'[40] She recommended to her girls that, even after they had left the school, they should enhance their own well-being, both physical and spiritual, by disciplined programmes of reading and study. She encouraged them in what she called 'the work of self-culture': 'Bear this first in mind, that to continue the work of education, of drawing out and developing your powers, is still your duty, and will be to the end of life.'[41] Ethics and philosophy were only formally taught to the young women who stayed at school beyond the age of 18, but Beale recommended philosophy, along with physiology and domestic and political economy, as a suitable subject of study for school leavers.[42] She thus demanded an extraordinary amount of effort and self-discipline from the girls under her care even after they had left the school. Sinclair, already habituated to a life dominated by long periods of solitary reading and learning, was sympathetic only up to a point. Her 1901 story 'Superseded' includes a description of the 'commanding personality' of Miss Cursiter, headmistress of a girls' school, whose lectures to her girls are very similar to those given by Dorothea Beale.[43] Miss Cursiter is a formidable and not entirely likeable woman, with 'an intelligence fervent with the fire of the enthusiast, cold with the renunciant's frost'.[44] Beale's temperament too was marked by an introspective mysticism, and an awkward courage, and like Miss Cursiter she was intent on modernizing women's education.[45] In 'Superseded' Miss Cursiter's advice to the girls and women at the school to

---

[40] Cited in Shillito, *Dorothea Beale*, 41.   [41] Beale, *A Few Words to Those Who Are Leaving*, 14, 6.

[42] See Beale, 'Introduction' to Beale, Soulsby, and Dove (eds.), *Work and Play in Girls' Schools*, 10–11; and Beale, *A Few Words to Those Who Are Leaving*, 8. It seems that Sinclair was among those who returned to school after they left for philosophy lessons. Janet Hogarth, who taught at the school from 1888 to 1891, remembered Sinclair as one of her philosophy pupils: 'We were fellow-learners rather than teacher and pupil, and she has since gone far ahead of me—witness her *Defence of Idealism*. But thirty-five years ago we sat side by side on a back bench in the College Hall, spelling out together the *Phaedo* and the *Apology*, whilst lessons on every sort of subject went on around us' (Courtney, *Recollected in Tranquillity*, 118).

[43] Sinclair, 'Superseded', 219. Miss Cursiter tells her girls to spend their evenings reading poetry, telling them that 'if your training has done nothing else for you it has taught you the economy of time' (ibid. 221–2).

[44] Ibid. 218.

[45] In 1856 Beale resigned her post as tutor at the newly founded Queen's College in London over a dispute about managerial control; and in the following year she was about to resign the headship of Casterton School in Yorkshire because she felt her hands tied by the restrictive attitudes of the governors, when they fired her. See Shillito, *Dorothea Beale*, 14–24. Miss Cursiter is keen to purge her staff: she 'would have liked to make a clean sweep of the old staff and to fill their places with women like Rhoda Vivian, young and

spend their evenings studying great literature causes the earnest middle-aged arithmetic teacher, Juliana Quincy, to drive herself to physical and mental collapse in an attempt to be worthy of the school. Juliana's doctor, with whom she is in love, inveighs against the evils of educating women against the grain of their physiological systems: 'Your precious system . . . sets up the same absurd standard for every woman, the brilliant genius and the average imbecile'.[46] The outcome of the story—Juliana's death—suggests that Sinclair was writing a cautionary tale about the ill effects of mental strain on women. She herself, while attracted to a life of study, was repeatedly laid up by exhaustion and overwork, and her enthusiasm for Beale's open and reflective approach to religious and philosophical issues was tempered by a recognition that Beale was not always sympathetic to the frailty of the bodies she had under her care.[47] Sinclair found Beale stimulating but also very taxing, and when her father died only a few months after she arrived in Cheltenham, and her mother more than ever needed her company and help at home, she seems to have agreed fairly willingly to come back at the end of the academic year.[48]

Mary Sinclair was by now a pretty, slender young woman, barely five feet tall. She wore her thick, chestnut hair in a plaited coronet, her black eyes were intense and watchful, and her voice was crisp and quiet. In later life she filled out into a 'compact little woman', dressed in dark colours—black, brown, and mauve—sometimes richly embroidered and set off with elaborate neckchains.[49] Virginia Woolf in 1909 remarked that she had 'little round eyes bright as steel', and James Walter Smith described her as 'a small and demure being' reminiscent of 'the prim mistress of some young ladies' finishing school': 'Her manner was as quiet as her dress. Her power—indefinable, all-observant, analytic—is to be found in her eyes; what those eyes miss isn't worth hiding or trying to hide.'[50] Sinclair observed the world from behind an almost 'immobile face', projecting a 'Buddha-like calm

magnificent and strong. . . . the new staff, modern to its finger-tips, was all but complete and perfect now' ('Superseded', 209).

[46] Sinclair, 'Superseded', 270.

[47] See e.g. a letter from Sinclair to Violet Hunt in 1908: 'Oh dear me—Virtue is never rewarded. I've felt it ever since I got up at 6 o'clock on Friday—I'm afraid I shall have to go easily and not work again for a bit' (Sinclair to Hunt, 24 Mar. 1908, in Violet Hunt Papers, Collection 4607, Division of Rare and Manuscript Collections, Cornell University).

[48] See Zegger, *May Sinclair*, 16. Mary in *Mary Olivier* is sent for by her mother after only three weeks at boarding school (MO, 141–2).

[49] Hyde, 'Miss May Sinclair', 1, UP, Box 48, fo. 525; Rascoe, 'Contemporary Reminiscences', 25.

[50] Cited in 'May Sinclair', in Dilly Tante (ed.), *Living Authors: A Book of Biographies* (New York: The H. W. Wilson Company, 1931), 373–4: at 374; Woolf to Lady Robert Cecil, 12 Apr. 1909, in *The Flight of the Mind: The Letters of Virginia Woolf*, i. *1888–1912*, ed. Nigel Nicolson and Joanne Trautmann (London: Chatto and Windus, 1975), 390.

and inscrutable charm': 'what she sees excites in her no apparent surprise, or, indeed, any visible emotion'. She seldom smiled, expressing amusement simply 'by slight muscular contractions at the corners of her eyes'.[51] Only cats, it seemed, could arouse her passion, and throughout her life she lavished affection on a succession of black toms.[52] Sinclair was always careful of people, as if each new acquaintance represented another potential source of danger. She could be generous, although she rarely gave way to impulse, and she once remarked to Catherine Dawson Scott that pity was her strongest emotion.[53] But the overall impression she gave was of someone defending herself against the world, and observing its antics from behind a carefully arranged mask: her friend novelist Ida Wylie remembered her as a 'shy, remote creature'.[54]

It was to a sadly diminished and financially stretched household that this attractive, withdrawn young woman returned when she came home from Cheltenham in 1882. William was now in Hull, and Frank was in India. Harold, Reginald, and Joseph were apparently still living with Amelia. But Joseph was restless: there were few opportunities for him in England. In 1885 he emigrated to Canada, and Sinclair never saw him again. As it turned out, this was only the first of many bereavements.

In the early 1880s, soon after Mary Sinclair returned home, what was left of the family moved back up north to be nearer their Liverpool cousins the Higgins, but in spite of the beauty of their surroundings (they were in the village of Gresford, near Wrexham), they were uncertain and apprehensive. Harold's health was not good: he was feverish, tired, and nauseous, and in September 1886, when he was 28, the family discovered that he had kidney disease, complicated by a congenital heart defect. Sinclair watched him weaken and was powerless to help him. On 28 August 1887, four days after her twenty-fourth birthday, he died. She scarcely had time to recover from this loss when she heard in a telegram from India that Frank had died suddenly, aged 32, on 18 April 1889. It was not even a heroic death: like Mark in *Mary Olivier*, Frank, reckless and extrovert to the end, was showing off at a party in the officers' mess, and suddenly collapsed with heart failure, caused by the same mitral valve irregularity which had killed his brother less than two years earlier.[55]

---

[51] Rascoe, 'Contemporary Reminiscences', 25.   [52] Ibid.

[53] C. A. Dawson Scott, 'Miss May Sinclair's New Novel', *Bookman* (London), 61 (Mar. 1922), 265–6: at 266.

[54] I. A. R. Wylie, *My Life with George: An Unconventional Autobiography* (New York: Random House, 1940), 178.

[55] See his captain's description of Mark's death in *Mary Olivier*: 'Peters is the heaviest man in our battery, and Major Olivier was carrying him on his back. We oughtn't to have let him do it. But we didn't know there

Sinclair, in spite of everything still her mother's closest companion, had to find some way to break it to her that her favourite son had died a farcical death.

The loss of her brothers and her mother's disapproval of her growing agnosticism only strengthened Mary Sinclair's reliance on intellectual life as a place where she could be sure of finding both solitude and comfort. In the wake of the deaths of Harold and Frank, the body appeared more and more to be a fragile and unreliable home. Not only did she begin to mistrust human biology, but the metaphysical basis of the world seemed uninviting and indifferent. Already aware of the ways in which science and reason might challenge the bases of religious faith, she explored with more and more urgency the possibility of some kind of reconciliation between theology and philosophy, between the emotions and the intellect, the body and the mind. She followed Beale's guidance, reading (and rereading) Plato, Aristotle, Kant, Hegel, Fichte, T. H. Green, and Schwegler's *Handbook of the History of Philosophy*.[56] Beale explicitly used Kantian concepts and vocabulary to try to entice Sinclair back to the Christian faith: 'The facts of conscience are to me quite inexplicable on any other hypothesis than that of One who is supremely good speaking to His children, not through "eye or ear", but directly. There is the unity of consciousness which makes memory possible, and moral judgment possible; and yet there is a secondary consciousness, the "categorical imperative", the ideal goodness, ever revealing to man a higher and better.'[57] Idealist philosophy seemed to offer Sinclair a number of ways to continue to believe in some form of transcendence without either abandoning her belief in reason as a means of knowing the world, or—what seemed to her to amount to the same thing—surrendering herself to a Christian creed which she could not fully uphold. As T. H. Green (who would become, in the early 1890s, one of her favourite philosophers) put it: 'No desire which forms part of our moral experience would be what it is, if it were not the desire of a subject which also understands: no act of our intelligence would be what it is, if it were not the act of a subject who also desires.'[58] Abandoned by almost all the men who had surrounded her as she grew, confined with a mother whose Christian belief was rigid and unsympathetic to those with doubts, Sinclair felt herself desperate to believe in a world that was moving not towards a

was anything wrong with his heart. He didn't know it himself. We thought he was fooling when he dropped on the floor' (MO, 304).

[56] Albert Schwegler, *Handbook of the History of Philosophy*, trans. James Hutchison Stirling (1847; 7th edn. Edinburgh: Edmonston, 1879). Dorothea Beale gives a list of recommended readings in philosophy, which includes Schwegler, in 'Philosophy and Religion', 211. At her death Sinclair bequeathed her copy of Schwegler, along with all her other philosophical texts, to the London Library.

[57] Beale to Sinclair, 5 Jan. 1887, in Raikes, *Dorothea Beale of Cheltenham*, 391.

[58] T. H. Green, *Prolegomena to Ethics*, ed. A. C. Bradley (Oxford: Clarendon, 1883), 135.

spiritual and emotional hinterland, but towards an ever more subtly harmonized system of human and divine relations. During the 1880s, she struggled to develop her own philosophy of mind.

Sinclair was also spending a great deal of time writing poetry. Publishing verse made little money, of course (she told Willis Steell that it did not have 'a liberal-paying market'), but—with William, Joseph, and Reginald still alive—she was not yet her mother's sole financial support, and could just afford to write what she wanted.[59] In 1886 her first collection, *Nakiketas and Other Poems*, appeared under the pseudonym of 'Julian Sinclair', and she was finally a published author.[60]

In *Nakiketas and Other Poems* Sinclair situates her philosophical concerns in the context of familial conflict, a battlefield she had come to know well. The long narrative poem 'Nakiketas', for example, describes a son who challenges his father to sacrifice him to the gods, and 'Apollodorus' explores the relation between knowledge, love, and death through the story of a man's relation to the woman who brought him up.[61] Even in these early works Sinclair sees family and sexual relationships defining the shape of philosophical endeavour. Like Mary Olivier, Nakiketas and Apollodorus learn in and through other people: their evolving epistemologies are also dramas of disappointment, hope, and fulfilment. As Sinclair wrote in 1893 of idealism, her early poetry aims at the 'annihilation of the distinction between the secular and the religious'.[62] The secular institutions of the family and of romantic love are seen here as shaping the quest for knowledge itself.

'Nakiketas' is based on a legend from the Katha-Upanishad, the third section of the Vedas, or ancient Hindu sacred literature. Sinclair's interest in the Vedas was first sparked by Beale, who was introduced to Hindu religion and philosophy when Indian student Pundita Ramabai arrived at Cheltenham Ladies' College in 1883. The first English translation of the Upanishads was published in 1832, but the late 1870s saw a revival of interest in them, with new translations by Robert Ernest Hume and philologist Max Müller appearing in 1877 and 1879. Both Beale and Sinclair were attracted to what

---

[59] Steell, 'Miss May Sinclair Tells Why She Isn't a Poet', 513.

[60] Boll notes that the 'somber pages' of *Nakiketas* show Sinclair searching 'for the authority to justify her agnosticism and for some kind of reconciliation between the Greek worship of vitality and the Eastern worship of death' (*Miss May Sinclair*, 39).

[61] Other poems in the collection include another long narrative poem, 'Helen', in which a woman unwittingly marries the man who was responsible for her father's financial ruin; 'George Eliot', which celebrates Eliot for being both 'manlike' in her learning and 'woman-weak to lean | On man's firm heart' (N, 71); and five short lyric poems, 'A Fable' (also published in *Cheltenham Ladies' College Magazine*, see n. 38, above), 'The Singer', 'Immortelle', 'Euthanasia', and 'Christapollo: In Memoriam Percy Shelley', which all, like 'Nakiketas', take up the question of life after death.

[62] Sinclair, 'The Ethical and Religious Import of Idealism', *New World*, 2 (Dec. 1893), 694–708: at 708.

Hume calls the Upanishads' 'system of intelligent monism', but Sinclair's version of the story of Nakiketas adapts and fleshes out the Vedic text with her own counter-narrative of the lost son who can express his feeling of being undervalued by his father only through a masochistic defiance and a fearless search for knowledge even beyond death.[63] 'Nakiketas' tells the story of the boy Nakiketas, son of Brahman Vagasravasa, who has pledged to sacrifice all his possessions, and all that he values, to the gods. Nakiketas is weary of the succession of religious rituals which make up his father's days, and he challenges his father to sacrifice him too, as his dearest possession. Enraged, his father agrees, and Nakiketas is slaughtered. Because Nakiketas has been left alone and unwelcomed for three days in the halls of death, Death, on his return, offers Nakiketas three wishes. Nakiketas's first wish is that he and his father might forgive and love one another again; his second wish is to know the nature of the sacrificial fire that leads to heaven; and his third wish is to know what happens after death.

Vedic philosophy allowed Sinclair to define an idealist position which had a specifically religious authority behind it. Sinclair's version of Nakiketas's story, in spite of the explicit reference to the Upanishads, and the poem's subtitle, 'Legend of the Katha-Upanishad', explores Western as well as Eastern philosophical discourses. Nakiketas's mind is described as a reflection of ideal presences and deities:

> a tranquil pool,
> Within whose twilight clearness he might see
> Sometimes the faces of the Bright Ones, shades
> And faint reflections of invisible things. (N, 2)

In the context of Hindu philosophy, these lines refer to the Brahma, or 'world-soul', expressing itself through Nakiketas (as Hume, author of the 1877 translation, explains, the Brahma is found not only in cosmic phenomena, but also in the 'organic and mental functions of the human person').[64] The Upanishads appealed to Sinclair precisely because the doctrine of the Brahma, or world-soul, did not distinguish between the human and the divine, or between the knowable and the unknowable world. But the phrase 'faint reflections' also suggests Platonic ideal forms and the noumenal world of Kant's philosophy. As Hume notes, the texts work their way towards a classic idealist position:

[63] *The Thirteen Principal Upanishads translated from the Sanskrit*, ed. and introd. Robert Ernest Hume (1877; rev. edn. Oxford: Oxford University Press, 1931), 2.

[64] Ibid., 'Introduction', 23.

Epistemological idealism must henceforth be the path travelled in order to reach the goal of an absolute unity. . . . Thus that world-ground, that unity of being which was being searched for realistically outside of the self, and which, as it was being approached, seemed to recede back into the illusory and into the unknowable, is none other than the self, which had eluded cognition for the reason that, as the subject of consciousness, it could not become an object.[65]

Consciousness becomes the harmonizing principle of the world.

But the danger of a belief in idealism is the fear that one may be lost in a world of deceptive illusion. Nakiketas walks 'as one who grasps in waking hours | After the feeble shadow of a dream' (N, 3). He can find no 'place' for the gods in whom his father believes, and his dissatisfaction with 'the empty sound of Vedic hymns' (N, 4) invokes Socratic ignorance as a kind of admission of defeat:

> The wise, the wise who taught us—what are they?
> Who know no more of death or life than I,
> Who know but this—that nothing can be known, . . . (N, 4)

Nakiketas's godless universe is also one in which epistemologies are baffled and fathers are neglectful. Believing despairingly that the self and its ignorance mark the limits of our world, he decks out his own body in an attempt to stage its puzzling centrality. The sterility of agnosticism is displaced into a defiant narcissism:

> He turned, and in his chamber shut him up;
> And thence, arrayed in all his costliest
> And fairest—purple, scarlet, chains of gold,
> Ankles and armlets, gemmed as for a feast,
> Went forth, to serve before the bidden guests.
>   There, when his father saw him, how he shone
> Above his boyhood's grace and loveliness
> In gorgeous hues, and jewelled; he waxed wroth,
> And cried, rebuking in his anger, 'Boy!
> Thou meanest insolence to me, and these
> My guests; such costly garb and ornament
> Beseem a prince—not one who stands to serve. (N, 5–6)

Sceptical of authority, Nakiketas challenges it not only by defying his father's instructions, but also by elevating the human body and its beauty above its allotted place in the socio-religious hierarchy. Far from renouncing the world, Nakiketas's loving adornment of his own body celebrates earthly

---

[65] Ibid. 42–3.

pleasures above all others. His bejewelled body stages excess: it shines '*above*
his boyhood's grace and loveliness' (N, 5, my emphasis). Nakiketas becomes
a symbol of compulsive over-investment in beauty, anticipating Wilde's
images of the doomed Dorian Gray (*The Picture of Dorian Gray* was serialized in *Lippincott's Magazine* in 1890).[66] His echoing of his dead mother's
looks, and his elaborate clothes, feminize him and focus the poem's erotic
interest around him, giving the poem a tone which runs quite counter to that
of the Katha-Upanishad from which Sinclair was working. 'Nakiketas'
explores the problem of the artist who has only his own body and mind with
which to work, the artist in a world which has no order and no beauty other
than that which comes from within himself. In drawing attention to himself
as a costly and coveted object, Nakiketas also dramatizes his own Oedipal
history, the resemblance to his dead mother which is his main attraction for
his father. His religious defiance—his insistence that his father second-
guess the gods by sacrificing his only son—is bound up, as Sinclair's was,
with a challenge to the parent for whom he is only a secondary object of
affection.

Nakiketas's demand that his father sacrifice him precisely because he
loves him also draws attention to the dynamics of filial self-sacrifice, a theme
to which Sinclair, already aware in 1886 that she would have to devote at
least the next few years of her life to caring for her mother, continually
returned in her fiction and her poetry. Nakiketas's sacrifice is literal where
Sinclair's was, of course, metaphorical, but in a poem from 1889 she wrote
about a woman whose death-in-life looking after her ageing father actually
does culminate in her demise:

> Oh, death in life! where possibilities
> Of everlasting love and lovelier thought,
> Flowers blasted before seed-time, come to nought!
> Oh! cruel waste of life that knows no birth,
> But dies in darkness—crueller than death
> That closes a long life-time, leaving faith,
> And hope, and loving memory upon earth.[67]

Nakiketas's masochistic offering of himself parallels the woman's gift of her
own life to her father.

---

[66] Sinclair herself published a poem called 'Decadence' in *Academy*, no. 1142 (24 Mar. 1894), 249, describing *fin-de-siècle* weariness in terms that are very similar to those used to describe Nakiketas: 'The gods and
heroes they are dust, and none | Knoweth their place, and love and light are gone | Where none can follow.'

[67] Sinclair, 'Custance of To-day', 208. The woman's situation parallels Sinclair's with her own father,
and later her mother, very closely: her 'one care' is 'How best to save him from himself, and raise | His
sordid spirit from the dust, or share | With him the shame of failure' (207).

The effect of Nakiketas's challenge is to make sure that his father cannot win. If he refuses to sacrifice Nakiketas, it can only be on the grounds that he is not his most treasured possession—an admission that would betray both himself and Nakiketas; and if he agrees, he must put to death his only son. Furthermore, the dividing-line between affection and possession is blurred. Does Nakiketas's father *own* him? Was Sinclair, unable to leave her mother because of their mutual emotional dependency, at the same time just another of the objects Amelia Sinclair salvaged from the wreck of her Rock Ferry home? Did Amelia demonstrate her love for her daughter by condemning her, like the woman in 'A Custance of To-day', to a life in her mother's shadow?

Nakiketas implicitly asks all of these questions. Unlike the Nakiketas of the Upanishads, who is concerned primarily not with his father's love for him, but with the love of the gods for his father, Sinclair's Nakiketas just wants to be reassured of his father's love and loneliness now that he is gone, and his wish is granted with a vision of his father in despair:

> Vagasravasa now, in loneliness,
> In ashes, couched on the rough jungle grass,
> Mourns his slain son with unavailing prayers. (N, 10)

Nakiketas is satisfied with this image of desolation. It marks his absence, defines his empty place. It also emphasizes the aggressive nature of his offer of himself. In Sinclair's hands the religious drama of the Katha-Upanishad becomes an Oedipal narrative which throws into relief the social and familial ramifications of religious practices. It is the complex structure of human emotions, as well as the cosmic order, which is at issue here.

This shift in emphasis is most pronounced in Sinclair's version of Death's reply to Nakiketas's question about the world beyond death. In the Katha-Upanishad, Nakiketas's question is posed in philosophical terms: he wants to know whether the dead can be said to have substance: ' "he [the dead man] exists," say some; "[h]e exists not," say others'.[68] In 'Nakiketas', however, Nakiketas is concerned only with his own self-consciousness and how he can come to know the limits of his world:

> And for I know my soul scarce lives, but lies
> As in a dream 'twixt wakening and sleep,
> Or betwixt sleep and wakening—tell me, thou,
> That which was hidden of old; say, whither wend
> The souls of men, . . . (N, 11)

---

[68] *Thirteen Principal Upanishads*, 344.

He lives in the world of illusion and representation, a world familiar to Sinclair through her work on Kant.[69] For Nakiketas, uncertainty about the nature of reality and of perception shifts—as it will so many times in Sinclair's later texts like 'The Intercessor'—into curiosity about the world of the dead. What is the nature of a world without bodies? Do the dead have bodies? How might we come to know them?

Death's answer places human thought squarely at the centre of the world:

> Knowledge is Being. Man lives but as he knows.
>
> .   .   .   .
>
> Vainly or well, in his gross element
> Man works, and from the clay of his own hands,
> Or dreams of his own soul, he shapes the gods. (N, 12–13)

This answer may at first look like a condemnation of human solipsism, but if we read it in context of both Sinclair's interest in, and the closeness of Vedic philosophy to, transcendental idealism, it becomes apparent that this is an early statement of views that Sinclair would not express openly in print until 1893. In the *Cheltenham Ladies' College Magazine* essay on Plato published in that year, she wrote that 'the presupposition of all thinking . . . is neither more nor less than the knowing subject, the self-creative activity of thought, the sole thing stable and certain'.[70] Death's answer echoes Kant's contention that human thought structures all perception according to its own necessary forms, space and time.[71] Sinclair's Death is an idealist, placing categories of human thought at the centre of the knowable universe.

'Apollodorus', the other major philosophical poem in *Nakiketas and Other Poems*, similarly takes up the relationship between perception, knowledge, and parental affection. The derivation of the title is unclear, and Sinclair gives no epigraph, but she may have been referring to the artist in Athens in the fifth century BC, who was one of the first to paint illusionistic pictures. The poem deals centrally with the relation of illusion to love. Apollodorus grows up with a beautiful maiden, who teaches him about the infancy of the world, but after some time, he is torn from her. When he is again free to travel, he seeks her, following the sound of her voice, but everywhere he goes, he sees only his own form reflected in the waters and the shadows. Just as he is about to give up hope, however, he hears her again, and the world is filled with her image. In celebration of their reunion he sings his 'Song of

---

[69] Sinclair is referring here to the Hindu idea of 'Maya', the world of illusion in which we are all trapped until we reach nirvana.

[70] Sinclair, 'Was Plato a "Dualist"?', 44.

[71] Kant develops this view most notably in *Critique of Pure Reason* (1781; rev. edn. 1787).

Life', but after three years, he tells her he wants to leave the hills and valleys for a while to sing her praises to other men. She tells him that he cannot leave her, and that night he dreams he sees her spinning a tapestry which bears the words 'Thou knowest me not. I am not that I seem'. He dreams once more, and this time the threads of the tapestry wind themselves around him, trapping him. He wakes in terror and deserts her. Tormented by deathly images of her, he finds her again, accuses her of deception, and she flees him. Finally, he has a dying vision of her hand in hand with death, and singing his 'Song of Death', goes happily to his grave.

This curious narrative bears traces of a number of literary influences: the style is reminiscent of both Keats and Milton, as is the section in which Apollodorus tries to embrace his loved one in a dream.[72] The description of Apollodorus' childhood, and the woman's close identification with a pastoral landscape, recall Wordsworth's 'Lucy' poems.[73] This is a story of a fall from innocence to experience, a transition from a world in which sensory perception is immediate and whole, to one governed by representation and loss. It would be possible to give a Lacanian reading of Apollodorus' upbringing, described in the poem in the following terms:

> with [Apollodorus]
> All thought and passion, life and love were one,
> And one their object—'twas a maid, whose face
> E'en in his infant dreams, bent dimly o'er
> His cradle, dimly beautiful; . . .
> Till rough hands rent him from her, and a scroll
> Was given him, and he was bound and bent
> Over its characters, and heard no more
> The maiden's legends; for her face was shut
> Out of his days. (N, 47)

As he grows, Apollodorus is severed from part of himself in the violent transition from an unmediated relationship with a woman to a world in which he is alone with, and in, language. This is the Kristevan as well as the Lacanian symbolic, in which he will have access only to traces of a quasi-maternal

---

[72] See e.g. 'Methought I saw my late espousèd saint', in John Milton, *Complete Shorter Poems*, ed. John Carey (London: Longman, 1968), 413–14: 'But O as to embrace me she inclined, | I waked, she fled, and day brought back my night'. See also Homer's *Odyssey*, bk. 10, ll. 204–9, in which Odysseus in Hades tries to embrace his dead mother: 'Thrice I sprang towards her, and my heart bade me clasp her, and thrice she flitted from my arms like a shadow or a dream' (Homer, *The Odyssey*, i, trans. A. T. Murray, Loeb Classical Library, no. 104, Cambridge, Mass.: Harvard University Press, 1919, 401).

[73] See e.g. 'Three years she grew in sun and shower', 1799, in *Wordsworth: Poetical Works*, ed. Ernest de Selincourt (London: Oxford University Press, 1936), 148: 'The stars of midnight shall be dear | To her; and she shall lean her ear | In many a secret place | Where rivulets dance their wayward round, | And beauty born of murmuring sound | Shall pass into her face.'

bodily presence: the woman's voice, her shadow. Even when he finds her again she will exist only in representations: in song, in dreams, in hallucinations. The poem explores the dilemma of a subject split off from itself, wrenched away from an originary state of unity: the self-conscious subject of Descartes, for example, or the alienated subject of Lacan. Essentially this is the drama of modernity, of the sceptical subject. As Schwegler puts it in Sinclair's textbook, the *Handbook to the History of Philosophy*, 'the originators of modern philosophy, Bacon and Descartes, began with scepticism'.[74] If for Apollodorus thought is the organizing principle of the universe, then thought is also always a form of mourning for the lost wholeness of the self. In Dorothea Beale's words: 'man is self-conscious, he can become an object to himself'.[75] To be conscious, to speak, is to be aware of your own difference from yourself. Like Apollodorus, we live in loss.

'Apollodorus', then, is largely an elegy for the unselfconscious subject. But it is also an anatomy of romance, a meditation on the relation of desire to representation. After their second rift, when Apollodorus announces his intention to leave the woman and sing her praises elsewhere, he has a vision of her singing and spinning. Her voice has been Apollodorus' erotic focus, who, in his search for her, pursued 'the faint sweetness of the sound' (N, 48). The noise of her spinning, however, drowns out her singing:

> The maiden of his love, before a wheel,
> Winding a fearful woof of her own hair,
> And singing as she span; while evermore
> The whirring and the noise of that great wheel
> Made dim her delicate music; in the woof
> Was wrought a running pattern, stars and suns,
> And crescents, shapes of birds and beasts and flowers,
> With their own hues . . . (N, 53–4)

As she spins her own hair into a tapestry, the material substance of her body is displaced into text, and her voice (the trace of Kristeva's semiotic 'chora'), is muffled by the sounds of her work.[76] Again loss is imaged as a fall away from the fullness of the body, and into representation. From a form of bodily merging or identification ('the light | Of her clear eyes was sight within his

[74] Schwegler, *Handbook of the History of Philosophy*, 150.

[75] Beale, 'Philosophy and Religion', 214.

[76] Hair carried a crucial symbolic significance for the Victorians. Maturity for women was indicated by binding the hair, or wearing it 'up', and mourning bracelets and other jewellery woven from the hair of dead loved ones were commonplace. Hair signifies both sexuality and mortality. See Elisabeth G. Gitter, 'The Power of Women's Hair in the Victorian Imagination', *PMLA* 99 (Oct. 1984), 936–54; and my 'Charlotte Mew and May Sinclair: A Love-Song', *Critical Quarterly*, 37 (1995), 3–17.

own, | And . . . her love was life within his limbs', N, 51) Apollodorus now sees their estrangement inscribed in and through her body.

His most horrifying vision comes when he dreams for the third time, and finds himself stifled by her hair:

> The mighty woof flowed downward from her form,
> And carpeted the ground, and rose again
> On every side close-woven like a wall
> Of pictured tapestry; while louder grew
> The whirring of her monstrous wheel, more vast
> The fearful web, that seemed to clutch and wrap
> Live creatures in its folds like summer flies;
> And as she swifter span, there as he stood
> Wove o'er and wrapped him shroudlike, horrible;
> Till blinded, pinioned, strangling, he awoke. (N, 54–5)

This scene too has its literary forebears: Tennyson's Lady of Shalott, for example, weaving her tapestry of the illusions which are all she can safely look at.[77] But in 'Apollodorus' this is a nightmare about not being able to escape from illusion: the pictures on the tapestry now seem like animals which have been trapped. These lines partially echo Nakiketas's plaintive remark, in the earlier poem, that he lives 'as in a dream 'twixt wakening and sleep' (N, 11), but they also represent at once the crisis of the desiring subject, whose desire is generated by the alienations of language, and of the agnostic philosopher, for whom the substance and logic of the material world are always in doubt. Apollodorus cannot escape the nightmare of body as text, of the displacement of experience into representation. His fear is that he will never again reach the real.

Terrified by his dream, Apollodorus flees the maiden. But now he is haunted by hallucinatory images of her grotesquely transformed body.

> She came to him
> At times, a blood-lipped phantom, hunger-eyed;
> At times, in all her ancient loveliness
> He saw her, hand-in-hand with Sin, go down
> To dance with Death before the gates of hell,
> Or stand, a thing diseased, whose leprous breasts
> Nourished a hidden brood—deformities
> And shapes of sin-begotten sickliness; . . . (N, 55–6)

---

[77] Alfred, Lord Tennyson, 'The Lady of Shalott', 1833, in *The Poetical Works of Tennyson, Cambridge Edition*, ed. G. Robert Stange (Boston: Houghton Mifflin, 1974), 27: 'But in her web she still delights | To weave the mirror's magic sights'.

Sinclair is here echoing Milton's *Paradise Lost* with its image of Sin and Death at the gates of Hell.[78] The woman's body has become grotesquely fertile, its life-giving potential suddenly terrifying and fatal. In a classic Kleinian (or pre-Kleinian) move, the maternal body has become a site of horror. It is as though representation—the dream of the tapestry—is inevitably followed by a vision of death, but a death which is crucially bound up with desire: the sexual body becomes both fecund and death-dealing.

At the end of the poem Apollodorus offers advice to those who come after him. He urges them to note that the soul both creates, and is sustained by, its own love-objects: 'as best the soul | Can bear to look upon Nature, she appears' (N, 66). His mistake was not to understand that the ideal takes many forms:

> I myself,
> In my imperfect vision, did divide
> That Being, and my spirit but desired
> According to its knowledge; now I know
> That One, the manifold in seeming fair! (N, 67)

In failing to arrive at an understanding of the relation of the One to the many, Apollodorus condemned himself to a life amongst phantoms and hallucinations. His advice reimagines the world of representation as one which does have some meaningful relation to an evolving unity or reality. The poem apparently shifts from a Kantian to a Hegelian understanding of the phenomenal world. As Schwegler puts it, Hegel 'conceived this universal [the Absolute] not as indifference, but rather as development, as a universal in which the principle of difference is immanent, and which uncloses itself into the entire wealth of the actuality exhibited by the worlds of mind and of matter'.[79] Apollodorus experienced the fall into representation as nightmare, but by the end of the poem he has found a way to explain his own alienation as only one moment in an evolving process of differentiation. According to Sinclair's own commentary on T. H. Green, Apollodorus' final speech is an act of self-assertion: 'The subject can only assert itself *as* subject by giving rise to an objective world of difference and change in which it is, so to speak, reflected back on itself from every side'.[80] In recognizing that the multiple images of his loved one were an expression of the 'manifold' (N, 67) of both the world and of his own evolving consciousness, Apollodorus comes to

---

[78] John Milton, *Paradise Lost*, bk. II (1667), ed. Alastair Fowler (London: Longman, 1968), 120–1: 'The one seemed a woman to the waist, and fair, | But ended foul in many a scaly fold | Voluminous and vast, a serpent armed | With mortal sting; about her middle round | A cry of hell hounds ... when they list, would creep, | If aught disturbed their noise, into her womb.'

[79] Schwegler, *Handbook of the History of Philosophy*, 315.

[80] Sinclair, 'Ethical and Religious Import of Idealism', 698.

understand the process of dialectical evolution. The thesis becomes its own antithesis and then arrives at a new synthesis. Love is defended as the dialectical principle by which the soul sustains itself:

> For dear life's sake itself the soul doth cling
> Unto the object of its sweet desire;
> For they are wed together; if the one
> Should flee, the other must pursue; if one
> Should change, the other changeth; for indeed
> The very law of life that binds in one
> The outer and the inner, needeth this; . . . (N, 67)

Without this dynamic of alienation and identification between desire and its objects, the soul would be unable to live. It finds its existence in the process of its own self-differentiation.

The volume *Nakiketas*, then, dramatizes the anguish of the Oedipal soul lost in a world of appearances. In both 'Nakiketas' and 'Apollodorus' philosophy comes to the rescue of religious doubt. It both confirms the protagonists' fears—that much of their experience is self-created or even delusional—and offers them a way of seeing those delusions as part of a higher process of evolution. Mary Sinclair, unable to adopt a religious creed in which she did not believe, continued to search for a secular form of belief, and in the 1880s idealist philosophy seemed to offer her one way into the kind of modern faith that she so much craved. But, as 'Nakiketas' and 'Apollodorus' imply, Sinclair could not separate her religious dilemmas from the familial situation in which she found herself. She rejected her mother's Protestant faith, and, in spite of Amelia's opposition to her philosophical studies, continued to read and to explore, knowing that she still needed to believe in something. When it seemed likely, as her brothers died one by one, that responsibility for her mother would eventually fall on her alone, her need for a spiritual life became even more acute. In 1912 she wrote that it was exactly the kind of self-sacrifice that she was called on to make that fostered the need for a spiritual life: 'Spirituality, so difficult for [man] to come by, has been positively thrust upon woman. Born of her sacrificial destiny, it has been expected of her, nourished in her, guarded by all the sanctions of her life. She has had time for it, all the time of all the ages.'[81] Mary Sinclair, alone at home with a querulous and hostile mother and one remaining brother, Reginald, could not find a spiritual life that satisfied her. As we shall see, her dilemma became even more acute as the century drew to its close. In the 1890s her agnosticism would cost her her marriage.

[81] Ead., 'Defence of Men', 560.

2

A Crisis of Love and Faith

=

MARY SINCLAIR was in many ways an unlikely candidate for the role of philosopher-poet. In 1886 she was living in obscurity in North Wales with her mother and Reginald, the last brother still at home, and few people knew that she was the author of *Nakiketas and Other Poems*, published in that year under the pseudonym 'Julian Sinclair'. In later years Sinclair would be acclaimed as one of the few brilliant women philosophers of her time—one of the only philosophers in England to defend idealist thought against the onslaught of mathematical philosophy and logic.[1] But in the late 1880s that kind of recognition was far in the future. Sinclair was still not sure of her own view of the world: the intellectual and emotional perplexity that had shaped *Nakiketas* continued to trouble her as she searched in vain for rational proof of God's existence. In the words of Edward Caird, a Scottish idealist philosopher whom Dorothea Beale recommended to Sinclair in 1893:

In face of the modern spirit of criticism, it is rarely possible for educated men, and for students of philosophy it is impossible, to rest for the entire support of their spiritual life upon the simple intuitions of faith. For them the age of unconsciousness is past, and they must call in the aid to reflection, if it were only to heal the wounds of reflection itself.[2]

---

[1] In 1917, after the publication of her book *A Defence of Idealism*, May Sinclair became a member of the Aristotelian Society for the Systematic Study of Philosophy (an accolade of which, according to her friend Ida Wylie, she was intensely proud) and, in 1923, a year after her book *The New Idealism* appeared, she was invited by John Henry Muirhead to contribute to a collection of essays by living philosophers, *Contemporary British Philosophy*. He noted that 'there is no other woman writer' on the list. See Boll, *Miss May Sinclair*, 19, and Wylie, *My Life with George*, 179. Sinclair's books on philosophy met with acclaim from figures such as Bertrand Russell (see Russell, 'Philosophic Idealism at Bay', *Nation and Athenaeum*, 31, 5 Aug. 1922, 625–6).

[2] Edward Caird, 'The Problem of Philosophy at the Present Time', Introductory Address to the Philosophical Society of the University of Edinburgh, 1881, in *Essays on Literature and Philosophy*, 2 vols. (Glasgow: James Maclehose and Sons, 1892), ii. 195. Dorothea Beale wrote to Sinclair in Dec. 1893 that she wished Sinclair could 'go to Oxford, and get to know Caird', who was Master of Balliol College. See Raikes, *Dorothea Beale of Cheltenham*, 392.

'The simple intuitions of faith' eluded Sinclair, who continued to depend upon 'reflection', even as it seemed to take her further and further from the spiritual certainty she craved.

Her second collection of poetry, *Essays in Verse* (published in January 1892), staked out some of the philosophical and theological positions open to her: Roman Catholicism, a Protestant belief in the 'double revelation' (EV, 9) of reason and faith, and a secular faith, German idealism. In 'Guyon' she tentatively endorses idealism as a substitute for religious belief, and, as if in recognition of this first public statement of her own agnostic philosophical position, it was in the signature to this volume that she first adopted the name by which she would henceforth be known. *Essays in Verse* was her first publication under the signature 'May' Sinclair. 'Mary' perhaps resonated too insistently with the Christian tradition of which she was now so unsure.

There were fresh departures in other areas as well. During the 1890s Sinclair encountered two new and significant influences: curate Anthony Deane, and Dixie Professor of Ecclesiastical History at Emmanuel College, Cambridge, Henry Melvill Gwatkin. Both men, like Beale, were intent on helping Sinclair to regain her lost faith. Her refusal to compromise on matters of belief established her as an unusually independent-minded woman— ironically, precisely the quality to which Deane and Gwatkin were attracted. But there was a price to pay: her relationships with both men collapsed when she finally abandoned Christianity altogether. In rejecting the demands of two men who loved her—each in his own way—she turned her back once and for all on her mother's world, in which women as a matter of course allowed men to do their thinking for them.

This period in May Sinclair's intellectual life was a crucial stage in her negotiation of modernity. Albert Schwegler comments in the *Handbook of the History of Philosophy* that 'a conviction of the impossibility of reconciling reason and revelation' marks the 'transition to modern philosophy', and Sinclair's commitment to reason over revelation marked her emergence as a thoroughly modern woman.[3] But she had some misgivings about that identity, fearing that it could lead simply to a decadent series of poses. Her first novel, *Audrey Craven* (1897), describes a woman whose public persona is as an intellectual.[4] But Audrey is a contradictory character, narcissistic and unfaithful as well as charming and impetuous. Sinclair was unsure how to go about shaping herself as a woman of the 1890s, and in her early

---

[3] Schwegler, *Handbook of the History of Philosophy*, 147.
[4] *Audrey Craven* was not published in the USA until 1906, after Sinclair had become a best-seller with *The Divine Fire* (1904).

writing we see her exploring the opportunities that were open to her, and their consequences.

The decade began with a move and a tragedy. After the deaths in 1887 and 1889 of her brothers Harold and Frank, Sinclair became more and more concerned about the health of the last brother left at home with her, Reginald. He seemed tired and lethargic; he was increasingly out of breath at the slightest exertion; when he was exhausted his lips developed a blue tinge. Sinclair's awareness that her two dead brothers had suffered from a congenital heart condition only intensified her worry over Reginald. In 1890 she, her mother, and Reginald moved south to a long, low house high above the sea on the South Devon coast in an attempt to improve Reginald's health. The climate there was gentler than in North Wales; the sea air might do him good. But all her efforts were in vain: Reginald died on 31 January 1891, several days after his thirtieth birthday. He was buried in the tiny churchyard at Salcombe Regis, a few miles along the coast. Now Sinclair's solitude with her mother was unrelieved. Desperately, she continued to write. Years later she told G. B. Stern that she had once had a breakdown when she tried to write in the same room as her mother.[5] Their tussles were relentless and intense.

Throughout 1891 as she wept and mourned for Reginald, Sinclair roamed the Devonshire moors, played Chopin on the piano, and worked doggedly on her next collection of poems.[6] Far from revealing the presence of God, her world, filled with sorrow and loss, seemed to demonstrate only his absence—or at least his cruel indifference. Sinclair faced the possibility that she might never feel confident of the existence of a transcendent deity. How then would she ever be able to make moral decisions? Where *Nakiketas and Other Poems* was largely concerned with the possibility that ours is a world of nightmarish and deceptive visions, *Essays in Verse* focuses on the question of individual freedom and moral autonomy. If agnosticism was itself immoral, as Sinclair sometimes feared, was an agnostic ethics possible? Following philosopher and social theorist T. H. Green, whose work she had read in the late 1880s at Beale's suggestion, she flirted with the idea of philanthropic socialism as the ethical fruition of idealist thought, but the unfinished plays of the early 1890s and *Audrey Craven* suggest that she found a socialist vision ultimately unsatisfying.[7] Even if charity work in the East End did make sense in terms of Green's vision of 'the concrete whole', it did not,

---

[5] Stern refers to this remark in a letter to Sinclair dated 15 June 1919, UP, Box 3, fo. 89.

[6] One of her few visitors during these years was Janet Hogarth, who recalled visiting Sinclair in Devonshire, where she 'found her walking the Devonshire moors, vaulting lightly over stiles, reading voraciously and turning scenes from Goethe's life into verse' (Courtney, *Women of My Time*, 52).

[7] Dorothea Beale suggested she should read T. H. Green in a letter in Dec. 1886: 'I don't think you will get any food in Spinoza. You say, may we not adopt Agnosticism and say of these problems honestly, "I will

for Sinclair, solve the problem of the individual subject's moral autonomy in a world defined by the power of thought.[8] Her endorsement of idealism as a substitute for religion in her first paid prose piece, 'The Ethical and Religious Import of Idealism' (1893), was largely based on the work of Green, but it still left open the question of the ethics of reason itself.[9] Where Dorothea Beale had believed passionately in the sanctity of thought and of philosophical enquiry, Sinclair continued to be preoccupied with the problem of the relation of philosophy to religious and ethical endeavour.

In 1891 Sinclair had no friends—other than Beale, who continued to counsel her from afar—with whom she could raise and discuss these questions. It was no doubt difficult for Sinclair to find like-minded people in the resort community of Sidmouth, and her mother, infuriated by her unfeminine interest in philosophy, discouraged and was ashamed of her daughter's challenges to religious orthodoxy. In the long opening poem in *Essays in Verse*, 'Guyon: A Philosophical Dialogue', Sinclair dramatizes her own internal debates, imagining what it might be like to be part of a group in which questions of morality and belief were routinely matters of controversy. Five university friends gather, seven years after they have left college, to reminisce over old times and to assess and argue with one another's philosophical positions. Two, Daniel and Merival, are Anglican parsons; another, Augustin, is a Roman Catholic; the fourth, Hamilton, is a rationalist; and Guyon, the fifth, is an idealist. Excited and disputatious, they argue over religion late into the night.

In using the dramatic form Sinclair places her poem squarely in a long tradition of Socratic enquiry. With a very different frame of reference, she echoes Oscar Wilde's reinvention of the philosophical dialogue in classic essays such as 'The Decay of Lying' (1889) and 'The Critic as Artist' (1890).[10] As in 'Nakiketas', with its description of the sumptuously dressed

give it up"? But you *cannot.* . . . You will not be able to give up philosophy. . . . I read a great deal of philosophy when I get time. Have you read Martineau's *Types of Ethical History*? If not, *do*. Also Green's *Prolegomena to Ethics*' (Dorothea Beale to Sinclair, Dec. 1886, in Raikes, *Dorothea Beale of Cheltenham*, 389). In 1888 the Cheltenham Ladies' College Guild, an organization of past pupils at the school, founded a philanthropic settlement in East London. The settlement moved into new premises near Shoreditch church in 1895 (see Shillito, *Dorothea Beale*, 56–7). *The Rector of Wyck* (1925) paints a satirical picture of the work undertaken by Matty's daughter, Milly, at just such a settlement. Manuscripts of Sinclair's unfinished play, *A Debt of Honour—A Tragedy in Three Acts* (1893–4) and notes for *Tancred of Adan: A Lyrical Drama* are preserved in UP, Box 18, fos. 347–51.

   [8] Green, *Prolegomena to Ethics*, 38.

   [9] The *New World*, which published 'The Ethical and Religious Import of Idealism', was an American periodical, and Sinclair said in a 1924 interview that she 'was paid what amounted in English money to nine pounds, and . . . felt very greatly encouraged' (Steell, 'May Sinclair Tells Why She Isn't a Poet', 513).

   [10] 'The Decay of Lying' (1889) and 'The Critic as Artist' (1890) were collected together with 'Pen Pencil and Poison' and 'The Truth of Masks' and revised versions published as *Intentions* (1891). See *The Artist*

young man, her work here uncannily shadows some of the major tropes of
the decadent poets and critics. But Sinclair adapts an ancient genre to contemporary philosophical, rather than aesthetic, concerns. 'Guyon' develops
and counters the Kantian vision in *Nakiketas and Other Poems* of a world of
perception shaped by the forms of human thought. By 1891 Sinclair was
leaning towards an anxious Hegelianism. Indeed, in an unpublished memoir
she refers to her continued 'absorption in Hegel' in 1895, and even in 1916
she describes a dream inspired by her recent reading of Hegel's *Logic*.[11] In
'Guyon' her question is double-edged: what room is there for revelation in a
world where reason is paramount, and how, in such a world, can we make
moral and ethical decisions?

It is clear as the poem develops that Guyon's contributions are meant to
provide the answer to the questions and disagreements of the other dis-
putants. Augustin's dismissal of reason and his espousal of the Roman
Catholic faith open him to the charge of superstition and irrationality. In this
poem whose only action is discursive, to be unable to argue is to be disabled,
and indeed Augustin is virtually silenced by Guyon's comment:

> Subtly you turn your argument, yet see
> Not that which every argument implies—
> That Reason is the organ Faith must use
> To justify herself. (EV, 9)

By challenging the authority of reason through reasoned argument, he
undermines his own discursive project from the start. Sinclair thus man-
oeuvres the proponent of faith over reason into an absurd and self-
contradictory position.

Reason in 'Guyon' is associated with the world of sense and of historical
evidence. This is its limit but also its strength: it is a synthesizing and organizing power. As Hamilton says:

>   Confined
> In the maze of sense . . .
> Reason is no keen discoverer
> Of truths not given; but of all she finds
> About her sets in order, brings from far
> Things disunited, joining them; . . . (EV, 8–9)

---

as Critic: Critical Writings of Oscar Wilde, ed. Richard Ellmann (Chicago: Chicago University Press, 1969),
290–320, 340–408.

[11] Sinclair, unpublished typescript, 'Reminiscences (Of Professor H. M. Gwatkin)', 2, in UP, Box 24,
fo. 456. For a description of her dream of Hegel, see the unpublished typescript of 'The Way of Sublimation',
also in UP, 14–15, Box 23, fos. 436–8.

This is an acknowledgement of the limits of practical reason along the lines of Kant's critique, but also—again following Kant—Hamilton implies that reason defines and makes intelligible the chaos of human experience. Through the power of reason, human autonomy and freedom are clearly expressed as secular matters: exactly the atheistic conclusion to which Merival objects.

Merival attempts a dualistic account of the world which endorses both faith and reason as twin poles of belief.

> If God has given
> A double revelation in His Word,
> And in His world of Nature and of man,
> I would accept them both. (EV, 9)

Hamilton, however, demolishes this cosmology with his argument that if the eternal or archetypal world reflects this one, it must be as morally mixed as the world in which we live. Hamilton's rejection of Merival's dualism reflects Sinclair's own Hegelian ambivalence about philosophies that rely on a division between, in her words, 'the sensible and intelligible worlds'.[12] Parallel worlds seemed to Sinclair to refuse any ultimate coherence, and to do away with the possibility of idealism (in every sense of the word).

It remains for Guyon to suggest a solution to the problem of dualism by his elaboration of a Hegelian view of the world. He agrees that reason can give 'no sign' (EV, 18) of any world beyond the one we know, but he asks why we should be so anxious to look for an 'ultimate reality' (EV, 18):

> The world that reason fashions through and through
> Is no phantasmal mockery, no cheat
> Palmed off on reason from behind the scenes
> Of consciousness. The soul that knows the world
> *Itself* through knowledge brings it to the birth,
> In thought upholds it and but perfects it
> In reason. Therefore reason cannot reach
> To a more real world beyond. Itself
> Being the one reality. (EV, 18–19)

Guyon argues here for the superfluity of faith in a world which is created and completed by the action of reason itself. Thought is itself infinite, Guyon argues, since it can recognize that the world around it is finite (EV, 19). There is thus no need for the concept of an infinite being, since human consciousness expresses and mediates the eternal. To Merival's objection that to

---

[12] Sinclair, 'Was Plato a "Dualist"?', 46.

identify infinity with the self implies that individual caprice rules the world,
Guyon replies that every soul partakes of a larger soul, so that the petty con-
cerns of selfhood are transcended by an evolving world-soul (like the
Brahma in 'Nakiketas').

> ... The Self I thought of, Merival,
> It is the highest Self made manifest
> In reason, where the human and divine
> First touch and close. (EV, 19–20)

This 'highest Self' is continually 'unfolding thousand-fold | This forward
vision of our consciousness | We call the universe' (EV, 20). Guyon's is a
progressive vision of a world gradually evolving towards the full realization
of some kind of world-consciousness. Indeed for him world and consciousness are almost indistinguishable, and Guyon's evolutionary vision
becomes as much a matter of the spirit as of the body. Just as Darwin,
Huxley, and Spencer had demonstrated the continued evolution of the world
towards an optimum, if unrealizable, state of internal balance, so Guyon,
following Hegel, sees the world as a dialectical progress towards a fully realized state of self-consciousness.[13] For an idealist like May Sinclair, these two
visions were virtually indistinguishable.

'Guyon' paves the way for what we might be justified in calling Sinclair's
'conversion' to idealism. But 'Guyon' is couched as a conversation: it is not
a definitive statement of Sinclair's own views. In 1893, however, in 'The Ethical and Religious Import of Idealism', she finally comes to an articulate reso-
lution of her own position. The article is an unqualified endorsement of
idealism as T. H. Green had redefined it, and as such it is an important mile-
stone in Sinclair's own development as a thinker. Sinclair approved of his
attitude to ethical enquiry, commenting in 'The Ethical and Religious
Import of Idealism' that 'Green held a metaphysical principle to be the only
possible foundation of ethics.'[14] His philosophy seemed to allay her anxieties
about the ethical possibilities of agnosticism. Green believed in Christianity
as a philosophy, rather than as a theology, and this allowed him to develop a
secularized form of philanthropy which anticipated the emergence of the
Labour party and the establishment of the Welfare State.[15] He established a

---

[13] May Sinclair's continuing interest in the evolutionary theories of writers such as Charles Darwin,
Herbert Spencer, and T. H. Huxley is explored in more detail in Chs 7 and 8 below. See also Susanne Stark,
'Overcoming Butlerian Obstacles: May Sinclair and the Problem of Biological Determinism', *Women's
Studies*, 21 (1992), 265–83.

[14] 'Ethical and Religious Import of Idealism', 695.

[15] See e.g. Green, 'Essay on Christian Dogma', in *Works of Thomas Hill Green*, ed. R. L. Nettleship
(London: Longman, Green and Co., 1888), iii. 161–85: at 182: 'Christian dogma, then, must be retained in

number of missions in the East End of London, and Sinclair drew on her knowledge of these for *Audrey Craven*.

May Sinclair found her discomfort with a faith based on revelation amply reproduced in Green's work. As Melvin Richter puts it, Green attempted to 'drop the traditional dogmatic theology of Christianity which was phrased in historical terms in favour of a restatement based upon Idealist meta-physics. By this means, he thought that he could remove the ostensible con-flict between the truths of science and the truths of religion.'[16] Sinclair explains that, according to his system, all subjects participate in the endless evolution of an eternal subject, and all have a 'surety of [their] regeneration' because of the basic divinity of the human soul.[17] Moral action is an expres-sion of our relation to the eternal subject and to all other thinking beings. To act morally is to recognize the basic identity of all human subjects in so far as they all participate in the eternal consciousness: 'No development and no culture of the individual is complete that does not take into consideration his relations to his brother-men. They are more than his brothers or his fel-lows—they are HE.'[18] An idealist agnosticism—one that recognizes a creat-ing intelligence, but not necessarily in its Christian form—can nonetheless give rise to an ethic of mutual responsibility which finds its expression in socialist institutions. Although May Sinclair does not emphasize this aspect of Green's thinking, he stressed the importance of social reform, and believed that the social order was continuous with the ideal relations of the immaterial world.[19] This provided a framework, at least, in which Sinclair could imagine the possibility of an agnostic ethics. T. H. Green offered a kind of secular theology, commenting in a letter of 1872 that he had 'def-initely rejected dogmatic theology for a certain sort of philosophy'.[20] As Sin-clair struggled with orthodox theology, she found Green's recasting of her questions in philosophical terms extraordinarily comforting. His were answers to which she would cling for most of her adult life. Idealism was

---

its completeness, but it must be transformed into a philosophy. Its first characteristic, as an intuition become abstract, must vanish, that it may be assimilated by the reason as an idea.' See also Melvin Richter, *The Pol-itics of Conscience: T. H. Green and his Age* (London: Weidenfeld and Nicolson, 1964), esp. 14 and ff., for more discussion of the relationship of Green's philosophy to the emergence of the Labour party.

[16] Richter, *Politics of Conscience*, 27.

[17] Sinclair, 'Ethical and Religious Import of Idealism', 706.   [18] Ibid. 702.

[19] See e.g. Green, *Prolegomena to Ethics*, 231: 'Thus in the conscientious citizen of modern Christendom reason without and reason within, reason as objective and reason as subjective, reason as the better spirit of the social order in which he lives, and reason as his loyal recognition and interpretation of that spirit—these being but different aspects of one and the same reality, which is the operation of the divine mind in man—combine to yield both the judgment, and obedience to the judgment, which we variously express by saying that every human person has an absolute value.'

[20] Cited in Richter, *Politics of Conscience*, 117.

precious to Sinclair because, in endorsing it, she could hold on to the aspects of Christianity she most cherished while dispensing with those that she found most difficult. When, in 'Guyon', Merival asks what bearing Guyon's 'misty mysticism' has on the everyday concerns of 'human life and conduct' (EV, 22), the idealist Guyon is ready with an answer. Since each 'life is lived | So much more truly in all other lives | Than in its own' (EV, 22), we are all ethically bound to recognize a common humanity.

> For the Self is gained
> Through knowledge, when the individual dies
> In its own vision of the One in All.
> Through lowly services; in common deeds
> Of daily kindness and of homely love.
>
> .   .   .   .
>
>   everywhere
> Self-abnegation is the starting-point
> For each, and union with the Highest Self
> The final goal of all. (EV, 22–3)

In arguing for common participation in a world-consciousness, idealism also encouraged a recognition of mutual responsibility, and of the necessity of sacrificing the self for the greater good of all. It could, as Sinclair wrote in 'The Ethical and Religious Import of Idealism', bring about the 'annihilation of the distinction between the secular and the religious', and realize 'the sanctity of the secular': 'Idealism offers us at least something like a satisfactory solution of the problems of knowledge, of the nature of the ethical ideal, of man's free will and moral responsibility, of egoism as against altruism, and, lastly, of immortality'.[21]

But this kind of heterodox faith set Sinclair apart from other less independent-minded young women. She was concerned that her own analytic and intellectual cast of mind might make it difficult for her to love wholeheartedly, or to be loved. In Sinclair's autobiographical novel *Mary Olivier* (1919) Mary's suitor complains about her preoccupation with philosophy: 'No woman who cared for a man would write the letters you do. I ask you to tell me about yourself—what you're feeling and thinking—and you send me some ghastly screed about Spinoza or Kant. Do you suppose any man wants to hear what his sweetheart thinks about Space and Time and the Dingan-sich?' (MO, 215). In another poem from *Essays in Verse*, 'Two Studies from the Life of Goethe', Sinclair tried to work out the relations between love and the intellect through the story of Goethe's romance with Frederika

---

[21] Sinclair, 'Ethical and Religious Import of Idealism', 708, 706.

Brion.[22] In the poem, it is Goethe's propensity for mental dissection which destroys his belief in his beloved: love, in other words, is destroyed by thought. Rational speculation can erode faiths other than that in God. In the poem Sinclair expresses her anxiety about the corrosive potential of the cerebral life, and dramatizes the moral dilemma which is posed in Goethe's autobiography (which Sinclair owned), and to which his Victorian biographers gave considerable attention.[23] Did he betray Frederika? Since he had stopped loving her, was he wrong not to marry her? Why did his love for her fade? Shaping the poem was Sinclair's own anxiety that her embrace of reason over revelation might condemn her to a life in which it was impossible to love without reservation.

In his autobiography, Goethe describes how, in the autumn of 1770, he made a trip with his friend Weyland to the village of Sesenheim, to visit Pastor Brion. Frederika was Brion's middle daughter, aged about 19, and she and Goethe formed an innocent, but passionate, attachment. However, when Frederika and her mother and sister visited Goethe in Strasburg in the early summer of 1771, Goethe began to have second thoughts, and his visit to Sesenheim in August 1771, although he did not say so explicitly, marked the end of his relationship with Frederika. Subsequently he wrote her a farewell letter, and then, eight years later, he revisited Sesenheim and saw her once more as a friend. Sinclair's poem is in two parts, the first written from the point of view of Goethe on his return to Frederika's village in 1779, eight years after his rejection of her, and the second written from the point of view of Frederika in 1772, a year after their separation. Frederika, in her anguish, has the last word, but we read her pain through the lens of Goethe's self-justification and remorse. Even the structure of the poem poses a moral question: what position should the reader take up in relation to the content of the two parts? Does the disruption of historical chronology—1779 preceding 1772—also mean a disruption of moral logic?

One of the most curious aspects of Goethe's account of the episode in his autobiography is his description of a vision he had as he rode away from Frederika's house in August 1771, knowing that he no longer wanted to be her lover.

---

[22] As well as 'Guyon' and 'Studies in the Life of Goethe', *Essays in Verse* contained a poem called 'Margery', in which a poet overcomes his self-doubt by becoming conscious of his oneness with a larger unity.

[23] Goethe's autobiography is listed among the books Ezra Pound selected from Sinclair's library after her death. May Sinclair knew German and she may have read *Dichtung and Wahrheit*, the title by which the text is known in German, in the original language (she owned Goethe's *Poetische Meister Werke* in German). See 'List of books as chosen by Ezra Pound, from the estate of the late Miss May Sinclair', HR, MS file (Norman, C) Misc. Sinclair also edited a collection of Goethe's aphorisms for the Priory Press Booklet series, published by Hampstead bookseller Sydney Mayle (*Thoughts from Goethe*, ed. May Sinclair, London: Priory Press, 1905).

When I reached her my hand from my horse, the tears stood in her eyes; and I felt
very uneasy. I now rode along the foot-path toward Drusenheim, and . . . I saw, not
with the eyes of the body, but with those of the mind, my own figure coming toward
me, on horseback, and on the same road, attired in a dress which I had never
worn,—it was pike-gray (*hecht-grau*), with somewhat of gold. As soon as I shook
myself out of this dream, the figure had entirely disappeared. It is strange, however,
that, eight years afterward, I found myself on the very road, to pay one more visit
to Frederica, in the dress of which I had dreamed, and which I wore, not from
choice, but by accident.[24]

Goethe offers no explanation of this bizarre episode, but it clearly struck a
chord with Sinclair. Although she does not mention the vision, the moment
she chose to dramatize from Goethe's inner life was that in 1779 just before
he set off along the footpath to Sesenheim; in other words, just before he
realizes that he is wearing the clothes in which he was attired in his vision
eight years earlier. We have already seen in Chapter 1 that in 'Apollodorus'
Sinclair explored the pain of the split subject. In Goethe's autobiography
she found another narrative of the alienation of the subject, this time a subject confronted by an uncanny version of itself. Goethe's prophetic vision
on the path to Sesenheim is a confrontation with his moral future, and the
limits of his moral will. Underlying Sinclair's elaboration of Goethe's inner
drama is an image of a man divided from himself by the inability to reconcile
his own actions with the 'moral law'.[25]

May Sinclair dramatizes Goethe's crisis as caused by his incapacity to
believe in, or to sustain, intuitive feeling. In the autobiography, Goethe
admits to envying Frederika's oneness with herself: 'Frederica always
remained equal to herself; she seemed not to think, nor to wish to think, that
the connection would so soon terminate.'[26] But he gives very little explanation of his own change of heart, in spite of the fact that after he wrote his
final letter to Frederika, 'the period of a gloomy repentance . . . was most
agonising, nay, insupportable'.[27] This reluctance to commit himself, even to
self-justification, encouraged biographers and interpreters of Goethe's life,
including May Sinclair, to speculate on what might have caused his love to
fade. The episode became a kind of ethical *Rorschach* test for commentators,
the contours of whose own lives can be seen defining the explanations they
offer. The tragic early marriage of George Henry Lewes, for example,
whose 1855 *The Life and Works of Goethe* Sinclair would certainly have

[24] *The Autobiography of Johann Wolfgang von Goethe*, 2 vols., trans. John Oxenford (Chicago and
London: University of Chicago Press, 1974), ii. 120.
[25] Sinclair, 'Ethical and Religious Import of Idealism', 701.
[26] *Autobiography of Johann Wolfgang von Goethe*, 118.   [27] Ibid. 143.

known (the free thinking Evadne reads it in Sarah Grand's *The Heavenly Twins*, 1893), haunts his lengthy justification of Goethe's action.[28] Because of the rigidity of the divorce law in the first half of the nineteenth century, Lewes was unable to divorce his wife Agnes, and as a result never married George Eliot, with whom he lived for many years. Lewes sympathetically explains Goethe's decision in the unabridged version of the *Life and Works* as the choice of life as a poet over life as a husband.

Eros, with folded wings and broken bow, was to him an image of fear. The choice lay between a quiet domestic life, and the career which ambition opened. . . . The affections, even in the affectionate, are powerless against the tyranny of Ideas. What is called the egoism of genius is but another name for tyranny of Ideas.[29]

This passage, with its emphasis on the figure of the poet, was left out of the more straightforwardly biographical abridged version of the life that went on sale in 1873; but the formulation would have appealed to May Sinclair, who was no stranger to the 'tyranny of Ideas'. Other late nineteenth-century biographers of Goethe followed Lewes's lead in declaring that Goethe had left Frederika because he felt marriage would be incompatible with his vocation as a poet. James Sime, for example, in his 1888 *Life of Johann Wolfgang Goethe*, noted that 'it was essential to the unfolding of his genius that his individuality should have free play'; and Herman Grimm, whose biography was translated into English in 1880, explained Goethe's loss of interest in Frederika by his growing 'consciousness . . . that his love, after all, existed only in imagination'.[30] If, as Lewes, Sime, and Grimm suggest, Goethe had left Frederika to pursue the life of the mind, his story was a perfect vehicle through which May Sinclair could explore the conflict between faith (an instinctive and unselfconscious belief in the loved one) and philosophy (which refused to take anything for granted). Sinclair's Goethe is hopelessly *fin de siècle*. He views his compulsion to analyse and to know the objects of his attention as a kind of disease, a destructive self-consciousness: the ennui of the divided self. In Sinclair's version, Goethe's poetic vocation is merely

---

[28] Sarah Grand, *The Heavenly Twins* (1893; repr. Ann Arbor: University of Michigan Press, 1992), 15. Sinclair met Sarah Grand with Katharine Tynan Hinkson in 1911. See Katharine Tynan, *The Middle Years* (London: Constable, 1916), 401.

[29] George Henry Lewes, *The Life and Works of Goethe*, 2 vols. (London: Daniel Nutt, 1855), ii. 145, 146. An abridged version, concentrating on Goethe's biography, was published as *The Story of Goethe's Life* (London: Smith, Elder and Co., 1873).

[30] James Sime, *Life of Johann Wolfgang Goethe* (London: Walter Scott, 1888), 44; Herman Grimm, *The Life and Times of Goethe*, trans. Sarah Holland Adams (Boston: Little, Brown and Co., 1880), 65. Grimm, unlike Lewes and Sime, is unsympathetic to this kind of disillusion: 'One would forgive him much; but to have broken the heart of such a maiden was inhuman' (67).

an excuse for his failure to love. The poem shows her preoccupied with the loveless scepticism of modernity, or, as *Audrey Craven* calls it, 'the malady of the century—the disease of thought' (AC, 135).

As Sinclair's Goethe waits in Strasburg before setting off to see Frederika, he ponders, Hamlet-like, on his own emotional vacillations.

> I was worse than fool;
> For downright folly has a certain force
> Of sightless perseverance; all its path
> Lies plain before it, trammelled by no doubt,
> It works straight on, looks not to right or left,
> And shapes a deed consistent with itself;
> So could not I. (EV, 28)

Doubt creeps in to create inconsistency and discontinuity, a self imperfectly expressed in its deeds. Indeed Goethe's confusion is with the nature of that self: what would it mean to shape a life consistent with the fractured emotional geography he finds within? In earlier poems, such as 'Nakiketas', 'Apollodorus', and 'Guyon', this difficulty has been resolved by imagining a self which is part of a higher consciousness, so that its internal inconsistencies signify nothing more than the evolutionary unfoldings of the universe. But here, Sinclair offers no such reassuring interpretation. She echoes Goethe and his biographers in her description of the lovers' countryside idyll, during which they feel themselves part of 'the universal Love that warms | The world's cold heart' (EV, 30). But Sinclair's Goethe cannot sustain this vision, cannot love without also wanting to know. 'The love that sought | Nearness of knowledge, in its seeking found | Fault and defect' (EV, 30). Is intimacy always a matter of knowledge? Was his desire to possess Frederika's secret an inevitable concomitant of his love, or a neurotic compulsion? Goethe knows that he related to her as he relates to the rest of the world:

> And so
> I gaze on everything till it unfolds
> Its inmost heart to me; and thus I learnt
> The secret of the bird's song, of the flower,
> The tree, the tiny insect in the grass,
> The very stars in heaven. Thus I looked
> Into that child's blue eyes till I compelled
> Their innocent confession. Through and through
> I looked, I searched her nature; with the rest
> She too became a study, put aside
> When finished, as it were. (EV, 31)

The difficulty with this kind of intimate probing is that it becomes not a gesture of love, but a gesture of mastery. Sinclair had wondered often enough whether her mother's expressions of love betrayed a desire to control her daughter, rather than (or as much as) to cherish her. How to distinguish between affectionate curiosity and a possessive desire to know someone else's weakness? A quasi-Wordsworthian attention like Goethe's to the natural world becomes profoundly anti-poetic when turned towards people; the self-discipline that poetic creation demands is misplaced in the chaos of human emotions. Goethe wonders how to combine his tendency towards 'coldest criticism' and his capacity for 'passion', and imagines:

> Some wondrous work
> Of exquisite proportion, where that sense
> Of fitness tames the lawless luxury
> Of young imagination which affects
> The sensuous grotesque. (EV, 35)

This ideal work would partake both of the poetic imagination and of love: each is a shaping power which must compose the violence of the material world and body into a form that partakes of the 'ideal' as well as of the 'world of things' (EV, 35). Such a harmonious form, though, is perhaps unsustainable in the post-Romantic era, and, as if to undermine Goethe's enthusiasm, the end of Goethe's section of the poem is followed not by his imagined 'wondrous work' but by Frederika's lamentation of seven years earlier. This, not a work of art, was the true result of his self-doubt.

The time-lapse is awkward. Goethe finishes by saying: 'Tomorrow I will ride to Sesenheim, | And see Frederica once before I go' (EV, 36). This is followed immediately by Frederika, seven years earlier in Sesenheim in 1772, turning over her keepsakes of Goethe and calling to her sister: 'No, sister, call me not; I cannot come' (EV, 37). It is as though Goethe can never make the trip he plans, for what he imagines is an excursion into the past, analogous to his momentary vision of the future several years earlier on the very same road. As he announces his intention to leave, the Frederika of the past calls out that she cannot come. The two are endlessly divided, hopelessly alienated, by the passage of time as well as by Goethe's ruthlessness.

The juxtaposition of the two lives also suggests the possibility of parallel or suspended worlds. Frederika's weariness and sorrow are described in vividly Tennysonian terms: 'I am so fretful grown | With sleeplessness, I can but weep to hear | The dreaded cock-crow' (EV, 39).[31] She fingers

---

[31] See e.g. Tennyson's 'Mariana' (1830): 'Upon the middle of the night, | Waking she heard the night-fowl crow; | The cock sung out an hour ere light' (*Poetical Works of Tennyson*, 8).

fetishistically the objects with which Goethe has left her: books, ribbons, and, especially, a lock of his hair (EV, 37). Her preoccupation with these traces of his presence is displaced into a fantasy of bodily suffering for his sake.

> And were he but—as some great men have been—
> Poor and despised, the world too ignorant
> To know his greatness, if this could have been,
> Oh, with what gladness had I suffered pain
> And hunger for him! (EV, 38)[32]

She wants her sense of the loss of his body inscribed on her own, as a material emptiness. Ravaged by hunger, her corporeal self will be as diminished as his body is for her, metonymically present only in the pathetically preserved curls of his hair.

Frederika's rhetoric, like that of Nakiketas, is one of self-sacrifice. She wants to be able to welcome her loss as a kind of recompense for all she has gained from Goethe.

> Once all my will was but that I could make
> Out of my own poor life some sacrifice,
> However slight, for one who gave me all
> His wealth, I bringing nothing in return. (EV, 38)

This is the classic Victorian heterosexual love-contract: the man brings wealth, the woman brings her body and her life. It was the classic filial contract as well: May Sinclair devoted her twenties and thirties to caring for her intolerant and exacting mother, in effect sacrificing her youth to her mother's demands. Yet Frederika has only intellectual and perceptual riches to show for her brief liaison with Goethe ('not a blade of grass | That grows by the wayside, but he did show | Some grace in it I never saw before', EV, 40), and her life is wasted. In fact, when Goethe left Frederika, she did indeed succumb to consumption for a time, and although she recovered, for a while her life hung in the balance.[33] This physical devastation is translated in May Sinclair's poem into an emotional fatigue and lifelessness, a woman denied the future she had imagined for herself. The 'ruinous sacrifice' (EV, 33) Goethe might have made, of his poetic vocation to his marriage to Frederika, is pitted against the sacrifice she nearly made, of her own vital force. The poem cannot decide between the two, and it ends with Frederika

---

[32] Years later Mary Olivier imagines doing something similar for her lover: 'she was mainly aware of a surpassing tenderness and a desire to immolate herself, in some remarkable and noble fashion, for Maurice Jourdain' (MO, 211).

[33] See *Autobiography of Johann Wolfgang von Goethe*, 213.

wearily answering her mother's call and taking up her daily tasks once again: 'Yes, mother. Yes, I come.' (EV, 41)

The compulsion to self-analysis which Goethe has already demonstrated in the first half of the poem is exposed in the second half as cruel and destructive. Rather than only imagining Frederika's sadness, as we have done when reading the first half, now we live it with her. Counterbalancing Goethe's persuasive rhetoric ('What if I had laid | A bond about my nature?', EV, 33) is the weight of Frederika's experience, her grief, her alienation, her boredom. This is the conflict between faith and reason again, recontextualized. For Goethe, love was, in the end, a 'mode of thought'; for Frederika, it was a 'mode of life'.[34] The poem stereotypically aligns thought with the masculine and feeling with the feminine, but this was a configuration that Sinclair challenged directly in her relationships with Anthony Deane and Henry Gwatkin, and in her first novel, *Audrey Craven*. Even in 'Studies from the Life of Goethe' the alignment is uneasy and troubled. Goethe is implicitly criticized for his failure to sustain or recognize the authority of emotion; Frederika is shown to be restless with her own ignorance. The poem articulates a frustration with the difficulty of bringing their two psychologies into any meaningful relationship with one another, the primal frustration of love. It was a frustration Sinclair was to experience at first-hand in her friendship with curate Anthony Deane.

In the summer of 1893 conflicts which had been, until then, mainly a source of intellectual frustration, became even more sharply personal. For it was then that Sinclair met, and rapidly became friends with, a man for whose sake she had to confront the question of her own belief once and for all. Anthony Charles Deane was seven years younger than May Sinclair, and when they met she was 30 and he was only 23, a Cambridge graduate who spent most of 1893 studying at Cuddesdon Theological College in preparation for his ordination in December 1893. He and his family were in the habit of spending the summers at Sidmouth, and Deane was fond of walking along the coast path to attend church at Salcombe Regis, the Sinclairs' local church, where the parson was, in Deane's words, 'sheer eighteenth-century and wholly delightful'.[35] May Sinclair, in spite of her religious doubts, continued to attend church during her mother's lifetime to avoid conflict with her, and it seems likely that Sinclair and Deane first made one another's acquaintance after one of the Sunday morning services. Deane had already published a substantial number of poems, sketches, and short stories in

---

[34] The phrase 'a mode of life rather than a mode of thought' occurs in a letter written to May Sinclair by Anthony Charles Deane, on 5 Feb. 1894 (UP, Box 1, fos. 21–2).

[35] Anthony C. Deane, *Time Remembered* (London: Faber and Faber, 1945), 47.

magazines such as the *Westminster Gazette*, *St James Gazette*, the *Globe*, and the *Pall Mall Gazette*. He read May Sinclair's *Essays in Verse* (which he diplomatically told her were 'very unusual, but very good indeed at their best') and, aware of the Sinclair family's precarious financial position, he helped Sinclair place her own poems and stories, telling her sternly that it was a mistake to publish without payment 'except for some very special reason'.[36]

His interest in *Essays in Verse* along with May Sinclair's natural bent for intellectual conversation and his own preoccupation with theological issues, meant that Deane and Sinclair soon became entangled in discussion and disagreement about the role of reason in Christian revelation. Deane, sure of his own position, worked on Sinclair to try to persuade her to ignore her doubts and return to God. Sinclair continued to worry away at the questions that had so vexed her during the writing of 'Guyon'. What was the relation between reason and faith? Could reason itself offer a system of belief? Her anxiety to reconcile the two was sharpened by her gradual realization that she was falling in love with Deane.[37] If she really was an atheist, or even an agnostic, Deane, only months away from ordination, would be unable seriously to entertain any thought of a romantic relationship with her. Their discussions were earnest and prolonged, made even more intense by their unspoken knowledge of how much was at stake for both of them. Years later Deane would nostalgically remind Sinclair of these early days:

Don't the Sidmouth days seem far away? And yet I can never think of them without pleasure, and regret. There's no place I love more—the old Sidmouth, with the friendly, frumpy, gossipy residents; the same faces day by day and year by year; the quaint shops, the Sunday climb to Salcombe church,—the walks on Mutter's Moor and, best of all, the misty evenings on the Esplanade, with the last of the light tinging the red cliffs, and the gentle wash of the full tide on the stones.[38]

Even as a happily married man Deane remembered Sidmouth as a mysteriously romantic place.

---

[36] Deane to Sinclair, 21 Oct. 1893; 10 Mar. 1894, UP, Box 1, fos. 21–2. In Oct. 1893 Deane sent her sonnets 'In Memoriam: Professor Jowett' to *Temple Bar*, and they were published in *Temple Bar*, 99 (Dec. 1893), 472. He also placed her 'Sonnet' in the *Cambridge Review* (23 Nov. 1893), 116 for which Sinclair was paid half a guinea. Sinclair's side of the correspondence has been lost.

[37] Evidence that Sinclair was in love with Deane has survived only by accident. In 1917 she responded to a request from Henry Gwatkin's widow Lucy by returning to her all the letters she had ever received from Gwatkin. She included a covering letter which, contrary to her intention, was preserved along with Gwatkin's letters. See Sinclair to Lucy Gwatkin, 31 July 1917, EC, fo. 539: 'Two [letters]—enclosed in an envelope—I keep back. I don't mind *your* reading them, but I sd. hate to have them published, for it is so very evident from them that I was in love with a parson who was *not* Professor Gwatkin.' The two letters to which she refers have not survived.

[38] Deane to Sinclair, 31 Jan. 1905, UP, Box 1, fos. 21–2.

In October 1893 Deane left Sidmouth for Cuddesdon, to prepare for his ordination. He and Sinclair continued their friendship in long and frequent letters, although her side of the correspondence has now been lost. Deane first raised the issue of Sinclair's religious faith when George Bentley, editor of *Temple Bar*, to whom Deane had sent Sinclair's sonnets on the death of Professor Jowett in October 1893, conveyed his concern that the sonnets expressed mildly unorthodox religious views. Sinclair dismissed Bentley's worries, but Deane, perhaps sensing that they disagreed on this matter, was more cautious, writing in November 1893: 'I agree that Bentley's anxiety as to your belief or its contrary is a trifle gratuitous. But it is carefulness (to excess) on the right side. . . . Of course I don't know what your views may be; or if you have ever studied Religion scientifically in the course of your metaphysical reading.'[39] When Deane returned to Sidmouth in January 1894 to visit his mother, he and Sinclair—to their mutual surprise and agitation—talked frankly about religion for the first time. To the lonely, confused Sinclair—'an unhappy woman', as she described herself, 'grappling, at Sidmouth, on a steep hillside, with the problem of the universe'—such open conversation must have come as an extraordinary relief.[40] Afterwards Deane insisted that the conversation was 'wholly unpremeditated' on his part, and apologized for 'talking "shop" ', but he had arrived bearing a copy of Robert Flint's *Theism* for Sinclair to read, and was clearly anxious to dissuade her from the feeling that her 'present mode of thought' was 'necessarily final'.[41] Sinclair was worried that her lack of orthodoxy had displeased him, but he assured her that he was 'in no way hurt, shocked, displeased, offended, grieved or put out—by our conversation on Wednesday; on the contrary, I enjoyed it'.[42] Deane was willing to listen and—even more significantly—he clearly cared about her. It seems unlikely that he ever explicitly declared his love; he may never have been sure himself just how he felt about Sinclair; but in the early months of 1894 he spent considerable time and energy writing long letters, recommending books, and climbing the steep path to Sinclair's house to engage her in intense and deeply felt debate. Even Sinclair's mother was forced to condone his visits. After all, he was now a curate of the Church of England.

Deane was sympathetic to Sinclair's doubts for a number of reasons. During his time as an undergraduate at Clare College, Cambridge, his faith

---

[39] Deane to Sinclair, 4 Nov. 1893, UP, Box 1, fos. 21–2.

[40] Sinclair, 'Reminiscences (of Professor H. M. Gwatkin)', 1, in UP, Box 24, fo. 456.

[41] Deane to Sinclair, 18 Jan. 1894, UP, Box 1, fos. 21–2. The book he brought her was Robert Flint, *Theism*, Baird Lectures for 1877 (7th edn., Edinburgh and London: Blackwood, 1889). He had recommended it to her in his letter of 4 Nov. 1893.

[42] Deane to Sinclair, 20 Jan. 1894, UP, Box 1, fos. 21–2.

had not always been unshaken. In his autobiography he describes how the
'materialistic arguments of Huxley and his followers were regarded as convincing by many clever undergraduates and younger dons; agnosticism
came to be taken as almost the necessary accompaniment of intellectualism'.[43] Sinclair's doubts were familiar to him: she was of course only one of
many who during those years came to reject the idea of God. Deane writes
that as an undergraduate he at first resolved to 'keep an open mind about the
truth of Christianity'; then later he began to feel that this 'attitude of neutrality' was 'ridiculous'. 'Of two things, one; either Christianity was true or
it was false. If it were true, it mattered more than anything else in the world.
If it were false, the sooner one abandoned it entirely the better. So . . . I set
myself to examine the evidence.'[44] Deane was also lucky enough to experience divine revelation. Soon after he decided that it was highly probable that
God existed, he had a 'profound spiritual experience', which he does not
describe in his autobiography, and which, he says there, he has never
described to anyone.[45] From then on the course of his life was set. It was perhaps because Deane was no stranger to doubt that Sinclair felt she could talk
to him. Deane took her arguments seriously even as he was not swayed by
them. He recommended books to her: Westcott's *An Introduction to the Study
of the Gospels*, and, as we have seen, Flint's *Theism*. Both books emphasized
what Merival in 'Guyon' had called the 'double revelation' (EV, 9) of science
and faith. Westcott laments 'the want of a clear and comprehensive view of
the mutual relations and influences of speculation and religion, as they have
been gradually unfolded by reason and revelation'; Flint argues that 'religion, in order to be reasonable, must rest on knowledge of its object'.[46]
Deane was concerned to expose Sinclair to arguments which squarely confronted her own dilemma: that belief in God could be bought only at the
price of belief in your own intellect. Both Westcott and Flint sought to
emphasize the relationship between intellectual rigour and the exhilaration
of faith. Flint's emphasis on the relation between knowledge and love
echoes Sinclair's vision in 'Apollodorus': that the object must be securely
known in order to be securely loved.

But Sinclair quarrelled even with Flint. In his final chapter Flint argues
for the necessity of revelation:

It is an indubitable historical fact that, outside of the sphere of special revelation,
man has never obtained such a knowledge of God as a responsible and religious

---

[43] Deane, *Time Remembered*, 61.   [44] Ibid.   [45] Ibid. 62.
[46] Brooke Foss Westcott, *An Introduction to the Study of the Gospels* (1851; 7th edn., London: Macmillan,
1888), 1; Flint, *Theism*, 2.

being plainly requires. . . . the science and philosophy even of the present day, dissevered from revelation, can produce no religion capable of satisfying, purifying, and elevating man's spiritual nature.[47]

In spite of his emphasis on the 'true light' of reason, Flint saw reason alone as an inadequate basis for faith.[48] Sinclair did not like the idea that religion might rest on feeling. Unused to trusting her own intuitions, suspicious of the sorrow which had been so large a part of her emotional life, Sinclair wanted to see evidence of, rather than merely to feel, the existence of God. How could she ever be sure that feelings were to be trusted, that what she felt was genuinely a revelation of God's presence, rather than a seductive illusion? Since, as an idealist, she was not even sure of the existence of material things outside the realm of human consciousness, how could she ever be certain about the existence of an immaterial world? Deane chastised her for demanding that Christianity somehow *prove* the existence of God:

Your two objections to the Christian Revelation are (a) that it 'does not provide a satisfactory solution of the most perplexing problems.' That is begging the question; 'satisfactory' is a subjective epithet. No intelligent Christian could maintain that every problem is explained; but no intelligent Christian could deny that ample reasons are given by Christianity why these problems should not be explained. Christianity's chief claim is not to be a riddle-solver, except within certain limits, but for the rest it puts an end to the anxiety which is ever looking for an answer, by giving rational grounds for the belief that they are intended to remain unsolved in this life.[49]

Since Sinclair maintained that she was partially convinced by the evidence of history, he tried to persuade her to allow herself the luxury of conviction by faith also:

I am glad that you regard the historic evidences of Christianity as strong, the more so, because doubts on this aspect of the question are objective . . . Whereas the metaphysical problems, of which you complain, are after all, subjective, and reading and speculation concerning them only lead, when carried beyond a certain point, to confusion worse confounded. The only remedy for them is that antiquated, despised but not quite extinct virtue—simple and childlike Faith. That must be the foundation; understanding will come after, and the two will then continually grow and mutually strengthen one another.[50]

So Sinclair struggled on, trying hard to suppress her instinctive scepticism and disbelief. Deane, hard at work in his first curacy in Barcombe, near

---

[47] Flint, *Theism*, 305, 311.   [48] Ibid. 302.
[49] Deane to Sinclair, 5 Feb. 1894, UP, Box 1, fos. 21–2.
[50] Deane to Sinclair, 18 Nov. 1894, UP, Box 1, fos. 21–2.

Lewes, avoided the subject of Christianity after the long letter of February 1894 (although he continued to write to her almost weekly) and concentrated on trying to place Sinclair's poems.[51] He did not visit Sidmouth again until September 1894.

By the time he returned, Sinclair had found yet another religious and professional mentor. Henry Melvill Gwatkin was Dixie Professor of Ecclesiastical History at Emmanuel College, Cambridge, a mesmerizing teacher who, like Dorothea Beale, was partly deaf and (unlike her) suffered from very poor sight.[52] Gwatkin, then aged 50, spent the summer of 1894 substituting for the vicar of All Saints' Church in Sidmouth, and when he gave a public lecture, Sinclair reported that 'Sidmouth was in a state of flattered excitement . . . and the All Saints' Schoolroom was packed.'[53] But Sinclair and her mother, shut away on their 'hill outside town', did not attend, and it was only because someone gave Gwatkin 'The Ethical and Religious Import of Idealism' that in July 1894 he 'climbed up [the] hill to see what could be done for [her]'.[54] Gwatkin's curiosity was whetted by the unusual phenomenon of a woman philosopher, one whose work had even made it into print, and he may also have sensed a challenge. If he could resolve the perplexity of this unusually intellectual and, by her own admission, 'unhappy' woman, he would have rendered a service both to religion and to Sinclair herself.

Their immediate conversation—no doubt because of the article—was about God. Gwatkin wrote to Sinclair on 12 July 1894 from Sidmouth: 'Yet I do not like to hear of "sliding back". . . . peace I fear will not be yours until you can give yourself up to the quickening and sustaining power of a love that is stronger and tenderer and far more near and real than any that mortals can lay before you.'[55] Like Deane, he hoped that Sinclair would find her way to an emotional awareness of God that would render her intellectual doubts superfluous. When Deane heard in the summer of 1894 that he had a rival as Sinclair's religious mentor, he was grudging, telling her that he had never met Gwatkin but that his book *Studies of Arianism* (1882) was 'sound but

---

[51] Deane describes his daily life in a letter to Sinclair of 25 May 1894 (UP, Box 1, fos. 21–2): 'What with two sermons each week, other writing, parochial work, cricket and numerous tennis parties, my time is very fully—albeit very pleasantly—occupied.' He sent her 'Song' to three different editors, who all rejected it, and he returned it to her on 26 Apr. 1894. It was finally published as 'Sea Whispers' in *Pall Mall Magazine*, 5 (Mar. 1895), 436.

[52] See Frank Stubbings, *Forty-Nine Lives: An Anthology of Portraits of Emmanuel Men* (Cambridge: Emmanuel College, 1983), sect. 38 [no page numbers], and Peter Slee, 'The H. M. Gwatkin Papers', *Transactions of the Cambridge Bibliographical Society*, 8 (1982), 279–83, for a brief biography of Gwatkin (1844–1916).

[53] Sinclair, 'Reminiscences (of Professor H. M. Gwakin)', 1, in UP, Box 24, fo. 456. Sinclair misdates the summer of their meeting as 1895.

[54] Ibid.

[55] Gwatkin to Sinclair, 12 July 1894, EC, fo. 541. Sinclair's letters to him have been lost.

dull'.[56] But Sinclair did not care. Part of her purpose in accepting Gwatkin's advice and support was the hope that he might be able to convince her where Deane seemed to have failed. Gwatkin knew that she was in love with a curate, and he understood the unhappiness to which agnosticism exposed her. Throughout 1894 and the year that followed he was intent on effecting and maintaining her conversion. In November 1894 his prayer that 'faith' will 'one day' be 'yours' seemed finally to have been answered, to his 'intense thankfulness'.[57] He reassured her that even now things might not be easy: 'The clouds may return—will return, but they cannot make light unseen if once your eyes have seen it.'[58] He even gave a measured endorsement to pantheism, remarking that it 'may well be a moment of a higher evolution'.[59] But Sinclair's sense of conviction did not last. Only a few weeks after she announced her conversion she was overcome by uncertainty again. Gwatkin encouraged her patiently: 'Keep your eyes on the light you have seen, and do not lose sight of it in the reaction you are now passing through. When the strain is lightened and your health is better, you will feel more and more the blessing that there is love above as well as round us.'[60] But Sinclair was beginning to be worn down by the struggle. In May 1895 Deane remarked that he hardly heard from her during the spring, and Gwatkin was worried about her too: 'Something in your weary letter seems to call for deeper and more tender sympathy than I ever gave you yet, or anything man can ever hope to give you. You are tired of arguments. . . . Uncertainty is a grievous trial. The answer is not in arguments, but in life. Only try; and you shall know it for yourself.'[61] But Sinclair was almost past trying. Deane had apparently lost interest in her religious life, although he continued to write—much less regularly—throughout 1895 and 1896, advising her on literary and publishing matters. In December 1896 he announced his engagement to someone else.[62] Sinclair's brief romance was over. But its memory haunted her: thirty years later she wrote a novel, *The Rector of Wyck* (1925), in which a young woman stifles her religious doubts in order to marry a young curate. As if to justify her own lonely life, Sinclair makes her heroine live to regret her limited life in a rural parish, and to long for her old

---

[56] Deane to Sinclair, 1 Aug. 1894, UP, Box 1, fos. 21–2.
[57] Gwatkin to Sinclair, 26 Oct. 1894, 12 Nov. 1894, EC, fo. 547.
[58] Gwatkin to Sinclair, 12 Nov. 1894, EC, fo. 548.
[59] Gwatkin to Sinclair, 6 Dec. 1894, EC, fo. 552.
[60] Gwatkin to Sinclair, 23 Dec. 1894, EC, fo. 553.
[61] Deane to Sinclair, 20 May 1895, UP, Box 1, fos. 21–2; Gwatkin to Sinclair, 13 Apr. 1895, EC, fo. 561.
[62] Sinclair wrote to Deane congratulating him in Jan. 1897 (see Deane to Sinclair, 17 Jan. 1897, UP, Box 1, fos. 21–2). Deane married Edith Maud Versturme on 5 July 1898. Deane later became Canon of Windsor and Chaplain to the King. The couple had no children.

life of philosophical debate and discussion in North London. There are consolations, though: Matty's marriage is long and happy. Throughout her life Sinclair continued to feel that she had traded sexual intimacy for intellectual independence. Most of the time she was proud of that choice, but *The Rector of Wyck* betrays her awareness of the pleasures and the comforts she had missed.

Religion and romance were not her only sources of worry during 1894 and 1895. Like Deane, Gwatkin was concerned about the level of financial constraint he found in the Sinclairs' household, and in July 1894, soon after he met her, he asked Sinclair to translate Rudolf Sohm's *Grundriss* (*Outlines of Church History*) from German into English, under his supervision, and for a fee of £20.[63] Sinclair agreed, but the work was far more taxing than she had anticipated. Originally she promised to have the book completed in six months, but after only a couple of months she was already writing to Gwatkin anxious that she would miss her deadline. When she did send him a draft of her translation in November 1894, he was worried about her: 'I am . . . concerned about some of the small slips, for they look to me like neither ignorance nor carelessness, but bad health—Do take care of yourself, for the strain on you just now must be very great. I shall not forgive you if you let this work overdo you.'[64] He wrote in January 1895 that he was concerned that their 'whole connexion . . . has been a heavy strain'. Twenty years later Sinclair, noting that he was referring to the patristic readings he was recommending, as well as the Sohm translation, annotated the letter: 'Heavens! They <u>were</u> a strain. I nearly died of them.'[65] But by March 1895 her labours were finally at an end and she was able to take a well-earned rest.

This was by no means the end of her troubles, however. In July 1895 she and her mother suffered yet another financial reversal. It is not clear exactly what happened: perhaps Amelia's tiny income was badly invested; perhaps their rent was raised way beyond their means; certainly May Sinclair was having little luck placing her poems and stories.[66] In any event, the two

---

[63] Gwatkin to Sinclair, 28 July 1894, EC, fo. 543.

[64] Gwatkin to Sinclair, 27 Nov. 1894, EC, fo. 550.

[65] Gwatkin to Sinclair, 1 Jan. 1895, annotation 1917, EC, fo. 554. In the 'Reminiscences (of Professor H. M. Gwatkin)' she notes that she 'read through the five volumes of Dorner's <u>Development of the Doctrine of the Person of Christ</u>, from beginning to end, to please him' (6, in UP, Box 24, fo. 456). She wrote humorously about the relationship between a young woman translator of German and the law researcher for whom she works, in 'Not Made in Germany', *Macmillan's Magazine*, 75 (Jan. 1897), 201–9.

[66] Gwatkin wrote in a letter of 1 Aug. 1895: 'I do not mind telling <u>you</u> that more than half of my own income was lost two years ago. Some may return, or more may follow. But yours is much worse than this' (EC, fo. 564). Sinclair preserved the manuscripts of a number of her unpublished poems, all dated between 1895 and 1898, with titles such as '1895', 'The Galilee of the Gentiles', 'Invocation', 'Mary Magdalene', 'Pictor Ignotus to the Original of his Madonna', 'Sappho', 'The Nineteenth Century', and 'To Ideal Beauty' (UP, Box 21, fos. 368, 372, 374–7, 384, 386).

women left Sidmouth for Eltham, East London, where Sinclair looked briefly for teaching work, before she and her mother were summoned to Hull where William, Sinclair's eldest brother (and father of six children, the youngest only 5) was seriously ill. Once again Sinclair watched as a brother weakened. Like Harold, Frank, and Reginald, William had a congenital heart defect, and his strenuous, outdoor life (he hated office work and, like his father, spent as much time as he could on his yacht) had strained his heart beyond recovery.[67] On 7 January 1896 he died and Sinclair had to fight not to despair. Gwatkin found her letters 'very touching, for all their courage'.[68] William had left his family ill provided for and Sinclair and Amelia were in no position to help. Desperately, Sinclair looked for work in London as a teacher, but her 'candour', as Gwatkin called it, about her religious views, was an obstacle and the one job offer she did receive was, in Gwatkin's words, 'not very great'.[69] It is possible that she did actually work for a few months at Miss Strong's High School for Girls in Baker Street, but if she did, her stay there was brief.[70] She was too shy really to enjoy teaching, and it was not where her real interests lay (she told Dorothea Beale in 1901: 'I cannot teach').[71] In March 1896 Gwatkin found her work revising a translation from Hungarian, for which she received £17, but she knew she could not sur-vive—physically or psychologically—as a translator.[72] There was one thing left to try: a career as a novelist. No record has survived of when or why Sinclair decided to experiment with fiction. T. E. M. Boll suggests that she was already working on her second published novel, *Mr and Mrs Nevill Tyson*, in 1894, and she may have completed the manuscript of *Audrey Craven* even before her brother's death.[73] She spent 1896 searching for a pub-lisher, and by the end of the year Blackwood's had agreed to take *Audrey Craven*. A few months later she and her mother moved into a house in Prim-rose Hill in London. Finally things seemed to be looking up.

Sinclair's debut as a published novelist marked the end of an era both in terms of her intellectual life and her emotional attachments. She and Deane,

---

[67] See Wilda McNeile to Boll, 24 June 1959, 13 Mar. 1960, UP, Box 48, fo. 529.

[68] Gwatkin to Sinclair, 6 Feb. 1896, EC, fo. 569.

[69] Gwatkin to Sinclair, 19 Feb. 1896, 7 Feb. 1896, EC, fos. 572, 570.

[70] On 8 Feb. 1896 Gwatkin wrote a letter of recommendation on Sinclair's behalf to Miss Strong, telling Sinclair on 2 Apr. 1896: 'Do not be too quickly discouraged as a leader of small bears. It is new work, and will have hitches' (EC, fo. 573). A week later he comments: 'you certainly seem to be making a good start' (10 Apr. 1896, EC, fo. 574).

[71] Sinclair to Beale, 11 Jan. 1901, Archive Department, Cheltenham Ladies' College.

[72] See Sinclair to Beale, 11 Jan. 1901, Archive Department, Cheltenham Ladies' College; and two letters from Sinclair to Macmillan, both dated 4 Nov. 1897, the Macmillan Archive, University of Reading, MS 1089.

[73] Boll, *Miss May Sinclair*, 51.

never explicitly involved, had gradually been drifting apart since the early months of 1895, and his engagement at the end of 1896 increased the distance that had already begun to widen between them. Sinclair and Gwatkin, however, had a peculiar affection for one another that was slower to fade. Gwatkin took his feelings for women seriously: in 1874 he had resigned his college fellowship rather than give up his attachment to the woman he later married (Cambridge fellows could not marry).[74] In spite of the twenty-year age gap between them, he and Sinclair were intimate in a way that Gwatkin suggested he had never experienced before, even with his wife.[75] He wrote to Sinclair a few months after meeting her: 'You cannot know how such delicate and gentle sympathy as yours is as a breath of life to a man who has done his work and fought his fight so much alone. We walk through life in masks.'[76] Sinclair confided in him in a way that was previously foreign to her character, and her vulnerability touched him: 'I cannot tell you how your trust draws me to you—for you are good indeed to me.'[77] When her brother died, Gwatkin found himself calling Sinclair 'my child': 'It is strange to take an old man's place to you; yet it seems to come naturally'.[78] His feelings for her were a complex mixture of mentor's, father's, and lover's: he wanted both to rescue her from her metaphysical limbo, and to help her withstand her mother's demands.[79]

Sinclair for her part remained profoundly grateful to Gwatkin throughout her life. She remembered his 'peculiar, searching, impersonal' kindness, and the gentleness and enthusiasm with which he went about the business of converting her.[80] Gwatkin's hospitality meant that she escaped her mother for days at a time when she went to Cambridge to work with him on her translations.[81] Their conversations had a hypnotic quality:

That very October [1894] the delightful Cambridge experience began; the exploring of the old Colleges; of the Library; the walks through the town, in the Backs; the lectures at Emmanuel—I can't conceive how he found time for all these things—; best of all, the long talks in his study in the house in Scrope Terrace; that well-known room lined with books from floor to ceiling. In summer and autumn it

---

[74] See Slee, 'H. M. Gwatkin Papers', 279.

[75] Boll suggests that Sinclair provided the intellectual stimulation that Gwatkin lacked in his marriage. See Boll, _Miss May Sinclair_, 50.

[76] Gwatkin to Sinclair, 26 Oct. 1894, EC, fo. 547.

[77] Gwatkin to Sinclair, 22 Nov. 1894, EC, fo. 549.

[78] Gwatkin to Sinclair, 6 Feb. 1896, EC, fo. 569.

[79] A letter of 23 Dec. 1894 suggests that Gwatkin had no great affection for Amelia Sinclair: 'Smooth speeches etc., and you must interpolate for me a civilized message for your mother' (EC, fo. 553).

[80] Sinclair, 'Reminiscences (of Professor H. M. Gwatkin)', 2, in UP, Box 24, fo. 456.

[81] Sinclair first visited the Gwatkins for the week of 15 Oct. 1894, and returned in Feb. 1896. See Gwatkin to Sinclair, 11 Sept. 1894, 19 Feb. 1896, EC, fos. 546, 572.

would be filled with a soft green light from the green garden; and there would be a cat—in the nineties, a large tight-coated tabby cat—curled up on one of the chairs or stationed in a hieratic attitude on the chimneypiece.

I would sit bolt upright in an armchair on one side of the fireplace (by the book-case where the Christian Fathers were), listening with the queer, strained intent-ness of conscious ignorance; and he would lie back, stretched out in his armchair, on the other side, and talk, and talk, in a low voice, with many pauses, while his idea crystalized [*sic*]; and very soon what you had once conceived to be the dullest period in the history of thought and in the world's history became miraculously alive. . . . Then, before you knew where you were, he had begun his work on your ignorance; not exposing it ruthlessly, but removing it gently and patiently, bit by bit, and putting in concrete ideas. He suggested in the politest possible manner that it was a poor thing to profess disbelief in Christianity before you had even tried to examine its historical foundations. He made you see that Christianity was an affair of history and psychology rather than of theological metaphysics; a question set-tled, not in Council Chambers but in the heart and soul of man, and that tracking down the evidence might be a pursuit almost as thrilling, in its way, as hunting the Hegelian Absolute through the mazes of the Triple Dialectic.[82]

This was, after Cheltenham Ladies' College, May Sinclair's second educa-tion. In effect, she was having informal tutorials with one of Cambridge's most eminent professors, a privilege she would not have had even if she had been able to enrol at Girton or Newnham.

But as Sinclair's interests shifted away from theology and philosophy towards fiction, Gwatkin felt himself disadvantaged and superfluous. As Sinclair says, 'He professed an almost superstitious abhorrence of "art" and "literature," the "works of Belial" ', and when she wrote to him after the publication of *Audrey Craven* to tell him she had 'sold [herself] unto Belial', he was unsurprised, but took her statement as a dismissal.[83] Twenty years later Sinclair remembered the abruptness with which their relationship ended: 'It is sad to see how suddenly the correspondence ceased when I abandoned myself to Belial for good.'[84] Sinclair's suspicions that Gwatkin was interested in her partly because he saw her as ripe for conversion must have been partly confirmed by his unceremonious abandonment of her, in spite of his reassurance in July 1896: 'Believe me, I never thought of you as a brilliant convert I might make—only as one I might be able to help, and whose sweetness to me has always deeply touched me.'[85] Not only Deane,

---

[82] Sinclair, 'Reminiscences (of Professor H. M. Gwatkin)', 2–4, in UP, Box 24, fo. 456.
[83] Ibid. 4–5; Gwatkin to Sinclair, 10 Nov. 1897, EC, fo. 583.
[84] Sinclair to Lucy Gwatkin, 31 July 1917, EC, fo. 539.
[85] Gwatkin to Sinclair, 6 July 1896, EC, fo. 577.

but Gwatkin too, were finally lost to her because of her refusal to compromise on matters of religious faith.

In turning from philosophical poetry to novel-writing Sinclair found herself simultaneously leaving behind the relationships that had sustained her
through the lonely years at Salcombe Regis. Neither Deane nor Gwatkin
could accept her as a secular thinker or writer, as one who was no longer
struggling with, but had finally rejected, the challenges of religious faith.
The publication of *Audrey Craven* temporarily eased the Sinclairs' financial
problems (the novel, which appeared in May 1897, was in a second edition by
October), but its bleak vision of the possibilities for *fin de siècle* womanhood
suggests that in spite of this first professional success Sinclair was conscious
of the emotional price she had paid to achieve it. Audrey is 'nothing if not
modern, the daughter of an age that has flirted with half-a-dozen ideals, all
equally fascinating' (AC, 326), but she is unable to remain faithful to any of
the men who love her, discarding them like outmoded ideas when she falls
prey to a new influence. She is preoccupied with metaphysics, 'a woman who
can look you in the face and ask you if you have ever doubted your own existence' (AC, 4), but her credibility as a philosopher is undermined in the novel
by her narcissism and her lack of integrity. The thinking woman here is
exposed as a façade, Audrey's pretensions to both intellectual and aesthetic
authority displaced by her beauty and her vanity.

Audrey's shortcomings suggest that, in spite of Sinclair's rejection of the
orthodoxy of her mother's generation, she remained suspicious of modernity, and especially of the idea of the modern woman. *Audrey Craven* is in
some ways a commentary on the phenomenon of the 'New Woman'.[86]
Audrey flouts convention; she insists on her right to an intellectual life (or
what, for her, passes for one); until the very end of the novel she claims the
right to choose her own partner in defiance of social convention. But where
many of the novelists Sinclair admired—George Gissing, Thomas Hardy,
Henry James, and George Meredith, for example—had portrayed the 'New
Woman' sympathetically, Sinclair, although fascinated by Audrey, is also
critical of her.[87] Like Anthony Deane, Sinclair associated the 'modern

[86] For discussions of the 'New Woman', see Ann Ardis, *New Women, New Novels: Feminism and Early
Modernism* (New Brunswick, NJ: Rutgers University Press, 1990); Gail Cunningham, *The New Woman and
the Victorian Novel* (London: Macmillan, 1978); Linda Dowling, 'The Decadent and the New Woman in the
1890s', *Nineteenth-Century Fiction*, 33 (1979), 434–53; Kate Flint, *The Woman Reader, 1837–1914* (Oxford:
Clarendon, 1993), ch. 11; Elaine Showalter, *A Literature of their Own: British Women Novelists from Brontë to
Lessing* (1977; rev. edn. London: Virago, 1982), ch. 7; Showalter, *Sexual Anarchy: Gender and Culture at the
Fin de Siècle* (New York: Viking, 1990), ch. 3.

[87] Sinclair wrote to Morley Roberts on 15 May 1906: 'I "discovered" Gissing for myself. I had never, in
my ignorance, heard his name when the title of New Grub Street attracted me to that book, the first of his I
ever read.' She especially liked *Born in Exile*: 'I cannot describe how it gripped & moved me—with an

heroine' with decadence.[88] In an 1899 review of Beatrice Harraden's *The Fowler*, for example, Sinclair implies that the modern woman is susceptible to unhealthy influences: 'Magnificent in physical and intellectual strength, modern to her finger-tips, with a beautiful healthy modernity, when first we are introduced to her Nora Penhurst is untouched by any taint of decadence.'[89] But she is soon seduced by an attractive but nihilistic lover who believes in nothing and lives only to exploit women. Audrey's story shows a woman who, like Harraden's 'fowler', is simply a collection of alluring surfaces. When a clergyman in *Audrey Craven* describes Langley Wyndham, a realist novelist, as 'very modern', he goes on to gloss the phrase: 'a decadent who would rather die with his day than live an hour behind it—who can't see that the future may have more kindred with the past than with the present. Mind you, I'm not talking of him, but of his school' (AC, 134–5). Audrey, like the 'school' of modern decadents, has no meaningful relationship with the past or even with her own history. In her, modernity reaches its degenerative nadir: her life is simply a flirtation with a series of different styles.

But in spite of Reed's generalization, Sinclair suggests that modernity is a gendered condition. Wyndham's cruel art lays Audrey bare when he publishes a realist novel whose central character is based on her, and Audrey, afraid of the ensuing publicity, flees London for the North Devon coast. Wyndham's decadence consists in his immoral disregard of both social and literary decorum, or, as Sinclair's friend Janet Hogarth put it, in his 'total absence of any sort of reticence': his writing 'made you see men and women, not as you imagined them, but as God made them. You saw, that is, the naked human soul, stripped of the clumsy draperies that Puritanism wraps round

agony of compassion. I think I was born in another sort of Exile and that made me understand' (UP, Box 3, fo. 76). She met Hardy in 1908 and expressed her appreciation of his work in her letters (see Ch. 4, below). Her essay on George Meredith appeared in the *Author* (1 June 1909), repr. in *Outlook*, 92 (19 June 1909) and in Annie Matheson, *Leaves of Prose with Two Studies by May Sinclair* (London: Humphry Milford at Oxford University Press, 1912), 301–15. She wrote to Charlotte Mew on 22 Apr. 1915 that Henry James had 'influenced me considerably' (HA).

88 Much of Deane's verse, including poems that were published during the period of Sinclair's friendship with him, reveals a conservative attitude to women. 'To the Modern Heroine' e.g. describes the New Woman, with her enjoyment of smoking, billiards, and intellectual debate, as 'insipid', 'deadly', and 'distasteful', and 'How It Strikes the "Contemporary"' satirizes the campaign for university degrees for women (see Anthony C. Deane, *Holiday Verses*, London: Henry and Co., 1894, 13–5, 32–4).

89 Beatrice Harraden had also been a pupil at Cheltenham Ladies' College, and when May Sinclair moved to Hampstead in Sept. 1898, Dorothea Beale put the two women in touch with one another. May Sinclair was very appreciative, writing to Beale on 2 Nov. 1898 that she liked Harraden 'so much' (Archive Department, Cheltenham Ladies' College); but Harraden was less enthusiastic about Sinclair, commenting that Sinclair was 'extremely "difficile"', more than I can express in words. . . . there is a certain metallic quality in her' (Harraden to Beale, quoted in Kamm, *How Different from Us: A Biography of Miss Buss and Miss Beale*, 211). The quotation is from May Sinclair, 'Miss Harraden's New Novel', *Bookman*, 16 (May 1899), 47.

it' (AC, 158).[90] Audrey is the victim of the masculine realist imperative which exposes her decadent condition: like Wilde's 'sphinx without a secret', Audrey is revealed as having no inner life.[91] 'Poor Audrey! Her own character was mainly such a bundle of negations that you described her best by saying what she was not' (AC, 90). Audrey is doomed to a life of performance, to what Joan Riviere thirty years later called the 'feminine masquerade': 'the feminine creature artless in perpetual artifice, for ever revealing herself in a succession of disguises' (AC, 124).[92] This is why Langley Wyndham is interested in Audrey: she epitomizes the 'modern woman' (AC, 282) in her teasing inability to develop a stable self. 'To find out what lay at the bottom of this shifting personality, what elemental thoughts and feelings, if any, the real Audrey was composed of . . . was [Langley's] plan of work for the year 1896' (AC, 125).

Audrey is contrasted in the novel with dedicated painter Katherine Haviland. Katherine like Audrey epitomizes a version of the 'New Woman': she lives an independently Bohemian life with her brother Ted—to whom Audrey is briefly engaged—in rooms in Pimlico. Her credo alienates her wealthy, conventional family: 'She believed that beauty is the only right or possible or conceivable aim of the artist, and she was ready to sacrifice a great deal for this belief. For this she slept and worked in one room, which she left bare of all but necessary furniture' (AC, 45). But Katherine exemplifies a form of modernity that still has a creative relation to some of the Victorian values by which Sinclair herself for the most part continued to live. When she realizes that Ted needs to go to Paris to study and improve his art, Katherine is prepared to lay aside her own career and spend her time doing commercial illustration to support Ted's artistic genius. Audrey, on the other hand, persuades Ted not to go, because she wants him to stay in London with her. Katherine spends the last hundred pages of the book patiently counselling and nursing Audrey's discarded lover Vincent because she is in love with him herself. As she contemplates her sacrifices for both Ted and Vincent she realizes that 'now she was giving up, not time alone, and thought, and labour, but love—love that could have no certain reward but pain. And she was still content' (AC, 276). Katherine symbolizes a modern femininity that has resisted the temptations of decadence: she achieves

---

[90] Janet Hogarth, 'Literary Degenerates', *Fortnightly Review*, 63 (1895), 586–92: at 589.

[91] In Oscar Wilde's story 'The Sphinx without a Secret: An Etching', a woman who has a mysterious appointment every afternoon is revealed after her death to have spent the time sitting alone in an empty room. See Wilde, *Complete Shorter Fiction*, ed. Isobel Murray (Oxford: Oxford University Press, 1980), 53–8.

[92] See Joan Riviere, 'Womanliness as Masquerade', 1929, in Victor Burgin, James Donald, and Cora Kaplan (eds.), *Formations of Fantasy* (London: Methuen, 1986), 35–44.

economic and intellectual independence while not relinquishing her capacity for loyalty and devotion. But Katherine's self-discipline and integrity are swept aside by Audrey's ruthless charm. If Audrey is an image of decadence, and Katherine of an alternative modern femininity that recognizes the worth of traditional values, it is Audrey, and her nihilistic version of the modern, that wins out in the end. Vincent has eyes only for her, and when her cruelty eventually kills him, even his posthumously published book is dedicated to Audrey.

Responses to *Audrey Craven* were generally favourable. Sinclair sent a copy to Anthony Deane, who thought it 'exceedingly clever' and was glad that Sinclair seemed 'to have escaped from the influence of German philosophers, at whose hands you have suffered many things, and whose stilted periods seemed to pursue you, at one time, even when you were writing fiction.'[93] But he objected to the portrait of the clergyman, Flaxman Reed, and Sinclair, perhaps in response, avoided satirizing clergymen in her fiction until near the end of her career.[94] Less ecclesiastical readers were more unequivocally admiring: daringly, Sinclair sent a copy of *Audrey Craven* to George Gissing, who loved it, and reviewers in the *Athenaeum* and the *Spectator* both praised its potential.[95] But May Sinclair was not entirely satisfied with *Audrey Craven*. She wrote to Dorothea Beale a few months after it came out that few of her reviewers had

'spotted' my moral idea—of self-revelation. Perhaps it is just as well . . . for I have not done the idea justice. It was impossible to develope [*sic*] it with a character like Audrey's to whom it would mean a blow to her vanity and nothing more. But I think a great deal might be made of it with a stronger character. However that was what I meant.[96]

Sinclair intended Audrey to be shocked by the revelations of Wyndham's novel into some kind of self-awareness. But she felt that in the end her characterizations were not quite in line with the novel's moral structure. Even as an experienced novelist, she continued to find the relation between

[93] Deane to Sinclair, 19 May 1897, UP, Box 1, fos. 21–2.

[94] Deane admonished Sinclair that far from being the kind of unworldly mystic that Sinclair depicts, the clergyman of a big parish 'has the most sturdy common-sense, the most penetrating sympathy, the most absolute correspondence of warm heart and cool head in his daily work' (Deane to Sinclair, 19 May 1897, UP, Box 1, fos. 21–2). Sinclair paints comic pictures of clergymen in *Mr Waddington of Wyck* (1921) and *A Cure of Souls* (1924).

[95] See George Gissing to Sinclair, 23 July 1897, UP, Box 1, fo. 34: 'Had you not told me it was your first novel, I should have thought it came from a hand already practised.' See also 'New Novels', *Athenaeum*, 110 (24 July 1897), 122; and 'Recent Novels', *Spectator*, 79 (28 Aug. 1897), 284. Sinclair was particularly pleased with the *Spectator* review (see Sinclair to Beale, 16 Sept. 1897, Archive Department, Cheltenham Ladies' College).

[96] Sinclair to Beale, 5 Oct. 1897, Archive Department, Cheltenham Ladies' College.

character and message awkward to handle: *The Helpmate* (1907) was criticized for being unconvincingly harsh on its inflexibly chaste heroine.[97]

In spite of its ambivalence about its central character, *Audrey Craven* does not wholly blame her for her own shortcomings. As Sinclair realized, its tone is uneven: Audrey is sometimes treated compassionately, and sometimes satirically. Sinclair's inconsistency reflects her confusion about different images of womanhood at the *fin de siècle*. In some ways, Audrey is not so different from Sinclair herself. Like Sinclair, she is 'looking for a revelation' (AC, 7); like Sinclair she insists on trying to determine the shape of her own life and beliefs. Although *Audrey Craven* is a far cry from other much more unequivocally feminist treatments of the predicament of the 'New Woman' in novels such as Sarah Grand's *The Heavenly Twins*, Mona Caird's *The Daughters of Danaus* (1894), or Ella Hepworth Dixon's *The Story of a Modern Woman* (1894), in it we see the first stirrings of the feminist consciousness which defined so much of Sinclair's later work. If Audrey fails to achieve self-realization or, in Sinclair's phrase, 'self-revelation', the novel suggests that this is partly the fault of the men with whom she becomes entangled: 'The men whose destiny she had tried to mould, who had ended by moulding hers, twisting it now into one shape, now into another, had done with it at last; they had flung it from them unshapen as before. There was no permanence even in destiny' (AC, 282). Audrey realizes wearily that 'woman, even modern woman, is the slave of circumstances and the fool of fate' (AC, 282). The men who tried to help Sinclair find her faith moved on, like Audrey's lovers, when she found herself finally unable to develop in the directions that they wanted. The satire of Audrey's empty-headedness is thus tinged with a certain pity. She may have been a contemptible parody of the kind of modern woman Sinclair admired, but the novel suggests that in spite of her attempts to exploit them, Audrey, like the self-sacrificing Katherine, was finally ill-used by men, prey as much as predator. Sinclair's experiences with Deane and Gwatkin left her with a feeling that only a thoroughly accommodating woman—like their two wives—could hope to achieve marital happiness.[98] Sinclair's prickly determination to evolve her own philosophy of life meant that she was ill-suited to the roles of wife and mother—at least as the men she loved defined them.

[97] See e.g. Eleanor Cecil's critique of *The Helpmate* (1907), in 'The Cant of Unconventionality', *National Review* (Nov. 1907); repr. *Living Age*, 255 (7 Dec. 1907), 579–89. I discuss this review in Ch. 3, below.

[98] Lucy Gwatkin did not share her husband's intellectual interests, and Maud Deane was a pretty, accomplished, and friendly woman who devoted her life to making sure that everything ran smoothly for her husband. See 'Source Materials on A. C. and Miss Maud Versturme', UP, Box 48, fo. 521.

Audrey Craven closes, perhaps surprisingly, with Audrey's marriage. Her husband is described as a 'nonentity' (AC, 325). The marriage 'seemed an ugly concession to actuality', an expression of Audrey's final embracing of 'a mature realism' (AC, 326–7). Audrey's story ends with her acceptance of compromise, the logical conclusion, Sinclair suggests, of the kind of morally bankrupt modernity for which Audrey has stood throughout the novel. 'Mature realism' was perhaps all that May Sinclair now hoped for, for herself. She ended the 1890s in as sceptical a state as that in which she entered them. Still mistrustful of feeling, still uncertain of the relation between emotion or desire and moral action, she had all the same managed to shift the terms of her own debate. The questions that preoccupied her at the end of the decade—the nature of 'femininity', the relation of the intellect to desire, the parameters of moral agency—were all related to those which she had started the decade by asking. But the context had changed. Rather than engaging in philosophical and theological debate, Sinclair had now reconstructed herself definitively as a novelist. She began to dissociate herself from her early poetry collections, telling Witter Bynner in 1905: 'I think nothing of them'.[99] Her career had finally begun.

---

[99] Sinclair to Witter Bynner, 29 Aug. 1905, HL, bMS Am 1891 (766).

1898–1908

3

Fame and the Literary Market Place

—

MAY SINCLAIR was simultaneously excited and uneasy at the idea of herself as a novelist. On the one hand, the discovery that she had enough talent
to earn money, however little, by writing fiction was immensely reassuring,
although it was many years before she felt completely secure.[1] On the other
hand, it meant that for the first time in her life the retiring Sinclair found herself exposed to the glare of publicity. The many advantages of being a
writer—access to the social networks of literary London, a new sense of her
own authority, pride at earning money—were made more fraught by
Sinclair's realization that now part of her intellectual and creative life was for
sale in a market that was much more savage and pervasive than that in which
her early poems and stories had appeared. Her image, personality, and life-
story (what she would reveal of it) were promoted along with her books: in
1898 the first publicity photograph of her was published with a brief biographical sketch in an advance notice for *Mr and Mrs Nevill Tyson*.[2] In a
newly competitive fictional market place Sinclair found herself struggling
with the idea of herself as someone with something to sell. She seemed to
have evaded one constraining institution (marriage) only to find herself
embroiled in another one (authorship). The novel which made her both
famous and relatively wealthy, *The Divine Fire* (1904), is ironically—but
perhaps appropriately—a critique of the bookselling industry in which she
was now earning her living. Acutely aware that she could not have been the
freethinking woman she wanted to be if she had married Anthony Deane,

[1] In Apr. 1908 Sinclair was offered £1,000 for the serial rights to *Kitty Tailleur*. She wrote to Otto Kyllmann, her editor at Constable, that she was sorely tempted by the proposal, even though she disliked the
magazine, the *Smart Set*, in which the novel would appear. '£1000 wd. make me independent at one stroke.
It's the precise sum wh., added to what I have already invested, wd. provide an income wh. I cd. live on if
my brain became permanently anaemic' (Sinclair to Otto Kyllmann, 10 Apr. 1908, General Manuscript Collection, Charles Deering McCormick Library of Special Collections, Northwestern University Library).

[2] 'New Writers: Miss May Sinclair', *Bookman* (London), 14 (Sept. 1898), 151.

Sinclair discovered that, as an author, she had to deal with the expectations of not just one but a series of men in the publishing business, at that date almost exclusively masculine.[3] Publishing, like marriage, seemed to demand that she sell, if not her soul, certainly her body (or at least its photographic image).

Sinclair used her fiction to develop and express her sense of frustration at the idea that the male world was continually seeking to co-opt her for its own purposes. She had alienated the men she loved because she would not accept their beliefs, and as she grew in confidence and fame, she continued the critique of men's treatment of women that had begun, somewhat hesitantly, in *Audrey Craven*. Part of the problem, in Sinclair's view, was that men were sadly inadequate to the task of supporting women in the way that they needed. How were women to reconcile their need for spiritual and sexual autonomy with the demands that men placed upon them? Women were not free as authors, as wives, as mothers, or even, as Sinclair knew to her cost, as daughters. Sinclair was soon recognized as a novelist who dealt with 'unpleasant' subjects, the small daily cruelties and the tragic denouements of married life.[4] In *Mr and Mrs Nevill Tyson* (1898) a young wife stops breast-feeding her son because of her husband's jealousy, with disastrous results; in *The Helpmate* (1907) the ascetic spirituality of a wife is responsible for her husband's acquisition of a mistress, and the subsequent death of a child; in *Kitty Tailleur* (1908) a courtesan kills herself out of self-disgust rather than marry the man she loves; and in *The Judgment of Eve* (1908) a man's refusal to relinquish his conjugal rights causes his wife to die in childbirth.

The publication and success of *Audrey Craven* in the summer of 1897 precipitated Sinclair straight into the turmoil of a literary industry that was in the process of rapid change. For fifty years novels had routinely been published in three-volume editions at a total cost of £1. 11s. 6d., a price which only libraries could afford. Only exceptional texts (Walter Scott's novels, for example) had print runs of more than about a thousand copies. But during the 1890s the book trade, along with journalism, was transformed

---

[3] Large numbers of women, of course, were well established at the end of the 19th cent. as novelists and even as critics, but very few were involved in the actual business of publishing (see e.g. Victor Bonham-Carter, *Authors by Profession*, 2 vols. (Los Altos, Calif.: William Kaufmann, 1978), i. All Sinclair's agents, editors, and publishers were men, apart from Florence Bate, who worked as a reader for Henry Holt, Sinclair's American publisher. At Holt's suggestion, Bate read some of Sinclair's stories in 1905 to see if she could help place them in magazines and thus increase publicity for *The Divine Fire*, which Holt published in 1904 (see Holt to Sinclair, 6 Jan. 1905 [misdated 1904], UP, Box 2, fos. 43–4, and Bate to Sinclair, 31 May 1905, UP, Box 1, fo. 4).

[4] Edward Clark Marsh, 'Miss Sinclair's *The Tysons*', *Bookman* (New York), 23 (July 1906), 535–6: at 536. Janice H. Harris notes that after *The Divine Fire*, 'Sinclair wrote a spate of novels and novellas all wrestling with the hot modernist topic of marriage' ('Challenging the Script of the Heterosexual Couple: Three Marriage Novels by May Sinclair', *Papers on Language and Literature*, 29, Fall 1993, 436–58: at 439).

into a highly commercial enterprise: the 'three-decker' novel was replaced by cheap 6s. editions, and reprints cost even less, with paperbacks selling for only 6d. or 7d.[5] As Rachel Bowlby puts it, 'More than at any time since the invention of printing and the beginnings of the first commodified literary genre, the novel, printed matter in general was becoming just another "novelty" to be devoured or consumed as fast as fashions changed.'[6] Gwendoline Keats ('Zack'), another Blackwood author whom Sinclair met in early 1898, refused to send the *Bookman* a publicity photograph, in protest at the 'whole modern spirit of self advertisement'; and Ford Madox Ford, who would become one of Sinclair's close friends, wrote in 1921 that the twentieth century ushered in for many authors a 'settled, gloomy conviction . . . that the Reader, the Public, should be coerced, municipally or otherwise, into the perusal of their works'.[7] Gissing, one of *Audrey Craven*'s admirers, was the most outspoken, and the most pessimistic, commentator on the 'professionalization' of authorship.[8] In Gissing's *New Grub Street*, for example, first published in 1891, Jasper Milvain comments that 'Literature nowadays is a trade. Putting aside men of genius, who may succeed by mere cosmic force, your successful man of letters is your skilful tradesman. He thinks first and foremost of the markets; when one kind of goods begins to go off slackly, he is ready with something new and appetising.'[9] Sinclair, anxious for money, but unused either to compromise or to self-promotion, had to find her way through this jungle with almost no help. Deane was the only one of her correspondents who had any experience of the publishing world, and shortly after the publication of *Audrey Craven* he sponsored her for membership in the Society of Authors.[10]

There were, however, several people who, because of *Audrey Craven*, saw her as a good commercial proposition. In December 1897 Sinclair was taken on by the first literary agent to operate in Britain, A. P. Watt, who had already represented Deane as well as Wilkie Collins, Walter Besant, Rider Haggard, Thomas Hardy, and Rudyard Kipling.[11] Literary agents were still

[5] Bonham-Carter, *Authors by Profession*, i. 71, 177.

[6] Rachel Bowlby, *Just Looking: Consumer Culture in Dreiser, Gissing and Zola* (New York and London: Methuen, 1985), 8. The first mass-circulation daily newspaper, the *Daily Mail*, was established in 1896.

[7] Keats to Sinclair, 8 July 1898, UP, Box 2, fos. 50–5; Ford Madox Ford, *Thus to Revisit: Some Reminiscences* (New York: Dutton, 1921), 10.

[8] Sandra Kemp, Charlotte Mitchell, and David Trotter, describe it this way in *Edwardian Fiction: An Oxford Companion* (Oxford: Oxford University Press, 1997), 323–8: at 324.

[9] George Gissing, *New Grub Street* (1891; New York: Modern Library Edition, 1926), 5.

[10] See Deane to Sinclair, 10 July 1897, UP, Box 1, fos. 21–2. The Society of Authors, founded in 1884, advised authors on matters to do with publishing contracts, and campaigned on issues such as copyright.

[11] See Deane to Sinclair, 24 Dec. 1897, UP, Box 1, fos. 21–2. Deane commented that now that Sinclair had Watt to look after her interests, he could 'gracefully retire, I think, from the post of literary

largely an unknown quantity, and Sinclair, who—like most authors in the
1890s—had agreed to Watt's terms without really knowing what she was
getting into, soon regretted it. Deane had already stopped using Watt by the
time he took Sinclair on, because he felt agents were financially disadvanta-
geous (although he was clearly ambivalent, and by July 1898 had signed on
with J. B. Pinker), and publishers, unsurprisingly, were generally hostile to
the idea.[12] They were used to having the advantage over unsuspecting
authors desperate, as Sinclair was, for even a small sum of money. *Audrey
Craven*, for example, was published under the half-profits system, in which
an author usually paid an initial sum in return for half the profits on all sales.[13]
But as Walter Besant pointed out at a conference organized by the Society of
Authors in 1887, the half-profits system was wide open to exploitation by
publishers who could fiddle their accounts and make a 'secret profit' on the
cost of paper, printing, binding, and advertising, as well as charging the
author an exorbitant 15 per cent for 'handling'. Besant maintained that
authors publishing in this way were more likely to end up with a quarter than
a half of the actual profits.[14] Sinclair thus made very little money from
Audrey Craven.

   She was in many ways, then, exactly the kind of author who needed an
agent. She had been recognized as a writer with potential, but timid, inexperi-
enced, and fresh from the provinces, she had little idea of how to negotiate.
However, even though she could not afford to ignore the financial side of her
new career, the frank commercialism of dealing with a publisher through an
agent made her embarrassed and fearful. She made the mistake of signing on
with Watt soon after the publication of *Audrey Craven*, and then using him to
negotiate with Blackwood, *Audrey Craven*'s publishers, for the rights to her
next novel, *Mr and Mrs Nevill Tyson*. In spite of her intellectual stubbornness
Sinclair hated confrontation, especially with people to whom she felt
indebted, and she became more and more anxious as Blackwood stalled for
months before finally offering a contract for *Mr and Mrs Nevill Tyson* in June

adviser'. See also Bonham-Carter, *Authors by Profession*, i. 168–9. A. P. Watt had been working as an
agent since 1875.

   [12] Deane to Sinclair, 24 Oct. 1897, 10 July 1898, UP, Box 1, fos. 21–2. J. B. Pinker started working as an
agent in 1896, and Curtis Brown in 1899 (see Bonham-Carter, *Authors by Profession*, i. 169). Pinker is famous
for acting as agent (and occasionally banker) for Joseph Conrad and H. G. Wells. See also James Hepburn,
The Author's Empty Purse and the Rise of the Literary Agent (Oxford: Oxford University Press, 1968). Henry
Holt, the American publisher of *The Divine Fire*, saw literary agents as regrettable evidence of the 'commercialization of literature . . . an inevitable accompaniment of tendencies in the modern evolution of commerce' (Holt, 'The Commercialization of Literature: A Summing Up', 566).

   [13] See George Blackwood to Sinclair, 25 Mar. 1905, UP, Box 1, fo. 9.

   [14] Bonham-Carter, *Authors by Profession*, i. 135.

1898.[15] Gwendoline Keats told Sinclair that Blackwood was 'a little hurt' at her signing on with Watt:

So I told him that you hated having [an agent], & had decided to drop him at the first opportunity; also that it had been only after being strongly advised to do so by another writer [Beatrice Harraden] that you had thought of employing an agent, & that you had never since ceased to regret having placed yourself in a position that might make those, who did not know you, think that you had been ungrateful for the many kindnesses he (Blackwood) had showed you.[16]

Sinclair was frightened that by seeming to chase profit she had lost Blackwood's trust, and relations between them were never very cordial again. *Mr and Mrs Nevill Tyson* was finally published in November 1898, and Beatrice Harraden told Dorothea Beale that nine months after publication, it had sold only 200 copies (Sarah Grand's *Heavenly Twins*, also a study of women's predicament in marriage, by contrast sold 20,000 copies in the first week when it appeared in 1893).[17] Blackwood reported a loss of £13 on the novel.[18] It seemed that Sinclair's modest literary success might already be a thing of the past.

Throughout 1898 and 1899, as *Mr and Mrs Nevill Tyson* flopped, Sinclair was depressed and anxious. She and her mother were quarrelling with their landlady at Ormonde Terrace, and in September 1898 they moved again, this time to 13 Christchurch Road, near Hampstead. Gwendoline Keats tried to lift Sinclair's flagging spirits: 'Don't lose heart just when you are on a good thing—You have more stuff in you than 9/10 of the writers nowadays. I know you must succeed in the long run—there is absolutely no other end possible for you.'[19] But Sinclair's problems were too pressing for even Keats's loyal support to cheer her. She was ill with flu for most of October 1899, and an offer by Richard Garnett, keeper of printed books in the British Museum, to publish a volume of her sonnets briefly lifted her spirits, but then came to nothing.[20] His son, publisher and critic Edward Garnett, helped her get more translation work, this time Theodore von Sosnosky's *England's*

[15] See letters from Gwendoline Keats to Sinclair between 25 Feb. and 5 July 1898 (UP, Box 2, fos. 50–5).

[16] Keats to Sinclair, 25 Feb. 1898, UP, Box 2, fos. 50–5. She mentions Harraden in another letter written later the same day.

[17] See Elaine Showalter, *A Literature of their Own: British Women Novelists from Brontë to Lessing* (1977; rev. edn. London: Virago, 1982), 205.

[18] See Beatrice Harraden to Dorothea Beale, 16 Aug. 1899, UP, Box 1, fo. 5 and Keats to Sinclair, 12 Oct. 1899, UP, Box 2, fos. 50–5. Sinclair seems this time to have negotiated an advance of £100 on royalties, an advance which the publishers never managed to recover. See Keats to Sinclair, 3 May 1898, UP, Box 2, fos. 50–5.

[19] Keats to Sinclair, 12 Oct. 1899, UP, Box 2, fos. 50–5.

[20] Sinclair was delighted that Garnett, 64 and a central figure in the London literary world, liked her sonnets. She wrote thanking him for 'the encouragement you have given me. It really has been more help

Danger: The Future of British Army Reform. Sinclair needed the money, but translating, as she had discovered when she was working on *Outlines of Church History*, was a great physical and mental strain. At least with the first book she had worked closely with Henry Gwatkin, and had punctuated the drudgery with visits to see him in Cambridge. The book on army reform held no interest for her, nor for Edward Garnett, whom she consulted occasionally only in the most perfunctory way.[21] Even Anthony Deane was concerned about her, writing at Easter 1901 that 'It is exasperating to conceive you translating grisly German books for starvation wages.'[22] Sinclair, labouring away at her translation, had little reason to feel cheerful or optimistic.

Her financial anxieties were compounded by an even more intense and personal worry when, in July 1900, her mother, now in her late 70s, suffered a serious heart attack and for two months was weak, confused, disoriented, and unable to take care of herself.[23] Although Sinclair and her mother had clashed many times during her childhood and adolescence, as her mother grew older, and Sinclair gradually assumed full responsibility for her, she became more and more protective and tender towards her (her pet name for her was 'the Lamb'). She had always been anxious to keep her from infection: when one of her nephews and nieces in Hull caught a minor illness while Sinclair and her mother were staying with them, Sinclair panicked and hurried her mother away.[24] Now her mother was seriously ill and needed full-time care. Sinclair, desperate to finish the translation, simply couldn't manage alone. She asked Edward Garnett to recommend a 'trustworthy person who should not be a professional nurse', and managed to find a maid who was, she told Dorothea Beale, 'a great help & comfort'.[25] Amelia Sinclair was 'a long time recovering' and even in January 1901 was still 'very weak', Sinclair told Beale.[26] Gwendoline Keats was sympathetic: 'How terribly hard for you & sad, I can't think of anything to say, damn it. That it should come when you need all your strength, pluck & time for your work. . . . The tragedy of it all makes my heart ache.'[27] It is possible that the

than you know. I knew no one but you who could speak with authority' (Sinclair to Richard Garnett, 20 Mar. 1900, HR, MS (Garnett, R) Recip).

  [21] See e.g. Edward Garnett to Sinclair, 15 Sept. 1900, UP, Box 1, fo. 28.

  [22] Deane to Sinclair, n.d. [Easter 1901], UP, Box 1, fos. 21–2.

  [23] See Sinclair to Dorothea Beale, 11 Jan. 1901, Archive Department, Cheltenham Ladies' College.

  [24] See Wilda McNeile to T. E. M. Boll, 24 June 1959, UP, Box 48, fo. 529, and Florence Bartrop to Boll, 26 Apr. 1960, UP, Box 48, fos. 518–19.

  [25] Edward Garnett to Sinclair, 8 Aug. 1900, UP, Box 1, fo. 28 and Sinclair to Beale, 11 Jan. 1901, Archive Department, Cheltenham Ladies' College.

  [26] Sinclair to Beale, 11 Jan. 1901, Archive Department, Cheltenham Ladies' College.

  [27] Keats to Sinclair, 23 Aug. 1900, UP, Box 2, fos. 50–5.

anguish Sinclair felt was intensified by the fact that she was having some kind of romantic relationship at the time of her mother's illness. In an undated letter which seems to have been written during the summer of 1900, Keats notes that although Sinclair has her work cut out for her on the translation, 'poor little beggar . . . is no end happy in other ways'.[28] Concrete evidence has long since disappeared, but the phrase 'the tragedy of it all', in the letter I quoted above, suggests that there may have been even more at stake for Sinclair than the death of an ageing parent and the tedium of uncongenial work. Certainly Sinclair's fictional alter ego, Mary Olivier, starts a sexual relationship around the time of her mother's stroke, and cannot marry her lover because she must stay at home to take care of her. But this remains speculative.

As Sinclair watched by her mother's sickbed, she was also awaiting the publication of her next book. Constable, who had contacted Sinclair 'off their own bat', as she put it, were scheduled to publish *Two Sides of a Question*, which consisted of the stories 'Superseded' and 'The Cosmopolitan', in February 1901.[29] Sinclair 'had just written the last words when my dear Mother's illness began, & I had neither the heart nor the time to re-write what need [*sic*] re-writing'.[30] On 22 February 1901, just a few days before the publication of *Two Sides*, Amelia Sinclair finally died. Overwhelmed with grief for the mother who—however disapproving and critical—was probably her closest emotional tie, Sinclair scarcely noticed the appearance of the book.[31] Her beloved sister-in-law Eleanor, the widow of her brother William, came south from Liverpool, where she had moved after her husband's death, to be with 'Mary May', as she called her, and to help with all the funeral and other arrangements. After Eleanor left Sinclair found herself for the first time in her life both alone and free.

Her days without the mother with whom she had lived for almost forty years were unusually isolated. The Irish writer Katharine Tynan Hinkson, prolific author of sentimental verse and poetry, who had befriended Sinclair in the summer of 1900, was concerned about her, writing to her after seeing her in January 1902: 'I hope you are feeling better my dear. You looked wan enough on Sunday. I wish you were not such a lonely little person. Perhaps it is good for the work, but it is bad for the human creature. And I have learnt to love her; began to love her from the first.'[32] Sinclair, who felt very close to

---

[28] Keats to Sinclair, n.d. [summer 1900], UP, Box 2, fos. 50–5.

[29] Sinclair to Edward Garnett, n.d. [Sept. 1900], HR, MS (Garnett, E) Recip.

[30] Sinclair to Hinkson, 1 Jan. 1902, JR.

[31] She told Hinkson a year later that she 'never took much interest in it' (Sinclair to Hinkson, 1 Jan. 1902, JR).

[32] Katharine Hinkson to Sinclair, 10 Jan. 1902, UP, Box, 2, fo. 41. In her autobiography Hinkson describes how 'Some time early in 1899 my husband had found "Mr. and Mrs. Neville Tyson" [*sic*] in a

Hinkson, reassured her that solitude was easier for her than it might have been for some women: 'You must not pity me too much for living alone. I can bear it better than most women can, & I have a great many things to do that I like doing, & life isn't long enough to get them all in! And then I have my friends. I cd. wish there were a few less miles between Hampstead and Ealing [where Hinkson lived].'[33] Sinclair's isolation (apart from a cat to whom she was entirely devoted) was unusual for her class and time, even though she seemed to accept it cheerfully enough. To some extent she chose to be alone: she dismissed her maid soon after her mother's death, probably for financial as much as emotional reasons, but even when she had more money she did not replace her, living in lodgings without a maid or companion until 1914.[34] Friends and acquaintances often commented on her reclusive tendencies. Ella Hepworth Dixon, author of *The Story of a Modern Woman* (1894), who met Sinclair around 1908, noted that 'She has always loved solitude, but once this inclination nearly lost her her life. She was found alone, in a high fever, stretched on a divan—absolutely helpless and having tasted nothing for several days. . . . [She] had a beautiful black cat in constant attendance.'[35] Even Arnold Bennett was struck by her isolation, writing in his diary: 'I rather liked this prim virgin. Great sense. She said she lived absolutely alone—not even a servant.'[36] The woman who had grown up sharing a house with her parents, five noisy brothers, a full staff, and several animals was now surrounded by the silence of empty rooms. All she had to listen to were her own thoughts.

When in late 1919 Sinclair's cat died the full extent of her emotional dependence on him became apparent. Dixon remarked that she was 'inconsolable', and Sinclair herself wrote several long, heartbroken letters to Catherine Dawson Scott (known as 'Sappho' after the long poem she published in 1889), describing how she had been summoned back to London from her writing retreat in Stow-on-the-Wold:

I came up on Wednesday & took Tommy home from the Vet's on my way. I had him for twenty-four hours. I can't tell you how awful those twenty-four hours were—knowing that the Vet wd. come the next day & chloroform him. . . . He

bundle of review books from the *St. James's Gazette*. We were both struck by the quality of it.' In the summer of 1900 Hinkson met Sinclair at a Women Writers' Dinner and their friendship began. Sinclair regularly cycled to Hinkson's house in Ealing for dinner and to go for walks. Hinkson appreciated not only Sinclair's modesty, but also her generosity and her lack of malice and envy. See Tynan, *Middle Years*, 292–4: at 292.

[33] Sinclair to Hinkson, 12 Jan. 1902, JR.   [34] Boll, *Miss May Sinclair*, 105.

[35] Ella Hepworth Dixon, '*As I Knew Them': Sketches of People I Have Met on the Way* (London: Hutchinson, 1930), 123. The incident Dixon describes occurred in 1909.

[36] Bennett, *Journal of Arnold Bennett*, 410–11.

didn't actually suffer under it, but the preliminary drug had to be given four times, he was so strong & full of vitality. And it seemed ages before the chloroform took effect & he went off—sobbing—to sleep in my arms.

The first dose of the drug paralysed his limbs but didn't affect his hearing, & I think in a way he knew me up to the last minutes of consciousness, & was content to be in my arms. I buried him that afternoon. . . . I don't think I can ever bear to see the house or my study where it happened, or the garden again. Even Stow is unbearable. The thought of it & the continual <u>seeing</u> it all over again has poisoned all my walks. And I can't work. I wish I cd. die; but I'm too strong.[37]

For a while she was obsessed with the idea of giving up her house in London and moving permanently to Stow, keeping just a couple of rooms in London as a pied-à-terre, but as her pain lessened she gradually abandoned the idea.[38] But the memory of Tommy's deathbed remained vivid, and in 1922 she worked it into *Anne Severn and the Fieldings*, where Anne sits up all night cradling a dying cat in her arms.

It seems to have helped Sinclair to describe Tommy's death in such vivid detail in her letters. But, perhaps partly because her feelings about her mother were so fraught and ambivalent, she left no such record of her emotional reactions to Amelia's death. Her response instead was to throw herself into her work, writing and revising the novel she had begun years earlier and then laid aside.[39] She was still very anxious about her career, telling Beale: 'I feel very hopeless sometimes, not so much because I'm afraid of failure in the vulgar commercial sense, though that seems pretty certain—I <u>am</u> afraid of not being able to make enough to live on by novel-writing, & having to give it up'.[40] Several times she pushed herself to the point of breakdown, writing to Katharine Hinkson in January 1902: 'I have been working hard on my long book, & I suppose I must have been overdoing it, for I've collapsed again.'[41] Two months before the book was finally finished in April 1904 Sinclair was again forced to rest. She told Hinkson: 'I must never go at it quite so hard again'.[42] She was ill on and off for the next eighteen months.[43] In an

[37] Dixon, *'As I Knew Them'*, 123; Sinclair to Catherine Dawson Scott, 28 Oct. 1919 and 2 Nov. 1919 (source of the citation), Beinecke Rare Book and Manuscript Library, Gen MSS 144, Box 1, fo. 22.

[38] See Sinclair to Scott, 5 Nov. 1919, Beinecke Rare Book and Manuscript Library, Gen MSS 144, Box 1, fo. 22.

[39] Deane enquired about 'Rickmann' (the name of the main character of *The Divine Fire* is actually 'Keith Rickman') in a letter of 28 Nov. 1899 (UP, Box 1, fos. 21–2). Sinclair told an interviewer for *Outlook* magazine that 'there were seven years between the commencement and finishing of "The Divine Fire", five years of which, however, were an interlude, during which she did shorter books, which meant less strain' ('Author of "The Divine Fire"', 728). On this reckoning she started work on the novel in 1897, just after she and her mother moved to London.

[40] Sinclair to Beale, 11 Jan. 1901, Archive Department, Cheltenham Ladies' College.

[41] Sinclair to Hinkson, 1 Jan. 1902, JR.   [42] Sinclair to Hinkson, 17 Feb. 1904, JR.

[43] See Sinclair to Witter Bynner, 29 Aug. 1905, HL, bMS Am 1891 (766).

attempt to recover her strength, she took a complete break, visiting her mother's family in Ireland in May 1904, and then spending the summer in Surrey, Cheltenham, the Cotswolds, and Sussex.[44]

But she was frightened and apprehensive about the reception of *The Divine Fire*.[45] Its publication was delayed until September 1904 because she had managed to find an American publisher, Henry Holt, willing to publish an independent US edition. She was delighted, especially since, she told Hinkson, Holt was 'very particular': 'there is such a dead set against English authors this year, & the length of the book was against it'.[46] But Holt made her nervous: he demanded minor revisions, and advised her to make extensive cuts (which she refused to do).[47] Even though the book would now reach a much larger audience than if it had appeared only in Britain, Sinclair was much less sure of its merits than she had been. The only aspect of the whole transaction that she welcomed unequivocally was her decision to dismiss her agent, A. P. Watt: 'the best day's work I ever did', she told Hinkson.[48] It can be no coincidence that *The Divine Fire*, Gissing-like, is concerned with the vulnerability of poverty-ridden authors, the corruption of the literary press, and the increasing commercialization of the bookselling trade. Sinclair was writing about the new world into which she had moved, but she was also continuing her interrogation of modern spiritual life. She told the Roman Catholic Katharine Hinkson that 'as I have no faith . . . I've had to make my own mysticism, & perhaps it's a queer thing'.[49] In *The Divine Fire*, characters search to preserve a sense of the sacred in everyday life. Greed and avarice are pitched against altruism and idealism in an attempt to find some meaningful relation between the laws of the market and the laws of faith and love. In effect, Sinclair was still looking for a modernity in which she could believe.

The Divine Fire is structured around the contrast between two spaces, a domestic library and a bookshop. The library belongs to the aristocratic father of Lucia Harden, who, while her father is abroad, pays to have it catalogued by Keith Rickman, a struggling poet and son of a bookseller who made his money in trade. We first see Keith in his father's new shop in the Strand. It is laid out like a department store, with lavish displays and plenty of artificial light:

The shop, a corner one, was part of a gigantic modern structure . . . Though the day was not yet done, the electric light streamed over the pavement from the huge

[44] See Sinclair to Hinkson, 6[?] May 1904 and 8 Aug. 1904, JR.
[45] See Sinclair to Hinkson, 8 Oct. 1904, JR.   [46] Sinclair to Hinkson, 8 Aug. 1904, JR.
[47] See Henry Holt to Sinclair, 13 July 1904, UP, Box 2, fos. 43–4.
[48] Sinclair to Hinkson, 8 Aug. 1904, JR.   [49] Sinclair to Hinkson, 12 Jan. 1902, JR.

windows of the ground floor; a coronal of dazzling globes hung over the doorway at the corner; there, as you turned, the sombre windows of the second-hand department stretched half way down the side street; here, in the great thoroughfare, the newest of new books stood out, solicitous and alluring, in suits of blazing scarlet and vivid green, of vellum and gilt, of polished leather that shone like amber and malachite and lapis lazuli. (DF, 10–11)

The shop is described in terms that align it with new commercial ventures such as Harrods in London or Galeries Lafayette in Paris. The reader is scarcely aware by the end of the paragraph that it is books that are on sale here: they are described first as mannequins wearing new suits of clothes, and then as pieces of jewellery. Rhetorically the books are interchangeable with a series of other commodities, or, as Marx put it, they figuratively 'metamorphose' into them.[50] Significantly, the terms of that figural metamorphosis are associated with the decorated bodies of women: clothes, jewellery.[51] But the bookshop, unlike the new department stores, is primarily a masculine space: the books are feminized to attract a male clientele. Keith is embarrassed by the flagrant commercialism of his father's shop: 'Surrounded by wares whose very appearance was a venal solicitation, he never hinted by so much as the turn of a phrase that there was anything about him to be bought' (DF, 12–13). He seeks to turn it into a place in which ideas are exchanged for free, a site for social gatherings and conversation: young men, who are 'not the least bit of good to the shop' (DF, 12), drift in and out to talk to him. The ambiguity of the phrase—'anything about *him* to be bought [my italics]'—hints at exactly his dilemma as an author who is trying to get published. Is it Keith or his writings that are for sale?

Shortly after this scene, Keith arrives at Court House to start working on Lucia's books. Lucia does not know, but Keith does, that her father has already mortgaged almost all of his property, including the library, to finance a debauched lifestyle overseas. Keith begins to fall in love with Lucia, and suffers agonies of remorse knowing that he is cataloguing the library in preparation for his father's company to buy it up from the financial agent who holds the bill of sale on it. The library is described in terms that recall Walter Benjamin's account of the 'auratic' object which modernity has left behind.[52] It has been gradually accumulated over centuries; its books are

---

[50] See Karl Marx, *Capital* (1867; trans. from 3rd German edn. Samuel Moore and Edward Aveling, ed. Friedrich Engels, rev. Marie Sachey and Herbert Lamm, in *Great Books of the Western World*, 50, Chicago, University of Chicago Press, 1952), sect. 2a, 'The Metamorphosis of Commodities'.

[51] See Bowlby, *Just Looking*, 27: 'a productive channel of investigation might be opened up by considering what woman as ideological sign, and women as subjects caught or participating in various levels of social relations, have in common with commodities—with the things which a buyer consumes.'

[52] See Walter Benjamin, 'The Work of Art in the Age of Mechanical Reproduction', 1936, in

rare and precious originals or first editions; it is a place devoted to the preservation and transmission of knowledge. If the bookshop is like a department store, the library is like a church:

The bookcases that covered the length and height of the walls were of one blackness with the oak floor and ceiling. The scattered blues and crimsons of the carpets (repeated in duller tones in the old morocco bindings), the gilded tracery of the tooling, and here and there a blood-red lettering-piece, gave an effect as of some dim, rich arabesque flung on to the darkness. At this hour the sunlight made the most of all it found there; it washed the faded carpet with a new dye; it licked every jutting angle, every polished surface, every patch of vellum. (DF, 65)

These books, unlike the ones in the Rickman shop, are holy objects. They shine in the dusk like stained glass windows, and whereas the bookshop is lit by electricity even during the day, this room is an alembic for sunshine. It is tempting to say that one space is cultural, the other natural, but maybe a more accurate distinction would be between the shop as a commercial, and the library as a historical, space. Later in the book Keith notes that 'the library belonged to [Lucia's] race and to their historic past' (DF, 145). Although the books can be sold, they are also inalienable: they belong to Lucia because she is her father's daughter, not because she paid money for them. The books in the shop, on the other hand, could belong to anyone: they are in transit, symptoms of the malaise of modernity. In David Frisby's words: 'The commodity form . . . symbolizes social relations of modernity. . . . The "phantasmagoria" of the world of commodities is precisely a world in motion, in flux, in which all values are transitory and all relations are fleeting and indifferent.'[53] The library, with its feudal associations with Lucia's family, resists this kind of shifting 'phantasmagoria'.

Keith's shame at his involvement in his father's designs on the library is bound up with his sense of Lucia as an ideal being, a woman with 'a luminous innocence, a piercing purity' (DF, 75).[54] He undercharges for his services because he longs to be near her; he refuses the gift of her hospitality, and stays at a nearby hotel while he works on the catalogue, because he feels embarrassed at the duplicity of his position. Lucia represents the possibility

Illuminations: Essays and Reflections, 1955, rev. edn. trans. Harry Zohn, ed. Hannah Arendt (New York: Schocken, 1969), 220, 221, 223: 'Even the most perfect reproduction of a work of art is lacking in one element: its presence in time and space, its unique existence at the place where it happens to be. . . . that which withers in the age of mechanical reproduction is the aura of the work of art. . . . Unmistakably, reproduction as offered by picture magazines and newsreels differs from the image seen by the unarmed eye. Uniqueness and permanence are as closely linked in the latter as are transitoriness and reproducibility in the former.'

[53] David Frisby, *Fragments of Modernity: Theories of Modernity in the Work of Simmel, Kracauer and Benjamin* (Cambridge, Mass.: MIT Press, 1986), 22–3.

[54] Zegger suggests that Lucia 'is a personification of the divine or the ideal' (*May Sinclair*, 30).

of non-commercial economies: economies of learning and of love. Throughout the book she is associated with the phrase 'divine fire', which means at once artistic genius and romantic passion. She becomes an image of poetic and ethical inspiration: 'Love between man and woman to her mind was a sort of genius; . . . the wind of the divine spirit blowing where it listeth, the kindling of the divine fire' (DF, 409). Pitched against this kind of anarchic freedom is the consolidating force of capitalism, which gives only the illusion of movement—what Marx called a '*perpetuum mobile*'—as goods circulate endlessly through the same few hands.[55] The library, for instance, when it passes into Keith's father's hands after Lucia's father's death, is quickly remortgaged to the same financial agent that Lucia's father had used.

Lucia's air of divinity and her ignorance, when Keith first meets her, of the imminent sale of the library place her symbolically outside the sphere of commodity relations. Keith is horrified at his father's acquisition of the library, and after his death, which leaves Keith penniless, Keith spends years in penury, trying to save the money to buy back Lucia's library and give it to her. Lucia's position at the centre of an economy based on the idea of the gift is contrasted with the status of the other women with whom Keith becomes entangled (Poppy, a music-hall actress and Flossie, a bank clerk to whom he is briefly engaged) who can both, in various ways, be bought. The figure of the prostitute or kept woman is a central preoccupation of *fin de siècle* novels—see, for example, Zola's *Nana* (1880), Gissing's *The Unclassed* (1899), Somerset Maugham's *Liza of Lambeth* (1897), and Stephen Crane's *Maggie: A Girl of the Streets* (1893)—as if femininity itself has come to be associated with bodies for sale.[56] Both Poppy and Flossie rely on their lovers to supplement their own meagre incomes, and as soon as one lover is exhausted, they replace him with another: Poppy becomes sexually involved with Pilkington, the financial agent who holds the bill of sale on the Harden library, almost before Keith has left her, and after Keith grows tired of her, Flossie neatly transfers her affections to Spinks, Keith's friend, with the connivance of the two men. Both women, without being prostitutes, in different ways trade on their bodies. As Horace Jewdwine, Lucia's cousin, comments, 'modern' passions are 'the passions of the divorce-court and the Stock Exchange' (DF, 482): centres of circulation in which women and money change hands.

---

[55] Marx, *Capital*, 60.

[56] See Rita Felski, *The Gender of Modernity* (Cambridge, Mass.: Harvard University Press, 1995), 4 and ff., for further discussion of this issue. One section of Charles Baudelaire's classic commentary on modernity, 'The Painter of Modern Life' (1863), is entitled 'Women and Prostitutes', as if the two are virtually indistinguishable. See Charles Baudelaire, 'The Painter of Modern Life', in *The Painter of Modern Life and Other Essays*, trans. and ed. Jonathan Mayne (London: Phaidon, 1964).

The novel has a proto-Marxist fascination with the phenomenon of money. Flossie works with banknotes that have been taken out of circulation:

Flossie was one of fifty girls who sat, row after row, at long flat desks covered with green cloth. A soft monotonous light was reflected from the cream-coloured walls against which Flossie's head stood out with striking effect, like some modern study in black and morbid white. . . . Hers was the lightest of light labour, the delicate handling of thousands of cancelled notes—airy, insubstantial things, as it were the ghosts of bank-notes, released from the gross conditions of the currency. Towards the middle of the morning Flossie would be immersed in a pale agitated sea of bank-notes. . . . It was almost mechanical labour, and for that Flossie had more than a taste, she had a positive genius. It was mechanical labour idealized and reduced to a fine art, an art in which the personality of the artist counted. (DF, 305–6)

Flossie is both art-object, her silhouette standing out in black against the wall like an Aubrey Beardsley print, and industrial artist. The worthless notes—'ghosts' of money, as Sinclair describes them—emphasize the secondariness of paper money, valuable only as a stand-in for the gold from which its value derives: as Marx put it, money 'serves only as a symbol of itself'.[57] Flossie's alienated and 'mechanical' labour in a sea of paper which is doubly alienated from the source of value (even its symbolic worth has been cancelled) throws into relief the transcendence of Lucia's world, full of value in and of itself.

As soon as Keith becomes aware of his preoccupation with Flossie, it is only a matter of time before he finds himself inevitably seduced into touching and then buying: as he kisses her, he feels that 'it was he who was being led; he who was being drawn, he who was being held—over the brink of the immeasurable, inexpirable folly' (DF, 322). She comes at a price—marriage; and Keith's 'genius', the part of him that is associated with Lucia and her library, looks on 'aghast' (DF, 323) as Keith commits himself to a sexual economy in which nothing is ever given away. Like a prostitute, Flossie is both commodity and consumer, and like a display in a shop, she cannot be fully enjoyed for free. She demands to get married not because she loves Keith, but because she wants to acquire a house of her own, and to reproduce herself: all her passion goes into imagining the daughter she longs for, Muriel Maud. A typical consumer, she loves the newest baby best: 'She's decent to the baby, but she's positively brutal to Muriel Maud', comments Keith's friend Maddox (DF, 576).

I have implied that Lucia and her library participate in an alternative, sacred order which is opposed to the commercialized world, symbolized by

---

[57] Marx, *Capital*, 60.

the bookshop, in which Poppy and Flossie live. But the novel also explores the interface between the order that Lucia stands for and the commercial world with which it is surrounded. We have seen that the library is mortgaged and sold twice, and Keith, although his real calling is poetry, buys it back by working for years as a hack journalist for an editor who believes that 'No art can hold out for ever against commercialism' (DF, 480). Keith, malnourished and dangerously ill, almost gives his life to get the library back, and even when he does finally raise the money to buy it by selling his own verse to an editor friend, it is no longer complete: he tells Lucia 'I'm sorry to say a few very valuable books were sold before the mortgage and could not be recovered' (DF, 546). *The Divine Fire* thus explores the charged intersection between the auratic art object and the literary market place. Where high modernism—Yeats, Eliot, Pound—explicitly sought to rescue art from the transience of the market by constructing it as changeless and detached, the earlier, proto-modernist art of the late nineteenth century was preoccupied with a more fraught, more immanent form of modernity, one that still half believed in the imbrication of the eternal values of art with the changing values of the material world.[58] The level of anxiety generated by this belief was often crippling: Gissing's letters, for example, chronicle his rage and despair at being unable to sell work he thought of as art.[59] To struggle as a writer, as Keith, Gissing, and Sinclair all did, was to struggle with the contradictions of pre-modernist culture itself, both at odds with, and dependent on, the dynamics of the market.

   Keith's relations with Lucia are plagued by these tensions. Shortly after he leaves her, he writes twenty-nine sonnets dedicated to her, but, unwilling to publish them because of their private nature, he leaves them to her in his will to do as she likes with.[60] They represent a potential financial resource, and he wants her to have them as 'partial payment of a debt' (DF, 304), the debt he

---

[58]   Recently scholars have begun to challenge the idea, popularized by Andreas Huyssen in *After the Great Divide: Modernism, Mass Culture, Postmodernism* (Bloomington, Ind.: Indiana University Press, 1986), that modernism was invested in the idea of an autonomous, detached art. See e.g. Kevin J. H. Dettmar and Stephen Watts (eds.), *Marketing Modernisms: Self-Promotion, Canonization, Rereading* (Ann Arbor: University of Michigan Press, 1996), 3: 'the dual trajectory of this book [is] both to reconsider the critically suppressed relationship between canonical modernists and the commercial marketplace, and to provide a metacommentary on other exclusionary and political effects devolving from such a pristine conception of modernist poetics, its dense and mysterious "purity."'

[59]   See e.g. Gissing's letter to Wells, 16 July 1898: 'I have hideous nights of sleeplessness, and wonder how the *devil* I am to live this life much longer', in *George Gissing and H. G. Wells: Their Friendship and Correspondence*, ed. Royal A. Gettmann (Urbana, Ill.: University of Illinois Press, 1961), 106; or Gissing's account of himself to his lover Gabrielle Fleury in late July 1898 (the letter is not dated): 'It is the life of a hermit; not a happy life; haunted with desires of the impossible, oppressed by great loneliness', in *The Letters of George Gissing to Gabrielle Fleury*, ed. Pierre Coustillas (New York: New York Public Library, 1964), 28.

[60]   Boll claims that Keith's sonnet sequence includes some of the poems Sinclair offered to Edward Garnett for the sonnet collection he hoped to publish (*Miss May Sinclair*, 179).

feels his father owes her since he bought her library at a fraction of its real value. But later, when Keith and Lucia meet again while he is engaged to Flossie, Keith decides to give the poems to Lucia so that she can see how wonderfully she has inspired him. Lucia asks if the manuscript she is holding is a copy, and Keith tells her it is the original, and the only one in existence. He objects to her suggestion of having a copy made: 'That would spoil my pleasure and my gift, too. It's only valuable because it's unique' (DF, 427). Lucia, however, refuses the gift. Keith will not allow her to believe that the poems are addressed only to an ideal, and she cannot accept them as love-poems to herself. 'I should feel as if I'd taken what belonged to some one else', she tells him (DF, 449). She sees the poems not as a gift but as a robbery. They are also—if unconsciously—a bribe, an attempt to buy her approval and love. Lucia, unlike her library, manages to resist being diminished by the commercial transactions into which even her lover seeks to tempt her.

Finally, Lucia simply offers herself to Keith. Keith, desperate to make restitution to Lucia, has told Flossie he must postpone their wedding so that he can put all his money towards buying the library back, at which news Flossie promptly leaves him for the more wealthy Spinks. Near the end of the novel, Keith visits Lucia to tell her he has finally managed to acquire the library. Lucia initially refuses to accept it, fearing to take advantage of the feeling she knows Keith has had for her. The two repeatedly try to disentangle the business aspects of their relationship from their feelings for one another: 'Try and think of it as a simple matter of business', Keith tells her; 'Don't think of our friendship . . . It's all pure business, as brutally impersonal as you like' (DF, 546, 547). But Lucia cannot accept the library until she feels she has something to offer in return. She holds out against him until she finally realizes that she loves him, and can give him her love in return for his gift of the library. The contradictory nature of their transactions is crystallized in the phrase 'free gift': 'Very slowly [Keith] realized that the thing he had dreamed and despaired of, that he dared not ask for, was being divinely offered to him as a free gift' (DF, 554).[61] The library which, as Keith tells her, 'isn't mine and is yours' (DF, 553), is paid for in the end by Lucia's affection. The logic of the market place now defines even the play of the 'divine fire'.

The Divine Fire appeared in September 1904 to lukewarm reviews in England and more enthusiastic ones in the USA. The Nation praised the novel's

---

[61] The ironies of the phrase 'free gift' in late 20th-cent. capitalism, in which 'free gifts' are only one more incentive to buy, demonstrate the extent to which modernity has become increasingly an economy of commodities.

analysis of the relationship between genius and its environment, and Holt wrote to Sinclair to tell her that the *Nation* reviewer had written him a personal letter saying that *The Divine Fire* was the best novel he had seen in a long time.[62] Frederic Taber Cooper in the New York edition of the *Bookman* described it as 'one of those rare books which give you so much to think about that you lay it down from time to time, only to find that you are compelled to take it promptly up again and persevere to the end . . . It is a book of very unusual quality.'[63] Soon Sinclair started to receive letters from editors and publishers anxious to serialize her next novel or to publish one or more of her stories: A. L. Sessions of *Ainslee's Magazine* in New York wanted 'a strong modern love story with a considerable degree of action and dramatic quality', and *Lippincott's Magazine* and *McClure's Magazine* were keen to look at any piece she might have.[64] But the novel was not yet making money, although Holt was cautiously optimistic, and Sinclair was still virtually penniless and struggling with translations for the *Cambridge Modern History*. She told Katharine Hinkson that if she fell behind, she was swamped by 'arrears'.[65] Nonetheless she was hopeful. If she could gather an audience in the vast American market her finances would be much more secure, and the Chace Act of 1891 had finally secured some limited copyright protection for foreign authors publishing in the USA.[66] She wrote to Hinkson: 'I hope soon there will be no need for me to do translations for anything. America is tuning up to a regular Hymn of Praise, & their best reviews are the ones that lay it on thickest. Mr Holt is full of hope & joy, & my publishers here are delighted; not at the actual sales (though these are more than we expected from the way the English reviews went), but at the prospect of sales & the warmth of Ricky's reception on "the other side".'[67] Holt was more tentative than Sinclair's letter implies, but he did tell her in December 1904 that in spite of initially disappointing sales, he still had 'confidence that the book will reach most of the comparatively limited class capable of appreciating it'.[68] His instincts were not always sound, however. He warned her that *The Divine Fire* 'could not make one of our phenomenal American "hundred-thousand" sellers', but in the end, the book sold around 200,000 copies.[69] Good reviews continued to appear in the US in early 1905 in the

[62] 'More Novels', *Nation*, 79 (24 Nov. 1904), 419–20; Holt to Sinclair, 25 Nov. 1904, UP, Box 2, fos. 43–4.

[63] Frederic Taber Cooper, '*The Divine Fire*', *Bookman* (New York), 20 (Feb. 1905), 553.

[64] *Lippincott's Magazine* to Sinclair, 9 Nov. 1904; S. S. McClure to Sinclair, 29 Nov. 1904, UP, Box 2, fo. 62; A. L. Sessions to Sinclair, 10 Dec. 1904, UP, Box 3, fo. 83. *Mr and Mrs Nevill Tyson* was serialized in *Ainslee's* in May and June 1906.

[65] Sinclair to Hinkson, 19 Dec. 1904, JR. [66] Bonham-Carter, *Authors by Profession*, i. 162.

[67] Sinclair to Hinkson, 19 Dec. 1904, JR.

[68] Holt to Sinclair, 28 Dec. 1904, UP, Box 2, fos. 43–4. [69] Ibid.; Zegger, *May Sinclair*, 31–2.

March issue of the *Bookman*, in the *Critic* (which called the novel 'brilliant'), and in the *Sewanee Review*.[70] Sinclair tried to analyse the reasons for her popularity in the USA in a letter to an unnamed American admirer of *The Divine Fire* in January 1905: 'Altogether I am simply amazed at the way it has been received on the other side of the water. What has specially pleased me is that you all seem to allow that I really had a right to choose my own subject & to treat it in my own way! (Can this be because you are a Republic?)'[71] The *Outlook* suggested two possible explanations 'offered by people of no small experience in publishing': 'The first thought it was our democracy that made the successful struggle of the poet Rickman against great obstacles peculiarly appeal to us, and the second that it was the growing tendency among the better-informed Americans to gain wherever possible either culture or profit as well as amusement from their reading.'[72] There were more practical explanations as well: Ford Madox Ford commented that sales of the book increased dramatically when the manager of Wanamaker's department store in New York decided to endorse it; and the novel may well have received more generous reviews in the USA than in the UK because critics assumed it was Sinclair's first novel (neither of her earlier books had yet been published in the USA).[73]

Immediate responses in England were more mixed. Katharine Hinkson was worried that she had offended Sinclair at Christmas 1904 with her 'want of sympathy' about *The Divine Fire*. She reassured her that it was 'a book of genius although I think it unequal in parts'; Sinclair for her part was glad of the encouragement but told her: 'if you had abused my book up hill & down dale while continuing to love the author, it wd. have made no difference to me'.[74] She had always been a little afraid of Hinkson, writing to her a year or so after they met: 'I can't quite realize that we are to be friends. At times I feel almost frightened, lest I sd. (as I know I do, & must) fall short of what your friend ought to be. I am horrid in some ways. I was particularly horrid the

[70] F. M. Colby, 'Miss Sinclair's *The Divine Fire*', *Bookman* (New York), 21 (Mar. 1905), 66–8; Olivia Howard Dunbar, 'Books Reviewed: Fact and Fiction', *Critic*, 46 (Feb. 1905), 183; 'Some New Novels: *The Divine Fire*', *Sewanee Review*, 13 (Jan. 1905), 119–20.

[71] Sinclair to an unnamed correspondent (Professor Carlton Lewis of Yale?], 21 Jan. 1905, HL, bMS Am 800.52 (230). Carlton Lewis is mentioned as 'my last misguided admirer' in a letter from Sinclair to Edward Garnett, 15 Jan. 1905, HR, MS (Garnett, E) Recip.

[72] 'Author of *The Divine Fire*', 728. Zegger echoes this analysis: 'In the United States . . . readers would naturally sympathize with a self-made man who bucked the English class system' (*May Sinclair*, 31).

[73] Ford Madox Ford, *Return to Yesterday* (New York: Liveright, 1932), 317. The anonymous reviewer in '*The Divine Fire*', *Reader*, 5 (Apr. 1905), 622–3, and William Morton Payne, in 'Recent Fiction', *Dial*, 38 (1 Jan. 1905), 18, both assumed *The Divine Fire* was a first novel.

[74] Hinkson to Sinclair, 24 Jan. 1905, UP, Box 2, fo. 41; Sinclair to Hinkson, 25 Jan. 1905, JR.

other day.'[75] Although Sinclair was evidently disappointed by Hinkson's reservations about the novel, Hinkson was one of the few people to whom she communicated personal—rather than professional—vulnerability, and that extra degree of intimacy and trust meant that Sinclair was able to accept Hinkson's critical opinions about her work. Anthony Deane, on the other hand, from whom Sinclair had long ago detached herself emotionally, was unreservedly enthusiastic about *The Divine Fire*, telling Sinclair that it was the 'very best book I have read for I don't know how long' and that he had 'no sort of reservation or qualifying criticism'.[76] But actual sales of the book in Britain were sluggish.

In February 1905, however, the book's commercial fortunes changed dramatically. Owen Seaman published a piece in *Punch* noting that *The Divine Fire*, which had received little critical response in Britain, was selling very well in the USA 'which has a vastly wider reading public, and, at times, a keener *flair* for genius'.[77] The *New York Times* followed up Seaman's article with an editorial and then a very favourable review, asking whether or not it was true that *The Divine Fire* was 'a best seller'.[78] Of course as soon as the question was asked the answer barely mattered: the publicity alone meant that sales, which had been growing steadily in the USA, escalated dramatically in both Britain and the USA. Soon May Sinclair found herself being fêted as a best-selling author. Ford Madox Ford noted that in the USA 'Parties were given at which examinations were held as to the speeches of the characters in Miss Sinclair's book. At others you had to wear about you some attribute suggesting its title.'[79] Literary agents J. B. Pinker and Curtis Brown both tried to get Sinclair on their books; Holt looked into publishing American editions of her earlier novels.[80] Sinclair began to recognize her own bargaining

---

[75] Sinclair to Hinkson, 8 Feb. 1902, JR.

[76] Deane to Sinclair, 31 Jan. 1905, UP, Box 1, fos. 21–2.

[77] Owen Seaman, 'Our Booking Office', *Punch*, 128 (1 Feb. 1905), 90.

[78] 'Topics of the Week', *New York Times*, 18 Feb. 1905, sect. 2, 97; H. I. Brock, 'Fire and Smoke', *New York Times*, 11 Mar. 1905, sect. 2, 150.

[79] Ford, *Return to Yesterday*, 317. Ford wore a fireman's helmet to one of these parties and aroused Sinclair's wrath: 'I took her home in a hansom from the house of one of the Garnetts in Highgate to her house in Kensington—a distance, I imagine, of ten miles but seeming a hundred. She refused to speak at all to me after I had told her.'

[80] See Sinclair to J. B. Pinker, 18 Feb. 1905, HA. She thanked Pinker for his interest but, mindful of the trouble she had run into with A. P. Watt and Blackwood's, told him: 'I am so entirely satisfied with my publishers, both in England & America, that I prefer to deal with them direct.' See also Curtis Brown to Sinclair, 4, 24, and 28 Mar. 1905, UP, Box 1, fo. 12, and Holt to Sinclair, 28 Mar. and 6 Apr. 1905, UP, Box 2, fos. 43–4. Holt wanted Sinclair to make considerable revisions to *Audrey Craven* before he would consider publishing it, largely so that he could copyright the American edition. Sinclair refused to do any more work on the novel, saying that it would be a 'waste of time. I could never again recapture the fresh interest' in it (cited in a letter from Holt to Royal Cortissoz, 12 May 1905, UP, Box 2, fos. 43–4). In the end Holt published *Audrey Craven* and *Superseded* in 1906. *Mr and Mrs Nevill Tyson* was published in the USA simultaneously by two different firms, Grossett and Dunlap, and B. W. Dodge, under the title *The Tysons* in 1906.

power: she played Pinker and Brown off against one another and finally settled on Brown to handle not only her novels (and reprints) but also her short
stories, something Brown was not usually willing to do.[81] A year after publication, *The Divine Fire* was still selling well, and Holt decided Sinclair should
go on a triumphal tour of the East Coast to meet her readers and prominent
American literati. The timing was unusual (so long after publication) but then
so was the sales profile of the novel, with its slow start (especially in Britain)
followed by a remarkable and sustained success on both sides of the Atlantic.[82]
Even in April 1905 Sinclair had not yet received any royalties and was still
struggling away with her German translations.[83] She told Katharine Hinkson
that she was 'overwhelmed with work wh. I hate & wh. I feel most unfit for'.[84]

In early September 1905 May Sinclair sailed for the USA. She stayed with
Winifred Holt, Henry Holt's daughter, in New York, and according to
Katharine Hinkson, Sinclair was lionized wherever she went:

America went mad over 'The Divine Fire.' Miss Sinclair was fêted and acclaimed
when she visited her American publisher, up and down the United States. The fair
Americans did things as extravagant as only they can do. Did I hear that at one of
the feasts in Miss Sinclair's honour there was a place reserved for 'Ricky' [Rickman]
of 'The Divine Fire' with a wreath of roses laid in it?[85]

In Boston in December Sinclair met Emerson, Charles Eliot Norton, and
William James, and she spent Christmas in Baltimore with Winifred Holt's
aunts. According to Boll, she was even invited to the White House, and went
out motoring with President Theodore Roosevelt.[86] She was also busy
working on a dramatization of *The Divine Fire* and negotiating with publishers (the play was never published), and she managed to secure an unusually
generous offer of £1,000 for a year-long serialization of her next novel in
the *Atlantic Monthly*.[87]

---

[81] See Brown to Sinclair, 28 Mar. 1905, UP, Box 1, fo. 12; Sinclair to Pinker, 15 May 1905, HA.

[82] S. S. McClure of *McClure's Magazine* wrote to Sinclair on 11 May 1905 pointing out that the *New York Globe* had just run a notice commenting that *The Divine Fire* had taken a year to achieve popular recognition (UP, Box 2, fo. 62). He advised her to serialize her next novel before publication in book form to make sure it was noticed right away. She took his advice, and *The Helpmate* was serialized in *Atlantic Monthly*, Jan.–Sept. 1907.

[83] Holt wrote on 28 Mar. 1905 that he was about to send 'in a few days' royalties on the first 2,000 copies (UP, Box 2, fos. 43–4). Technically, he could have held back 75% of what he owed her until Apr. 1906, but he was worried that she would be poached by another publisher in the meantime. On 21 Apr. 1905 he told her he would send royalties on a further 1,000 copies as soon as he could (UP, Box 2, fos. 43–4). For each 1,000 copies sold Sinclair received £46. 1s. 6d. (Sinclair's financial statements, UP, Box 42, fo. 494).

[84] Sinclair to Hinkson, 12 Apr. 1905, JR.   [85] Hinkson, *Middle Years*, 293.

[86] Boll, *Miss May Sinclair*, 77–8. Zegger, however (*May Sinclair*, 23, 151), maintains that the invitation was extended but not accepted.

[87] Sinclair to Kyllmann, 12 Dec. 1905, General Manuscript Collection, Charles Deering McCormick Library of Special Collections, Northwestern University Library.

But Sinclair's nervous pleasure in her own success was shadowed by yet another personal tragedy. In mid-November, while she was in New York, she heard that her last surviving brother, Joseph, aged 50, had died in British Columbia several weeks earlier, on the day Sinclair's ship docked in the USA. Like her other brothers, Joseph suffered from mitral valve disease, and died shortly after catching pneumonia. Sinclair had been moving around so much that the news had taken weeks to reach her, but when she did finally hear 'it was a great shock' and 'put everything else out of my head'.[88] There was nothing that she could do to ease her grief. She had no other siblings with whom to share the news, and she had never met Joseph's Canadian family (indeed in letters she even seems unaware of the existence of Joseph's youngest child, born in 1896).[89] She felt responsible for her teenage nephews' welfare, telling Otto Kyllmann, her editor at Constable's, that she must 'work rather hard for a little while'.[90] True to form she had already set up a study in Winifred Holt's apartment, and was writing in the intervals between parties and calls. The incessant curiosity and scrutiny to which she was subjected was even more unwelcome now that she was both unhappy, and keen to get to work. Unsurprisingly, she did not always make a good impression, especially at large parties. When she was seated next to Mark Twain at an official dinner on 5 December to celebrate his seventieth birthday, at the end of the evening Twain thanked her in exasperation for a 'remarkably interesting silence'.[91] Katharine Hinkson noted that 'Miss Sinclair's silence amazed the Americans. . . . she had made a fine art of silence when she did not wish to speak.'[92] But in more intimate settings she did better. In Boston she met and quickly became attached to Annie Fields and Sarah Orne Jewett. Fields and Jewett had been living together in a 'Boston marriage' since the death in 1881 of Fields's husband, James T. Fields, who had been editor of the *Atlantic Monthly*, which serialized Sinclair's *The Helpmate* in 1907. Both women were novelists, older than Sinclair (Fields by thirty years and Jewett by fourteen), and Sinclair was touched and a little flustered by their kindness to her. When she wrote to Fields thanking her for

[88] Sinclair to Richard Garnett, 13 Dec. 1905, HR, MS (Garnett, R) Recip.; Sinclair to Kyllmann, 24 Nov. 1905, General Manuscript Collection, Charles Deering McCormick Library of Special Collections, Northwestern University Library.

[89] In the letters to Garnett and Kyllmann cited above she refers repeatedly to 'my nephews'. But in a family tree drawn by Harold Sinclair, one of William Sinclair's sons, Joseph's children are shown as Harold, born 1890, Reginald, born 1891, and Helen, born 1896 (UP, Box 42, fo. 493).

[90] Sinclair to Kyllmann, 24 Nov. 1905, General Manuscript Collection, Charles Deering McCormick Library of Special Collections, Northwestern University Library.

[91] Zegger, *May Sinclair*, 23. The dinner was described in a souvenir issue of *Harper's Weekly* (23 Dec. 1905). See Boll, *Miss May Sinclair*, 76–7.

[92] Hinkson, *Middle Years*, 293.

her hospitality she told her: 'I shall always account you & Miss Jewett, if I may, among the friends who stand for the most & the best', and to Otto Kyll-mann, she described Fields as 'the dearest, sweetest old lady [who] made me feel at home before I'd been two hours in her house.'[93] But she still just wanted to go back to England. She told Richard Garnett that she had to 'struggle against incessant temptations to take the next steamer home', and she burst into tears in front of Kyllmann's friend Booth about her awkward exchange with Witter Bynner over the article he had planned.[94]

On 20 January 1906 Sinclair finally sailed for England. Otto Kyllmann's father invited her to stay with him in Watford while she looked for a place to live, but she was anxious to 'settle down steadily' to work, and took rooms at 8 Willow Road in Hampstead.[95] Family responsibilities were soon weighing heavily upon her again: in April her beloved sister-in-law Eleanor, William's widow, died suddenly in Liverpool, and Sinclair rushed north to help her nephews and nieces.[96] Eleanor left six children, the youngest only 16, and Sinclair, who had always been close to her brother's family, assumed responsibility for them as well as for Joseph's children in Canada. William's children remained her closest family ties until her death.

For Sinclair aunthood went some way towards filling the gap left by childlessness. So many of her novels explore the feelings of women without children that it seems likely that she was herself preoccupied with, and regretful, about her childless state. She wrote of Charlotte Brontë, with whom, as I explain in Chapter 4, she identified intensely, that the key to her nature was her 'love of children':

We are face to face here, not with a want in her, but with an abyss, depth beyond depth of tenderness and longing and frustration, of a passion that found no clear voice in her works, because it was one with the elemental nature in her, undefined, unuttered, unutterable. . . . All her life, I think, she suffered because of the perpet-ual insurgence of this secret, impassioned, maternal energy. (TB, 63, 66)

Sinclair understood through experience that the longing for a child could be

[93] Sinclair to Annie Fields, 24 Dec. [1905], The Huntington Library, San Marino, California, FI 3822; Sinclair to Kyllmann, 12 Dec. 1905, General Manuscript Collection, Charles Deering McCormick, Library of Special Collections, Northwestern University Library.

[94] Sinclair to Richard Garnett, 13 Dec. 1905, HR, MS (Garnett, R) Recip.; Sinclair to Kyllmann, 12 Dec. 1905, General Manuscript Collection, Charles Deering McCormick, Library of Special Collections, Northwestern University Library. Witter Bynner had drafted an article based on letters from Sinclair, and a conversation he had with her in New York. Sinclair was very distressed by its revelatory tone and telegraphed Bynner forbidding publication. See Introduction, above, for further discussion of this incident.

[95] Sinclair to Kyllmann, 25 Dec. 1905, General Manuscript Collection, Charles Deering McCormick Library of Special Collections, Northwestern University Library.

[96] See Sinclair to Morley Roberts, 28 Apr. 1906, UP, Box 3, fo. 76.

at the centre of a woman's sexual being. In some of her novels women respond even more erotically to babies than they do to men. In *Mr and Mrs Nevill Tyson* Molly Tyson's childless intellectual friend, Miss Batchelor, 'instinctively' holds out her arms for Molly's baby, and 'when he cried she held him all the closer' and 'let him explore the front of her dress with his little wet mouth and fingers'.[97] In *The Helpmate* a woman is moved to make love to her husband by the touch of a child's hand on her breast. It seems that Sinclair was for much of her life as invested in maternal as in heterosexual erotics, and she worried about the relationship between the two. How could women control their erotic responses to children and disentangle them from their sexual feelings for men? Could a woman be a good mother *and* a good wife?

The novels of the early years of the twentieth century are all fairly sceptical about heterosexual relations. In the story that preceded *The Divine Fire*, 'The Cosmopolitan', published with 'Superseded' in *Two Sides of a Question* (1901), Sinclair returned to the idea that men found it difficult to understand and to love women whose desires ran counter to their own. Sinclair told Dorothea Beale that the 'question' of the title was femininity, and that the two stories were 'studies in opposite feminine types'.[98] As we saw in Chapter 1, Juliana Quincy of 'Superseded' is displaced by a new generation of assertive and independent women. Frida, the protagonist of 'The Cosmopolitan', is 'in love with life', in spite of a dreary existence spent ministering to a stultifyingly boring father.[99] At the end of the story, having abandoned her father and spent a year on a yacht with a woman friend, she tells her suitor: 'you are incapable, not of loving perhaps, but of loving a certain kind of woman the way she wants to be loved.'[100] Frida demonstrates to the central male character the inadequacy not only of his preconceptions about women, but also of his capacities for affection. But Sinclair was not always certain where the blame for this state of affairs really lay. *The Helpmate* analyses the effects of masculine incontinence on women's sense of their own sexuality, and on relations between mothers and their children, but it is as critical of the wife's position as of the husband's. This time the distinction is not between the chaste ideal and the woman who is for sale (as it was in *The Divine Fire*) but between a woman whose chastity is as destructive as the freer sexuality of the women with whom she is in competition. The apparent moral ambiguity of the novel troubled many reviewers: the

[97] Sinclair, *The Tysons* (1898; US edn. New York: Holt, 1907), 86.
[98] Sinclair to Dorothea Beale, 11 Jan. 1901, Archive Department, Cheltenham Ladies' College.
[99] Sinclair, 'The Cosmopolitan', in *Two Sides of a Question*, 107.   [100] Ibid. 175.

celibate wife is dealt with much more harshly than her unchaste husband. *The Helpmate* analyses the difficult politics of sexuality itself.

The novel opens in a marriage bed. Anne Majendie, after a few happy days of honeymoon, overhears guests in her hotel talking about her husband Walter's pre-marital affair. Horrified, she retreats into religion and celibacy, insisting that her husband pay with a life of penitence for what he has done. During a stroll in the woods Anne is temporarily aroused by the beauty of the landscape and the touch of a little child they meet on their walk, and she yields to Walter. As a result of this encounter, Anne gives birth to a daughter, Peggy. Walter, who adores Peggy, is still cold-shouldered by Anne, and in the end succumbs to the attractions of Maggie, a seamstress, whom he sets up as his mistress in a remote farmhouse in the marshes. Anne and Walter discover that Peggy has mitral valve disease, and that she must be protected from distress and shock. Walter spends one last night with Maggie, and then tells her that he must end their relationship. But it is too late. During the night, Peggy, hysterical with fear at her father's absence and convinced that he is dead, dies. Anne accuses Walter of killing her, and he gets drunk and suffers a stroke. In her fear for him, and her remorse, Anne finally understands that it was her coldness which caused all the trouble between them, and even, indirectly, was responsible for Peggy's death. Anne and Walter are reconciled, and we assume, although we are not told, that he recovers.

The Helpmate ran into trouble even before publication. Sinclair wrote to Morley Roberts while she was still working on the manuscript: 'You sd. see the opening of my new novel, where I've gone straight to the roots of the matter & cut preliminaries.'[101] The novel was serialized in the *Atlantic Monthly* before being published as a book, and the editors objected to a sentence in the first instalment describing Walter's clothes hanging over the back of a chair (implying, presumably, that he had gone to bed naked).[102] Sinclair duly removed the clothes (which were reinstated in the book version). All the same, the publication of the novel in 'the chaste columns of the *Atlantic*' (one of the most conservative and prudish of the American periodicals) was a landmark event in the history of American magazine publishing: Helen Haines in *What's in a Novel* called it the end of 'the age of reticence' in America.[103]

[101] Sinclair to Morley Roberts, 15 May 1906, UP, Box 3, fo. 76.

[102] See Sinclair to Kyllmann, 9 Oct. [1906], General Manuscript Collection, Charles Deering McCormick Library of Special Collections, Northwestern University Library.

[103] Helen E. Haines, *What's in a Novel* (New York: Columbia University Press, 1942), 48. For a discussion of the discourse of 'reticence' in turn-of-the-century American journalism, see Rochelle Gurstein, *The Repeal of Reticence: A History of America's Cultural and Legal Struggles over Free Speech, Obscenity, Sexual Liberation, and Modern Art* (New York: Hill and Wang, 1996), 146–71.

The novel was unusual among contemporary texts for its open sympathy towards extramarital philandering (compare, for example, Henry James's *The Ambassadors*, 1903, and *The Golden Bowl*, 1904, in which sex outside marriage is treated with much more caution, or H. G. Wells's 'New Woman' novel, *Ann Veronica*, 1909, which depicts Ann's would-be lover Ramage as a clumsy womanizer). *The Helpmate* is highly critical of the Victorian ideal of the sexless woman, an ideal Sinclair saw persisting even into the early decades of the twentieth century. In 1912 she declared that 'the pass we have come to, the extreme shakiness of man's standard of sexual morality today, is largely due to the debilitating, the disastrous influence of the Early and Mid-Victorian woman'.[104] Anne is an example of a woman who 'preys with her strength, with her comparative coldness and security of temperament, upon passions whose violence and significance she realizes only as so much tribute to her power'.[105] She is heavily punished by the plot and the rhetoric of the novel, which explicitly lay responsibility for the death of her child and the serious illness of her husband at her door: by his sickbed she realizes she 'had ruined him as surely as if she had been a bad woman. He had loved her, and she had cast him from her, and sent him to his sin. There was no humiliation and no pain that she had spared him' (H, 425). When Anne finally understands that she has mistakenly 'come to look upon flesh and blood, on the dear human heart, and the sacred, mysterious human body, as things repellent to her spirituality' (H, 426), she decides that her spiritual infidelities have been even more serious than her husband's minor misdemeanours.

In spite of Anne's failings, Sinclair is sympathetic to her feeling of sexual contamination:

Anne felt that her union with Majendie had made her one with that other woman, that she shared her memory and her shame. For Majendie's sake she loathed her womanhood that was yesterday as sacred to her as her soul. Through him she had conceived a thing hitherto unknown to her, a passionate consciousness and hatred of her body. She hated the hands that had held him, the feet that had gone with him, the lips that had touched him, the eyes that had looked at him to love him. (H, 7)

Her awareness of Walter's previous lover means that Anne can no longer hold on to a sense of her own sexual agency. Boll suggests that her jealousy and her feeling of connection with the other woman make it impossible for her to claim her own desire: 'The scandal threatens to expose her own healthy animalism, because it forces her to identify herself with Lady Cayley',

---

[104] Sinclair, 'Defence of Men', 562.   [105] Ibid. 561–2.

her husband's former mistress.[106] Her husband's illicit pleasure thus estranges her from her own legitimate desires.

Anne can only endure both Walter's desire and her own when they are displaced into the longing for children. She and Walter encounter a beautiful baby at a cottage in the woods. Anne takes it in her arms:

It turned to her, cuddling. Through the thin muslin of her bodice she could feel the pressure of its tender palms.

Majendie stood close to her and tried gently to detach and possess himself of the delicate clinging fingers. But his eyes were upon Anne's eyes. They drew her; she looked up, her eyes flashed to the meeting-point; his widened in one long penetrating gaze.

A sudden pricking pain went through her, there where the pink and flaxen thing lay sun-warm and life-warm to her breast. (H, 109–10)

Anne allows Walter access to her because she cannot quite distinguish between her arousal by the touch of the child, and by the 'penetrating' power of Walter's gaze. She will not allow herself to enjoy Walter unless her desire has been stimulated and sanctioned by a feeling she perceives as holy: the desire for a child. Maternal sexuality is tangled up, and provides an alibi for, her sexual responses to her husband. Anne allows Walter to make love to her in the shadows cast by the trees. But when they return to the town, she returns to her religious observances: 'after all, she was only a spiritual voluptuary' (H, 185); 'The trembling woman who had held him in her arms at Westleydale had never shown herself to him again' (H, 117). Without the sanction of a beneficent nature all around her, Anne retreats again, afraid that she is only another object on display in Majendie's house: 'this house of which she was the mistress did not in the least belong to her. . . . It was full, the whole house was full, of portraits of the Majendies' (H, 212). As long as she feels like another commodity that Walter has collected—one in a series of women—she can reinhabit neither her body, nor her home. It takes a double tragedy for her to realize that sexual love is itself a form of spiritual experience: 'there is no spirituality worthy of the name that has not been proven in the house of flesh' (H, 427).

Reviews of the novel were favourable, but many judged it slightly disappointing after the splendours of *The Divine Fire*. H. I. Brock in the *New York Times Book Review* and William Morton Payne in the *Dial* both saw it as a

---

[106] Boll, *Miss May Sinclair*, 190. See also Harris, 'Challenging the Script of the Heterosexual Couple', 448: 'In [*The Helpmate*], Sinclair envisions homoeroticism, autoeroticism, and heterosexual desire as complexly reinforcing each other.'

comedown, largely because of its 'confusion of moral values'.[107] The
Athenaeum, for example, noted that 'in her anxiety to be fair to the man [Sin-
clair] has placed the woman in a light so peculiarly unamiable as to make his
failings appear in comparison mere trifles'.[108] Lady Eleanor Cecil, wife of a
prominent Tory peer, judged the novel immoral, arguing that it sought to
persuade its readers that 'adultery with a little shop-girl . . . is the redeeming
agent'.[109] Sinclair was annoyed that most of the reviews (which she described
as 'bad') had not seen that Anne's character softened as the novel progressed:
'I do agree with you in sympathizing with Anne', she wrote to Sarah Orne
Jewett: 'I think it was awful for her. So awful, that I felt that she cd.n't help
being like that. Very few of my critics, so far, have noticed that I have made
her softer as the book goes on, that she is capable of great tenderness through
her maternal nature, & that, half the time, her conscience is fighting with her
tenderness.'[110] Sinclair conceived the novel as a sympathetic treatment of a
woman who is forced to deny herself to her husband because of his sexual
iniquity, but, uneasily aware that 'men are, on the most favourable showing,
what we have permitted them to be', she did not paint as critical a picture of
Walter as she might have done.[111] Her attempts to be fair to men were seen as
insincere: Eleanor Cecil suggested that the 'unconventional' morality of the
novel was simply a sensationalizing gimmick to increase sales.[112] Sinclair was
stung by these unenthusiastic responses. The next two texts she wrote were
unequivocally critical of men's sexual predations and hypocrisy, as if she had
decided that moral subtlety in the area of sexual relations would inevitably be
mistaken for caricature or, to use Eleanor Cecil's word, 'cant'.[113]

As *The Helpmate* rolled off the presses of the *Atlantic Monthly*, Sinclair was
busy reconstructing her life as a financially secure, relatively well-known
novelist and single woman. In August 1907, the month *The Helpmate*
appeared in book form, she moved after years in rented rooms into a flat of
her own in Edwardes Square in Kensington. She wrote to Sarah Orne Jewett:

Here I am, all alone, in an enormous studio (in proportion to me) wh. serves for
everything except a bath-room & bed-room (I've turned the tiny dining-room into

---

[107] H. I. Brock, '*The Helpmate* a Noteworthy Book', *New York Times Book Review* (24 Aug. 1907), 510;
quotation from William Morton Payne, 'Recent Fiction', *Dial*, 43 (16 Oct. 1907), 250–1: at 251.

[108] '*The Helpmate*', *Athenaeum*, 4165 (24 Aug. 1907), 204.

[109] Cecil, 'The Cant of Unconventionality', 584. Virginia Woolf, who was a friend of Eleanor Cecil's,
was unsure about the logic of her attack on *The Helpmate*, writing to Violet Dickinson: 'I think it is fairly
clear that the whole of Nelly's objection to Miss Sinclair is a moral one. She thinks that Miss S. holds a bad
man to our admiration. . . . I think her position is quite tenable *if* she could explain her reason for thinking
that morality is essential to art—But this she refuses to do' (n. d. [Nov. 1907], *The Flight of the Mind*, 317).

[110] Sinclair to Sarah Orne Jewett, 29 Aug. 1907, HL, bMS Am 1743 (198).

[111] Sinclair, 'Defence of Men', 562.   [112] Cecil, 'The Cant of Unconventionality', 585–6.

[113] See Cecil's title, 'The Cant of Unconventionality'.

a bath-room)—it is the funniest flat you ever saw, but <u>it's mine, & nobody but me can get into that bath</u>. You don't know what that means if you haven't lived, as I have, for ten years in rooms—other people's rooms. And there is joy & pride & general up-liftedness in the possession of yr. own front-door.[114]

To Hinkson she was a little more restrained, remarking only: 'It really is rather funny—the idea of <u>me</u> in a big studio 30 ft by 30—all alone!'[115] The death of her mother and the increase in her income gave her much greater mobility as well as more privacy and comfort. She spent most of the summer of 1907 in a cottage on the Sussex Downs, and from 1907 onwards she routinely spent several months a year away from London.[116] This flexible, independent life, coupled with her growing interest in the suffrage movement, sharpened her sense of the compromises many married women had to make. As review after review of *The Helpmate* questioned her moral sympathies, she wrote her most trenchant analysis yet of sexual relations within marriage, *The Judgment of Eve*. This time there was no mistaking her meaning. Aggie, the central character, after giving birth to six children is told by a doctor that she must have no more, but out of pity she yields to her husband's wheedlings and is killed by the subsequent pregnancy. Her husband mourns: 'It would have been better . . . if I had been unfaithful to her. *That* wouldn't have killed her.'[117] This novel is squarely on Aggie's side, even as it implies her judgement—in marrying the intellectual clerk Arthur rather than the good-natured farmer John—is at fault, since John unlike Arthur spares his wife unwanted pregnancies. But Aggie is also at the mercy of the same force which in *The Helpmate* used Anne 'for an end beyond herself' (H, 117): 'It was as if Nature had conceived a grudge against Aggie, and strove, through maternity, to stamp out her features as an individual'.[118] Women's bodies are used by both men and Nature in ways that erase women's autonomy and deprive them of privacy—that privacy which Sinclair so prized.

Maternity was the pivot of Sinclair's analysis of women's complex sexual predicament. Many of the novels of her mid-career suggest that a successful

---

[114] Sinclair to Sarah Orne Jewett, 29 Aug. 1907, HL, bMS Am 1743 (198).

[115] Sinclair to Hinkson, 2 Aug. 1907, JR. Her excitement was tempered by the discovery that her upstairs neighbour was a musician who practised regularly. She wrote jokingly to Kyllmann that she would have to get up at 5 a.m. in order to write (Sinclair to Kyllmann, 1 Sept. 1907, General Manuscript Collection, Charles Deering McCormick Library of Special Collections, Northwestern University Library).

[116] 'I'm living in a peaceful spot, on a goose-green, close under the Sussex Downs, where the air is like the air of heaven' (Sinclair to Hinkson, 11 July 1907, JR). The smogs of London had a bad effect on Sinclair's health: she wrote to William Rothenstein on 9 Feb. 1919: 'I <u>must</u> have a place to work in, where I can fly when London gets too poisonous & thick' (HL, bMS Eng 1148 (1377)). In the same letter she writes of spending 'five months in the year' in her retreat.

[117] Sinclair, *The Judgment of Eve* (New York and London: Harper, 1908), 120. The novella first appeared in *Everybody's Magazine* (Sept. 1907) and in a supplement to the *Lady's Realm* (Dec. 1907).

[118] Ibid. 89.

marriage is incompatible with contented motherhood. In *Mr and Mrs Nevill Tyson* Molly's connection to the baby is in direct conflict with her sexual involvement with her husband; in *The Helpmate* the love of a child is both sensually thrilling, and one of the means by which Anne is brought low (she realizes that 'God has taken her child from her that she might see', H, 428); and in *The Judgment of Eve* too many children destroy the parents' relationship. In the novel that followed *The Judgment of Eve*, *Kitty Tailleur* (1908), published in the USA as *The Immortal Moment: The Story of Kitty Tailleur*, reformed courtesan Kitty horrifies herself by caressing her fiancé's small daughter. Sinclair defended the scene by saying it had nothing 'to do with [Kitty's] "badness"—only with her "earthliness", so to speak; & she, poor thing, mixed it all up with her "badness"', but the novel itself seems less certain of the distinction, as though women's sensuous investments in children have a problematic relationship with their sexual connections with men.[119]

Kitty Tailleur suggests that Kitty's desires have been shaped by masculine demands. The novel opens with brother and sister, Robert and Jane Lucy, observing Kitty and her companion, who are staying at the same hotel. Kitty is continually stared at as she moves around its reception rooms. She is like one of the books in Rickman's bookshop, an object made for display: 'There was something terrible to [Bunny, her companion] in their entry, in their passage down the great, white, palm-shaded, exotic room, their threading of the ways between the tables, with all the men turning round to stare at Kitty Tailleur' (KT, 20). Like an article in a department store, Kitty is always illumined and reflected in 'monstrous mirrors' (KT, 21). She lives her life in the dazzle of a 'horrifying publicity', an object designed to be consumed by the eyes of others, and, implicitly, available for their consumption and possibly possession. The association of the fallen woman with the commodity could not be made more plain.

Part of the problem with Kitty, in Bunny's view, is that she has so internalized her own commodification that she seems deliberately to court the gaze of others: 'The public eye, so far from pursuing Kitty, was itself pursued, tracked down and captured. Kitty couldn't let it go. Publicity was what Kitty coveted' (KT, 31). Kitty is a creature of the modern moment, a woman like Audrey Craven who exists only in her own performances. But it is impossible for Kitty to acknowledge the part she plays in staging herself: first she tells Bunny that she was 'born' conspicuous (KT, 23), and then accuses Bunny herself of attracting attention to them through her self-consciousness. In Kitty, modern femininity has reached a point of alienation

---

[119] Sinclair to Kyllmann, 8 [9?] Mar. 1908, General Manuscript Collection, Charles Deering McCormick Library of Special Collections, Northwestern University Library.

at which it can no longer recognize or name its own processes: eros and artifice are fused.

Robert is fascinated by Kitty's performances. Although rumour has it that Kitty is a kept woman, Robert proposes marriage to her and she accepts, filled with longing for his two little daughters by his first wife (now dead). The passage in which Kitty repudiates her own desire for them is one of the most curious that Sinclair ever wrote. The movement for male chastity had put child prostitution on the political agenda, but Sinclair chooses to dramatize the sexualization of children not from a man's, but from a woman's point of view.[120] Anne's sexual response to a baby in *The Helpmate* was unproblematic because it was very clearly experienced in the context of her desire for her husband. But Kitty, not yet married and with a history of illicit sexual liaisons, is a much more confusing case:

Then some perverse and passionate impulse seized her to wake the child. She did it gently, tenderly, holding back her passion, troubling the depths of sleep with fine, feather-like touches, with kisses as soft as sleep. . . . Kitty's troubling hand turned [Barbara] from her flight down the ways of sleep. . . . Kitty rose, lifting the child with her from the bed. She held her close, pressing the tender body close to her own body with quivering hands, stroking the adorable little face with her own face, closing her eyes under the touch of it as she closed them when Robert's face touched hers. She was aware that she had brought some passionate, earthly quality of her love for Robert into her love for Robert's child.

She said to herself, 'I'm terrible; there's something wrong with me. This isn't the way to love a child.' (KT, 248–9)

Kitty's 'perverse impulse' and her roving hand 'trouble' the sleeping child, and perhaps the reader too: Kitty's ex-lover insists that Robert will be afraid that Kitty will contaminate his children, and Kitty, although she has earlier insisted that she 'wouldn't hurt them for the world' (KT, 203), in the scene quoted above suddenly fears her own sexual responses. It is possible to read this scene as a kind of symbolic Oedipal drama, in which it is not the desire of the child, but the desire of the mother which is at stake. Freud was at this date just beginning to elaborate a theory of women's desire for children which equated it with their desire for men.[121]

---

[120] Sheila Jeffreys notes that 'A determination to transform male sexual behaviour was a predominant theme of the constitutional and militant suffrage campaigners in the intense phase of feminist activity leading up to the First World War' (*The Spinster and her Enemies: Feminism and Sexuality 1880–1930*, London: Pandora, 1985, 45). The National Union of Women's Suffrage Societies declared that suffrage stood for 'The Cause of Purity—we want to put down the White Slave Traffic, to protect little children from assaults, and to save our boys from hideous temptations' (cited ibid. 45).

[121] Freud first formulated the idea of penis envy in 'On the Sexual Theories of Children' (1908). In 1917 he suggested that a woman's wish for a child was the displaced expression of the wish for a penis. Penis envy

The ambiguously tender quality of Kitty's passionate affection for the child complicates the reader's sense of her 'badness', as Sinclair wanted, but it also suggests that she cannot love without wanting to touch. In spite of Sinclair's obvious sympathy with Kitty and her desire to put her disreputable past behind her, the scene with Barbara implies that Kitty's capacity to express love has been irredeemably corrupted by her relationships with men.[122] Sinclair makes Kitty responsible for her own childlessness. Kitty is described as feeling 'the pang of the motherhood she had thwarted and disowned' because she has chosen never to marry (KT, 250). Where maternal feelings are ultimately the mode of Anne's redemption, Kitty is beyond salvation by these means, since even her responses to children are no longer pure.

Because she fears that Robert will discover her history, and reject her as an unfit wife and mother, Kitty finally tells Robert the truth and breaks off their engagement. Robert offers to support her financially without making her his mistress; she tells him that in her experience no man would be capable of that. Then, in her despair, she throws herself from a cliff and dies. The responsibility for Kitty's tragic end is placed squarely on men's shoulders. Jane Lucy delivers a trenchant speech to Kitty's former lover as they wait for news of Kitty at the end of the novel: 'You are responsible. It's you, and men like you, who have dragged her down. You took advantage of her weakness, of her very helplessness. You've made her so that she can't believe in a man's goodness and trust herself to it' (KT, 310). Kitty's ambiguous desires and tragic end turn her into a kind of test case for feminism.

Some reviewers, including William Morton Payne, the *Dial* reviewer who had liked *The Divine Fire* and *The Helpmate*, judged *Kitty Tailleur* sentimental and immoral.[123] Janet Hogarth, Sinclair's old friend from Cheltenham who was working at the Times Book Club when *Kitty Tailleur* was published, noted that when she sent a copy of the novel to 'a missionary station in West Africa' by mistake, the 'missionary wrote, more in sorrow than in anger, that he had found it necessary to make a solemn holocaust of that piteous little study of a woman with a past.'[124] Having secured her reputation

---

causes the little girl to turn away from her mother and take her father as her primary love-object, in the hope that he will give her a penis and/or a child: 'the wish for a penis and the wish for a baby would be fundamentally identical' ('On Transformations of Instinct as Exemplified in Anal Eroticism', 1917, in *Standard Edition of the Complete Psychological Works of Sigmund Freud*, trans. and ed. James Strachey, London: Hogarth, 1966–74, xvii. 127–33: at 129).

[122] As Janice H. Harris notes, 'Sinclair's attempts to resolve [the scene] lead her in contradictory directions' ('Challenging the Script of the Heterosexual Couple', 452).

[123] William Morton Payne, 'Recent Fiction', *Dial*, 45 (1 Nov. 1908), 296.

[124] Courtney, *Recollected in Tranquillity*, 179–80.

with *The Divine Fire* Sinclair could afford to take some risks. She tried hard
to find a balance between the indulgent attitude to men's behaviour about
which reviewers had complained in *The Helpmate*, and the more trenchant
analyses in *The Judgment of Eve* and *Kitty Tailleur*. But she was ambivalent
herself. Her personal experience did not seem to her to authorize a radically
defensive feminist discourse, although she was attracted to the campaign for
women's suffrage, and even participated in it on and off between 1907 and
1912. But she never forgot the five brothers who had been her main source of
affection during her childhood, and in spite of her residual resentment, she
could not condemn even Anthony Deane for standing by his beliefs as stead-
fastly as she, in the end, stood by her own. Alone in her studio in Kensington, she wondered what it meant that she could now, finally, call herself a
professional writer who depended on no one either financially or emotionally. She found the key to her own self-reconstruction in the lives of the
Brontë sisters, who also faced criticism for their attempts to unravel the
responsibilities of men and women to each other, and like her were assumed
to be men.[125] Their lives and works offered her an ideal opportunity to reflect
on her own feelings about the literary market place, celibacy, creativity, and
childlessness.

[125] The unnamed correspondent who wrote her a fan letter about *The Divine Fire* assumed she was a man.
See n. 71, above.

4

Celibacy and Psychoanalysis

===

IN EARLY 1907, just after the serialization of *The Helpmate* began, May Sinclair watched a suffragist march attended by her friends Beatrice Harraden, Alice Meynell, Aphra Wilson, and probably Evelyn Sharp.[1] She told Otto Kyllmann that she was 'willing to stand up & be shot dead opposite the Carlton Club—if that wd. really benefit all future generations of my sex—but I haven't the courage to march in that procession!'[2] Sinclair did indeed make an unlikely suffragist. The two novels she published in 1908, *Kitty Tailleur* and *The Judgment of Eve*, are outspoken enough about men's oppressive treatment of women to show that she was at least partly in sympathy with the movement for women's rights, but her reluctance to appear in public or to draw attention to herself meant that she was ill-suited to the activist life. Her natural inclination was to communicate her support by writing from the unbroken peace of her little studio in Kensington, looking down over the green grass of the square. She wanted to find a way to support the suffrage movement without becoming too involved in the life of the streets and of the prisons. The Brontë sisters became more and more important to her as women who had successfully combined secluded lives and an outspoken, passionate response to the cramped conditions of women's existence. Sinclair believed that their lives demonstrated the close connection between creativity and celibacy for women. She was now 45, and it seemed unlikely that she would ever find a husband with whom she could be satisfied. She used the stories of the Brontë sisters to justify her own emotional isolation, becoming more and more interested in the poetics of celibacy, and in the

---

[1] Alice Meynell (1847–1922) was a poet; Aphra Wilson was an editor at Hutchinson's, Sinclair's publishers after 1912; Evelyn Sharp was a writer and member of the Women's Suffrage and Political Union, who introduced herself to Sinclair in May 1906 (see Sinclair to Sharp, 15 May 1906, Bodleian Library, Oxford, MS Eng. lett. d. 276, fos. 174^r–175^v). For Beatrice Harraden, see Ch. 2 n. 89.

[2] Sinclair to Kyllmann, 9 Feb. 1907, General Manuscript Collection, Charles Deering McCormick Library of Special Collections, Northwestern University Library.

relationship between sexuality and the imaginative life. When in 1913 she had the opportunity to become involved with the Medico-Psychological Clinic, the first clinic in Britain to offer psychoanalytic treatment, she did not hesitate. She had long been interested in the charged dynamics of family life and in the vicissitudes of sexual development, and the idea of a mental underworld inhabited, in Freud's words, by ghosts 'like the shades in the Odyssey', appealed to her interest in shadow-states.[3] Her reading in psychoanalytic theory sharpened her sense that artistic production and sexual impulses sprang from one source, but it also intensified her belief that only the chosen few ('geniuses') could benefit from the kind of isolation she herself embraced. When she revisited the story of the Brontës in her 1914 novel *The Three Sisters* she made it clear that for ordinary people sexual frustration could be as corrosive as over-indulgence.

Sinclair's participation in the women's suffrage movement began partly because so many of the women she knew were committed to the campaign. She attended her first suffrage procession, as we have seen, because a number of her friends were marching in it. A year went by before she finally plucked up the courage to become actively involved herself. In March 1908—almost overwhelmed by shyness and embarrassment—she stood with Violet Hunt on a street corner in Kensington rattling a collecting-box, and in the same month she went into print as a supporter of the suffrage movement, joining with suffragist playwright Elizabeth Robins in a 'Message' in the first issue of the suffragist periodical *Votes for Women* : 'it is impossible to be a woman and not admire to the utmost the devotion, the courage, and the endurance of the women who are fighting and working for the Suffrage to-day. And I am glad and honoured to have this opportunity of recording my whole-hearted sympathy with them and with their aims.'[4] Because Sinclair's own primary commitment had always been to her writing (out of economic necessity as much as anything), she was as concerned with the protection—or improvement—of women's right to work, as with their right to vote. She joined the Women's Freedom League in 1908 largely out of indignation at a proposed government scheme to prevent married women accepting paid employment.[5] When she did finally join a suffrage march on

    [3] Sigmund Freud, *The Interpretation of Dreams*, 1899, in *Standard Edition*, iv. 249.

    [4] For more details about her experiences with the collecting-box, see Ch. 1 n. 9. See also Sinclair, 'Message', *Votes for Women*, 1 (Mar. 1908), 79. The first serious episode of suffragette violence—stoning the windows of 10 Downing Street—occurred on 30 June 1908. See Leslie Parker Hume, *The National Union of Women's Suffrage Societies 1897–1914* (London: Garland, 1982), 50.

    [5] See Boll, *Miss May Sinclair*, 88; and Sinclair, unpublished fragment on women's suffrage, 11, UP, Box 24, fo. 452. The Women's Freedom League was committed to 'a forceful, unbending but essentially reasoned appeal to abstract principles' (see Sandra Stanley Holton, *Suffrage Days: Stories from the Women's Suffrage Movement*, London: Routledge, 1996, 144, 168).

18 June 1910, it was as a woman *worker*: she walked proudly under the banner of the Women Writers unit.[6] If Ella Hepworth Dixon, who was also involved in the suffrage movement and a friend of Sinclair, is to be believed, the diminutive Sinclair actually *carried* the banner 'for many miles' and 'seriously hurt herself'.[7] Sinclair allowed her membership in the Women's Freedom League to lapse after only one year, but she was still active in the movement until 1912, telling Hugh Walpole in that year that she was 'swallowed up in a suffrage pamphlet I've been writing [*Feminism*]', and writing to Mary Johnston and Theodore Roosevelt to gather signatures for a petition protesting against the sentencing of suffragettes as common criminals rather than political prisoners:

Whatever you may think of the latest action of our militants, you cannot fail to see how immense is the importance of the principle involved.

That my country sd. disgrace itself before all other nations by sentencing political offenders as felons is more than anybody who cares for common justice can bear.

I have asked Mr. Roosevelt for his signature & the President's [Taft].

Good cheek—but it's worth while risking a rebuff. <u>Time</u> is of the utmost importance . . . I enclose some forms in case you cd. get other signatures. We want none that are not of national importance.[8]

This letter, however, was one of the last public actions she took in defence of the suffrage movement. She took Edward Garnett to a Women Writers' Suffrage League dinner on 2 July 1913, but as violence and militancy increased, she became more alienated, and more cautious in her support.[9] When the First World War broke out in 1914 she, along with thousands of others, seems to have lost interest in the suffrage campaign altogether. In 1917 she published a novel, *The Tree of Heaven*, in which she is highly critical of its methods and its mass appeal.[10]

Her commitment to the movement had in fact always been somewhat ambivalent.[11] Sometimes she worried that enfranchisement would make it

[6] Boll, *Miss May Sinclair*, 89.   [7] Dixon, '*As I Knew Them*', 124.

[8] Sinclair to Hugh Walpole, 12 Apr. 1912, UP, Box 3, fo. 91; and to Mary Johnston, 11 May 1912, Special Collections Department, University of Virginia Library, fol: May Sinclair to Mary Johnston 1904, 1907, 1912, Box Number 6, Collection No. 3588. Sinclair may have met Roosevelt when she visited the USA in 1905–6 (see Ch. 3, above). The suffragettes had been sentenced as ordinary felons from the first arrests and imprisonments in Oct. 1906, but Mar. 1912 saw an escalation of militant action, with the first attacks on private property (shop windows in the West End) (see Hume, *National Union of Women's Suffrage Societies*, 30, 132).

[9] Sinclair to Edward Garnett, 24 June 1913, HR, MS (Garnett, E) Recip.

[10] I discuss this novel in detail in Ch. 5, below.

[11] Diane F. Gillespie notes that Sinclair's suffrage essays and her fiction recreate 'a confused transitional period during which theories are affirmed and challenged and during which, she fears, individual women are being harmed as much as helped by efforts on their behalf' (' "The Muddle of the Middle": May Sinclair on Women', *Tulsa Studies in Women's Literature*, 4, Fall 1985, 235–51: at 235).

harder, not easier, for her to earn her living as a novelist. She was afraid that if women got the vote, she would be interrupted by canvassers in the middle of the morning and constantly distracted by political concerns. In December 1908 she wrote in *Votes for Women*: 'I have no hesitation in stating that if I were not a mere novelist I would be a suffragette, in Holloway or out of it. As a mere novelist every selfish desire and selfish ambition is against the Suffrage. For the position of an *un*married woman novelist, earning enough to live on, cannot be improved, and may be injured, "when we get the vote".'[12] But Sinclair also predicted that a finer art would come from 'the genius of enfranchised womanhood', and in an unpublished piece she admitted that 'questions of abstract justice' overrode her personal resistance to taking up a public civic role:

Personally, I have no political consciousness or conscience; I like being taxed because it makes me feel prosperous when I am least so, and I should hate to be represented; the privileges and rights of citizenship would bother me more than its burden, and I doubt if I should see political righteousness on either side. But I see a great deal of political unrighteousness in withholding from women who <u>are</u> citizens all powers of citizenship, powers which any Government would give to any tramp tomorrow if giving them would keep itself in power.[13]

If she was ambivalent, then, it was because she was basically uninterested in party politics, and worried that the franchise would make even more demands on her mental energy than she was already feeling. She was also uneasy from the outset about the tactics of the Women's Suffrage and Political Union, writing a private letter of protest to Emmeline Pethick-Lawrence about a meeting at the Albert Hall in late 1908 when a suffragette lashed out at the face of a steward with a whip.[14] But the idea that women should have some say in determining the shape of their own lives—whether politically, sexually, or emotionally—was one with which she was utterly in agreement, and she made no secret of that fact. Even Edith Wharton, usually sympathetic to fictional explorations of constraints on women's lives, seems to have 'rather shied away from' Sinclair because of her reputation as a feminist, although she did meet her at least once when she was in London in 1908.[15]

---

[12] Sinclair, 'How It Strikes a Mere Novelist', *Votes for Women*, 2 (24 Mar. 1908), 211.

[13] Ibid.; unpublished fragment on women's suffrage, UP, Box 24, fo. 452, 9–10.

[14] Sinclair to Evelyn Sharp, 14 Dec. 1908, Bodleian Library, Oxford, MS Eng. lett. d. 277, fos. 67ʳ–68ʳ. Violet Hunt describes the meeting in her autobiography: 'Later on came the terrible Albert Hall meeting, when a girl near me suddenly slashed out with a whip and cut the face of the steward, and that of one of my friends who was trying to silence or carry her out. Mrs. Meynell and Mrs. C. F. G. Masterman and I, all three ardent for the Cause, sat in a box and wept to see our friends so mauled in the arena below—Miss Evelyn Sharp hustled' (*Flurried Years*, 42).

[15] *The Letters of Edith Wharton*, ed. R. W. B. and Nancy Lewis (New York: Scribner, 1988), 8, 168.

   Sinclair's ambivalent response to attempts to gain the vote partly reflected
her sense of harassment now that she was a well-known and popular novelist. She had a reputation of being sympathetic to younger, lesser-known
writers, and she was besieged by letters and requests for help. Her fears,
however unfounded, that enfranchisement would simply mean that even
more people wanted her support, indicate the extent to which the struggle to
protect her mental space had become a constant preoccupation. Writing at
the pace she had set herself exhausted her, but she could not afford to relax
her efforts. She spent the summer of 1908 motoring in Normandy and
yachting in Scotland, probably with Evelyn Underhill, but then, partly
because she was still supporting her nieces and nephews, had to be 'rather
economical' with money.[16] She continued to lose time to illness, and during
an extended trip to Cannes, Rome, Venice, and Florence in the spring of
1910, paid for by the proceeds of *The Creators*, which was in the middle of its
serial run in *Century* magazine, she was so 'unwell and "nervy"' that she had
to refuse most of her invitations.[17] Furthermore, she had been warned by a
doctor in October 1908 that she had severely strained her heart by cycling,
and told that she must avoid strenuous exercise in the future. This made it
hard for her to see even close friends. She told Katharine Hinkson: 'My stupid
heart is out of order—strained with cycling again—& it makes everything
difficult & uncertain for the time being. I cd.n't walk from the station . . . Oh
dear, I'm so miserable.'[18]

   Even more galling was the fact that the ride that she blamed for her cardiac problems was one she took with Thomas Hardy when she met him for
the first time in October 1908. The two cycled together from Dorchester to
Weymouth, a distance of about ten miles. By all accounts they enjoyed one
another's company: Hardy wrote to Edward Clodd that he had found Sinclair 'a charming companion', and Sinclair told Hinkson that she had 'lost
her heart to [Hardy] hopelessly'.[19] Hardy, who was a good twenty years
older than Sinclair, was dismissive of her doctor's concerns, but she continued to be cautious.[20] A year after their first meeting Sinclair tried to entice

---

[16] Sinclair to Annie Fields, 19 Sept. 1908, The Huntington Library, San Marino, California, FI 3820.

[17] Sinclair to Linda Villari, 15 Apr. 1910, Bodleian Library, Oxford, MS Eng. lett. d. 492, fos. 63–4.

[18] Sinclair to Katharine Hinkson, 27 Oct. 1908, JR. After a while, though, she decided to ignore the doctor's orders, telling H. G. Wells on 16 Oct. 1915: 'I've damaged my heart cultivating [hard exercise] recklessly & I recover & go on' (University of Illinois Library at Urbana-Champaign).

[19] Thomas Hardy to Edward Clodd, 12 Oct. 1908, *The Collected Letters of Thomas Hardy*, ed. Richard
Little Purdy and Michael Millgate, iii. *1902–1908* (Oxford: Clarendon Press, 1982), 344; Sinclair to
Hinkson, 15 Oct. 1908, JR.

[20] See Hardy to Sinclair, 12 July 1909, *Collected Letters of Thomas Hardy*, iv. *1909–1913* (Oxford: Clarendon Press, 1984), 31–2.

Hardy on to Evelyn Underhill's yacht with her when she docked in Weymouth in July 1909, but Hardy was busy in London with an operatic production of *Tess of the d'Urbervilles*.[21] Although Hardy repeatedly urged
Sinclair in the autumn of 1909 to return to Max Gate, and the following summer the two exchanged invitations in London, Hardy's wife was jealous and
resentful of her husband's preference for Sinclair, and they seem not to have
met again.[22] But Sinclair, happily oblivious of these complications, was
pleased to have earned his respect and liking, and observing the quiet tranquillity of his life in the country may have encouraged her to take a house
away from London herself in 1912.[23]

Sinclair's meeting with Hardy coincided with the beginning of her
lengthy editorial involvement with the Brontës. Sinclair used the sisters'
narratives—both their lives and their works—to explore feelings and issues
which were very close to her heart. She was not alone in feeling that there
were unusually close parallels between their life-stories and her own. Like
the Brontës', her own life was 'prefaced' and punctuated 'by memorial
inscriptions': Sinclair's biographer could, like Gaskell, begin her story 'with
a funereal five-fold reiteration of "HERE LIE THE REMAINS" '.[24] As we have
seen, the similarities between Charlotte Brontë and Sinclair were particularly strong: like Brontë, Sinclair was the last surviving sibling in her family,
she spent many years in rural isolation caring for a grieving, difficult parent,
and she achieved literary celebrity only in middle life.[25] Her reviewers and
friends also saw some affinity between Sinclair's life and ideas and those of
her Victorian forebears. Janet Hogarth, who first met Sinclair at Chel-

[21] Sinclair to Hardy, 9 July 1909, Thomas Hardy Memorial Collection, Dorset County Museum; Hardy
to Sinclair, 12 July 1909 (see n. 20, above). Sinclair was relieved in the end that he had not come: 'it is just as
well you cd.n't. We were two days in Portland Harbour, with a gale outside; & we were all but caught in the
Race going round Portland Bill on Saturday night. I was all alone with the sailors; having landed my sea-
sick friends [Ernest Rhys, editor of the Everyman series, his wife, and Sinclair's cousin] at Swanage; & very
glad I was that I had not succeeded in luring you into this peril. As it was, I'm afraid I thoroughly enjoyed it'
(Sinclair to Hardy, 21 July 1909, Thomas Hardy Memorial Collection, Dorset County Museum).
[22] See Hardy to Sinclair, 1 Aug. 1909, 16 Sept. 1909, and 23 June 1910, *Collected Letters of Thomas Hardy*,
iv. 38, 45, 101. Florence Dugdale, who became the second Mrs Hardy, wrote in response to an invitation
from Edward Clodd on 11 Nov. 1910: 'Now, if you wanted to give Mr TH. a really happy time, you should
ask Miss Sinclair, & I could gently intimate to him that Miss Sinclair was so anxious to be there with him,
. . . etc etc. Poor Mrs H. says she *won't* have her at Max Gate, & so what is poor Mr T.H to do?' (*Letters of
Emma and Florence Hardy*, ed. Michael Millgate, Oxford: Clarendon Press, 1996, 66).
[23] In Oct. 1912 Sinclair rented a cottage in Reeth in Swaledale, North Yorkshire, about fifty miles north
of Haworth (see Maurice Hewlett to Sinclair, 16 Oct. 1912, UP, Box 1, fo. 40). She routinely spent several
months a year there, writing and walking on the moors.
[24] Sinclair, 'Introduction' to Elizabeth Gaskell, *The Life of Charlotte Brontë* (New York: Dutton, 1908),
pp. xiv, xii.
[25] Sinclair was 41 when *The Divine Fire* was published. *Jane Eyre*, Charlotte Brontë's first published
novel, appeared in 1847 when Brontë was 31. It met with immediate acclaim.

tenham Ladies' College and was one of the few people to visit her in the 1890s in Salcombe Regis, wrote of Sinclair's early years as a writer:

There can have been few literary beginnings so independent of outside help, since the Brontës sat scribbling in the kitchen at Haworth. Indeed, there are aspects of Miss Sinclair's work which almost suggest a Brontë reincarnation. The strong creative instinct, the innate poetry, the sense of landscape, the clean and fearless portrayal of human passion, all had their prototypes in the work of that fate-driven trio of sisters, to whom Miss Sinclair felt drawn by so close an affinity that for a time she made her home in their country.[26]

In 1916 William Lyon Phelps described *The Divine Fire* as a posthumous work by Charlotte Brontë: 'In the year 1904 Charlotte Brontë revisited the glimpses of the moon, wrote a strange novel called *The Divine Fire* and returned to the Elysian Fields. She signed the work by the then unfamiliar name of May Sinclair.'[27] Biographically and stylistically the parallels between Sinclair and Charlotte Brontë seemed obvious not only to her friends but also to readers who had never even met her.

The sisters appealed to Sinclair for a number of reasons. First, she was driven by the conviction that their lives—especially Charlotte's—had been misunderstood. Where critics such as Margaret Oliphant and Clement Shorter had suggested that Charlotte's genius was released by her hopeless love for Paul Héger, Sinclair was intent on demonstrating that Charlotte had never been in love with anyone.[28] It was important to her to justify her own emotional isolation. If she could show that the Brontës' genius had been nourished by their celibacy, she could turn her own solitude into a professional advantage rather than a source of sorrow. Secondly, their independence and that of their heroines reinforced Sinclair's emerging political consciousness: she hailed their novels as the origins of modern feminism. And thirdly, their tragic stories appealed to the side of her that was increasingly preoccupied with the elegiac and the supernatural. She told Annie Fields in December 1910 that she was 'writing short stories—stories of all queer lengths & all queer subjects; "spooky" ones, some of them. I like doing them!', and in 1914 she joined the Society for Psychical Research.[29] To

---

[26] Courtney, *Women of My Time*, 53.

[27] William Lyon Phelps, 'The Advance of the English Novel', *Bookman* (New York), 43 (May 1916), 306–7: at 306.

[28] See Margaret Oliphant, 'The Sisters Brontë', in ead. et al., *Women Novelists of Queen Victoria's Reign: A Book of Appreciations* (London: Hurst and Blackett, 1897), 45–6; Clement Shorter, *Charlotte Brontë and her Circle* (1896; 2nd edn. London: Hodder and Stoughton, 1908), and *Charlotte Brontë and her Sisters* (London: Hodder and Stoughton, 1905). I discuss these texts and Sinclair's response to them in more detail below.

[29] Sinclair to Annie Fields, 9 Dec. 1910, The Huntington Library, San Marino, California, FI 3819. See Boll, *Miss May Sinclair*, 105, for discussion of her membership in the SPR.

Sinclair the Brontës symbolized both a raw and forward-looking feminist consciousness, and the endurance of terrible grief.

During the years before the First World War Sinclair became firmly established as an expert on the Brontës. She published introductions in 1908 to editions in the new Everyman series of *The Life of Charlotte Brontë*, *Jane Eyre*, and *Shirley*, in 1909 to *Villette*, in 1910 to *The Professor*, in 1914 to *The Tenant of Wildfell Hall*, and in 1921 to *Wuthering Heights*.[30] A request from her publisher Constable to write a 'slight monograph' for their Little Biographies series produced the full-length *The Three Brontës* in 1912.[31] Sinclair's books were representative of a broader renewal of critical and journalistic interest in the sisters. In 1908 Clement Shorter, editor of the *Sphere*, published a second edition of his 1896 book *Charlotte Brontë and her Circle*, in 1905 his *Charlotte Brontë and her Sisters* appeared, and in 1910 he edited the first volume of the *Complete Works of Emily Brontë*, which included seventy-one previously undiscovered poems.[32] Novelist Mary Ward was active as a Brontë editor at this period as well, writing introductions to three volumes of *The Life and Works of Charlotte Brontë and her Sisters* between 1906 and 1910.[33] There were various reasons for this increased interest in the Brontës. The start of a new century encouraged reassessments of the great Victorian authors, and the Brontë sisters were especially attractive because they posed most acutely many of the questions asked by the increasingly active pre-war movement for women's rights. On a more practical level, the explosion of mass publishing meant that new series like Everyman were keen to put out new cheap editions of the classics as quickly as possible. Sinclair's personal

[30] The Everyman series was founded by J. M. Dent in 1906, and edited by Sinclair's friend literary journalist and Welsh translator Ernest Rhys (1859–1946). The series was designed to offer classics at an affordable price, and by 1946 it numbered almost 1,000 volumes. The scale of the operation offered innumerable opportunities to writers turned editor like Sinclair. See Bonham-Carter, *Authors by Profession*, i. 177, and Kemp, Mitchell, and Trotter, *Edwardian Fiction*, 340. Sinclair's introductions appeared in Charlotte Brontë, *Shirley* (London: Dent, 1908); Charlotte Brontë, *Jane Eyre* (London: Dent, 1908); Elizabeth Gaskell, *The Life of Charlotte Brontë* (London: Dent, 1908); Charlotte Brontë, *Villette* (London: Dent, 1909); Charlotte Brontë, *The Professor* (London: Dent, 1910); and Anne Brontë, *The Tenant of Wildfell Hall* (London: Dent, 1914). All were simultaneously published in New York by Dutton. Sinclair seems to have written the introduction to *Wuthering Heights* first, in 1907 (see typescript in the possession of Peter Assinder, Sinclair's great-nephew), but Everyman were already preparing to publish an edition of the novel by Ernest Rhys himself, and another one, including some of Emily Brontë's poems, with an introduction by Margaret Lane, both in 1907, and Sinclair's edition did not appear until 1921, and then only in Britain.

[31] See Sinclair to Clement Shorter, 9 Dec. 1911, The Brotherton Collection, Leeds University Library. The book was published as *The Three Brontës* (London: Hutchinson, 1912).

[32] Shorter, *Charlotte Brontë and her Circle*, *Charlotte Brontë and her Sisters*, and *Complete Works of Emily Brontë*, i. *Poetry* (London: Hodder and Stoughton, 1910). See also R. W. Crump, *Charlotte and Emily Brontë*, *1846–1915: A Reference Guide* (Boston: G. K. Hall, 1982).

[33] *The Life and Works of Charlotte Brontë and her Sisters*, ed. Mrs Humphrey Ward (London: Smith, Elder & Co., 1906–10).

predilection for Charlotte, Emily, and Anne found itself happily matched by economic and cultural conditions.

The key term in Sinclair's work on the Brontës is 'modern'. Struggling herself with what it meant to be a woman whose emotional allegiances were to a Victorian culture that had frustrated and constrained her, Sinclair interrogated over and over again the ways in which the Brontës had anticipated the values of an age they would not live to see. Repeatedly Sinclair stresses that the sisters and their heroines were pioneers of modern femininity. 'Little Jane' Eyre, for example, 'in spite of . . . her tendency to refer to herself as a "dependent", remains to this day young and splendid and modern to her finger-tips'; 'Shirley Keeldar is the ancestress of the great modern heroines, big-souled, unsentimental, and untamed'; Charlotte Brontë became 'more complex and, unconsciously, more modern; she advanced nearer and nearer to the searching analytic light'; and 'Mrs. Huntingdon [in *The Tenant of Wildfell Hall*] is, if not the first, one of the first of the long line of insurgent modern heroines'.[34] Unlike Audrey Craven, the Brontës and their creations represented the constructive possibilities of the kind of resistant Victorian woman May Sinclair herself had been. The 'modern heroine' is associated in Sinclair's mind with a rebelliously analytic spirit which refuses to submit to masculine control. Jane Eyre challenged the 'ancient and formidable tradition' that 'No woman should know her own nature until some man (and *he* must be her husband) reveals it to her'.[35] Instead, Jane insisted on both determining her nature for herself and on revealing it to Mr Rochester unasked: 'Jane offended. She sinned against the unwritten code that ordains that a woman may lie till she is purple in the face, but she must not, as a piece of gratuitous information, tell a man she loves him; not, that is to say, in as many words' (TB, 129). Sinclair is scathing about the feminine subterfuge which would have been Jane's only other recourse: the Victorian woman 'may exhibit every ignominious and sickly sign of [love]; her eyes may glow like hot coals; she may tremble; she may flush and turn pale; she may do almost anything, provided she does not speak the actual words' (TB, 129–30). In the 1912 essay on feminism Sinclair described this as a form of emotional manipulation which is even worse than masculine bullying: 'the extreme shakiness of man's standard of sexual morality to-day, is largely due to the debilitating, the disastrous influence of the Early and Mid-Victorian woman. Her wilful ignorance, her sentimentalism, her sex-servility, amounted to positive vice, and could only be productive of viciousness in the unhappy males exposed

---

[34] Sinclair, 'Introduction' to *Jane Eyre*, p. xii; 'Introduction' to *Shirley*, p. xlv; 'Introduction' to *Villette*, p. xv; 'Introduction' to *The Tenant of Wildfell Hall*, p. ix.

[35] Sinclair, 'Introduction' to *Jane Eyre*, p. ix.

to it.'[36] Jane Eyre, on the other hand, like Helen Huntingdon, 'slammed the door of [her] bedroom . . . in the face of society and all existing moralities and conventions'.[37] Both characters anticipated a world in which women would articulate their own desires clearly and without equivocation.

Sinclair was well aware of the costs of that kind of candour. She believed that Charlotte and Anne Brontë symbolized the desperation of anachronism: they were imprisoned in a world which they had outgrown. Unaware that her religious struggles and her passion for intellectual pursuits were typical of her generation, Sinclair herself felt like a misfit in the provincial society in which she moved before coming to London in 1896. But she had at least finally settled into a world in which she was easily identifiable as a successful and independent writer, even if her reclusive tendencies and her primness did sometimes raise eyebrows. Anne, on the other hand, had died before her talent was fully recognized, and Charlotte had enjoyed only a few months of marriage before dying during her first pregnancy. Sinclair used the Brontës' more acute deprivation to reflect on her own, noting that 'though in many respects an ultra-Victorian woman, rigid in Victorian Puritanism and at the same time saturated with Victorian sentiment, Anne belongs even more than Charlotte, more than Emily, to the twentieth century'. 'She *does*', writes Sinclair, 'represent something, if it is only the restless misery of women born into the Victorian age before their time.'[38] The eponymous heroine of Anne's novel *Agnes Grey*, is, in Sinclair's words, although 'only an inarticulate, a feeble, tremulous and lachrymose Jane Eyre . . . every bit as frank and unveiled an example of woman suppressed and frustrated, squirming in her intolerable prison house', and the 'spirit of the twentieth century' speaks even through Agnes: 'in Agnes Grey it is a forlorn, sad spirit, subdued and almost inarticulate, a voice moaning rather than crying in the wilderness; yet it is there.'[39] In spite of her gentleness, Anne Brontë had 'an immense, a terrifying audacity': she was 'an insurgent in religious thought', and Sinclair believed that her 'melancholy' was a 'pathological' form of 'religious doubt' (TB, 47–9). Sinclair, who had also been driven to despair by her inability to realize the presence of God, saw her own predicament mirrored in Anne's divided affinities. In spite of her sympathies with Anne, however, the youngest Brontë sister had little real appeal for Sinclair. Although she exemplified some of her early difficulties, she was not a figure whom Sinclair admired. Several times Sinclair notes that she had 'no genius': 'Her gentle insignificance served her well' (see TB, 47, 51). It

[36] Sinclair, 'Defence of Men', 562.   [37] Sinclair, 'Introduction' to *The Tenant of Wildfell Hall*, p. ix.
[38] Ibid., pp. viii, vii.   [39] Ibid., p. viii.

was Charlotte, not Anne, with whom Sinclair really identified, and who offered her the best opportunity for self-analysis and self-justification.

Charlotte Brontë represented to Sinclair a genius that was moulded not by erotic feeling for a man, but by intimate family relationships established in childhood. It was crucial for Sinclair to prove that Charlotte Brontë's gifts as a novelist were independent of any feelings she might have had for Paul Héger, the schoolmaster with whom she worked while she was in Brussels, since if Sinclair could show that, she could argue that women who were romantically unattached could be at least as good writers as those who were in love. A number of pages of both *The Three Brontës* and the introductions are devoted to disproving statements by critics such as Angus Mackay and J. Malham-Dembleby that Charlotte loved Héger, and that her unrequited love inspired the flowering of her talent into *Jane Eyre*.[40] Sinclair suggested a different reading, one that acknowledged the influence of Charlotte's sisters (especially Emily). She was convinced that the desire to find a romance at the root of Charlotte's creative powers belittled her as a writer and as a woman:

her genius was the thing that irritated, the enigmatic, inexplicable thing. Talent in a woman you can understand, there's a formula for it—*tout talent de femme est un bonheur manqué*. So when a woman's talent baffles you, your course is plain: *cherchez l'homme*. Charlotte's critics argued that if you could put your finger on the man you would have the key to the mystery. This, of course, was arguing that her genius was, after all, only a superior kind of talent. (TB, 82)

Sinclair's contention that Charlotte was free of all romantic attachments was an attempt to protect her from the grudging praise of critics who were unwilling to see *Jane Eyre* as 'solitary and . . . unbegotten'.[41] Sinclair believed it was the product of a domestic and an inner life rich enough to give Charlotte Brontë the material she needed without the dubious benefit of stimulation from the heterosexual world. She saw not Héger but *Wuthering Heights* as the catalyst of *Jane Eyre*:

It is not possible that Charlotte, of all people, should have read *Wuthering Heights* without a shock of enlightenment; that she should not have compared it with her own bloodless work; that she should not have felt the wrong done to her genius by her self-repression. Emily had dared to be herself; *she* had not been afraid of her own passion; she had had no method; she had accomplished a stupendous thing

---

[40] Angus Mackay, *The Brontës: Fact and Fiction* (London: Dodd Mead, 1897); J. Malham-Dembleby, *The Key to the Brontë Works: The Key to Charlotte Brontë's 'Wuthering Heights', 'Jane Eyre', and her Other Works* (London: Walter Scott Publishing Co., 1911). Malham-Dembleby maintains that Charlotte wrote *Wuthering Heights*, and that the relationship between Cathy and Heathcliff dramatizes that between herself and Héger. Sinclair eventually responded directly to this argument in 'Who Wrote *Wuthering Heights*?', *Bookman* (London), 66 (May 1924), 97–8. She decided it was Emily.

[41] Sinclair, 'Introduction' to *Jane Eyre*, p. x.

without knowing it, by simply letting herself go. And Charlotte, I think, said to her-self, 'That is what I ought to have done. That is what I will do next time.' And next time she did it. (TB, 146)

Sinclair stressed the intellectual exchanges between the sisters. It was not just, as she wrote of Emily and Anne, that they 'were inseparable', pacing 'up and down the parlour of the Parsonage' with 'their arms round each other's shoulders' (TB, 50): it was also that all three sisters were in different ways try-ing to understand and to interpret the world, and learning from one another through reading, discussion, and thought. They grew not only through experience but also through debate and study, activities that had been so cru-cial and so painful to Sinclair during those lonely years at Salcombe Regis.

Sinclair believed that sexual intimacy could actually hinder women in their pursuit of artistic excellence. She was adamant that in spite of her late brief marriage, Charlotte Brontë was for most of her life resolutely opposed to sharing her life with a man. Sinclair argued this partly in response to Margaret Oliphant's description of Charlotte as 'a plain-faced, lachrymose, middle-aged spinster, dying, visibly, to be married, obsessed for ever with that idea, for ever whining over the frustration of her sex' (TB, 20). Sinclair's dislike of Oliphant's categorization of Brontë as morbid and neurotic was part of a broader defence of celibacy which she pursued in her 1912 book, *Feminism*, written for and published by the Women's Suffrage League. She saw in Oliphant's account of 'an undesired and undesirable little spinster pining visibly and shamelessly' (TB, 67) a forerunner of the views of such notable opponents of women's suffrage as Sir Almroth Wright, Professor of Experimental Pathology at the University of London.[42] Wright published a letter in *The Times* on 28 March 1912 which stated that 'the mind of woman is always threatened with danger from the reverberations of her physio-logical emergencies. It is with such thoughts that the doctor lets his eyes rest upon the militant suffragist. He cannot shut them to the fact that there is mixed up with the woman's movement much mental disorder; and he cannot conceal from himself the physiological emergencies which lie behind.'[43] Wright followed current medical practice in assuming that women were agi-tating for the vote partly as a way of releasing frustrated sexual energies. Sin-clair argued indignantly that men were just as prone to 'physiological emergency' as women, and that female sexual abstinence did not necessarily lead to hysteria. Almroth Wright wrote, announced Sinclair, 'as if all women (and men, too) in whom the sexual instincts are not conspicuous and dom-

    [42] In *The Three Brontës* Sinclair quotes extensively from Oliphant, 'The Sisters Brontë', esp. 45–6.
    [43] Sir Almroth Wright, letter to the editor, *The Times* (28 Mar. 1912), 7–8: at 7. His *The Unexpurgated Case against Woman Suffrage* was published in 1913.

inant were necessarily incomplete; whereas they very often are the *most complete* types of all, as possessing that Will the existence of which Sir Almroth Wright either denies or ignores'.[44] She believed women who were not preoccupied with the duties and emotional strains of marriage and motherhood were more likely to achieve intellectual and creative autonomy. Writing off the suffragettes as frustrated spinsters (many of them, as Sinclair pointed out, were in any case married), or Charlotte Brontë as pathologically sexually deprived, was a classic way of disabling them as activists.[45] Sinclair noted that 'the very fact that the unattached have most leisure and opportunity for agitation sufficiently accounts for their presence in this movement; . . . its causes are economic, sociological, individual, anything in the world . . . except sexual'.[46] To suggest that the suffragettes were motivated by their sexual appetites was just another version of the Charlotte Brontë/Héger travesty: as Sinclair put it, *cherchez l'homme*.

Even when on 29 July 1918 what remained of the Charlotte Brontë/Héger correspondence—four love letters written by Brontë—were published for the first time in *The Times*, Sinclair continued to argue that Brontë's feelings were not the source of her creative impulse. She acknowledged that 'I am bound to unsay much that I have said, and to admit that some passionate element, innocent and unconscious, was, for all its innocence and unconsciousness, present unmistakably in Charlotte Brontë's feeling for her "Master".'[47] But she stood by her contention that Charlotte's 'genius owed nothing to her "master", that (in spite of her brief obsession) it was independent of all that he could do to her or make her feel. The proof is the use, the deliberate and unimpassioned use it made of him.'[48] By insisting that Charlotte's genius exploited rather than being exploited by her feeling for Héger, Sinclair managed to use the evidence of the letters to suggest that genius was a stronger force than love—that love was, indeed, potentially irrelevant to women's creative talent. She may have been stung by the review of *The Helpmate* in the November 1907 issue of *Outlook*, which suggested that she needed a 'wider knowledge of life' before she would be ready to tackle subjects such as marital sex.[49] Her aim in writing on the Brontë sisters was to show that women (and, indeed, men) did not need a broad range of experience in order to write with genius.

The values Sinclair espoused in her work on the Brontës also shaped *The*

[44] Sinclair, *Feminism* (London: Women's Suffrage League, 1912), 12.
[45] Ibid. 15.   [46] Sinclair, fragment on women's suffrage, 13, UP, Box 24, fo. 452.
[47] Sinclair, 'The New Brontë Letters', *Dial*, 55 (1 Nov. 1913), 343–6: at 344 (repr. as an introduction to the 2nd edn. of *The Three Brontës* in 1914).
[48] Ibid. 346.   [49] 'The Season's Books', *Outlook*, 87 (23 Nov. 1907), 621–2: at 622.

Creators, the novel she was working on alongside her Brontë introductions in late 1908 and throughout 1909. It was serialized in _Century_ magazine between November 1909 and October 1910 under the editorship of Richard Gilder, and subsequently published in volume form in both Britain and the USA.[50] Sinclair started thinking about it in September 1908, writing to Annie Fields: 'I am planning a long—really very long—novel. It will be harder to write than anything I've done since The Divine Fire, & I must not talk about it—in case it doesn't "come off ". It is one that I've had in my mind for years & I have not felt ready for it till now.'[51] The central character, celebrated novelist Jane Holland, lives like Sinclair herself on the 'top floor in the old house in Kensington Square. To make sure her splendid isolation, she had cut herself off by a boarded, a barricaded staircase, closed with a door at the foot' (C, 5). Evelyn Underhill warned Sinclair: 'I suppose by the way you are prepared to hear everyone say that Jane is you? Because I'm sure that they will!'[52] Jane certainly dramatizes many of Sinclair's fears and questions about female creativity. Her closest friend, writer George Tanqueray, tells her that her fame has made her vulnerable to the demands of 'Awful people, implacable, insatiable, pernicious, destructive people. The trackers down, the hangers-on, the persecutors, the pursuers. . . . You let everybody prey on you' (C, 7, 8).[53] He urges her to protect herself from interruption and distraction even if it means a drop in income. Jane's worst enemy, however, is not other people, but herself. In spite of knowing, as her writer friend Nina insists, that 'if any woman is to do anything stupendous, it means virginity' (C, 106), Jane marries editor and critic Hugh Brodrick, partly—in true Sinclairian style—because her body thrills to the touch of a child: 'at the touch of the child's body, a fine pain ran

---

[50] Sinclair and Henry Holt fell out over the sale of the serial rights to _The Creators_. In 1924 Sinclair told Willis Steell that Holt was 'a fine man, but an autocrat; oh, awfully arrogant. . . . when the Century Company wished to buy the serial rights of a novel, Mr. Holt refused to sell; and, because I couldn't afford to lose the money, I was obliged to take the book away from him' (Steell, 'May Sinclair Tells Why She Isn't a Poet', 513). Holt blamed Sinclair's agent, Curtis Brown, including Sinclair among a number of authors who were 'yanked away from me by their agents, with some help from very enterprising members of the trade' (Henry Holt, _Garrulities of an Octogenarian Editor, with Other Essays Somewhat Biographical and Autobiographical_, Boston: Houghton Mifflin, 1923, 212).

[51] Sinclair to Annie Fields, 19 Sept. 1908, The Huntington Library, San Marino, California, FI 3820.

[52] Evelyn Underhill to Sinclair, n.d. [1909?], UP, Box 3, fo. 90. A review in _Current Literature_ suggested that George Tanqueray was based on George Meredith ('_The Creators_', _Current Literature_, 49, Dec. 1910, 690–1: at 690). But there were other contenders for that role: Ford Madox Ford heard rumours that he might have been the 'point' in actual life out of which the character of George Tanqueray developed (see Ford to Edgar Jepson, 28 Oct. 1910, _Letters of Ford Madox Ford_, ed. Richard M. Ludwig, Princeton: Princeton University Press, 1965, 45). Ezra Pound, who also knew Ford, wrote to Sinclair while he was reading _The Creators_: 'Mind you I can't or I haven't yet been able to read as an outsider. Nos amis déguisés despite your valliant [_sic_] and courteous efforts!' (Pound to Sinclair, 11 Mar. 1911, UP, Box 3, fo. 74). It seems likely that Tanqueray is based on a number of Sinclair's acquaintances.

[53] Ezra Pound, who became Sinclair's friend in 1909, expressed the same fear to her: 'people _impose_ on you' (see H.D., _End to Torment_, New York: New Directions, 1979, 9). See the opening of Ch. 6, below.

from her finger-tips to her heart' (C, 267). But once she is married, and especially once she is a mother, she no longer cares about writing, and the novel
she produces in the early months of her marriage is a disappointment. As a
married woman she can no longer write in perfect freedom:

> According to her code and Tanqueray's she had sinned a mortal sin. She had con-
> ceived and brought forth a book, not by divine compulsion, but because Brodrick
> wanted a book and she wanted to please Brodrick. Such a desire was the mother of
> monstrous and unshapen things. In Tanqueray's eyes it was hardly less impure than
> the commercial taint. . . . She had done violence to her genius. She had constrained
> the secret and incorruptible will. (C, 287)

The metaphoric conception and gestation of the book out of her pleasure
with Brodrick means that its roots are in the corrupt soil of the body, rather
than the 'divine fire' of the mind. Jane's desire to write is at war with her
desire for family life: 'Married she served a double and divided flame' (C, 318).
Sinclair wrote of Emily Brontë that 'it was through her personal desti-
tution that her genius was so virile and so rich' (TB, 200), and Jane can only
write if she severs 'the tie of flesh' (C, 328) between herself and her baby,
and, even more ominously, herself and her husband. The novel even implies
that Jane's second child is weak and nervous because she worked on a novel
during her pregnancy with him. In spite of her sympathetic rendering of
Jane, Sinclair evidently intended her novel as a cautionary tale for women.[54]
The Creators makes it clear that domestic, maternal, and sexual responsibilities make it very difficult—even impossible—for women writers to produce
their best work. The notion of the 'divine fire' from Sinclair's early novel is
now put to work in justification of Sinclair's own ascetic lifestyle.

One of the reasons for the incompatibility of life as a writer and life as a
wife and mother is that creative genius is, in Sinclair's view, a masculine
force. As I noted above, she described Emily Brontë as 'virile', and Nina in
The Creators goes even further, telling Jane:

> Doesn't it look, Jinny, as if genius were the biggest curse a woman can be saddled
> with? It's giving you another sex inside you, and a stronger one, to plague you.
> When we want a thing we can't sit still like a woman and wait till it comes to us, or
> doesn't come. We go after it like a man; and if we can't get it peaceably we fight for
> it, as a man fights when he isn't a coward or a fool. And because we fight we're done
> for. And then, when we're done, the woman in us turns and rends us. (C, 105)[55]

---

[54] As Boll remarks, 'Jane's situation as a wife and mother introduces a problem: whether or not a woman
novelist to whom the quality of her writing, not her happiness as a person, is the supreme desideratum,
should marry' (*Miss May Sinclair*, 201).

[55] Sinclair may well have identified with Nina, who continually loses the men she loves to other women,
as well as with Jane. Nina burns her sleeve and arm while making tea for a man she loves, and cries out: 'If

The figure of genius as an irresistible force was a commonplace at this period. Swinburne in an 1894 volume on Charlotte Brontë which Sinclair read when she was working on *The Three Brontës* describes it as a 'subtle and infallible force of nature' which 'compels us without question to positive acceptance and belief'; Sinclair's friend novelist Violet Hunt thought of it as 'a state permanently bordering on frenzy, a beatitude which entails certain pains and penalties that no one else can shoulder'.[56] But Sinclair felt that women were at particular peril from this 'force of nature', since it ran counter to their instincts to love and to nurture. In her view the 'pains and penalties' Hunt wrote about were magnified for women in whom the impulse to bear children could be primitive and anguished, as it may well have been for Sinclair herself. When she is first married and no longer writing Jane feels estranged from herself. Recalling herself two years earlier, writing alone in her attic, she feels 'a shock of surprise, of spiritual dislocation. She was positively asking herself, "What am I doing here?" ' (C, 286). It is impossible for her to satisfy both aspects of her self. George Tanqueray, on the other hand, who also marries during the course of the novel, neglects his wife both socially and sexually because he is absorbed in his work, but feels no more than a slight guilt about it. The conditions of women's lives mean that their creative and their sexual impulses are in constant conflict in a way that is rarely true for men.[57]

Sinclair believed that when a novelist was truly 'creating', as she called it, the world of the imagination rendered the material world irrelevant.[58] When Jane embarks on writing a new novel, she is at the mercy of 'the consuming and avenging will':

For the world of vivid and tangible things was receding. The garden, the house, Brodrick and his suits of clothes and the unchanged garment of his flesh and blood, the child's adorable, diminutive body, they had no place beside the perpetual, the

---

you had a body like mine . . . you'd be glad to get rid of it on any terms' (C, 234). Sinclair herself had burnt 'a lace sleeve & part of my arm on an oil-stove while engaged in the sacred rites of hospitality' about six years earlier (Sinclair to Hinkson, 14 Nov. 1903, JR).

[56] Algernon Charles Swinburne, *A Note on Charlotte Brontë* (1894; new edn. New York: Haskell House, 1970), 6, 9; Hunt, *Flurried Years*, 17. See Christine Battersby, *Gender and Genius: Towards a Feminine Aesthetics* (Bloomington, Ind.: Indiana University Press, 1989) for further discussion of the concept of 'genius'.

[57] As Jane Eldridge Miller puts it in her reading of *The Creators*: 'as the novel develops, it becomes clear that the writing experiences of the men and the women are vastly different, and that although creativity may not distinguish between genders, gender ultimately determines the circumstances of creativity in important ways' (*Rebel Women: Feminism, Modernism and the Edwardian Novel*, London: Virago, 1994, 190).

[58] One of the classic late Victorian and Edwardian distinctions between genius and talent was that genius was 'creative', whereas talent merely observed. Swinburne e.g. wrote that 'mere intellect . . . is constructive' while 'pure genius' is 'creative' (*Note on Charlotte Brontë*, 6–7). Sinclair wrote in *The Three Brontës*: 'It was true enough of Charlotte that she created. But of Emily it was absolutely and supremely true' (199). The title of *The Creators* obviously alludes to this distinction.

ungovernable resurgence of her vision. They became insubstantial, insignificant. The people of the vision were solid, they clothed themselves in flesh. (C, 347)

The retreat into an immaterial world which is in many cases more engrossing than the world of the senses meant that novelists such as Jane lost all interest in the life they shared with husband or child. Sinclair used this theory of creativity to support her conviction that experience was irrelevant—even inimical—to the realization of creative genius: 'Experience?' Jane exclaims: 'Experience is no good—the experience you mean—if you're an artist. It spoils you. It ties you hand and foot. It perverts you, twists you, blinds you to everything but yourself and it. I know women—artists—who have never got over their experience, women who'll never do anything again because of it' (C, 268). If imaginative life replaces and even surpasses life in the world, then there is not necessarily any meaningful relationship between the two. Sinclair's account of her own creative processes in a 1905 letter to Witter Bynner suggests that, like Jane Holland, she needed to withdraw from the buzz of everyday life to 'see' the characters of her next novel:

And it was only the other day that I took the trouble to observe <u>how</u> a new novel comes & grows. I had been empty of ideas for a year & a half (chiefly through illness) & I despaired as I've despaired dozens of times before of ever writing anything again. Then—I was on a mountain in Wales at the time (not that the mountain had anything to do with it)—when, suddenly, as if a door had been opened into some room, I saw the people, the characters that had been hidden away somewhere in the back of my brain, refusing to show up, that were mere nameless outlines foreshadowing rather than embodying the motif of the book—I saw them alive in the most living moments of their life, acting out their drama, with their souls, their emotions & thoughts, transparent to me without the medium of words. . . . That's the way they always come. And until I get there, & see those people so, completed before a phrase has gone to their making, I can do nothing with them.[59]

Sinclair claims she must be able to enter a parallel world before she can start to write, a parallel world in which she can observe without participating in the events of the characters' lives. Jane too, after a period when she writes nothing, sees the central character of her next novel while she is sitting quietly alone in her garden: he 'arose with the oddest irrelevance out of the unfathomable peace. She could not account for him, nor understand why, when she was incapable of seeing him a year ago, she should see him now with such extreme distinctness and solidity' (C, 112). Neither woman can engage with the activities of the world around them as long as they are

---

[59] Sinclair to Witter Bynner, 29 Aug. 1905, HL, bMS Am 1891 (766). The novel she 'saw' on the mountain was *The Helpmate*.

immersed in the dramas of another world of their own making. As Sinclair wrote in *The Three Brontës*, to 'the supreme artist the order of the actual event is one thing, and the order of creation is another. Their lines may start from the same point in the actual, they may touch again and again, but they are not the same, and they cannot run exactly parallel' (TB, 165). An intense absorption in one 'order' made it impossible to participate in life in the other.

Writing *The Creators* was a long and difficult process, although at first things seemed to be going well. In January 1909 Sinclair was in Sussex cheerfully working on the novel: 'I've finished about one-third of my new novel, wh. will be longer than "The Helpmate"; nearly as long, I'm afraid, as "The Divine Fire". It has been more joy to do than anything since the days of Ricky [Rickman in *The Divine Fire*] . . . There's really some interest in having a good solid piece of work stretching in front of you.'[60] But when in March 1909 the novel was accepted for serialization by the *Century* magazine, Sinclair suddenly found herself working to other people's timetables.[61] Because *The Creators* was being serialized while Sinclair was still working on it (unlike *The Helpmate*, which was finished before the serialization even started), Sinclair had to keep going, however exhausted she felt.[62] And since the magazine wanted to illustrate the story, her deadlines were even earlier than she had expected. She complained to Richard Gilder, editor of *Century* magazine in which the novel appeared: 'this Artist, my hated rival, is to be set upon me to hound & harry me from chapter to chapter, to clamour for "copy" . . . to be about my path, & (in spirit) about my bed.'[63] Sinclair was unused to interference with her own creative processes, and the stress was almost too much for her. In June 1909 she was admitted to a nursing home for three weeks. She told Gilder that her 'illness was purely physical & only required rather more care than I cd. get in my servantless flat', but there were rumours that she had suffered a minor mental collapse, and Sinclair's defensiveness to Gilder suggests that in fact nervous strain was a factor in her ill health.[64] She felt constantly constrained by the magazine's insistence that she keep each instalment to a certain number of pages, and each draft

---

[60] Sinclair to Fields, 9 Jan. 1909, The Huntington Library, San Marino, California, FI 3821.

[61] Sinclair discusses her acceptance of the *Century* contract, and the timing of the instalments, in a letter to Richard Gilder on 10 Mar. 1909, HR, MS (Sinclair, M) Letters.

[62] Sinclair wrote to Gilder on 13 June 1909: 'Never again will I begin even to arrange for a serial before the whole book is written', HR, MS (Sinclair, M) Letters.

[63] Sinclair to Gilder, 7 Apr. 1909, HR, MS (Sinclair, M) Letters.

[64] Sinclair to Gilder, 13 June 1909, HR, MS (Sinclair, M) Letters. She wrote again a week later, sending him the first few instalments of the novel, and telling him: 'If you hear alarming reports of me, don't believe them. I'm as fit as ever. I have not had either "a nervous breakdown", or an "operation", but I'm credited, so I hear, with both!!! My "Nursing Home" was a purely preventive measure, & entirely successful' (Sinclair to Gilder, 25 June 1909, HR, MS (Sinclair, M) Letters).

had cuts marked in blue ink that she hoped the editor would not have to carry out.[65] When she discovered that in fact she was writing under the maximum, and the magazine was *still* making cuts, she was furious, and tried to insist that Gilder print an editorial note explaining that the serial version of the novel was an abridgement of the volume edition.[66] The first instalment finally appeared in November 1909, and Sinclair hated the accompanying illustration, telling Gilder that it looked like the illustration to 'the "Tale of a Village Inn", & how the horny-handed son of the blacksmith took to drink in consequence of the heartless coquetry of the innkeeper's daughter' (see pl. 13).[67] But Gilder never saw the letter: he died suddenly on 18 November. Sinclair was mortified that 'the last letter I ever wrote to him sd. have seemed to express dissatisfaction with arrangements wh. had been considered with so much care', and she was relieved that at least he never knew the extent of her irritation with the pictures.[68] After Gilder's death Sinclair felt more alienated from the novel than ever. At least when Gilder was alive, in spite of her frustration with the magazine's deadlines and demands, she felt sure that she had at least one appreciative and grateful reader. She told Annie Fields that the writing of the novel had been 'long & difficult. . . . I am grieved that I did not finish it in time for Mr. Gilder to read it all. A great deal of the pleasure I sd. have had in its appearance has gone now.'[69]

In spite of Sinclair's hopes that the novel would be seen as another *Divine Fire*, it received fairly mixed reviews when it was published as a book in September 1910. The *Athenaeum* was hesitant, suggesting that it was 'a measure of the author's success in arousing our sympathy that we feel distressed when the conclusion leaves this problem only half-resolved'; the *Times Literary Supplement* wryly observed that the 'comedy' of the book's subtitle (it was called *The Creators: A Comedy*) must lie in the characters' believing themselves to be geniuses; Carter Irving in the *New York Times Book Review* thought it obnoxious and complained about the 'portentous seriousness' with which women novelists regarded their own work; and William Morton Payne of the *Dial*, who had welcomed *The Divine Fire*, found *The Creators* unconvincing.[70] Only the *Independent* took its message seriously, but even it

[65] Sinclair to Gilder, 25 June 1909, HR, MS (Sinclair, M) Letters.

[66] Sinclair to Gilder, 4 Sept. 1909, HR, MS (Sinclair, M) Letters.

[67] Sinclair to Gilder, 1 Nov. 1909, HR, MS (Sinclair, M) Letters.

[68] Sinclair to Mr Underwood-Johnson (Gilder's temporary successor at the *Century*), 14 Dec. 1909, HR, MS (Sinclair, M) Letters.

[69] Sinclair to Fields, 14 Dec. 1909, The Huntington Library, San Marino, California, FI 3816.

[70] 'The Creators', *Athenaeum*, no. 4328 (8 Oct. 1910), 415; 'The Creators', *Times Literary Supplement* (29 Sept. 1910), 350; Carter Irving, 'Miss Sinclair's *Creators*: A Novel from which We Learn Much about the Imaginary Writers of Wonderful Books', *New York Times Book Review*, 22 Oct. 1910, 584; William Morton Payne, 'Recent Fiction', *Dial*, 49 (16 Oct. 1910), 287–8.

complained about the novel's pomposity.[71] Sinclair was hurt, perhaps particularly so about negative responses to this novel because it dealt with issues so
close to her heart. Hinkson expressed her sympathy, telling Sinclair: 'don't
wear yourself out', and Sinclair told Hardy that her reviews 'depressed me
for about ten days after my book came out'. In a rare moment of self-
revelation—and perhaps of envy of Hardy's cosy domestic life—she
acknowledged that her solitary state made her vulnerable: 'I haven't any one
at home to say "It doesn't matter".'[72] It was ironic that it should be reviews
of the book in which she defended celibacy most forcefully that provoked
her to express regret that she had no one to share her disappointment.

The reviews of *The Three Brontës* in 1912 comforted Sinclair to some
extent for the discouraging reception of *The Creators*. Getting the book into
print in the first place was not easy. Sinclair wrote to Otto Kyllmann at Constable's in March 1912 to tell him that much to her regret (and trepidation—
she hated writing letters like this) she had accepted an advantageous offer
from Hutchinson of an advance on her next three novels. She tried to convince him that losing her would be to the firm's commercial advantage in the
long run:

Even if yr. firm were prepared to 'plunge' to this extent, I wd.n't let you try, for I'm
sure you'd lose on it. This man thinks he isn't going to lose—& he has been told
how small my sales are. He's 'plunging' with his eyes well opened.

I simply can't tell you how sorry I am to leave you; I wd. not do it, if either
America paid as well as it did once, or I had not such heavy & unexpected family
claims constantly occurring & likely to occur. For the last six years, whenever these
offers came I've refused them—solely on yr. account. But now I must think of my
own people. And I'm rather in difficulties myself.

Sinclair may have been frustrated by Constable's failure to publicize her
novels widely enough in Britain: she told Kyllmann pointedly that the 'firm
I'm thinking of has pledged itself to "push" my books for all it is worth'.[73]
Founded in 1887 on the crest of the publishing wave, Hutchinson was anxious to expand, and it catered to a slightly less highbrow taste than Constable, who had published Walter de la Mare, George Gissing, and George
Meredith, as well as May Sinclair.[74]

---

[71] 'Shall a Genius Marry?', *Independent*, 69 (1910), 1156–7.

[72] Hinkson to Sinclair, 27 Oct. 1910, UP, Box 2, fo. 41; Sinclair to Hardy, 31 Oct. 1910, Thomas Hardy
Memorial Collection, Dorset County Museum.

[73] Sinclair to Otto Kyllmann, 8 Mar. 1912, General Manuscript Collection, Charles Deering McCormick
Library of Special Collections, Northwestern University.

[74] Kemp et al., *Edwardian Fiction*, 326–7.

In switching firms, Sinclair was slightly shifting gear, but for such a well-established author it scarcely mattered. When she signed the contract with Hutchinson, Constable, who had been preparing to publish *The Three Brontës*, immediately cancelled their plans for the book. Hutchinson, however, quickly took it over and brought out *The Three Brontës* within three months of signing it, in June 1912. Critical response was swift and appreciative. G. K. Chesterton in the London *Nation* and *New York Times Book Review* thought that Sinclair had surpassed even Elizabeth Gaskell as a biographer of Charlotte Brontë; William E. A. Axon in the *Bookman* praised it for 'suggestions that cannot be ignored'; the *Independent* called it a 'remarkably acute and sympathetic study'; and W. E. Simonds in the *Dial* described it as 'vivacious, dramatic, frank, and unconventional'.[75] When reviewers did have reservations, they were always about the depth of Sinclair's own investment in the material: the *Literary Digest* thought she saw the sisters 'through colored glasses which allow no faults', and a review in the *Nation* astutely speculated that Sinclair might have admired the Brontës not so much for their work, as for the extent to which they rebelled against the limitations placed on women's intellectual lives at that period.[76] It was true, of course, that the sisters spoke as much to Sinclair's personal concerns as to her interests as a critic and a biographer. Perhaps this—coupled with the strain and unfamiliarity of writing for serialization—was responsible for the contrast between the styles of, and the reviewers' responses to, *The Three Brontës* and *The Creators*. *The Creators* is longer and less lively than *The Three Brontës*, as if Sinclair was overwhelmed by the message she was trying to convey.

One of the reasons for the popularity of *The Three Brontës*, and some of what makes it so readable even today, is that it is written partly as a ghost story. As she began work on *The Three Brontës*, Sinclair was simultaneously engaged in writing what she described to Annie Fields as 'stories of all queer lengths & all queer subjects; "spooky" ones'.[77] She had always been interested in apparitions (she told H. G. Wells that she had seen a ghost as a child), and she was intrigued by the idea of a fourth dimension, of an immaterial world in which the dead moved and had their being and which the living could rarely see.[78] During that first childhood reading of *The Life of Charlotte Brontë*

[75] G. K. Chesterton, 'The Weird Sisters: GKC Reviews May Sinclair's Life of the Brontës', *New York Times Book Review*, 22 Sept. 1912, 515 [repr. from the London *Nation*]; William E. A. Axon, 'The Three Brontës', *Bookman* (London), 42 (Aug. 1912), 212; 'The Three Brontës', *Independent*, 73 (28 Nov. 1912), 1254–5: at 1254; W. E. Simonds, 'The House of Brontë', *Dial*, 53 (1 Nov. 1912), 329–30: at 329.

[76] 'As to the Brontë Family', *Literary Digest*, 45 (2 Nov. 1912), 811–12: at 811; 'Emily Brontë', *Nation*, 96 (30 Jan. 1913), 104–6: at 104.

[77] Sinclair to Annie Fields, 9 Dec. 1910, The Huntington Library, San Marino, California, FI 3819.

[78] See Sinclair to H. G. Wells, 16 Oct. 1915, University of Illinois Library at Urbana-Champaign: 'the

it was the spectral figure of Emily, rather than those of her more approach-able sisters, which appealed most strongly to Sinclair's imagination. At that age she had little interest in the literary activities which became so central a feature of her response to the Brontës in adult life.

I skipped all the London part, and Charlotte's literary letters. I had a very vague idea of Charlotte apart from Haworth and the moors . . . But, for all that skipping and forgetting, there stood out a vivid and ineffaceable idea of Emily; Emily who was tall and strong and unconquerable; Emily who loved animals, and loved the moors; Emily and Keeper, that marvellous dog; Emily kneading bread with her book propped before her; Emily who was Ellis Bell, listening contemptuously to the reviews of *Wuthering Heights*; Emily stitching at the long seam with dying fin-gers; and Emily dead, carried down the long, flagged path, with Keeper following in the mourner's train. (TB, 278)

Emily's death, the stilling of that magnificent body, was central to Sinclair's response to her. Unlike her sisters, Emily could not be pressed into the ser-vice of twentieth-century feminism. Instead she seemed to Sinclair like a kind of quintessential lost object. 'Charlotte destroyed all records of her sis-ter', Sinclair notes, and so Emily 'stands apart in an enduring silence, and guards for ever her secret and her mystery' (TB, 194, 193). Sinclair returns over and over again to the image of Emily arranging her hair on the day of her death: 'she sat before the fire, combing her long, dark hair, and . . . the comb dropped from her weak fingers, and fell under the grate'; 'Emily in her mortal illness, sitting by the hearth, combing her long hair till the comb slips from her fingers' (TB, 35, 193). The association of Emily, combing her hair like a siren, with the work of death ('driven by her immortal passion for life, she fought terribly', TB, 35) allows Emily Brontë's last moments to memor-ialize the enigma of sexual difference itself. As Clement Shorter put it in 1896, she is 'a sphinx whose riddle no amount of research will enable us to read'.[79] Even writers who shared none of Sinclair's feminist sympathies fell prey to the lure of Emily's hapless ghost: anti-suffragist Mary Ward, for example, wrote in 1899 of her visit to the Brontë parsonage that as 'one

only time I ever saw an apparition (& it was sufficiently appalling) I wasn't a bit afraid. It simply seemed the most natural thing in the world. I was only a child & there wd. have been no shame in being afraid; but I sim-ply wasn't.' Evelyn Underhill's *The Grey World* (London: Heinemann, 1904) is about a dead child who weeps to return to the earth, is sent back, but repeatedly slips back into the world of the dead: 'His helpless little soul slipped its leash, the walls of sense trembled and melted, and he was back again in the horrible country of silence and mist. . . . he was in another dimension' (24). *The Divine Fire* and *The Grey World* were reviewed together by H. I. Brock, 'Fire and Smoke', *New York Times*, 11 Mar. 1905, sect. 2, 150, and Sinclair liked *The Grey World* so much that she sent a copy to Annie Fields and Sarah Orne Jewett for Christmas 1905 (see Sinclair to Fields, 24 Dec. [1905], The Huntington Library, San Marino, California, FI 3822).

[79] Shorter, *Charlotte Brontë and her Circle*, 146.

mounts the stone staircase, with one's hand on the old rail, suddenly ghosts are there. Emily mounts before one, clinging to the rail, dragging her wasted frame from step to step.'[80] Something about Emily's early death, and her proud independence and reserve, haunted the late Victorian and Edwardian imagination as, Jacqueline Rose has suggested, Sylvia Plath haunts us today.[81]

In 1911 Sinclair began a ghost-story, 'The Intercessor', which grew out of her fascination with Emily Brontë's tragic spectre. 'The Intercessor', first published in the *English Review* in July 1911, tells the story of archivist Garvin's stay as a lodger in a remote farm in Yorkshire. One night, he hears a child crying (although there are none living in the house), and a few nights later he sees her beating on the open door of the bedroom of the farmer's wife:

At this hour of the newly risen moon there was light on the landing like a grey day. He saw a girl child standing on the garret stair. It had on a short nightgown that showed its naked feet. It was clinging to the rail with one hand.

Its face was so small, so shrunken and so bleached, that at first its actual features were indistinct to him. What *was* distinct, appallingly distinct, was the look it had; a look not to be imagined or defined, and thinkable only as a cry, an agony, made visible.

The child stood there long enough to fix on him its look. At the same time it seemed so withdrawn in the secret of its suffering as to be unaware of him.

It descended the stair, went close past him, and crossed the landing to the women's room.

Now on these hot August nights the door was left half open, leaving a wide passage way into the room. Garvin could see it. He looked for the child to go in where its mother lay. Instead of going in it stood there motionless as if it kept watch.

Then all at once it began crying, crying and beating on the open door with its tenuous hands, beating and pushing as against a door closed and locked.

It was then that Garvin knew.

The creature gave up its efforts at last and turned from the door sobbing. Garvin could not see its face now, for it had raised its arms and held them across its forehead with the backs of the hands pressed against its weeping eyes. Thus blinded, it made its way across the landing towards Garvin's door, and passed by him, still unaware, into his room.

He went in and shut to the door. The child was standing by the foot of the bed as if it watched somebody who slept there. It stayed, watching, while Garvin undressed and got into bed. Then—Garvin was not frightened nor even surprised at what happened then; he seemed to have expected it—the little creature climbed up the

---

[80] Mary Ward, 'Introduction' to Charlotte Brontë, *Shirley* (London: Harper's, 1899), p. x.
[81] Jacqueline Rose, *The Haunting of Sylvia Plath* (London: Virago, 1991).

bedside and crept in beside him. He felt, flesh to flesh, its body pressed to his body, the palms of its hands upon his breast, and its face hidden against his side. (I, 137–9)

The local doctor finally explains the family's history: Effy's mother, angry at her husband's lack of interest in her after Effy's birth, stopped allowing the child to sleep with her in her bed. Every night, the little girl beat despairingly on her mother's door. When Effy, on one of her nightly trips to the servant's bed for comfort, found her father and the servant making love, she developed a disease akin to epilepsy, and during one of her seizures, she fell from a window into the stone tank in which she drowned. Out of pity, the ghost is visible only to visitors, like Garvin ('the intercessor' of the story's title). When Effy's ghost finally does appear to her mother in an apparent attempt at reconciliation, the mother shrieks and tries to fend her off. That night she gives birth to a dead child. She refuses to relinquish it for burial, and asks repeatedly for Garvin. When he comes, Effy follows him into the room and, as Garvin gently removes the body of the baby from its mother's breast, Effy slides into the baby's place and finally receives her mother's embrace.[82]

Even after so many years 'The Intercessor' still has the power to shock, partly because of the uncompromising way in which it represents maternal rejection—one of Sinclair's own earliest memories—and the bottomless sorrow of childhood. Its debts to Emily Brontë are obvious. The Yorkshire setting, the remote farmhouse, the arrival of a lodger, Garvin's spelling out of the date and the initials above the door, and the ghost of a child who clamours for entry all appear near the opening of *Wuthering Heights*. Effy's spectre recalls at once the ghoulish Catherine Earnshaw at the window, Emily Brontë herself (whose nature, in Charlotte's words, was 'simpler than a child's'), and even her elder sister Maria Brontë, dead at 12, of whom Sinclair wrote: 'She was the first of the children to go down into the vault under Haworth Church; you see her looking back on her sad way, a small, reluctant ghost, lovely, infantile, and yet maternal' (TB, 11).[83]

Effy's story can be read as a kind of Brontëan Gothic parable about the

[82] Sinclair was unable to find a magazine in the USA willing to handle 'The Intercessor'. She knew it was good, and she was very anxious that it should reach her large and loyal American audience. She wrote to Hinkson in frustration: 'I can't publish the best short story I ever wrote or shall write—in America. They're shocked at the subject' (22 Feb. 1911, JR). American sensibilities were apparently more sensitive to depictions of child-ghosts, unloving mothers, and stillborn babies lying at the breast than were the jaded British. 'The Intercessor' was eventually published in the USA as 'The Intercession: A Novel' in *Two Worlds* (Sept. 1926), and then reprinted as the title-story in *The Intercessor and Other Stories* (London: Hutchinson, 1931; New York: Macmillan, 1932).

[83] 'Stronger than a man, simpler than a child, her nature stood alone', Charlotte Brontë, 'Biographical Notice of Ellis and Acton Bell', written for the 2nd edn. of *Wuthering Heights* and *Agnes Grey*, 1850; repr. in Emily Brontë, *Wuthering Heights*, ed. William M. Sale, Jr. and Richard R. Dunn (3rd edn. New York: Norton, 1990), 318.

temporality of family histories. Garvin is a historian working on a 'County History'. He has 'had his nose in a hundred parish registers, sifting the dust of oblivion for a clue to some forgotten family' (I, 114). Effy teaches him that there are other histories to be written, not of 'forgotten families' but of the people that families have tried to forget. Effy represents all that her family cannot assimilate, reminding it both of its sexuality (her illness and death were caused by witnessing her father and his lover together, in a kind of displaced primal scene) and of its mortality. Effy's expulsion is the family's attempt to defend itself against its own history, as well as against the ravages of both parents' desire. Her appearances expose family life as a drama defined by an unwilling but inescapably traumatic engagement with the past. Her visits to Garvin's bed remind him that if he were to write the true history of a family, it would be based not on the evidence of parish registers, but on the traces of its ghosts.

Effy's ghost also represents the troublingly remote insistence of the dead Emily Brontë. In spite of her horror of revelatory biography, Sinclair was committed to the project of commemorating the Brontës' works and even to recreating their lives so that their suffering, their solitude, and their genius would never be forgotten. But Effy is implicated in the death of her infant sibling: her continued half-presence in the house is ruthless and destructive. Since her mother will not acknowledge her, even in death, Effy needs the child to die in order that she can receive a maternal embrace in its place: 'As Garvin stooped suddenly and lifted the dead child from the bed, he saw Effy slide through his hands into its place. In Mrs. Falshaw's eyes there was neither any fear nor any discernment of the substitution . . . Her arms pressed the impalpable creature, as it were flesh to flesh' (I, 196–7). Effy's haunting resolves her own anguish but kills the child for whom the enveloping arms were originally intended. It is hard not to read the story as an allegory of Sinclair's barely conscious feeling of her own insignificance in the wake of the mysterious presences that preceded her: Emily Brontë, Charlotte Brontë, and even her own long-dead sister Gertrude. Emily's ruthlessness and indifference were intimidating: 'Strangers received from her an impression as of a creature utterly removed from them; a remoteness scarcely human' (TB, 195). Charlotte and Anne both offered Sinclair the reassurance of beliefs that were in some way connected to—even anticipating—her own, but she could find no way to make sense of Emily's mystery, her silence, her disgusted contempt of death. Of all the sisters Emily seemed to offer Sinclair the least, threatening her hard-won sense of literary achievement and emotional and cultural belonging. She was like an obstinately mute ghost.

'The Intercessor' was one of Sinclair's most effective 'spooky' stories, and it was also a significant turning point in her intellectual development, anticipating as it did many of the psychoanalytic concepts that were so central to Sinclair's work after she became involved with the Medico-Psychological Clinic in 1913. Her interest in ghosts and ghost stories grew partly out of her conviction that it is impossible ever to leave the past behind. She was fascinated with the Brontës' lives because, like her own, they were shaped by intense childhood attachments that persisted into adulthood. Sinclair wrote in the introduction to Gaskell's *The Life of Charlotte Brontë*:

A woman cannot get away from her family even in its absence. She may abandon it; it may abandon her; but she is bound to it by infrangible, indestructible bonds. It, and all it has done to her or for her, has an enduring life in her memory. However much abandoned or ignored, its persistence there endows it with immortality.[84]

No doubt it was partly this conviction of the determining power of familial bonds that made her so receptive to psychoanalytic theory when she first came across it in the months before the First World War. Psychoanalytic theory addressed some of the same issues as spiritualism: psychic images— usually of family members—lie concealed in the unconscious like ghostly figures in another dimension, and, like a seance, an analysis calls them up. Freud himself, of course, was very interested in the occult and in spiritualism: indeed his work was first discussed in Britain in 1893 by the President of the British Psychical Society, Frederic Myers.[85] When in the mid-1920s Sinclair was regularly attending spiritualist sessions run by Catherine Dawson Scott, she summoned her brother Frank—dead in India in 1889—and was concerned that what she saw was simply a trick played by her own unconscious:

I was very anxious to get proof of [the spirits'] presence, something that cd.n't be explained away as yr. or my subconsciousness. So on Wednesday night I called to Frank & asked if he cd. show a light in my room in a place where it cd.n't come from the outside.

Nothing happened on Wednesday night but last night I'd no sooner called to Frank when a bright rod of light appeared, intensely pulsating, with a steady light below, in the very place I had asked for. It remained some time.

Then I asked him to take it away. This didn't happen all at once, but presently the light began to flicker & struggle, & when I bent forward to see if there were anything in the front window that was causing it, it went out suddenly.[86]

[84] Sinclair, 'Introduction' to *The Life of Charlotte Brontë*, p. xiii.

[85] See Ernest Jones, 'Reminiscent Notes on the Early History of Psycho-Analysis in English-Speaking Countries', *International Journal of Psycho-Analysis*, 26 (1945), 8–10: at 8.

[86] Sinclair to Catherine Dawson Scott, 9 Oct. 1925, Beinecke Rare Book and Manuscript Library, Gen. MSS 144, Box 1, fo. 22. Scott, an ardent spiritualist, refers to her 'sittings' with Sinclair in her account of the materialization of, among others, her own dead husband (see *From Four who are Dead*, London: Arrowsmith, 1926, 31). Sinclair wrote the introduction to the volume.

For the next five months Frank apparently continued to appear regularly, in various different guises, until in February 1926 Sinclair thought of an 'infallible test':

My brother was a gunner. I'm going to put a question about artillery wh. only a gunner could answer. A friend, a gunner, has given me a good one: What happens if a gun is fired at an angle of 45° when you increase yr. elevation? If I get the right answer I shall know it is really Frank, because it cd.n't be even in my subconsciousness. But if I don't get the right answer I'm afraid I shall conclude there's nothing in it.[87]

Tantalizingly, no evidence has survived of the ghost's answer. But the episode testifies to Sinclair's vivid sense of the links between the supernatural and the psychoanalytic worlds. In 1917 she described the unconscious as 'the haunted world below our waking consciousness'.[88]

The 'spooky stories' that she started to write in late 1910 thus paved the way for Sinclair's transition in 1913 into psychoanalytic ways of thinking about the psyche and the family. When her ghost stories were published as a collection in 1923, four years after the publication of Freud's 'The "Uncanny"', Sinclair chose for her volume the resonantly psychoanalytic title *Uncanny Stories*. 'The Intercessor' could be read as a description of the literal 'return of the repressed'. As Freud wrote in 1923, 'the character of the ego is a precipitate of abandoned object-cathexes and . . . it contains the history of those object-choices'.[89] Effy's sad story is an insistent reminder of the centrality of abandoned love-objects to the constitution of all families and all identities.

Boll tells us that May Sinclair probably originally became involved with the Medico-Psychological Clinic (or Brunswick Square Clinic, as it was later known) because of her friendship with Jessie Murray, a doctor who, like Sinclair, was active in the suffrage movement.[90] Ernest Jones, who came

---

[87] Sinclair to Scott, 28 Feb. 1926, Beinecke Rare Book and Manuscript Library, Gen. MSS 144, Box 1, fo. 22.

[88] Sinclair, *A Defence of Idealism* (New York: Macmillan, 1917), 8.

[89] Freud, *The Ego and the Id*, 1923, in *Standard Edition*, xix. 3–66: at 29. Freud first wrote about the ego forming through the introjection of lost objects in 'Mourning and Melancholia' (1917). See also Rebecca Kinnamon, *May Sinclair's Fiction of the Supernatural*, Ph.D. thesis (Duke University, 1974). Kinnamon notes that Sinclair's 'later tales are the result of her conscious efforts to propagate the discoveries of modern psychology' (127).

[90] See Boll, 'May Sinclair and the Medico-Psychological Clinic of London', *Proceedings of the American Philosophical Society*, 106 (Aug. 1962), 310–26: at 312. This article is the only substantial source on the clinic, and it is the source of most of the information in this section. I only cite sources other than Boll. Jessie Murray's publications include Murray and Henry Noel Brailsford, *The Treatment of Women's Deputations by the Police. Copy of Evidence collected by Dr Jessie Murray and Mr H. N. Brailsford, and forwarded to the Home Office by the Conciliation Committee for Women's Suffrage* (London: Woman's Press, 1911), and

across Freud's work in a 1903 review, had first used psychoanalytic methods in his practice in 1905, but the Brunswick Square Clinic was the first British institution devoted to psychotherapy, and explicitly committed to psycho-analytic methods.[91] Jessie Murray, along with her companion Julia Turner, Constance E. Long, Hector Munro, and a number of others started planning the clinic in 1913, and Sinclair was one of its founding members (she was later appointed to the Board of Management). In the early days the clinic was based in Murray's and Turner's shared house in Endsleigh St, and opened just three afternoons a week for, in the words of its first prospectus, the 'treatment by medical and psychological means of functional nervous dis-eases and of functional disorders accompanying organic diseases'.[92] The fee was 2s. 6d. a session (about the same amount that May Sinclair spent on bus fares in an average week). During these first months Sinclair's job was to search for suitable premises. When in July 1914 she managed to acquire the lease on 30 Brunswick Square, electrical and other equipment was installed so that psychotherapeutic treatment could be supplemented by 'Electric Baths' (to stimulate the muscles and general metabolism in cases of hyster-ical paralysis and neurasthenia), massage, relaxation, and—occasionally—drug treatments. By 1917 the clinic had built up a substantial clientele among shell-shocked soldiers, many of whom were housed in a residential unit next door to the main clinic, where they were offered psychotherapy, electrical and other treatments, and, in the words of a 1919 report, 'occupation-therapy' (one of the earliest uses of the term): 'handicrafts, the plastic arts, music, recitation, dancing, games, gardening'.[93] The clinic advertised itself as a 'centre for treatment for those who ought not to be dependent on the charity of our Hospitals, and who are, nevertheless, unable to pay the fees usually charged for private treatments of the necessary kind', noting:

It is almost a national disgrace that there should not yet be in England a centre for the organised use and further trial of the many methods already at the command of Psychotherapy. All of these are being more and more extensively used in England,

'Introduction' in Marie Carmichael Stopes, *Married Love: A New Contribution to the Solution of Sex Difficul-ties* (London: Putnam, 1918). Although the majority of people associated with the clinic had a medical back-ground, one student, Ella Freeman Sharpe, who later became a well-known Freudian analyst, originally trained as a teacher of English. See Ella Freeman Sharpe, *Collected Papers on Psycho-Analysis*, ed. Marjorie Brierley, introd. Ernest Jones (1950; repr. New York: Brunner/Mazel, 1978), p. v. Dean Rapp notes that 'the literary community was amongst the most receptive groups in the elite to psychoanalysis' ('The Early Discovery of Freud by the British General Educated Public, 1912–1919', *Journal of the Society for the Social History of Medicine*, 3, Aug. 1990, 217–43: at 222).

[91] Jones, 'Reminiscent Notes', 9.

[92] 'Proof' Prospectus, 1914, quoted in Boll, 'May Sinclair and the Medico-Psychological Clinic of London', 314.

[93] 'The Medico-Psychological Clinic Report', quoted ibid. 318.

but the high fees which are necessarily charged for private treatment put them out of the reach of people of small means, a class particularly liable to break down nervously and mentally owing to economic pressure. Here is a crying need. The Medico-Psychological Clinic hopes not only to meet this need, but to do more.[94]

After the outbreak of war medical staff donated their services for free, and the clinic relied—not very successfully—on fees and private contributions to pay the rent and cover its maintenance costs. Sinclair, in spite of her lawyer's misgivings, donated the very substantial sum of £500 in early 1914, before the clinic had even opened.[95] In 1916 she was for a while the sole contributor—to the tune of £30—to 'a Fund for Nerve-Shocked Soldiers to pay their 2/6 fees for treatment at the Medico-Psychological Clinic (we've been so successful with civilians)'.[96]

It is difficult now to be sure what kind of psychotherapeutic treatment these early patients—mostly soldiers—were receiving. At first Julia Turner handled most of the analyses, with some assistance from Jessie Murray. Portions of Freud's work had been appearing in translation in Britain from 1909 onwards, and in 1911 David Eder presented the first paper on psychoanalytic treatment in England to the Neurological Section of the British Medical Association (they all walked out).[97] But in 1913 the range of psychoanalytic texts that was available in English was still severely limited. Murray's and Turner's practice seems to have been an eclectic blend of French, Swiss, American, and Viennese methods: in the words of a 1917 circular, the clinic offered 'the various forms of mental analysis, and re-synthesis which are known as *Psychological Analysis* (Janet, Morton Prince, &c.), *Psycho-Analysis* (Freud and Jung, &c.), and as *Therapeutic Conversation and Persuasion* (Dejerine, Dubois, &c.), *Re-Education and Suggestion* in the hypnoidal and hypnotic states'.[98] Neither Murray nor Turner had ever undergone analysis

---

[94] Medico-Psychological Clinic, 'Special Appeal in Time of War', 8 Oct. 1917, quoted ibid. 317.

[95] Robert Singleton Garnett, son of Richard Garnett, erstwhile director of the British Museum Reading Room, brother of critic and publisher Edward Garnett, and a personal friend of Sinclair's, wrote to her on 27 Jan. 1914 expressing his concern: he asked whether the clinic had an insurance policy for its employees, and added: 'I scarcely follow why your £500 has been put down at so early a stage. What is it wanted for and where is it? Was it wanted for "preliminary expenses"? . . . After the [inaugural] Meeting has taken place & the business has taken more shape, I should be pleased to see you—I think you should know more of the liabilities of Directors before you go much further' (UP, Box 1, fo. 29).

[96] Sinclair to Marie Belloc Lowndes, 11 Mar. 1916, HR, MS (Lowndes MAB) Recip.

[97] See Jones, 'Reminiscent Notes', 10.

[98] 'Special Appeal in Time of War', quoted in Boll, 'May Sinclair and the Medico-Psychological Clinic of London', 317. Accents are omitted in the original. 'Rational psychotherapy' is described in Paul Dubois, *The Psychic Treatment of Nervous Disorders: The Psychoneuroses and their Moral Treatment*, trans. and ed. Smith Ely Jelliffe and William A. White (1905; 6th edn. New York: Funk and Wagnalls, 1909), 223 ff. Dubois's practice combined Weir-Mitchell's rest-cure (isolation, inaction, and overfeeding) with '*the education of the will*, or, more exactly, *of the reason*' (35). Dubois was Professor of Neuropathology at the

themselves, or been formally trained (although Murray did attend lectures by Pierre Janet), and the two women seem to have evolved their own exuberant, idiosyncratic, even (given Murray's allegiance to the suffrage movement) feminist strategies. They emphasized the curative role played by conscious efforts of will and, long before Melanie Klein came to Britain, they stressed the part played by anxiety, rather than sexuality, in the development of mental disorders.

It was not long before the staff of the clinic realized that in order to treat all the patients who sought their help, they needed more psychoanalysts. When July 1915 Jessie Murray established a formal training programme for young students of psychotherapy it was Sinclair who coined the term 'orthopsychics' which later appeared in the organization's title, the Society for the Study of Orthopsychics.[99] Students at the Society took a three-year course, which included undergoing a training analysis, attending lectures on subjects such as biology, general and experimental psychology, and comparative religion, writing a thesis, and starting supervised work with patients. Of the 30 students who trained at the Society for the Study of Orthopsychics, 24 were women. The clinic was thus an important centre for those who wished to train as analysts but were not medically qualified.

The Medico-Psychological Clinic, with its variety of therapeutic models, was relatively quickly superseded. It was in the year of its foundation, 1913, that committed Freudian Ernest Jones set up the London Psycho-Analytic Society, the institution which would eventually replace the Medico-Psychological Clinic after the death of Jessie Murray in 1920.[100] Initially the two societies developed side by side. The Medico-Psychological Clinic followed Murray's lead in its commitment to the training of lay analysts, in the varied nature of its therapeutic methods, and in its belief in physical treatments. The London Psycho-Analytic Society, on the other hand, dedicated itself much more specifically to the promotion and discussion of Freudian psychoanalysis. When in 1921 James Glover, one of the analysts at the clinic, returned to London after his analysis with Karl Abraham in Berlin, the clinic, in severe financial difficulties, had already reduced the scale of its operations. Jessie Murray had died young of cancer in 1920. Glover, now an ardent convert to formal psychoanalysis, insisted that the residential unit,

University of Berne. Déjerine, who worked with Charcot at the Salpêtrière hospital in Paris, attempted the 'building up and the redirecting of the personality': the physician's role 'is that of a lay confessor, or a moral director'. See J. Déjerine and E. Gauckler, *The Psychoneuroses and their Treatment by Psychotherapy*, trans. Smith Ely Jelliffe (1913; 2nd edn. Philadelphia and London: J. P. Lippincott, 1915), 299, 302.

[99] Boll, 'May Sinclair and the Medico-Psychological Clinic', 316.
[100] Vincent Brome, *Ernest Jones: Freud's Alter Ego* (New York: Norton, 1983), 105.

with its gardening parties and its dancing evenings, be closed down, and he proposed that what remained of the clinic should affiliate with the British Psycho-Analytical Society. But Julia Turner, loyal to Murray's memory, and determined not to compromise the more relaxed and eclectic practices by which she had set such store, refused to cooperate. The rift between Glover and Turner gradually destroyed both the clinic and the society. The Brunswick Square premises closed in 1922 and the clinic was formally liquidated in 1923. For a while Glover (later joined by his brother Edward) and Turner stubbornly continued to run separate training programmes based in their own homes, but soon even those fizzled out. The Glovers—now members of the British Psycho-Analytical Society—and Ernest Jones were shortly embroiled in a fight with the British medical establishment to defend the legitimacy of psychoanalytic treatment, and the ad hoc nature of the institution where so many of their associates had received their initial training would not have helped their cause. Nor, one suspects, would the dominance in the early movement of so many outspoken, intellectual— even, in the case of Murray and Turner, possibly lesbian—women. So the clinic was quietly repressed from psychoanalytic histories and from analysts' autobiographies. Boll notes that there are no references to it in any medical register or directory of public clinics, and neither Ernest Jones nor his biographer Vincent Brome mention it in their accounts of the early days of the BPAS.[101] However, almost all the best-known names in early British psychoanalysis—James Glover, Ella Freeman Sharpe, Mary Chadwick, Marjorie Brierley, Nina Searl, Sylvia Payne, and Susan Isaacs—trained there, and received their first analysis from Julia Turner.

The openness of analysts such as Jessie Murray and Julia Turner to eclectic and informal methods encouraged Sinclair to develop her own idiosyncratic versions of classic Freudian and Jungian formulations like repression and sublimation.[102] The flexibility which characterized the practice of the Medico-Psychological Clinic was crucial to someone like Sinclair who— always sceptical even when she was at her most fascinated—was reluctant simply to adopt psychoanalytic ideas without revising them to suit her own philosophy. Although Sinclair herself was never analysed and was involved with the clinic in a purely administrative role, she was intellectually as well

[101] Boll, 'May Sinclair and the Medico-Psychological Clinic', 311; Ernest Jones, *Free Associations: Memories of a Psycho-Analyst* (New York: Basic Books, 1959); Brome, *Ernest Jones*, 120.

[102] Zegger notes that 'Sinclair's use of psychoanalytic ideas does not follow any literal textbook pattern' (*May Sinclair*, 71). Julia Turner was the author of *The Psychology of Self-Consciousness* (1923), *The Dream on the Anxiety Hypothesis* (1923), and *Human Psychology as Seen through the Dream* (1924), all published in London by Kegan Paul, Trench, Trübner and Co. *The Psychology of Self-Consciousness* was reviewed by Turner's former patient and trainee, Ella Sharpe, in *International Journal of Psycho-Analysis*, 6 (1925), 78–9.

as practically committed to it, and her writing from 1913 onwards shows her engaging in her own form of psychoanalytic thinking.[103] Indeed, psychoanalytic concepts saturated her thinking to such an extent that she would eventually be described by Katherine Mansfield as an example of a writer whose work had suffered 'the eclipse of psychoanalysis'.[104]

The first novel in which Sinclair experimented with psychoanalytic models of the family and of identity was *The Three Sisters* (1914).[105] Although the parallels with the Brontë family are slim (the story concerns the three daughters of a parson in North Yorkshire), the title is an obvious reference to *The Three Brontës*, published two years earlier and reissued in a second edition alongside *The Three Sisters* in 1914.[106] In the novel Sinclair, perhaps influenced by Breuer's contention that 'sexuality [is] one of the major components of hysteria', makes it clear that celibacy is not invariably a good thing, especially for women who, unlike Emily Brontë and Jane Holland, are not 'geniuses'.[107] Unsatisfied sexual appetites, Sinclair suggests, can make such lesser beings ill, induce them to lie to and betray their loved ones, and encourage them to manipulate men into a state of dulled dependency. The novel is thus to some extent a revisiting of the issues Sinclair explored in *The Creators*. She had of course already considered the possibility that sexual abstinence might be spiritually and emotionally unhealthy: in *The Helpmate* (1907) Anne and Walter Majendie's child dies because of her mother's refusal to allow her husband into her bed. But in *The Three Sisters* Sinclair's new psychoanalytic enthusiasms are evident in the fact that she now sees sexual frustration as a medical and a psychic, rather than a spiritual and a social, problem. She told novelist Marie Belloc Lowndes that when 'a passionate desire for love . . . is thwarted, a morbid physical condition is set up. Unhappiness is a direct cause of a well-known fearfully common uterine disorder, wh. frequently incapacitates women from bearing children.'[108]

---

[103] Occultist Dion Fortune, who worked at the clinic for a while, wrote that May Sinclair 'attended the lectures there, and then wrote her psychological novels; but she did not see the routine work of the treatment rooms, nor the records of the follow-up file' (Dion Fortune, typescript, '*THE WINGED BULL*': *A Study in Esoteric Psychology*, 217). I am grateful to Simon Buxton for this reference.

[104] Katherine Mansfield, 'Ask No Questions' [review of Sinclair's *The Romantic*], *Athenaeum*, no. 4721 (22 Oct. 1920); repr. in *Novels and Novelists*, ed. John Middleton Murry (London: Constable, 1930), 274–9: at 274.

[105] The novel on which Sinclair was working as she became involved with the clinic was *The Combined Maze* (1913), a naturalistic novel in the manner of H. G. Wells about the difficult and sordid marriage of a poverty-stricken and debt-encumbered clerk. I discuss this novel in more detail in Ch. 6, below.

[106] Boll claims that '*The Three Sisters* bears no sign of imitating a single trait of the Brontës. . . . The closest borrowing from Brontëan actuality is the Reverend' (*Miss May Sinclair*, 226).

[107] Josef Breuer, 'Theoretical', in id. and Freud, *Studies on Hysteria*, in Freud, *Standard Edition*, ii. 244.

[108] Sinclair to Marie Belloc Lowndes, 20 July 1912, HR, MS (Lowndes MAB) Recip.

Psychoanalysis seems almost to have brought her round to Sir Almroth Wright's point of view.

The Three Sisters, like D. H. Lawrence's *The Rainbow* (1915) and *Women in Love* (USA 1920, UK 1921), recalls the popular family sagas of writers such as John Galsworthy in the novels of *The Forsyte Saga* (published 1906 onwards) and Arnold Bennett in the Clayhanger series (1910–18). Lawrence and Sinclair, however, both concentrated on groups of siblings and used stories of their parallel sexual developments to comment on the adverse effects of sexual repression and family life. Lawrence had originally intended to call *Women in Love*, *The Sisters*, but, as he wrote to Catherine Carswell in 1916: 'May Sinclair having had *Three Sisters* it won't do'.[109] Sinclair recognized that Lawrence and she shared the belief that sex was mystic and redemptive, and was outraged by the suppression of *The Rainbow* in 1915.[110]

The Three Sisters tells the story of Gwenda, Mary, and Alice, who are all in love with the village doctor, Steven. Each sister has a different strategy for attracting his attention: Mary plans to be 'kind and sweet and womanly'; Gwenda is conscious—and immediately ashamed—of wanting to walk out on the moors so that Steven will see her as a 'wild, strong girl'; and Alice thinks: 'I will make myself . . . [s]o ill that they'll *have* to send for him' (TS, 10). Alice does indeed become ill, refusing to drink her milk—the symbolic residue of her dead mother and absent stepmother—until she develops cardiac arrhythmia. Steven sees her reluctance to eat as a symptom not a cause, telling Gwenda: 'She's been starving herself because she's ill. It's a symptom. The trouble is not that she starves herself—but that she's been starved' (TS, 77). Later, when Alice's father maliciously tells Alice that Steven has been seen with Gwenda, Alice becomes ill in earnest, and once again Steven diagnoses her illness as the result of sexual and emotional deprivation: 'she'd be all right—perfectly all right—if she was married' (TS, 181). Alice's illness is hysterical and it turns out that it is not Steven himself, but sexual pleasure, that she craves: sex and then marriage and children with local farmer Jim Greatorex quickly put her right.

Sinclair's account of Alice's illness and cure deviates significantly from the classic Freudian position. Indeed in 1910 Freud explicitly warned analysts against the kind of literalizing analysis Sinclair (and Steven) so

---

[109] D. H. Lawrence to Catherine Carswell, 10 Aug. 1916, *The Letters of D. H. Lawrence*, ed. Aldous Huxley (New York: Heinemann, 1932), 364.

[110] Sinclair wrote in response to an enquiry in 1924: 'I did write something in defence of Mr. D. H. Lawrence's "Rainbow". I said that the suppression of this book was a crime, the murder of a beautiful thing. But I don't know where or when it appeared, if it appeared at all. I rather think I wrote it in a letter' (Sinclair to Professor McDonald, 7 Oct. 1924, HR, MS (McDonald, ED) Recip).

confidently offer in *The Three Sisters*. He was critical of an analyst who told a divorced female patient suffering from anxiety-states that 'she could not tolerate the loss of intercourse with her husband, and so there were only three ways by which she could recover her health—she must either return to her husband, or take a lover, or obtain satisfaction from herself'.[111] Freud warned that the physician's exclusive emphasis on 'the somatic factor in sexuality' oversimplified the case: 'we reckon as belonging to "sexual life" all the activities of the tender feelings which have primitive sexual impulses as their source . . . For this reason we prefer to speak of *psychosexuality*, thus laying stress on the point that the mental factor in sexual life should not be overlooked or underestimated.'[112] Sinclair's stress in *The Three Sisters* on Alice's physical release (she easily switches her affections from Steven to Jim) aligns her with the 'wild' analyst who understands sexual deprivation to be a purely physiological frustration. In some ways, then, Sinclair's understanding of psychoanalytic concepts was oversimplified. She was—however unintentionally—a popularizer of a fairly crude version of Freudian thought.

Yet in other ways—ways that even Freudian psychoanalysis had not yet anticipated—her understanding of the kind of sexual displacements that take place between parents and their adult children was remarkably subtle and original. Alice's father is a repressed and lascivious man who is partially responsible for the deaths of his first two wives: 'He was told that Mother would die or go mad if she had another baby. And he let her have Ally'; 'Frances . . . died of that obscure internal trouble which he had so wisely and patiently ignored' (TS, 28, 20). His third wife leaves him because she is afraid of him, and after her departure his frustration at being unable to remarry saturates the house. Although he is largely 'unconscious of his real thoughts, his real motives, his real likings and dislikings', he has an instinctive understanding of Alice's plight, since it is so close to his own: 'something in him, obscurely but intimately associated with Robina [his third wife], responded to that sensual and infernal tremor' of Alice's piano music (TS, 21–2). When Alice starves herself the vicar knows exactly what is going on, telling Gwenda: ' "Do you suppose I don't know what's the matter with her?" . . . the stiff, straight moustache that guarded his mouth lifted, showing the sensual redness and fulness of the lips' (TS, 78).

Alice plays out her father's own repressed desires as part of her role in an Oedipal triangle in which she is identified with the wife he has lost. When he interrupts her gazing dreamily at herself in the mirror in his bedroom, his

---

[111] Freud, ' "Wild" Psychoanalysis' (1910), in *Standard Edition*, xi. 221–7: at 221.   [112] Ibid. 222–3.

face is reflected in the hand-mirror that belonged to Alice's mother: 'the look on her father's face was awful because it was mysterious. Neither she nor her instinct had a word for it. There was cruelty in it, and, besides cruelty, some quality nameless and unrecognisable, subtle and secret, and yet crude somehow and vivid'. Alice drops and shatters the mirror and the look disappears, passing 'out of his face as if a hand had smoothed it' (TS, 89), as though his desire can overcome its repression only through her narcissism. When he fiercely opposes Alice's marriage to Greatorex—even though she is pregnant and the couple are in love—Gwenda, the only character who is not at the mercy of her own unconscious, challenges him to untangle his own motivations from Alice's, saying: 'No man ought to say that of his own daughter. How does he know what's her own and what's his?' (TS, 285).[113] The strain of the argument is so great that the vicar has a stroke and finally secures his ownership of at least one of his daughters, Gwenda, who has no choice but to renounce marriage and take care of him.

As Jane Eldridge Miller points out, *The Three Sisters* was in many ways a transitional text for Sinclair.[114] Where she had explicitly planned *The Creators* as a lengthy novel, and resented editorial pressure to cut, *The Three Sisters* is much briefer. She told Hugh Walpole in January 1913 that his novel *Fortitude* was too long: 'I wish you cd. have kept it a bit tighter & cleaner, but that's merely personal taste & you know the particular little craze I've on just now', and she explained to Duneka, editor of *Harper's*, that 'a perfect craze for elimination is on me at present'.[115] Psychoanalytic theories such as Freudian dream interpretation taught her that single images could resonate throughout a narrative and convey much more than was apparent at first glance. *The Three Sisters* concentrates much more than her earlier work on the inner life, perhaps as a result of her long meditation on the Brontë sisters, with their 'inner life, tumultuous and profound in suffering' (TB, 192). The novel paves the way for her later psychological texts such as *Mary Olivier: A Life* (1919) and *Life and Death of Harriett Frean* (1922). But its forward-looking promise was eclipsed somewhat by the outbreak of war two months before its publication in October 1914. Reviews were favourable but readers'—and reviewers'—attention was somewhat distracted, and no one commented specifically on the alteration in her style, although all praised the

[113] Zegger points out that the novel attempts to distinguish between the 'subconscious drives and ill-understood motives' of both Mary and Alice (who later displaces her fear of her husband onto her father), and the rational self-discipline of Gwenda (*May Sinclair*, 69–70).

[114] Miller, *Rebel Women*, 194–5, 198–202.

[115] Sinclair to Hugh Walpole, 28 Jan. 1913, HR, MS (Walpole, H) Recip; Sinclair to Duneka, 21 Mar. 1913, HR, MS (Sinclair, M) Letters. Walpole (1884–1941) was a literary journalist and novelist, and *Fortitude* (1913) was his first popular success.

writing.[116] But by the time *The Three Sisters* appeared, May Sinclair herself had other preoccupations. When England joined the Great War in August 1914, and Hector Munro at the Medico-Psychological Clinic solicited Sinclair's help in assembling an ambulance unit and taking it to Belgium, Sinclair lost interest in everything else. By the time *The Three Sisters* appeared she had already spent several weeks at the front.

[116] See e.g. 'Fiction for November', *New York Times Book Review*, 19 (8 Nov. 1914), 485–6, which likened the novel to Greek tragedy and *Wuthering Heights*; '*The Three Sisters*', *Athenaeum*, no. 4539 (24 Oct. 1914), 424, which commented on Sinclair's 'notable gift for psychological analysis'; Frederic Taber Cooper, 'Some Novels of the Month', *Bookman* (New York), 40 (Jan. 1915), 552–7, who called it a 'sympathetic and probing study of feminine psychology' (557). Where reviews were critical, it was of the novel's morbid sensibility and emphasis on sexual feeling (see '*The Three Sisters*', *Saturday Review*, 99, 2 Jan. 1915, 18; 'Fiction', *Spectator*, 113, 12 Dec. 1914, 854).

1908–1918

5

War

=

THE OUTBREAK of war in August 1914 radically changed May Sinclair's sense of priorities. Although she continued with her customary activities—writing, working for the Medico-Psychological Clinic, going back and forth between London and her little house in Yorkshire—she felt that the war had irreparably altered both her own consciousness and the world in which she lived. She told Gilbert Murray, Regius Professor of Greek at Oxford, that she would never write a book like *The Three Sisters* again: 'The War will leave none of us as it found us.'[1] It quickly came to represent to her—as to so many others—the possibility of a new and more vivid life, one in which the usual conventions were suspended, and one which gave opportunity for close contact with men in vulnerable states.[2] Sinclair had stood on the sidelines of emotional and sexual dramas like the Ford Madox Hueffer/Violet Hunt scandal, she had participated in raising children only obliquely as an aunt, but she was determined that this time events would not pass her by.[3] On 25 September 1914 she went out to the front in Belgium with an ambulance

---

[1] Sinclair to Gilbert Murray, 29 Oct. 1914, Bodleian Library, Oxford, MS Gilbert Murray 25, fos. 126–7.

[2] Robert Wohl notes that there was a widespread feeling 'among young men of [Rupert] Brooke's class and education . . . of exhilaration and "being gathered up" ' (*The Generation of 1914*, Cambridge, Mass.: Harvard University Press, 1979, 92).

[3] Sinclair was a staunch supporter of Violet Hunt and Ford Madox Hueffer (later Ford) when in Feb. 1913 an English court ruled that the two were not legally married, and that Violet therefore could not use the name 'Violet Hueffer'. Violet, who appears to have gone through a form of marriage ceremony in Germany and to have believed herself to be Hueffer's wife, was in despair, and news of the court ruling was splashed all over the English papers. Sinclair wrote to Hueffer: 'If it's a question of "volcanoes", I'd rather take a bungalow on the edge of yours, than row for five minutes in the same boat with Mrs. Elsie Hueffer [Hueffer's first wife, who brought the suit against Hunt]. I'm sick of the world we live in, with its cowardice & hypocrisy, & abominable, poisonous, sham morality' (Sinclair to Hueffer, n.d. [1913], HA). But she also counselled Violet, on behalf of the Women Writers' Committee (which included Marie Belloc Lowndes, Evelyn Sharp, and novelist Mrs W. K. Clifford), to stay in France until the scandal had blown over (Sinclair to Hunt, 10 May 1913, HA). Hunt and Hueffer ignored her advice and returned home in June. See Joan Hardwick, *An Immodest Violet: The Life of Violet Hunt* (London: André Deutsch, 1990), 111–22.

unit. Two and a half weeks later she was ordered to go back to England, ostensibly to collect more funds, and then was told that the unit had no further use for her. Her disappointment and humiliation at being once again pushed aside—just as she had been during childhood football games with her brothers—was sharp and deeply felt. She dealt with it by writing repeatedly about the war in the years that followed, publishing an account of her weeks in Belgium in *A Journal of Impressions in Belgium* (1915), as well as no fewer than six novels which are either set at the front or prominently feature the war in their narratives.[4] Her brief time in action gave her access, for the first time in her life, to a world of violence in which lives were at stake and in which men and women mingled with a new sense of freedom. 'Personally,' she wrote to Arthur Adcock on 28 February 1915, 'I feel as if I had never lived, with any intensity, before I went out to [the war] in the autumn.'[5]

An eagerness to go out to the war as a way of escaping the boredom and monotony of bourgeois life was common among educated young men in 1914. Rupert Brooke's feeling that it offered him and his peers a chance to turn 'as swimmers into cleanness leaping, glad from a world grown old and cold and weary' was echoed by many of his contemporaries.[6] But Sinclair's expression of the same enthusiasm was unusual because she was at least twice Rupert Brooke's age, and a woman. Ironically, her experiences in Belgium served only to reinforce her sense of herself as superfluous and anachronistic—a hangover from the Victorian age. She told Katharine Tynan Hinkson that she was delighted with Hinkson's description of her in her autobiography as a swift runner: 'It was because they thought I cd.n't run that the two bravest women in our Field Ambulance Corps refused to let me go with them on an expedition to a battle-field that I'd set my heart on— The hardest luck I'd ever had! If only I were thirty or even twenty years younger I sd. be in Belgium now.'[7] In her fiction and non-fiction the war figures both as a climactic and mystical experience of personal autonomy, and as a crucial development of the modern world from which she was prematurely and unjustly excluded.

---

[4] *A Journal of Impressions in Belgium* was first published in three instalments in the *English Review* in May, June, and July 1915. The 'Day Book' in which Sinclair made notes while she was actually in Belgium, and which she used as the basis for the *Journal*, is in UP, along with a holograph draft of the *Journal* itself (Box 21, fos. 388–98). Her war novels are *Tasker Jevons* (1916, published in the USA as *The Belfry*), *The Tree of Heaven* (1917), *The Romantic* (1920), *Anne Severn and the Fieldings* (1922), *The Rector of Wyck* (1925), and *Far End* (1926).

[5] Sinclair to Adcock, 28 Feb. 1915, UP, Box 1, fo. 1.   [6] Cited in Wohl, *Generation of 1914*, 89.

[7] Sinclair to Katharine Hinkson, 9 Nov. 1917, JR. Hinkson wrote in her 1916 autobiography: '[Sinclair] used to run races on Hampstead Heath with a small boy, outstripping him, for she was swift as Atlanta' (Tynan, *Middle Years*, 292).

British women, always a multiple and contradictory constituency, as Sinclair knew, disagreed over the war from the start.[8] The suffrage movement, whose militancy in the years immediately preceding the war had, some said, paved the way for public acceptance of a far more destructive project of national violence, definitively split over the issue of whether or not to support the war efforts of a government which had failed to support its demand for a women's vote.[9] Women could not enlist as soldiers, but they could train as nurses or VADs and get out to the war that way. Those who stayed at home often found themselves doing the jobs of the men who had left for the continent. Still others attempted to continue their pre-war lives with as little change as possible. Sandra Gilbert has suggested that women were liberated by the widespread absence of men from their domestic and working lives, although she does point out that as well as their 'sexual glee' women felt intense anxiety and guilt at having got what they wanted at so many men's expense.[10] But despite the government's efforts to recast the roles of mother, wife, and indeed of 'woman' in the mould of war, women remained confused and fiercely divided.[11] Almost all Sinclair's war novels focus either on women's experience or on men's observation of women's behaviour during the war. For Sinclair, as for her country, the definition of the object 'war' entailed the redefinition of the category 'woman'. This in turn demanded a renewed labour of self-definition, as her sense of her own sexual and spiritual identity was newly inflected by the changes she perceived around her and within herself.

From the first days Sinclair was outspoken in her support for the war. On

[8] Sinclair wrote in an untitled, unpublished typescript fragment on women's suffrage: 'Woman, as [the anti-suffragists] have conceived her, does not exist. . . . there is not and never will be any Woman's Vote. After all, that formidable, preponderating multitude of British females is made up of individuals who, for all political purposes, are individuals first and women afterwards. So far are they from thinking, feeling, or acting alike that their probable behaviour under enfranchisement is far more difficult to predict them [*sic*] was that of the Working Man before the Reform Bill' (6, 7, UP, Box 24, fo. 452).

[9] See Gillian Beer's analysis of pacifist Vernon Lee's resistance to suffragette militancy on exactly these grounds, in 'The Dissidence of Vernon Lee: *Satan the Waster* and the Will to Believe', in Suzanne Raitt and Trudi Tate (eds.), *Women's Fiction and the Great War* (Oxford: Clarendon Press, 1997), 107–31: at 113. The Pankhursts, leaders of the suffrage movement, split over the issue of support for the war. Emmeline and Christabel Pankhurst instructed suffragettes to abandon their protests and threw all their weight behind the war effort; Sylvia Pankhurst, on the other hand, became active in the pacifist movement and continued her work with working-class communities in the East End of London. See Holton, *Suffrage Days: Stories from the Women's Suffrage Movement*, 209–26.

[10] Sandra Gilbert and Susan Gubar, *No Man's Land: The Place of the Woman Writer in the Twentieth Century*, ii. *Sexchanges* (New Haven: Yale University Press, 1989), 264.

[11] See e.g. the 'Little Mother's' letter, 'A Mother's Answer to "A Common Soldier" ', which was widely circulated for propaganda purposes, and reprod. in Robert Graves, *Goodbye to All That* (1929; repr. New York: Anchor, 1985), 228–30, and A. E. Foringer's poster, *The Greatest Mother in the World*, repr. in Claire M. Tylee, *The Great War and Women's Consciousness: Images of Militarism and Womanhood in Women's Writings, 1914–1964* (London: Macmillan, 1990), pl. 6.

18 September 1914 twenty-five writers signed an 'Authors' Declaration' in *The Times*, stating that 'Great Britain could not without dishonour have refused to take part in the present war.'[12] Among the twenty-five were four women, May Sinclair, Jane Ellen Harrison, Flora Annie Steel, and Mary (Mrs Humphry) Ward. At this stage Sinclair, like many others, saw the war as a form of moral and emotional cleansing, not just in terms of Britain's foreign policy but also in terms of social and cultural life within the nation's boundaries.[13] In an unpublished paper called 'Influence of the War on "Life and Literature" ', she wrote:

For there is no doubt that these [emotional] values were precisely what we were beginning to lose in 'life and literature', along with Religion, that is to say with our hold on Reality, before the War. Most of us—with the exception of one or two poets—were ceasing to live with any intensity, to believe with any conviction incompatible with comfort, and to feel with any strength and sincerity. Yet we were all quite sincerely 'out for' reality without recognising it when we saw it and without any suspicion of its spiritual nature.

And Reality—naked, shining, intense Reality—more and not less of it, is, I believe, what we are going to get after the War.[14]

This feeling of explosive and cathartic change was summed up in an article Sinclair contributed to the magazine *Woman at Home* in February 1915. The war, she wrote, 'came to us when we needed it most, as an opportune postponement if not the end of our internal dissensions—the struggle between Unionists and Nationalists, between Capital and Labour, between the Suffragettes and the Government, between Man and Woman'.[15] In casting the coming of the war this way, she summarily dismisses all the radical confrontations of the pre-war period: the struggle for Home Rule in Ireland, the birth of the Labour party, and the fight for women's suffrage. In Sinclair's work the war is divorced from wider contexts. Even after reading all of her war fiction, the reader barely knows who was fighting who, and certainly is never given any analysis of why, or to what end. In order to think of war as she did, as an opportunity for intense, authentic *personal* experience, it was necessary that she should refuse to consider its significance as a political event. Sinclair, usually so sceptical and resistant, was oddly uncritical of the politics that led up to and framed the conflict. She simply wanted to be part of it.

---

[12]   See Samuel Hynes, *A War Imagined: The First World War and English Culture* (London: Bodley Head, 1990), 27.

[13]   See ibid. 13, for a discussion of Edmund Gosse's similar response to the outbreak of war.

[14]   Sinclair, 'Influence of the War on "Life and Literature" ', unpublished typescript, 2, UP, Box 25, fo. 481.

[15]   Sinclair, 'Women's Sacrifices for the War', *Woman at Home*, no. 67 (Feb. 1915), 7–11: at 11.

At first Sinclair was unsure about going out to the war. Within days of England's declaration of war on Germany on 4 August, Hector Munro, one of the directors of the Medico-Psychological Clinic, decided to equip an ambulance unit for service at the front, and while he was in Belgium scouting things out Sinclair was put in charge of organizing financial support for the venture. She wrote to Marie Belloc Lowndes asking her to use her influence in getting Munro's appeal for funds printed in the national press:

We've got together an <u>Ambulance Motor</u> Corps, equipped, with five men & five women, to go over where they're wanted most, & do whatever is most wanted. We've done it all by our private subscriptions & efforts, but we shall have to make <u>some</u> appeal for more money to take over.

The Times has printed letters from people about whether you sd. wear mourning for heroes or not, it has allowed every noodle in the country to air his or her views, but it found no room for a sane & practical suggestion of mine as to the care of our <u>recruits</u>. . . . <u>Can</u> you help us?[16]

Sinclair did not, at this stage, know that she herself was to be one of the party. According to her published journal of her experiences in Belgium, Munro challenged her to accompany him not long before the unit was due to leave:

I remember . . . the Sunday evening when the Commandant [Munro] dropped in, after he had come back from Belgium. We were stirring soup over the gas stove in the scullery—you couldn't imagine a more peaceful scene—when he said, 'They are bringing up the heavy siege guns from Namur, and there is going to be a terrific bombardment of Antwerp, and I think it will be very interesting for you to see it.' I remember replying with passionate sincerity that I would rather die than see it; that if I could nurse the wounded I would face any bombardment you please to name; but to go and look on and make copy out of the sufferings I cannot help—I couldn't and I wouldn't, and that was flat. And I wasn't a journalist any more than I was a trained nurse.

I can still see the form of the Commandant rising up on the other side of the scullery stove, and in his pained, uncomprehending gaze and in the words he utters I imagine a challenge. It is as if he said, 'Of course, if you're *afraid*'—(haven't I told him that I *am* afraid?).

The gage is thrown down on the scullery floor. I pick it up. And that is why I am here on this singular adventure. (JI, 14–15)[17]

[16] Sinclair to Marie Belloc Lowndes, 17 Sept. 1914, HR, MS (Lowndes, MAB) Recip.

[17] Britain joined the war in Aug. 1914 as a protest against German violation of Belgian neutrality. Namur in western Belgium fell on 23 Aug. When Sinclair went out to Belgium in late Sept. 1914 the Germans were already in control of most of south-eastern Belgium and were pushing west and north. The Germans began a heavy bombardment of Antwerp, where many of the Belgian troops had retreated, on 28 Sept. and it fell on 10 Oct. The Munro Ambulance Corps arrived in Ghent on 26 Sept., visited Antwerp briefly on 4 Oct., and withdrew from Ghent early on 12 Oct., just ahead of the German advance. Sinclair left Belgium on 13 Oct.

After her initial resistance, Sinclair appears to have given in without much of a struggle. She was already preoccupied with the war, giving half of all her wartime earnings to the war effort, and dreaming nightly of 'an interminable spectacle of horrors: trunks without heads, heads without trunks, limbs tangled in intestines' (JI, 7).[18] She wrote to Charlotte Mew in August 1916: 'I can't imagine anything more awful than . . . the state of mind that doesn't believe [in the war], & that can imagine that anything that's been thought & written (within the last twenty years, anyhow) more important than the winning of the War!'[19] She was poised to subordinate even her writing to the war effort. In spite of her fear of violence and her worry that she could make no useful contribution, a part of her clearly also saw the war as her last chance for adventure. Joining Munro's corps was Sinclair's only hope of seeing any action. Already 51, she was too old to train as a VAD or with the Red Cross. She had no experience of war and little experience of nursing, other than with her brothers, whose gradual weakening from heart failure hardly prepared her for the kind of mutilations she might see on the Belgian front. Yet on 25 September 1914 she found herself on the boat to Belgium.

The Munro Ambulance Corps was remarkable for many things, apart from numbering among its members an apparently useless middle-aged woman. Its Commandant, Hector Munro, like many others who wished to put together ambulance and other units, had to jump through many hoops to get the Corps out to Belgium in the first place. Women in particular were viewed with suspicion: Mrs St Clair Stobart, who had founded the Women's Convoy Corps in 1907, was not sent out to the Balkan war in 1912 because the British Red Cross refused to accept any women, even those who were already trained, as Mrs St Clair Stobart's were, along Royal Army Medical Corps lines.[20] At the beginning of the 1914–18 war, the British War Office was still very resistant to the idea of women in the battle zone. It refused to authorize either the Scottish Women's Hospital Units, founded by Elsie Inglis in 1914, or Flora Murray and Louisa Garrett Anderson's Women's Hospital Corps, which went to Paris in September 1914 under the auspices of the French Red Cross.[21] Munro's Corps included an unusually large number of women. As the Baroness de T'Serclaes, one of his original recruits, commented: 'the founder and leader of the corps, Dr Hector Munro, was an

[18] See Sinclair to Lowndes, 17 Sept. 1914, HR, MS (Lowndes, MAB) Recip, for information about her wartime donations.

[19] Sinclair to Charlotte Mew, 25 Aug. 1916, HA.

[20] David Mitchell, *Women on the Warpath: The Story of the Women of the First World War* (London: Jonathan Cape, 1966), 152–3.

[21] Ibid. 178–88.

eccentric Scottish specialist, one of whose primary objects seemed to be leadership of a feminist crusade, for he was far keener on women's rights than most of the women he recruited.'[22] When the war correspondent Philip Gibbs encountered the Munro Corps shortly after Sinclair had left it, he noticed with surprise the number of women in it:

They did not seem to me at first sight the type of woman to be useful on a battlefield or in a field-hospital. I should have expected them to faint at the sight of blood, and to swoon at the bursting of a shell. Some of them at least were too pretty, I thought, to play about in fields of war among men and horses smashed to pulp. It was only later that I saw their usefulness and marvelled at the spiritual courage of these young women, who seemed not only careless of shell-fire but almost unconscious of its menace, and who, with more nervous strength than that of many men, gave first-aid to the wounded without shuddering at sights of agony which might turn a strong man sick.[23]

It was this sort of attitude that men like Munro and women like the Baroness de T'Serclaes, who later became famous as one of the Heroines of Pervyse, had to face. She describes the astonishment of the other women in the party (including May Sinclair) when she and fellow-recruit Mairi Chisholm arrived at Victoria Station in knickerbocker khaki suits: 'The others were slightly scandalized—one could see it in their furtive glances . . . it was difficult for these gentle ladies, who wore correct costumes and picture hats, to think there could really be any need for stepping right outside the conventional lines, at all events until they got to the war zone.'[24] When, after she left the Munro Corps, she applied for permission to set up an Advanced Dressing Station just behind the front lines, the Baroness was told by the Admiral that as a woman she would not 'stand the strain'. She told him that 'because I was a woman I could stand strain and hardship (I nearly asked him if he had ever heard of childbirth)'.[25] But all the same there may have been something in Philip Gibb's comments. Munro, mistrustful of officialdom, did not want trained nurses. He was anxious to attract young women who were adaptable and adventurous. In he end he took only four of his 200 applicants, and of those four, only one, Mrs Knocker (who later became the Baroness), was a trained nurse.[26]

[22] Baroness De T'Serclaes, *Flanders and Other Fields: Memoirs of the Baroness de T'Serclaes*, M. M. (London: Harrap, 1964), 37.

[23] Philip Gibbs, *The Soul of the War* (London: Heinemann, 1915), 173.

[24] *The Cellar-House of Pervyse: A Tale of Uncommon Things from the Journals and Letters of the Baroness de T'Serclaes and Mairi Chisholm*, ed. G. E. Mitton (London: A. and C. Black, 1916), 1–2.

[25] De T'Serclaes, *Flanders and Other Fields*, 63.   [26] Mitchell, *Women on the Warpath*, 126.

Munro was a charismatic leader. Several of the women with whom he worked commented on his comic appearance, his disorganization, and his charm. Baroness de T'Serclaes describes him as 'a likeable man and a brilliant impresario, but wonderfully vague in matters of detail, and in appearance the very essence of the absent-minded professor'.[27] Impatient with his carelessness, de T'Serclaes left the Munro Corps to set up her own operation in Pervyse soon after May Sinclair's departure. Sinclair seems to have been more susceptible. In an entry in the manuscript version of the journal, which was not included in the printed book, she notes that Munro is 'not only a psychologist & psychotherapist, but a "psychic", & he has the "psychic"'s uncanny power over certain people (they are generally women)' (29). His invitation to her over an intimate dinner at her house to come to Belgium with him clearly flattered her and made her feel that he really wanted her company. But his motives were most likely primarily economic. Since the corps was unable to secure official backing until the last minute (Sinclair notes that they were rejected by the War Office, the Admiralty, and the British, American, and French Red Cross, JI, 1), they were in serious need of money, and all four women recruits paid their own way (Baroness de T'Serclaes records that Mairi Chisholm, a fanatical motorcyclist, sold her motorbike to raise funds).[28] There was a further financial emergency even after the corps had finally secured the support of the Belgian legation and was reorganizing itself as a commission of inquiry into the condition of Belgian refugees (JI, 3). In a passage omitted from the published journal, Sinclair notes that 'our Treasurer, three days before the Corps had arranged to start for Belgium, had started for America, leaving all our funds safely locked up in his private account at his bank' (3). Munro knew that in January 1914 Sinclair had invested the considerable sum of £500 in the Medico-Psychological Clinic. He knew that she had money; he knew also that she was sympathetic to the idea of women's rights, and had written articles and a pamphlet in support of the suffrage movement. He must have imagined that she would be keen to support a feminist venture, not to mention the added incentives of her own excitement about the war and her prior connection with Munro through the clinic. If he could convince her to come to Belgium with him, she would be even more likely to give the unit substantial financial support.

Given this kind of pressure, it is almost certain that May Sinclair made some kind of financial contribution. Habitually self-effacing but eager to help others with loans and gifts, it is not surprising that her published journals do not mention the fact or the degree of her support. But Marie Belloc

---

[27] De T'Serclaes, *Flanders and Other Fields*, 37.   [28] Ibid.

Lowndes, who was in close touch with Sinclair at the time, suggests in her autobiography that the ambulance corps was originally Sinclair's idea:

There must have been an extraordinarily noble streak in this remarkable writer.... She went on writing books, all more or less successful, until the outbreak of the war in 1914. She then, with her savings, started an ambulance, putting in charge of it a brilliant medical man, who, she felt, had not had his chance in life. She must have left this man completely free to select his staff, and herself occupied, in the little party which accompanied him, a post which she called that of 'the scribe'.[29]

Whether or not it was Sinclair who first had the idea of putting together an ambulance corps, the fact that it was she who provided the initial funds for its equipment and transport helps to explain her unlikely presence in Belgium during the first weeks of the war. It was unclear even to Sinclair exactly what her role in the corps would be: 'they've called me the Secretary and Reporter, which sounds very fine, and I am to keep the accounts (Heaven help them!) and write the Commandant's reports, and toss off articles for the daily papers, to make a little money for the Corps' (JI, 4). But, as Sinclair herself notes, she knew nothing of accounting, and was not a trained journalist or reporter. In the end she sent no news reports back to Britain during her brief time in Belgium, and spent much of her time unpacking and packing Munro's bags. The Baroness de T'Serclaes did not understand what she was doing there:

she was a very intellectual, highly strung woman who managed to survive only for a few weeks before the horrors of war overcame her and she was sent home. Her functions were not entirely clear: I think she was to act as secretary to Dr Munro, though she could only have had the effect of making his own confusion slightly worse, and there was an idea that she might help to swell the corps' tiny finances by writing articles for the Press about its work.[30]

Sinclair was superfluous not only to the war effort, but to the unit to which she belonged as well. Only money could buy her the proximity to war that she craved, but money could not buy her youth or expertise.

Because her role was so ill-defined, Sinclair spent a lot of time in Belgium doing nothing. She wrote to Ezra Pound a couple of days after she arrived in Ghent: 'What I'm suffering from principally at this moment is boredom.... it is very boring for the Secretary who sees nothing—nothing at all, & does nothing but sit snug in the Flandria Palace... & write reports of actions in wh. secretaries are not called upon to take a part.'[31] As the others went out to Alost,

[29] Marie Belloc Lowndes, *A Passing World* (London: Macmillan, 1948), 196.

[30] De T'Serclaes, *Flanders and Other Fields*, 37–8.

[31] Sinclair to Ezra Pound, 29 Sept. 1914, Beinecke Rare Book and Manuscript Library, Ezra Pound Papers, Box 48, fo. 2136.

Quatrecht, and Zele to retrieve the wounded, periodically coming under fire themselves, Sinclair served dinner to the crowds of Belgian refugees gathered at the Palais des Fêtes and fretted about her hours of inactivity.

Keeping the Corps' accounts only takes two hours and a half, even with Belgian and English money mixed, and when I've added the same column of figures ten times up and ten times down, to make certain it's all right (I am no good at accounts, but I know my weakness and guard against it, giving the Corps the benefit of every doubt and making good every deficit out of my private purse). Writing the Day-Book [daily record of events]—perhaps half an hour. The Commandant's correspondence, when he has any, and reporting to the British Red Cross Society, when there is anything to report, another half-hour at the outside; and there you have only three and a half hours employed out of the twenty-four, even if I balanced my accounts every day, and I don't. (JI, 68)

On 1 October Sinclair was told she could no longer even work at the Palais des Fêtes in case she introduced infection into the Military Hospital there. Instead, she was put in charge of replacing the soiled linens in the ambulances. In exasperation, she finally told Munro she 'might as well be taken prisoner by the Germans . . . since that would, at least, give [her] something to write about' (JI, 89). Munro grudgingly agreed to let her come out with one of the ambulances. But in spite of his promise he continued to drag his feet. It was not Munro, but one of the official war correspondents who finally took her out on 7 October to see the devastation at Baerlaere. Munro did not include her in an ambulance trip until 8 October, a week after he had first consented to having her with him.

It was on that day that Sinclair, as she puts it, encountered her 'first wounded man' (JI, 170). In a small village near Lokeren she went with two Belgian stretcher-bearers to bring back an injured man from one of the outlying houses. When the stretcher-bearers put down the stretcher to rest, Sinclair impatiently grabbed the poles of the stretcher herself. Knowing that she could never carry it, the bearers wearily took up their burden once more, and Sinclair followed them back to the ambulance where she watched Munro dress the soldier's wound. The following day Sinclair seized her chance again when in the afternoon a new ambulance, sent by the British Red Cross to the Munro Corps, was called out to Melle while all the other corps members were away. In Melle she watched while five wounded men were treated and loaded into the ambulance. To her disappointment the village was not shelled while she was in it. On 10 October Munro took her back to Melle, now right on the edge of the German lines, where there were still two German wounded lying in a field within range of the German guns.

When Sinclair tried to board the ambulance to go with the others to get the men she was physically pushed out of the car by the Baroness de T'Serclaes: 'Mrs. Torrence [the name Sinclair gives to Mrs Knocker, later the Baroness], having the advantage of me in weight, height, muscle and position, got up and tried to push me off the step. As she did this she said: "You can't come. You'll take up the place of a wounded man" ' (JI, 214). Sinclair found herself standing in the street as the ambulance roared away. So far, although she had been out with the ambulance three times, she had never been in any danger or taken any central role in the rescue or the care of dying men. The following night she felt even more inept as she struggled to take care of a wounded British soldier in the hospital in Ghent. She was unable to lift him; she disturbed him with her continual coughing; she annoyed the doctors and nurses by summoning them continually. The next morning she was removed from the case. Her brief career as a nurse was over.

But Sinclair barely had a chance to regret it. Antwerp had fallen to the Germans on 10 October while she sat with the dying man, and German troops were expected to enter Ghent within hours. The Corps was ordered to pack their bags and retreat, and in the middle of the night of 11 October they left for Ecloo, halfway between Ghent and Bruges. Sinclair, obsessed with the wounded man she had nursed so unsuccessfully, announced when they arrived at Ecloo that she was returning to Ghent to be with him. When she tried to board a train to Ghent she had once again to be physically restrained: 'the Chaplain, who is abominably strong, put his arms round my waist and pulled me off' (JI, 260). Sinclair was furious but there was nothing she could do. When the Corps arrived in Ostend they discovered that they only had funds for another few days. 'So it was more or less settled amongst us that somebody would have to go over to England the next day and return with funds, and that the supernumerary Secretary was, on the whole, the fittest person for the job' (JI, 272). When another woman was temporarily appointed Secretary, Sinclair 'saw nothing sinister about this arrangement . . . It seemed incredible to me that I should not return' (JI, 273). But as she saw the cliffs of Dover looming in the distance she suddenly hated them because they were not the coast of Flanders, 'Which would be absurd if I were really going back again. Yes, I must have had a premonition' (JI, 288). All too soon she realized that her trip to England was an elaborate trick to get rid of her. She never saw military action again, and had to resign herself to ' "fluffing" wool for surgical swabs' and writing stories instead of heroically pulling men from the field of battle.[32]

[32] Sinclair to H. G. Wells, 16 Oct. 1915, University of Illinois Library at Urbana-Champaign.

Sinclair's time in Belgium was dominated by her desperate desire to be under fire rescuing the wounded, and the equally strong determination of her fellow workers to keep her away from situations in which she would simply be in the way. Sinclair wanted to experience danger because of the extraordinary sensations it provoked in her. She described the feeling in a letter to H. G. Wells:

Danger's different, there's always a fascination about it. But out there there's something more, I've tried to describe it, but I can't, it's an awfully intimate thing, only, at the bad moments, such as they were, it was as near ecstasy as it cd. be. And yet that isn't it, either; really, it's like nothing on earth so much as the approach of the beloved person; there's gladness & desire in it. I've only had it once before & that was when a doctor broke it to me that he was afraid I had cancer—wh. is I suppose the thing one dreads above all possible diseases. I hadn't got it, but for twenty-four hours he (& I) thought that it was so. It's as if life were hiding something, keeping something from you all the time, & at every prospect, no matter what prospect, of breaking through you rejoice.[33]

Descriptions of excitement like this were commonplace in men's writings about the war, but for a woman to express such greed for adventure and for sensation was unusual.[34] The war offered Sinclair a form of sexual, almost mystic fulfilment which she would have found it difficult to experience in any other setting. In the *Journal* she describes the feeling of mounting tension as the Corps approached Ghent for the first time as an almost orgasmic form of pleasure:

A curious excitement comes to you. I suppose it is excitement, though it doesn't feel like it. You have been drunk, very slightly drunk with the speed of the car. But now you are sober. Your heart beats quietly, steadily, but with a little creeping, mounting thrill in the beat. The sensation is distinctly pleasurable. You say to yourself, 'It is coming. Now—or the next minute—perhaps at the end of the road.' You have one moment of regret. 'After all, it would be a pity if it came too soon, before we'd even begun our job.' But the thrill, mounting steadily, overtakes the regret. It is only a little thrill, so far (for you don't really believe that there is any danger), but you can imagine the thing growing, growing steadily, till it becomes ecstasy. Not that you imagine anything at the moment. At the moment you are no longer an observing, reflecting being; you have ceased to be aware of yourself; you exist only in that quiet, steady thrill that is so unlike any excitement that you have ever known. (JI, 12–13)

[33] Ibid.
[34] See Paul Fussell, *The Great War and Modern Memory* (Oxford: Oxford University Press, 1975), 114–15 and 270–2 for references to masculine accounts of ecstasy under fire.

Sinclair's anxiety to go with the others into battle zones grows out of her appetite for this sensation, a sensation which engages both mortality and sexuality. Her description here suggests that the battlefield is a place where bodies become known not only in their vulnerability, but also in their strength and their capacity for stimulation. Presumably she hoped that in Belgium everything would fall into place around her new sense of 'superior reality' (JI, 167). Certainly this happens for a number of her characters. 'Khaki', for example, in the story of that name, redeems his absurd life by enlisting in the Boer War and proving that, as his friend puts it, he was 'in love with danger'.[35] In a story Sinclair wrote shortly after she returned to England in 1914, 'Red Tape', the central character believes (wrongly, it turns out) that the man she is in love with has enlisted, and fantasizes about the war as 'one immense, encompassing sheet of shells and bullets that converged on Mr Starkey in the middle of it. It was there, in the middle of it, that she desired to be.'[36] In imagining her own body at the centre of the war's violence, Sinclair hoped that it would also be at the centre of a field of sexual energy.

But the female body has a complex relation to this fantasy and to this sexualized war aesthetic. The broken, decomposed bodies of the trenches are all male. It was hard for women to put their own bodies at the symbolic centre of the conflict, as Sinclair appears to have wanted. In many of her novels, and in the *Journal*, a sexualized relation to a soldier or doctor at the front mediates the vexed relationship of women's bodies to the conflict. Heteroerotic relations—whether they are between a nurse and a patient, or between lovers—become entangled, in Sinclair's work, with women's desire to take part in the war. For example, in *Tasker Jevons: The Real Story*, the first novel Sinclair published after returning from the war, Jevons's wife Viola insists on training as a nurse and following him out to the front, much to his annoyance. 'They're [women] *all* trying. You should just see the bitches—tumbling, and wriggling and scrabbling with their claws and crawling on their stomachs to get to the front—tearing each other's eyes out to get there first.'[37] It is unclear whether the novel's sympathies lie with Viola's desire to be with her husband, or with her husband's irritation at her presence. Jevons's biography is modelled very closely on Sinclair's: the dates of his

---

[35] Sinclair, ' "Khaki" ', *English Review*, 15 (Sept. 1913), 190–201, repr. in *Tales Told by Simpson* (London: Hutchinson, 1930), 13–25: at 21.

[36] Sinclair, 'Red Tape', *Queen: The Lady's Newspaper* (14 Nov. 1914), 802–3: at 802; repr. in Trudi Tate (ed.), *Women, Men and the Great War* (Manchester: Manchester University Press, 1995), 199–209.

[37] Sinclair, *The Belfry* (New York: Macmillan, 1916), 266. The novel was simultaneously published in the UK as *Tasker Jevons: The Real Story*.

time at the front are almost identical to hers, like her he is too old to enlist, like her he finds that although no one will support his scheme to command his own ambulance unit, people are keen to use his money and his fame as a writer to support their own schemes. There is some sympathy too in the novel's account of the narrator's sexual confusion: 'I was a man and I should have been thinking of those men; and here I was, compelled against my conscience and my will to think of this woman.'[38]

Yet Viola, the wife who so annoys him, also recalls Sinclair. Excised passages from her journal imply that she was sexually attracted to Munro and followed him out to the war just as Viola followed Jevons. She felt that she had come to Belgium at his invitation, and was then jealous and humiliated when it became clear that he preferred to work with the younger women in the unit. When Sinclair saw Munro going out in an ambulance with one of the young women recruits, she was, in her words, 'absurd enough to feel the tight, agonising grip of pain, such as a creature might feel if it found itself betrayed' (JI, 89). Munro's indifference to her once they actually arrived in Belgium undermined her fantasy that, through him, she would experience the war at first-hand, both materially, as a nurse, and symbolically, as the lover of someone whose body was continually under fire. In fact he—with the support of the Baroness de T'Serclaes—did his best to keep her away from the battlefields. His apparent lack of concern about her plight only intensified her frustration. In an unpublished passage she wrote: 'it has turned out exactly as I thought it would when I told the Commandant that I sd. be no earthly use to him or his ambulance' (77a); even in the published *Journal* she wrote that she felt like a 'large and useless parcel which the Commandant had brought with him in sheer absence of mind, and was now anxious to lose or otherwise get rid of' (JI, 281). In a passage partly omitted from the published *Journal*, she describes accusing him of encouraging flirtatious behaviour among the recruits (passages that were cut from the published version are in italics):

And as no young woman of modern times is going to let herself be outdone by young Haynes [an ambulance driver], you must expect to find Ursula Dearmer [Mairi Chisholm] in the middle of the road [exposed to shell-fire] too. You cannot suppress this competitive heroism of young people. The roots strike too deep down in human nature. *They are bound up with the primordial instinct of flirtation. (The Commandant intimates, with every appearance of outraged dignity, that this is an instinct wh. so far as he is concerned has no existence. I go on relentlessly.) All the same it exists, & no psychologist or psychotherapist can afford to ignore it. But (I have led up*

---

[38] Sinclair, *Belfry*, 277–8.

gently to my point) for our present purposes we may. In the modern young man and woman competitive heroism has completely forgotten its origin and is now an end in itself. *Heaven bless you, they mean nothing by it. (The Commandant is slightly paci-fied.) But if you don't happen to like it you must not take any more mixed pic-nic parties to Termonde, that is all*. (JI, 79; unpublished draft, 70)

Unable to accuse him directly of seducing her into following him out to Belgium and then abandoning her, she displaces her indignation into a picture of desire run rampant in the group he is charged with leading. As Marie Belloc Lowndes writes of Munro's refusal to allow Sinclair to return to Belgium: 'Though I do not think she was in love with him, this treacherous conduct on his part in a sense broke her heart.'[39]

The *Journal* and passages from Sinclair's 1922 novel *Anne Severn and the Fieldings* suggest that her jealousy fastened on the Baroness de T'Serclaes as the woman who had displaced her in Munro's affections. The Baroness was clearly impatient with Sinclair and, as we saw, it was the Baroness, not Munro, who pushed her off the ambulance in Melle as it left to pick up wounded men. In *Anne Severn* the Baroness is reconstructed as a jealous and manipulative woman who has the Commandant at her beck and call. Anne is edged out of the ambulance corps in which she has distinguished herself by her heroism by her adoptive sister-in-law, Queenie, who is afraid of being shown up by her. A letter from one of the drivers tells Anne: 'We're all furi-ous here at the way you've been treated. I've resigned as a protest . . . Queenie doesn't want you about when the War medals are handed round. Everybody sees that but old Cutler [the Commandant]. He's too much gone on her to see anything. She can twist him round and round and tie him up in knots' (AS, 116). It may be that Sinclair was jealous of Munro's reliance on—and possible attraction to—the Baroness, who was after all the only properly trained member of the unit, and that it was easier for her to criticize the Baroness than Munro, who had after all been a close friend. In *Anne Severn* Sinclair reworked the story of her own abrupt expulsion from the Corps into a tale of sordid jealousies and betrayals. She even allowed the 'Secretary' to make a cameo appearance:

We picked up two more stretcher-bearers in Ostend and a queer little middle-aged lady out for a job at the front. Cutler took her on as a sort of secretary. At first Queenie was so frantic that she wouldn't speak to her, and swore she'd make the Corps too hot to hold her. But when she found that the little lady wasn't for the

---

[39] Lowndes, *Passing World*, 197. Both Sinclair's companion in later years, Florence Bartrop, and Sinclair's niece Wilda McNeile wrote that Sinclair was 'not fond' of Munro, and she had few dealings with him socially after the war was over. See Florence Bartrop to T. E. M. Boll, 3 Mar. 1960, UP, Box 48, fos. 518–19, and Wilda McNeile to Boll, 24 June 1959, UP, Box 48, fo. 529.

danger zone and only proposed to cook and keep our accounts for us, she calmed down and was quite decent. Then the other day Miss Mullins came and told us that a bit of shell had chipped off the corner of her kitchen. The poor old thing was ever so proud and pleased about it, and Queenie snubbed her frightfully, and said she wasn't in any danger at all, and asked her how she'd enjoy it if she was out all day under fire, like us. (AS, 111–12)

Giving some elements of her own story to Miss Mullins, and others to Anne, Sinclair revised her own experiences and rewrote her own role as both harmlessly altruistic and recklessly brave. Even she knew that, however unjust her dismissal had been, her activities in Belgium had fallen far short of heroic. But it must have comforted her to write an alternative version of her tale of embarrassment and humiliation.

However, even her less heavily embellished description of events in the *Journal* was disputed by other witnesses of the Corps' activities. A stiff exchange of letters with Miss Ashley-Smith, a nurse travelling with the Munro Corps who turned back at Ecloo to return to Ghent during the retreat, shows that Sinclair's and Ashley-Smith's memories of the incident were in sharp contrast. Miss Ashley-Smith (by now Mrs McDougall) objected to a passage from one of the extracts from the *Journal* that had appeared in the *English Review* which suggested, in her view, that she had abandoned one of her patients when she left Ghent with the Munro Corps at Sinclair's invitation: 'As you cannot possibly have forgotten Mr. Foote was at the Hôtel Flandria under the care of Mrs. Knocker (a trained nurse!), yourself and the other ladies of your party . . . why should you revive an unpleasant episode by attempting to put the cowardice or panic or whatever it was on to me.'[40]

Sinclair published a Note clearing up the misunderstanding with the next extract of the *Journal*, and Mrs McDougall accepted her apology. But in her own copy of the published volume, now preserved in the Imperial War

[40] Mrs G. A. McDougall to May Sinclair, 12 June 1915, UP [not catalogued]. The offending passage in the journal appears in the *English Review*, 20 (June 1915), 309, when Sinclair describes inviting Miss Ashley-Smith to join the Munro Corps in their retreat from Ghent: 'She would not consent to come with us at first, because one of her four British is too ill to be moved. But the nuns persuaded her that he would be as well looked after as if she were there, and that she would do no good by remaining.* [The asterisked footnote reads: 'She heroically went back to Ghent from Ecloo the next morning and stayed there till the death of one of her patients.'] An editorial note was added to the July 1915 number as follows: 'Miss Sinclair writes in connection with a footnote, page 309, of the June number, that it is open to misconstruction. The fact is that Miss Ashley-Smith did not leave the patient referred to, and could not have left him, seeing that he was not in any sense her patient at the time' (*English Review*, 20, July 1915, 476). In the published volume the episode is described in greater length and in slightly different terms. Mrs G. A. McDougall published her own account of her wartime experiences in *A Nurse at the War: Nursing Adventures in Belgium and France* (New York: McBride, 1917).

Museum in London, Mrs McDougall continued to fume, scribbling corrections and exclamations all over the margins of her book. According to her, Sinclair falsified many of the details of the story of the group's flight from Ghent. In the *Journal* Sinclair writes that at Ecloo she and Miss Ashley-Smith spent 'a long time discussing which of us is going back to Ghent' (JI, 298). But Miss Ashley-Smith annotated the sentence crossly: '<u>Rot</u> There was no discussion I was on my way wh. I met them [the Munro Corps] [*sic*]'. In response to a footnote of Sinclair's claiming that Munro had his own plan for returning Miss Ashley-Smith wrote: 'biggest lie of the lot!' (JI, 298). Faced with the statement that Sinclair 'got on [the train] too, to go with her' (JI, 300), she scrawled exasperatedly: 'Tiens tiens! Dear me! I never saw this happen! . . . She said she wd. come if I waited till she got her 2 suitcases!!' She disagreed too with Sinclair's account of the Munro Corps' concern with her own safety after she had left. Sinclair maintained that they would all have returned to Ghent to fetch her back again had they not telephoned and learnt both that Miss Ashley-Smith had arrived safely, and that 'no more women were to return to Ghent' (JI, 303). Beside this last comment Miss Ashley-Smith wrote 'I don't <u>think</u>!', and she also noted that 'the wires were cut' and 'There were no calls going thru' & no one to know of my safe arrival!' She was even scornful of the Munro Corps' haste in leaving Ghent, scrawling on page 307: 'they panicked the whole lot of them—there was no danger for a few days' and 'they had no orders to leave Ghent when they did it was sheer funk [*sic*]'. It is impossible now to reconstruct precisely what happened: either woman could be misremembering or deliberately distorting the truth. Both were hypersensitive to accusations of cowardice and of shirking their responsibilities to the wounded men in their care. Sinclair fantasized about the pleasures of battle, but there may also have been something about her behaviour which suggested that she was, understandably enough, less than enthused at the prospect of participating in it in the flesh.

Sinclair's *Journal* was among the first wartime women's diaries to be published in Britain. Gladys Lloyd's *An Englishwoman's Adventures in the German Lines* had appeared soon after the war began in 1914, and the anonymous *Diary of a Nursing Sister on the Western Front*, Monica Dearmer's *Letters from a Field Hospital*, and Sarah MacNaughton's *A Woman's Diary of the War* all came out in 1915. The *Journal* was unusual in dwelling on what it felt like to be a spectator of, rather than an actor in, the scenes of violence unfolding in Belgium and France (among the diaries and autobiographical essays published in Britain in 1915 only Mildred Aldrich's *A Hilltop on the Marne*, 1915, was told from the point of view of a woman who was not a nurse). Most reviewers of Sinclair's *Journal* welcomed Sinclair's concentration on psychology and characterization. Florence Finch Kelly in the *Bookman* noted that the *Journal* was 'surely one of the most curious records of war experience of all the many that have been written. For, in the first place, it is instinct with temperament and, in the second, it applies to the portraying of experiences with a Field Ambulance Corps the method of the analytical, psychological novelist.'[41] The *Spectator* described her portraits of the other women as 'triumphs of characterization', the *Dial* noted that 'one knows the whole staff as thoroughly as one knows any of the characters of Miss Sinclair's novels', and the *North American Review* called it 'the most genuine and vital piece of writing that has come from the war area'.[42] The *Nation*, however, found it shrill and personal.[43] It fell to Rebecca West, with whom Sinclair became friends around this time, to identify what was really at stake in the text:

No triumph of good work that may come to Miss Sinclair will ever make up to her for the discovery that the artist is unfitted for the life of action. And yet every page of this gallant, humiliated book makes it plain that while it is glorious that England should have women who walk quietly under the rain of bullets it is glorious too that England should have women who grieve inconsolably because the face of danger has not been turned to them.[44]

Sinclair wrote, West remarked, as if she were 'a little girl sitting on a tin trunk at a railway station and watching the people go by'.[45]

Sinclair returned on 13 October to an England that was already caught up in war fever. In March 1914 she had moved out of her little studio flat in Kensington into a small house on Blenheim Road in Hampstead and, for the first time in her adult life, she had acquired a maid, Nellie Bartrop (Nellie's sister Florence took over when Nellie left Sinclair's employ in 1919). When Zeppelin raids on coastal towns began in early 1915 (London was first bombed on the night of 31 May 1915), Sinclair continued, out of loyalty, to spend most of her time in London with Bartrop and her beloved black cat, even though she had her little cottage in Reeth to retreat to, and a standing invitation from Katharine Hinkson to join her in Ireland.[46] On rare trips north for writing retreats, she felt uncomfortable, writing to Hinkson from Yorkshire in June 1915: 'though I adore these hills & these green fields, I can hardly bear to be

[41] Florence Finch Kelly, 'Eye Witnesses of the War', *Bookman* (New York), 42 (Dec. 1915), 462–6: at 465–6.

[42] 'Heroines of the War', *Spectator*, 115 (9 Oct. 1915), 477; Benjamin M. Woodbridge, 'Belgium's Agony', *Dial*, 60 (20 Jan. 1916), 72–4: at 73; 'New Books Reviewed', *North American Review*, 211 (Nov. 1915), 779–81: at 780.

[43] 'Books on the War', *Nation* (NY), 101 (11 Nov. 1915), 576. Some of Sinclair's more recent critics have expressed an equally negative response: Tylee e.g. in *The Great War and Women's Consciousness*, calls the *Journal* 'narcissistic and myopic' (30).

[44] Rebecca West, 'Miss Sinclair's Genius', *Daily News* (24 Aug. 1915); repr. in *The Young Rebecca: Writings of Rebecca West 1911–1917*, ed. Jane Marcus (London: Macmillan, 1982), 304–7: at 307.

[45] Ibid. 304.   [46] Sinclair to Hinkson, 23 May 1915, JR.

here—to see the young men going about as if there wasn't any war, & the bean-feasts [parties] coming up from Darlington'.[47] She told Hinkson in 1917 that 'pacifism is the one awful temptation we have to steel ourselves against. To me it's the worst conceivable treachery to the men who've fought & died since 1914, & to their wives & mothers & children. It's real pity & real tenderness to fight on & save the world.'[48] She was reluctant to be away from London partly because she had no intention of missing things, and she occupied her time getting the *Journal* into print (she gave all her royalties to the National Committee for Relief in Belgium), helping to make medical supplies, and writing novels in enthusiastic support of the war.[49] She was committed to the war effort partly out of a sense of family responsibility. She told Hinkson: 'You may wonder how I can endure to write. But I cd.n't endure <u>not</u> to write & to have no power to help the things I want to help, or to support my nephew if he comes home disabled from the War'.[50] In fact, not one but three of her nephews enlisted. Two died in 1915 aged respectively 34 and 25 (William, son of her eldest brother William who had settled in Hull, and Harold, son of her brother Joseph in Canada). The third, Harold Lumley, also one of William's children, spent most of the war in POW camp, was invalided out in 1918 at the age of 30, and collapsed with pneumonia, arriving at Sinclair's house in London and requiring devoted nursing for several months. As Sinclair anxiously followed news of the war she was uncomfortably aware that young men for whom she felt responsible—and two of whom at least she loved (she may never have met Joseph's son)—were in danger when her own attempt at self-sacrifice had been spurned. Her safety depressed her. In the months that followed her return to London, under the influence of her new friendship with poet Charlotte Mew, she wrote three poems about being away from the danger of war.[51] 'Field Ambulance in Retreat: Via Dolorosa, Via Sacra', first published in December 1914, describes the retreat from Ghent and—à la Wilfred Owen—the beauty of the 'red and white harvest' the 'dripping ambulance' gathers from the fields. As the troops retreat:

> our shining, beckoning danger goes with them,
> And our joy in the harvests that we gathered in at nightfall in the fields;
> And like an unloved hand laid on a beating heart
> Our safety weighs us down.[52]

---

[47] Sinclair to Hinkson, 29 June 1915, JR.   [48] Sinclair to Hinkson, 9 Nov. 1917, JR.
[49] See Sinclair to Lowndes, 15 Aug. 1915, HR, MS (Lowndes, MAB) Recip.
[50] Sinclair to Hinkson, 23 May 1915, JR.
[51] I discuss her relationship with Charlotte Mew in detail in Ch. 6, below.
[52] 'Field Ambulance in Retreat: Via Dolorosa, Via Sacra' was first published in Hall Caine (ed.), *King*

The unwanted caress of the 'hand' of safety implicitly contrasts with the excitement and desire with which the implied speaker of the poem approaches danger. Sinclair's second war poem, 'Dedication (To a Field Ambulance in Flanders)' (dated 8 March 1915) appeared as the epigraph to the book version of the *Journal*, and speaks even more directly to her own experience. 'Danger' is personified as an alluring presence who summoned the speaker into battle and 'when I came within sight of her, | She turned aside, | And hid her face from me' (JI, no page numbers). The speaker thus cannot number her own among the 'names' of those who went under 'the thunder of the guns, the shrapnel's rain and the curved lightning of the shells':

> I do not call you comrades,
> You,
> Who did what I only dreamed.
> Though you have taken my dream,
> And dressed yourselves in its beauty and its glory,
> Your faces are turned aside as you pass by.
> I am nothing to you,
> For I have done no more than dream.

Like *Anne Severn and the Fieldings*, the poem accuses the other members of the corps of stealing Sinclair's honour, and although the aggression is contained at the end by an appropriate eulogy ('In the high places of Heaven, | They shall tell all your names'), the poem remains an indictment of those who consigned her to the margins of her own dream. 'After the Retreat', published in the special imagist number of the *Egoist* in May 1915, mourns the passing of her time at the front: 'If only I could see again | The house we passed that day.'[53] There was nothing left for her to do now but make cotton swabs for the troops, worry, and write.

After *Tasker Jevons*, published in February 1916, she moved on to another project, less closely tied to her own experiences of the war, with which she felt much more comfortable. Telling Marie Belloc Lowndes that Janet Hogarth had thought *Tasker Jevons* her best novel to date, she commented: 'Quite honestly, I don't. . . . But I like the book I'm writing now better than all of my books put together. And I hope—if it comes off—it'll be better than any of them.'[54] The book she was working on, *The Tree of Heaven*, drew

---

Albert's Book (London: Hodder and Stoughton, 1914). It was reprinted in the 2nd edn. of Jacqueline Trotter (ed.), *Valour and Vision: Poems of the War 1914–1918* (London: Martin Hopkinson, 1923), 43–4 (all proceeds from this volume went to the Incorporated Soldiers and Sailors Help Society), and in Catherine Reilly (ed.), *Scars upon my Heart: Women's Poetry and Verse of the First World War* (London: Virago, 1981), 98–9. The quotation comes from p. 98 of this edn.

[53] Sinclair, 'After the Retreat', *Egoist*, 2 (1 May 1915), 77.
[54] Sinclair to Lowndes, 11 Mar. 1916, HR, MS (Lowndes, MAB) Recip.

not only on her experiences at the front but also on her ambivalent relationship with the suffrage movement and on her strengthening involvement with the imagist movement in poetry, which I discuss in detail in the next chapter. *The Tree of Heaven* was in many ways a synthetic project for Sinclair: the novel attempts to make sense of—and integrate—all the diverse aspects of her experience over the preceding couple of years. In it she suggests that the suffrage movement, the war, and avant-garde art are all part of the same cultural configuration she calls the 'vortex'. The novel is concerned with the Harrison family, and especially with the experience of the three children, Michael, Nicky, and Dorothy, as they grow up in the 1900s and face the war as young adults. In 1910, Dorothy hosts a meeting of the fictitious 'Women's Franchise Union' and in 1912, like the central character in H. G. Wells's novel *Ann Veronica* (1909), inadvertently participates in a suffragette raid on the House of Commons, and is imprisoned in Holloway gaol. When the war begins, Dorothy trains with the Red Cross and, after the death in the trenches of her fiancé Frank Drayton, joins an ambulance unit which is sent out to Belgium—like the Munro Corps—in September 1915. Michael is a poet, and becomes involved with a group of avant-garde artists centred around the house of poet Lawrence Stephen. When war breaks out, he embraces pacifism and refuses to enlist, in spite of his family's pressure. Nicky becomes an engineer and invents an early prototype of the tank.[55] He enlists as soon as the war begins, and his death finally provokes Michael to become a soldier. At the end of the novel, Michael too is killed.

The Tree of Heaven was in many ways an unashamedly propagandistic novel. Sinclair's glorification of the spiritual uplift of war was typical of much of the popular fiction of the era (Cicely Hamilton in *William—An Englishman*, 1919, for example, skates over the violent episodes of her story in order to concentrate on her protagonists' determination to win what she saw as a 'just' war). Sinclair chose to ignore the spate of diaries, autobiographies, and novels from 1915 onwards that emphasized the war's brutality and the powerlessness of both the men and the women who, after 1916, were compelled to take part (Mary Hamilton's *Dead Yesterday*, 1916, explicitly criticizes one of its central characters for exulting in the war as if it were merely a pageant put on for his entertainment). Sinclair continued to see the war as a route to self-realization, and even in 1917 longed to return to it.

Although the title of *The Tree of Heaven* suggests that its central image will be the tree in the family garden under which the Harrisons regularly

---

[55] See Trudi Tate, *Modernism, History and the First World War* (Manchester: Manchester University Press, 1998), 120 ff., for a discussion of literary and cultural responses to the first deployment of the tank in Sept. 1916.

gather, in fact the book's governing symbol is the vortex. Sinclair derived the image from the manifesto of the Vorticist movement, of which her friend poet Ezra Pound was one of the leaders. Vorticism came into being when in 1913 Wyndham Lewis and others split off from Roger Fry's Omega workshop and founded their own Rebel Art Centre in 1914. This soon closed as resentments between Lewis and the Centre's patron, Kate Lechmere, intensified, but the group, still centred around Lewis, Pound, and sculptor Henri Gaudier-Brzeska, continued to work on the magazine that would become their mouthpiece, *Blast: The Review of the Great English Vortex*, whose first issue appeared in June 1914. Many of the views expressed by characters in Sinclair's novel echo those expressed in *Blast*.[56]

Sinclair's attraction to the aesthetic theories of the Vorticists is somewhat paradoxical. The *Blast* group were unlikely allies for Sinclair, with their iconoclastic aesthetic theories and their uncompromising rejection of conventional forms. Although Sinclair became more experimental as a novelist in the years following the war (*Mary Olivier: A Life*, 1919, for example, is characterized by its innovative, fragmentary prose), *The Tree of Heaven* — in which she is most sympathetic to the Vorticists—is conventionally structured, and, although written in a somewhat sparer style than some of Sinclair's previous novels, fairly traditional in its form—just the kind of book the Vorticists despised.[57] The first issue of *Blast* included in its list of the 'blasted' some of Sinclair's closest friends: poet Alice Meynell and her family, for example. But along with her allegiance to more conservative literary and social circles like that of the Meynells and even Hueffer and Hunt, Sinclair was also susceptible to the mockingly flirtatious charm of Ezra Pound. She supported him financially and, as we shall see in the next chapter, published favourable reviews of the imagist poets, with whom Pound was also closely involved. Her feelings were thus fairly evenly divided between attraction and exasperation. When in 1917 she wrote a defence of T. S. Eliot's poetry at Pound's request she had to tread very carefully not to betray her own contradictory responses:

Mr. Eliot is associated with an unpopular movement and with unpopular people. His 'Preludes' and his 'Rhapsody' appeared in *Blast*. They stood out from the experimental violences of *Blast* with an air of tranquil and triumphant achievement;

---

[56] Information in this paragraph comes from William C. Wees, *Vorticism and the English Avant-Garde* (Manchester: Manchester University Press, 1972), and Jo Anna Isaak, *The Ruin of Representation in Modernist Art and Texts* (Ann Arbor: UMI Research Press, 1986).

[57] Sinclair wrote to Arthur Adcock on 16 Jan. 1918: 'Years ago I came to see that [*The Divine Fire*] was "too rhetorical & too diffuse" ' (UP, Box 1, fo. 1).

but, no matter; it was in *Blast* that they appeared. That circumstance alone was disturbing to the comfortable respectability of Mr. Waugh and *The New Statesman*.[58]

She did not number herself among those who were disturbed by the poetry, but she was nonetheless sympathetic to their point of view.

The ambivalence of her attitude to Vorticism is expressed in her modification in *The Tree of Heaven* of the image the Vorticists had done so much to publicize. For them, the vortex was an image of the triumph of form over the tumbling energies of chaos. As Gaudier-Brzeska put it in the first issue of *Blast*, 'VORTEX IS ENERGY', and, as William C. Wees suggests: 'Stable and self contained, yet suggesting whirling concentrations of energy, the Vortex in the pages of *Blast* symbolised primordial force restrained by the shaping power of art.'[59] The vortex was a primal, but self-sustaining, economy, with its own aesthetic of contained movement and speed. It exemplified the geometric cleanliness of line that philosopher and art-critic T. E. Hulme, never explicitly embraced by the Vorticists but often seen as paving the way for them, had advocated in his 1913 lecture on 'Modern Art and its Philosophy'. Developing a theory of abstraction, Hulme called for 'a new complex geometrical art', one exemplified in Gaudier-Brzeska's sculpture, in which the interrelationships of planes give each piece its own taut aesthetic unity.[60]

In *The Tree of Heaven* the vortex is less an image of aesthetic containment than of a moral and psychological abyss. At a suffrage meeting Dorothy speculates on her friend Rosalind's uncritical devotion to the cause:

Rosalind would always be caught and spun round by any movement that was strong enough. She was foredoomed to the Vortex.

That was Dorothy's fault. It was she who had pushed and pulled the slacker, in spite of her almost whining protest, to the edge of the Vortex; and it was Rosalind, not Dorothy, who had been caught and sucked down into the swirl. She whirled in it now, and would go on whirling, under the impression that her movements made it move.

The Vortex fascinated Dorothy even while she resisted it. She liked the feeling of her own power to resist, to keep her head, to beat up against the rush of the

---

[58] Sinclair, ' "Prufrock: And Other Observations": A Criticism', *Little Review*, 4 (Dec. 1917), 8–14; repr. in Scott (ed.), *Gender of Modernism*, 448–53: at 449. Sinclair is writing in response to Arthur Waugh, 'The New Poetry', *Quarterly Review* (Oct. 1916), 226 (repr. in Michael Grant (ed.), *T. S. Eliot: The Critical Heritage*, i, London: Routledge, 1982, 67–9), a review of an anthology in which 'The Love-Song of J. Alfred Prufrock' appeared. For more extensive discussion of Sinclair's essay on Eliot, see Ch. 6, below.

[59] Henri Gaudier-Brzeska, 'Vortex', *Blast*, 1 (20 June 1914), 156; Wees, *Vorticism and the English Avant-Garde*, 177.

[60] T. E. Hulme, 'Modern Art and its Philosophy', 1913, in *Speculations: Essays on Humanism and the Philosophy of Art* (New York: Harcourt Brace, 1924), 94.

whirlwind, to wheel round and round outside it, and swerve away before the thing got her.

For Dorothy was afraid of the Feminist Vortex, as her brother Michael had been afraid of the little vortex of school. (TH, 123–4)

The vortex here stands not for definition and dynamism, but for amorphousness and the loss of the individual will. Frances thinks of her children being swept into 'the unclean moral vortex' (TH, 156): the vortex is an image of degeneration, of uncontrolled appetites—whether sexual or political—and of approaching chaos. It may be that Sinclair, outspoken in her fiction but prim and reserved in her everyday life, is adapting the Vorticist image here as an implicit criticism of the Vorticist move into abstract art and its repudiation of an art that recognized and celebrated humane values. Certainly the Vorticists' way of life represented a break from the relaxed and stable country-house social scene of the Edwardian period to which Sinclair had become accustomed, and the Vorticists and those associated with them—artist Mark Gertler, for example—often led freer sexual lives than the writers of her own generation with whom Sinclair was involved (Hueffer and Hunt were, of course, a notable exception).[61] But Sinclair was not usually critical of the sexual mores of others—indeed, she supported the dubious union of Hueffer and Hunt, and if this version of the vortex was intended as a slur on the lives of Pound and his allies, it was heavily submerged. There was another way in which Sinclair was critiquing the Vorticist agenda, however. The Vorticists insisted on their commitment to the individual. The opening statement of *Blast* described Vorticism as 'an art of individuals', and in a piece in the *Egoist* in August 1914, Pound wrote: 'The Vorticist movement is a movement of individuals, for individuals, for the protection of individuality.'[62] But for Sinclair the vortex represents a centripetal force that denies individual autonomy. Dorothy's objection to the 'feminist vortex' is that it draws women in and deprives them of the ability— or the right—to make their own judgements. Even more ominously, it allows them to *imagine* that they have preserved their independence of mind (Rosalind believes it is she who makes the vortex turn).

The image of the vortex expresses Sinclair's fear of the idea of a permeable subjectivity. In part, it was her growing familiarity with psychoanalytic theory that stimulated her anxiety. As I noted in Chapter 4, one of the most radical innovations of psychoanalysis was to suggest not only that the psyche was discontinuous and inevitably irrational, but also that it was peopled by the spectral presences of those we have known and loved. Freud wrote in

---

[61] See n. 3, above.   [62] See Wees, *Vorticism and the English Avant-Garde*, 122.

1923, 'the character of the ego is a precipitate of abandoned object-cathexes and . . . it contains the history of those object-choices'.[63] The aspect of psychoanalytic theory with which Sinclair's work was most in tune was its image of the psyche as a surface which could absorb and transform objects from the external world. As 'The Intercessor' suggests, this idea frightened as well as fascinated her. This was in part a result of her peculiarly Victorian brand of agnosticism. Her resistance to an irrational form of belief was fed by her aversion to the idea of a mind that had been invaded by something beyond its control. Reason was the force which disciplined both what went on within the mind, and what entered it from without. A 1912 short story, 'The Flaw in the Crystal', describes the inner corruption of healer Agatha Verrall, whose failure to keep her own thoughts chaste allows the evil personality of one of her patients to merge with her own. A lapse in mental discipline renders the mind vulnerable to the corrupting force of others: Agatha feels 'as if the walls of personality were wearing thin, and through them she felt him trying to get at her'.[64] The vortex is an image for this kind of experience when it occurs en masse.

The Tree of Heaven is unwavering in its condemnation of this kind of leeching of individual energy. Dorothy definitively rejects the suffrage movement when she realizes that because of her politics she has deprived herself of several years of her lover's companionship: the novel is critical of any public commitment that displaces private lives. In fact, it is almost critical of the public sphere itself. Its only word for social relations other than the sexual or the familial is 'the vortex', and political movements—the suffrage movement, even the war—are valued only if they somehow enhance private life. The novel is dismissive or evasive of its own responsibility as historical record, giving precise but wholly inaccurate dates for events in the suffrage movement.[65] The philosophical paradox with which Sinclair was wrestling in the context of her feelings about the war, then, was her indifference to public events, and her horror at the idea of collective action itself, coupled with her fascination with the idea of the war. As she told Marie Belloc

[63] Freud, *The Ego and the Id*, 29. Freud first wrote about the ego forming through the introjection of lost objects in 'Mourning and Melancholia' (1917). In early 1916 Sinclair was writing the psychoanalytic commentaries which appeared as 'Clinical Lectures on Symbolism and Sublimation', I, *Medical Press* (9 Aug. 1916), 118–22; II, *Medical Press* (16 Aug. 1916), 142–5.

[64] Sinclair, 'The Flaw in the Crystal', *English Review*, 11 (May 1912), 189–228 (also published as *The Flaw in the Crystal*, New York: Dutton, 1912); repr. in *Uncanny Stories* (New York: Macmillan, 1923), 163.

[65] e.g. the raid on Parliament in which Dorothy takes part, and the huge procession when she and others are released from Holloway prison, is dated July 1912. In fact there was no such large procession in July 1912. By 1912 the suffragettes had switched to more militant activities such as arson and window-breaking. Nor was there an organization called the Women's Franchise Union. The nearest was the Women's Franchise League, which was no longer active by the 1910s.

Lowndes in November 1917, 'I can't . . . join in anything collective. . . . I do really think artists sd. be held exempt from undertakings that they aren't suited for'.[66] In 1919 she wrote to Catherine Dawson Scott of 'the hatred that I have of being identified with movements & with sets'.[67] It was the same ambivalence that she had struggled with in relation to the suffrage movement before the war.

Sinclair was not alone during these years in expressing distaste for mass movements. Two years before the publication of *The Tree of Heaven*, Trotter had published his collection *Instincts of the Herd in Peace and War*, sections of which had already appeared well before the war but which Trotter considered was an appropriate volume in wartime given the problem of sustaining national 'morale'.[68] It was perhaps of this volume that Sinclair was thinking when she described Michael's dislike of 'the collective, male odour of the herd' at his boarding school (TH, 86). The war stimulated a significant interest in crowd theory. William McDougall, who acted as a medical consultant for the Medico-Psychological Clinic, published *The Group Mind* in 1920, and Freud's own *Group Psychology and the Analysis of the Ego* appeared in 1921.[69] Sinclair's concern with the intersection of the individual and the crowd was typical of psychology and psychoanalysis as disciplines. She differed from thinkers such as Trotter or Freud, however, in linking crowd theory to contemporary theories of abstract art. In *The Tree of Heaven*, the vortex of the crowd—absorbing all comers—is juxtaposed with a Vorticist art which seeks to express movement through the combination of different planes. In Sinclair's work crowd theory becomes a matter of aesthetics.

It was one of the commonplaces of Victorian ideologies of the crowd that they expressed the lower side of man. Trotter, who links 'gregariousness and suggestibility', notes that contemporary texts on suggestion stressed the 'lower' qualities which emerge either during hypnosis or in the midst of a crowd: the personality called into being by suggestion is 'irrational, imitative, credulous, cowardly, cruel, and lacks all individuality, will, and self-control'.[70] McDougall, in *The Group Mind*, describes the crowd as primitive, like a wild beast or child. Freud cites McDougall, and himself notes the

[66] Sinclair to Lowndes, 9 Nov. 1917, HR, MS (Lowndes, MAB) Recip.

[67] Sinclair to Catherine Dawson Scott, Beinecke Rare Book and Manuscript Library, 28 Oct. 1919, Gen. MSS 144, Box 1, fo. 22.

[68] W. Trotter, *Instincts of the Herd in Peace and War* (New York: Macmillan, 1915), 7.

[69] William McDougall, *The Group Mind, a sketch of the principles of collective psychology with some attempt to apply them to the interpretation of national life and character* (London: G. P. Putnam and Sons, 1920); Sigmund Freud, 'Group Psychology and the Analysis of the Ego', 1921, in *Standard Edition*, xviii. 67–143.

[70] Trotter, *Instincts of the Herd*, 26–7.

regressive nature of groups, and the 'collective inhibition of intelligence in groups'.[71] Human behaviour in crowds, then, is a step back down the evolutionary chain. Implicit in much of this work is a critique of war itself. Trotter saw war as the superlative expression of the 'herd instinct', calling it a 'disreputable and disastrous legacy of the brute and the savage, undesirable in civilised life'.[72] Sinclair partly reproduces this version of things in her account of the London crowd that greets England's declaration of war on Germany: 'Part of this crowd was drunk; it was orgiastic; it made strange, fierce noises, like the noises of one enormous, mystically excited beast; here and there, men and women, with inflamed and drunken faces, reeled in each other's arms; they wore pink paper feathers in their hats' (TH, 282). But she also describes this particular crowd as one that gravely shoulders a political responsibility. The crowd expresses England's emotional and moral diversity: 'It was an endless procession of faces; grave and thoughtful faces; uninterested, respectable faces; faces of unmoved integrity; excited faces; dreaming, wondering, bewildered faces; faces merely curious, or curiously exalted, slightly ecstatic, open-mouthed, fascinated by each other and by the movements and the lights; laughing, frivolous faces, and faces utterly vacant and unseeing' (TH, 282–3). The people who throng London's streets are responsible and aware, as well as childlike and narcissistically innocent. This group is evolving away from the excited 'herd' of Trotter's description towards a sense of civic—and military—duty. For Sinclair, war both draws out, and corrects, the regressive tendencies of the crowd.

Thus Sinclair, unlike Boris Sidis, Le Bon, Trotter, or Freud, makes a special case for war.[73] War's crowds—of anxious citizens, of troops, of the wounded—are exempted from the opprobrium in which Sinclair generally holds mass movements. The crowd at the suffragette banquet celebrating the release of Dorothy and the other prisoners, for example, is unregenerate. When the prisoners enter the banquet hall, the crowd greets them with a strange, atavistic sound, 'a savage and a piercing collective sound, . . . a clear tinkling as of glass or thin metal, and a tearing as of silk, and a crying as of children and of small, slender-throated animals' (TH, 223). The sound

[71] Freud, 'Group Psychology and the Analysis of the Ego', 117, 85.

[72] Trotter, *Instincts of the Herd*, 28.

[73] Le Bon, *Psychologie des Foules*, 1895, repr. as *The Crowd*, ed. Robert A. Nye (New Brunswick, NJ: Transaction, 1995) and Boris Sidis, *The Psychology of Suggestion: A Research into the Subconscious Nature of Man and Society* (1898; repr. New York: D. Appleton, 1920) laid the groundwork for the work by Trotter, McDougall, and Freud that followed. As Laura Stempel Mumford points out, in *The Tree of Heaven* 'war is the only legitimate public activity' ('May Sinclair's *The Tree of Heaven*: The Vortex of Feminism, the Community of War', in Helen M. Cooper, Adrienne Auslander Munich, and Susan Merrill Squier (eds.), *Arms and the Woman: War, Gender and Literary Representation*, Chapel Hill, NC: University of North Carolina Press, 1989, 168–83: at 177).

shatters and divides (breaking glass, tearing silk); it is childlike and bestial. To Dorothy 'that collective sound was frightful' (TH, 224). Its full horror is exemplified in the behaviour of Dorothy's maiden aunt, overtaken by the 'collective song' as the crowd bursts into the March of the Women. She screams: 'Her head was thrown back; and on her face there was a look of ecstasy, of a holy rapture, exalted, half savage, not quite sane' (TH, 225). Emmeline's excitement is purely in response to the crowd and the song (she has never been active in the suffrage movement). The feminist enthusiasm of the crowd is embodied à la Almroth Wright in the hysterical outburst of a frustrated and elderly woman, and Dorothy's later renunciation of suffragism as a waste of the time she could have spent with her male lover confirms the novel's scepticism about many of the suffrage movement's aims and methods. As Dorothy asks during a 1910 meeting of the Women's Franchise Union, 'Are we not then to fight with our tongues and with our brains?' (TH, 119) Just as Sinclair was uncertain of the role she could play as a *writer* who supported the suffrage, so Dorothy is resistant to the militant actions of the group to which she belongs.

If the collective aspect of the suffrage movement was distasteful to Sinclair, the war was potentially even less attractive. But she was faced with the task of reconciling the fact of her resistance to mass activities with her desperate desire to participate in one of the largest mobilizations of populations that Europe had ever seen. The war presented her with a paradox: it was at once an example of the intolerable collectivity of public life, and an object intimately marked by the separate investments and experiences of all those who had been through it. Sinclair uses the character of Michael in *The Tree of Heaven* to work through some of these contradictions. Michael initially refuses to enlist because of his horror of the 'herd' of war and of its apparently unthinking obedience. At these moments in the novel the war too becomes an emblem of the degenerate 'vortex': 'the immense vortex of the War' (TH, 299). Michael thinks of it as one of 'the loathsome violences of the collective soul':

From his very first encounters with the collective soul and its emotions they had seemed to Michael as dangerous as they were loathsome. Collective emotion might be on the side of the archangels or on the side of devils and of swine; its mass was what made it dangerous, a thing that challenged the resistance of the private soul. . . . Michael . . . was afraid, not of the War so much as of the emotions of the War, the awful, terrifying flood that carried him away from his real self and from everything it cared for most. (TH, 327)

Michael's mistrust here is similar to the unease of the young May Sinclair confronted with a religion that demanded her faith without her rational acquiescence. Both Michael and Sinclair are apprehensive about losing the discipline of privacy. They fear the vortex of the crowd, and the intimacy of identification with so many other souls. But Michael finally enlists, after his beloved brother Nicky is killed in action. The novel's descriptions of Nicky's and Michael's feelings at the front manage to negotiate the awkward contradiction of Michael's eventual pleasure in the experience of battle. In *The Tree of Heaven* a solitary mysticism offers an escape from the vortex of mass warfare. Michael describes his feelings in a letter to Nicky's widow Veronica, who herself has telepathic powers. 'But suppose it is your nerves. Why should they tingle at just that particular moment, the moment that makes *animals* afraid? Why should you be so extraordinarily happy? Why should the moment of danger be always the "exquisite" moment?' (TH, 395–6) Sinclair was of course drawing on her own experiences in Belgium when she wrote these passages. But in *The Tree of Heaven* descriptions like Michael's are used to challenge the idea of war as a materialization of the 'herd instinct'. Sinclair manages to make sense of her desire to participate in the war, in spite of her deep mistrust of mass movements, by describing it as a profoundly private experience of quasi-mystical ecstasy, in which the soul merges not with other people but with 'Reality' itself. In reinventing war in this way she also evacuates it of any political dimension: it becomes an internal object, a zone of heightened sensation and of self-discovery, to which wider contexts are simply irrelevant. As Rebecca West wrote in her review of the *Journal*, 'one cannot imagine Miss Sinclair presuming to express an opinion upon international affairs'.[74] For Sinclair, 'international affairs' were not what the war was about.

This image of a war of sensation allows Sinclair to reimagine the soldier's body as emblematic of Vorticist moves towards a more abstract art. As Michael says: 'It's all curiously quiet and steady. . . . Your body may be moving violently, with other bodies moving violently around it; but *you*'re still' (TH, 395). This sounds very much like an image of Pound's or Gaudier-Brzeska's vortex, with its whirling outer rim moving in towards a still centre. Michael's words also recall the words of one of his sculptor friends in London, who talks about the visual representation of movement in terms that almost exactly replicate those of the Cubists and the Vorticists. Paul Monier-Owen, evidently based on Gaudier-Brzeska, speaks of an aesthetic of 'decomposition':

---

[74] West, 'Miss Sinclair's Genius', 305–6.

By decomposing groups of figures you compose groups of movements. . . . It can't
be done unless you break up your objects . . . It can't be done unless you dislocate
their lines and masses as I dislocate them, so as to throw them all at once into those
planes that the intact body could only have traversed one after another in a given
time. (TH, 243–4)

This broken body reorganizes time and space to produce what Monier-
Owen calls 'rhythm', a rhythm which depends on the intersection of violent
movement and stillness. 'You have to choose between the intact body which
is stationary and the broken and projected bodies which are in movement',
says Monier-Owen (TH, 244). Michael's ecstasy in battle—his sense of
being, in the words of T. S. Eliot, at 'the still point of the turning world'—is
partly born out of a Vorticist aesthetic, in which the motion of the body is
expressed as a kind of transcendental immobility.[75] It is this transcendence
which militates against the war as vortex. These 'decomposed' bodies—a
grotesquely accurate term for the bodies of war—generate vortices of their
own, concentrating the power of their own movement in the feeling of stillness at their centre. The centre of the war is reconceptualized: it is no longer
a centripetal force drawing everything and everyone to itself, but a space in
which any number of individual bodies can experience their own private
vortex. Sinclair's version of the Vorticist body overcomes the intensification
of the 'herd instinct' associated with mass movements: the aesthetic of the
broken, decomposed body—the body at war—allows men (and, in theory,
women) to enter the war and refind themselves there on their own terms.

   The Tree of Heaven pleased some reviewers with its enthusiastic endorsement of fighting as a spiritually satisfying experience. The *New York Times
Book Review*, for example, noted that its 'study of the psychological effect of
the war on Michael is done with remarkable sureness and subtlety'.[76] Others
found it 'very partial', and felt that Sinclair's concentration on 'the pervasive
consciousness that makes a family' masked her ignorance of and callous lack
of concern about war's brutality.[77] Sinclair was especially grateful for a
review by Frank Swinnerton which went beyond consideration of the content to discuss the form of the novel. She was still aiming for 'simplicity &
concentration', but she felt that *The Tree of Heaven* was 'not direct <u>enough</u>,
concentrated <u>enough</u>'.[78] As well as her commitment to supporting the war in

---

[75] T. S. Eliot, 'Burnt Norton', 1935, *Four Quartets*, in *Collected Poems 1909–1962* (London: Faber and
Faber, 1974), 191.
[76] 'The War in England and Germany', *New York Times Book Review*, 27 Jan. 1918, 29.
[77] Herbert J. Seligmann, 'May Sinclair, Sentimentalist', *Dial*, 64 (23 May 1918), 489–90.
[78] Sinclair to Arthur Adcock, 16 Jan. 1918, UP, Box 1, fo. 1. Swinnerton's review appeared in *Bookman*
(London), 53 (Jan. 1918), 137. Other reviews also mentioned the book's 'imagistic' technique. See

2. Frank Sinclair, May Sinclair's favourite brother, who died in India in 1889 aged 32.

1. Amelia Sinclair, May Sinclair's mother.

3. The house in Rock Ferry near
Liverpool where May Sinclair
lived until she was 7.

4. Dorothea Beale, headmistress
of Cheltenham Ladies' College,
who acted as May Sinclair's philosophy teacher and spiritual
advisor, in 1886.

5. May Sinclair in 1898, the photo that was used in publicity for her second novel, *Mr and Mrs Nevill Tyson*.

6. Anthony Deane, the curate with whom May Sinclair was later in love, while he was still at Wellington College in 1885. Deane is on the extreme right, holding a violin.

7. Henry Melvill Gwatkin, Regius Professor of Ecclesiastical History at Emmanuel College, Cambridge. He tried to help Sinclair regain her Christian faith in 1894–5.

8. William Sinclair, May Sinclair's eldest brother, and his wife Eleanor. She and Sinclair were very close.

9. The family of William and Eleanor Sinclair, c.1900 (William had died in 1896). Clockwise from left: Francis, Wilda, William (who was killed in 1915), Eleanor, Eleanor (junior; known as Nora, and May Sinclair's favourite niece), Harold, Agatha.

10. Gwendoline Keats ('Zack'), novelist and friend, in 1898.

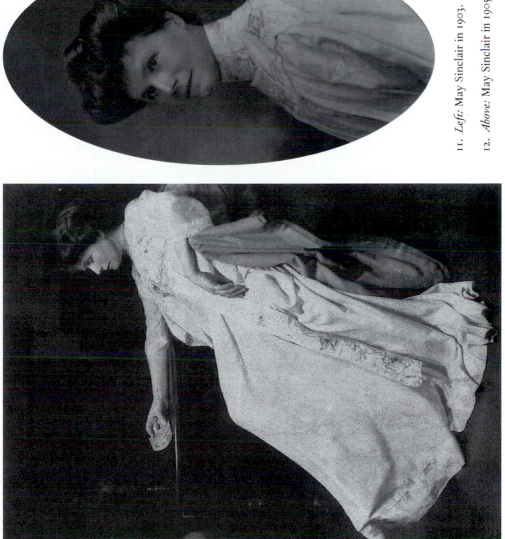

11. *Left*: May Sinclair in 1903.

12. *Above*: May Sinclair in 1905.

13. *Left*: illustration to the first instalment of *The Creators* in *Century* magazine, November 1909. Sinclair particularly disliked this picture.

14. *Above*: Katharine Tynan, Irish writer, in 1897–8. She befriended Sinclair in 1900 after reading *Mr and Mrs Nevill Tyson*.

15. Thomas Hardy, Sinclair's cycling companion, in 1913.

16. Charlotte Mew, with whom Sinclair had an awkward friendship in the years before the First World War, in 1923.

17. Ezra Pound in 1913. He became Sinclair's friend and protégé in 1908.

18. Richard Aldington, poet and friend, 1931.

19. May Sinclair in the 1920s.

20. May Sinclair outside her writing hut in Stow-on-the-Wold, 1920s.

21. *Above*: May Sinclair with her cat.

22. *Left*: May Sinclair in the 1920s.

23. *Right*: May Sinclair in the late 1920s.

24. May Sinclair and Florence Bartrop, her companion during her last years.

25. Letter from May Sinclair to Katharine Tynan Hinkson, 1 January 1902.

the fiction she published during the war years, Sinclair was also tentatively experimenting with fictional technique. Her most radical attempt at innovative narrative was *Mary Olivier: A Life*, the novel which followed *The Tree of Heaven*, but *Mary Olivier* returned to a pre-war setting, as I note in Chapter 7, where I discuss the novel fully. It was as if the formal innovation to which Sinclair aspired was incompatible with the message she wanted to convey of a just war in which all moral beings should participate. It was not possible to write heroic prose in the fragmented, sceptical style of the modernist novel.

Sinclair was working on *Mary Olivier* as the war dragged to a close in the autumn of 1918. But as soon as she had finished it, and the war was finally over, she started working on another novel, *The Romantic*, which returned to the sad tale of her own experiences on the front. Perhaps the cessation of hostilities freed her up to explore one last time what had really happened in Ghent in late September and early October 1914. Certainly she would not have been able to write *The Romantic* if she had still felt obliged to celebrate the courage of the Allied troops. In her workbook for the novel, Sinclair wrote: 'The war has brought out his [the central character's] latent savagery & brutality. His frustrated sex avenges itself in cruelty to [blank]. To himself he blames her for his own break-down.'[79] The erotic exhilaration she experienced near the battlefields is counterbalanced by the possibility that men who lack sexual confidence will be unable to perform well under fire. If courage is somehow linked—as it was in her mind—to heightened sexual awareness, those who instinctively avoid physical arousal will have no way of confronting the imminence of death. In some ways *The Romantic* reinforces the message of both *The Helpmate* and *The Three Sisters*, that an openness to sexual pleasure is essential for mental and moral health. But in *The Romantic* John's disgust at sexual desire is a betrayal not just of the woman who loves him, but also of the Allied cause.

The Romantic tells the story of Charlotte Redhead, a woman who, as the novel opens, has just been dropped by the married man with whom she was sexually involved. On a country walk she runs into John Conway, who, like her, is interested in learning to farm. Together they find jobs working on a farm in the Cotswolds, and gradually realize they have fallen in love with one another. Charlotte confesses that she has been with another man, and John tells her he is relieved, since, as an experienced woman, she will not need sexual initiation from him. They agree to be a couple, but not to become lovers. When the war breaks out, they form a small ambulance corps

Lawrence Gilman, 'The Book of the Month. May Sinclair's New War Novel', *North American Review*, 207 (Feb. 1918), 284–8; F.H., 'The Rendezvous with Death', *New Republic*, 14 (2 Feb. 1918), 28–9.

[79] Notes for *The Romantic*, Workbook 2, UP, Box 39.

and, sponsored (like the Munro Corps) by the Belgian Legation, leave for Belgium. John is initially thrilled by the sensation of danger, but it gradually becomes clear to Charlotte that he would rather abandon her and wounded men than risk his own life. Several times he lies to her and leaves her in villages under fire because he is too much of a coward to come back for her. Eventually he is shot in the back and killed by the servant of a wounded Belgian captain he was too cowardly to help. McClane, the psychiatrist leader of the rival ambulance corps at the hotel they are staying at, explains John's psyche to Charlotte. He was a degenerate, he says: 'he couldn't live a man's life' (R, 199). The novel ends with Charlotte joining McClane's corps instead.

Charlotte is from the first intensely attracted to John's body and face: 'The young body, alert and energetic; slender gestures of hands. The small imperious head carried high. The spare, oval face with the straight-jutting, pointed chin. Honey-white face, thin dusk and bistre of eyelids and hollow temples and the roots of the hair. Its look of being winged, lifted up, ready to start off on an adventure' (R, 18). With John, Charlotte imagines she can experience first the earth (as a farmer), and then the war, as adventures that will bring her new feelings and new sensations. In Belgium, she is continually overtaken by feelings of pity and tenderness for the soldiers she works with. Supporting a wounded Belgian, she 'could feel nothing but the helpless pressure of his body against hers, nothing but her pity that hurt her and was exquisite like love' (R, 103). The English countryside too moves her to feelings of affection: 'And the hills—look at them, the clean, quiet backs, smoothed with light. You could stroke them' (R, 26). She assumes that she and John together will share these kinds of communion, opening themselves up to feelings and people beyond their usual limits.

But John's response to the countryside is excited and sadistic.[80] He sees it as a challenge: 'fighting with things that would kill you if you didn't. Wounding the earth to sow in it and make it feed you' (R, 26). In true Freudian fashion he cannot disentangle love and aggression, and he tells Charlotte that beauty and kindness have always grown out of some 'damnable cruelty' (R, 27). John's reactions to Charlotte, as their relationship develops, bear all the traces of this ambivalence. In fantasy, danger attracts him. When they hear the guns in the distance, Charlotte feels that they are 'locked close, closer than their bodies could have joined them, in the strange and poignant ecstasy of danger' (R, 79). But the reality of wounds,

---

[80] See Sharon Ouditt, *Fighting Forces, Writing Women: Identity and Ideology in the First World War* (London: Routledge, 1994), 68, for further discussion of this aspect of John's character.

blood, and most of all fear, make John turn pale and run. As Charlotte puts it:

John's cowardice was not like other people's cowardice. Other cowards going into danger had the imagination of horror. He had nothing but the imagination of romantic delight. It was the reality that became too much for him. He was either too stupid, or too securely wrapped up in his dream to reckon with reality. It surprised him every time. And he had no imaginative fear of fear. (R, 170)

Sinclair's interest in this psychic configuration, a configuration that was clearly not Sinclair's own (she was haunted before she went out by visions of mutilated bodies) but which nonetheless spoke to her enough that she made John the focus of her novel, suggests that the war raised issues for her about the relationship of fantasy to reality, that 'Reality' which she at first believed the war would deliver. Perhaps she used John as a way of working through some of her own fear of sexual intimacy. For the first time, in insisting on being close to a man (Munro) to whom she seems to have been attracted, and on experiencing something (the war) which was never really meant for her, she was confronted with the intensity of her own desires. But like John's, Sinclair's war was not what she had expected. Whether she had, as she claims, repeatedly tried to go out with the ambulances, or whether, as Miss Ashley-Smith suggests, she was reluctant, frightened, and disorganized, the romances she had expected did not materialize, either with Munro or with the idea of herself as a solitary, exultant hero.

Repeated humiliations reminded of her marginal status as an untrained, undesirable middle-aged woman. Her anxiety to be in Belgium was made to seem ridiculous and even ugly, like Viola's in *Tasker Jevons*. Like Jevons, John can't stand to be made aware of Charlotte's—or any woman's—sexuality: 'I loathe those women. There's Alice Bartrum—I saw her making eyes at Sutton over a spouting artery. As for Mrs. Rankin they ought to intern her. . . . Gwinnie hangs her beastly legs about all over the place. So do you' (R, 136–7). John is made to articulate some of the hostility towards women that Sinclair constantly associates with the battlefield, but he was also a character with whom she could identify. As a coward, whose face turns 'sallow-white and drawn and glistening' (93) bringing in the wounded from the battlefield, John is scorned and marginalized. Sinclair's interest in him as a character reveals her concern for those who are left out of the 'herd', as Trotter called it: women and men who are disabled in some way—age, physique, psychic make-up.[81]

[81] Trotter himself was anxious about those who for some reason were left out of the 'herd': 'The peace of mind, happiness, and energy of the soldier come from his feeling himself to be a member in a body solidly

Sinclair clearly saw and applauded bellicosity as an essential component in healthy masculinity (compare, for example, Rose Allatini's *Despised and Rejected*, published in 1918 and immediately prosecuted for sedition, which indicts the brutality of its heterosexual male characters). As McClane explains, John could never feel like a man. His degeneracy was a kind of feminization, an inability to 'live a man's life' (R, 199). His repudiation of women and his excitement at the idea of war are both reaction-formations, attempts to compensate for the inadequacy of his masculinity. As McClane explains it: 'His platonics were just a glorifying of his disability. All that romancing was a gorgeous transformation of his funk. . . . [*ellipses in original*] So that his very lying was a sort of truth. I mean it was part of the whole desperate effort after completion. He jumped at everything that helped him to get compensation, to get power' (R, 200). John's cowardice and his gender dysfunction are explained away as congenital conditions, rather than responses to the war. Although the war is at the centre of the novel it is oddly peripheral to John's psychology, as though Sinclair could not bear to give it the centrality it would seem to demand. Like John she both invoked the erotic intensity of war and fled it; simultaneously complained that she could not reach it, and wished that it would not reach her. It was both a loved and a hated object, one which constructed her as a problem, or, at best, an irrelevance, and yet which she could not let alone.

The Romantic was almost her final fictional statement about the war, and the last text she wrote to be constructed around it.[82] She took some care with it, consulting Richard Aldington about the accuracy of some of the scenes.[83] But it was as though, having written it, there was little more of interest to be said. Reviews were favourable, although, as Corrine Yvonne Taylor points out, some noted that the novel 'comes perilously close to becoming a case study rather than an imagined work of art'.[84] Others welcomed its psycho-analytic bent: the review in the *Spectator*, for example, called it 'a notable achievement in psychoanalysis', and Frederick Taber Cooper declared that it had been 'a long while since a purely degenerate type of man has been so consistently and relentlessly portrayed'.[85] But most reviews did not see it as

---

united for a single purpose. . . . the presence of a large class who are as sensitive as any to the call of the herd, and yet cannot respond in any active way, contains very grave possibilities. The only response to that relentless calling that can give peace is in service; if that be denied, restlessness, uneasiness and anxiety must necessarily follow' (*Instincts of the Herd*, 144, 148).

[82] In both *The Rector of Wyck*, and *Far End*, characters are killed in the war, but their experiences there are not described in any detail.

[83] Sinclair to Scott, 20 Mar. 1920, Beinecke Rare Book and Manuscript Library, Gen MSS 144, Box 1, fo. 22.

[84] Taylor, 'Study of May Sinclair', 94.

[85] '*The Romantic*', *Spectator* (London), 125 (13 Nov. 1920), 641; Frederic Taber Cooper, 'The Coward', *Publishers' Weekly*, 98 (18 Sept. 1920), 657.

a war novel at all. In later years, even Sinclair herself seems to have come to see the war as historically and culturally ephemeral. In a 1924 interview in the USA she stated:

I don't think our literature was at all affected by the war, though I am not prepared to say this positively. Of course, when our men came back after years of fighting they did not want serious things. They danced and played, trying to forget the horrors they had lived through. Perhaps they read the lightest literature at that time. But it was only a temporary state of mind.[86]

Characteristically she divorces 'the war' from the processes of historical transformation, and presents it merely as a slight interruption to literary history. Once Sinclair had made a definitive statement about the psychic geographies war configured, she simply put it behind her. The war had not, in the end, delivered the personal and cultural transformations she had at first hoped for. After all, why should life be more 'real' in war-torn Belgium than anywhere else? If it was passing her by, it passed her by just as much on the front as it did back in civilian society.

---

[86] Ryan Walker, 'May Sinclair Talks of Everything Except Herself', *New York Times Book Review*, 18 May 1924, 2.

6

Experiments in Poetry

=

A FEW years before the outbreak of the war that affected May Sinclair so profoundly, she received an unexpected early morning call from fellow writers Richard Aldington, H.D., and Ezra Pound. When Sinclair 'opened the studio apartment door', H.D. reports, her 'somewhat Queen Mary bang or fringe was done up in curl papers'. H.D. 'tugged at Richard's sleeve to suggest that we go home, but Ezra had already swung on into the studio. May Sinclair made no reference to her early morning appearance.' Sinclair's composure in the face of this invasion reveals both her habitual politeness, and the extent to which she felt at home with, and attracted by, her friends' Bohemian unpredictability. On this occasion Pound whirled through her rooms 'flinging books from a table in May Sinclair's studio on to an inaccessible shelf that ran under the high sloping roof'. Pound was indignant on Sinclair's behalf, telling her 'people impose on you'.[1] The books were all gifts from aspiring young poets and novelists, who had sent them to Sinclair in the hope of securing her advice and support.

There was more than a little irony in Pound's taking it on himself to protect Sinclair, since he had been one of her protégés, and had been accepting substantial gifts from her, ever since he arrived in London from the USA as an unknown writer in 1908. H.D. was also just beginning her career as a poet, and was overawed by meeting the famous May Sinclair. Sinclair was more than twenty years older than H.D. (in 1911 Sinclair was 48, Pound and H.D. were in their mid-twenties, and Aldington was only 19), but she was disarmed by Pound's flirtatious charm, by H.D.'s whimsical intelligence, and by Aldington's kindness and good looks. Harold P. Collins, future editor of the *Adelphi* magazine, described watching 'a highly nervous H.D., at a dinner she gave for May Sinclair in 1924, completely bewitch the older

---

[1] H.D., *End to Torment*, 9–10.

woman. H.D. concealed her social timidity with laughter and wizardry, and that touch of the rebellious, gifted poet that May Sinclair, with her sedate modesty, could not resist.'[2]

Sinclair's fondness for these young rebels meant that she was willing to defend their work in public, even when that involved aligning herself with unpopular literary movements such as imagism in poetry. Such gestures had significant unforeseen consequences for her own work. Her interest in contemporary poetry, sparked by Pound and his associates, gradually transformed her own aesthetic practice until, with *Mary Olivier: A Life* (1919), she herself became one of the leaders of literary modernism. As Sinclair watched the development of imagism, and, because of her connection with the Medico-Psychological Clinic, read more and more widely in psychoanalytic theory, she pondered the relationship between poetic and psychological modernity, between the philosophy of the imagists and of the psychoanalysts in whose thought she was immersing herself. Imagism offered her a way out of the ornate metrics and melodrama of late Victorian poetry, but as she worked through its relation to psychoanalytic ideas, she eventually grew weary of its spareness. Psychoanalysis, with its careful description of the rhythms and textures of the mind, increasingly grounded Sinclair's aesthetic practice. All the same she found it hard to renounce Victorian aesthetics altogether. Sinclair's evolution into a modernist novelist, coupled with her nostalgic attraction to Victorian literary, especially poetic, styles, meant that during the transforming years of the First World War she found herself caught in a contradiction she described as characteristic of modernity itself.

Her most substantial statement of the paradox of modernity did not appear until 1921, in her review essay on Richard Aldington's poetry.[3] The article looked back over Aldington's career, and it must also have seemed to Sinclair like a retrospective of her own. Aldington like Sinclair had served in the First World War, the only man in their immediate circle to do so, and he cautiously acknowledged their war experience as a bond between them, writing to John Cournos from a military training camp in August 1916:

---

[2] Pound's letters to Sinclair are full of an affectionate irony (see my discussion later in this chapter of his response to her article on his work). Collins's words are quoted in Barbara Guest, *Herself Defined: The Poet H.D. and her World* (New York: Doubleday, 1984), 149. A number of people have speculated that Sinclair was a little in love with Aldington, partly because Richard Nicholson, Mary Olivier's lover, is said to have been modelled on him (see e.g. Guest, *Herself Defined*, 63). Florence Bartrop, Sinclair's companion and housekeeper for the last thirty years of her life, told Sinclair's biographer Theophilus Boll that she thought Sinclair could have loved Aldington 'in perfect physical innocence', and remembered his frequent visits and 'an atmosphere of emotion' between them. See Boll, *Miss May Sinclair*, 119–20.

[3] Sinclair, 'The Poems of Richard Aldington', *English Review*, 32 (May 1921), 397–410.

'Little May is very sweet, and seems to understand in a way, but her sense of duty is too ever-present!'[4] An early draft of the Aldington essay reveals that Sinclair was even more preoccupied with the role of war in Aldington's poetic development than the published piece suggests: she worried that 'a paralysing fear of spiritual mutilation' must have gripped him and his fellow soldier poets as they tried to preserve their creative gifts intact.[5] But she did not blame the war exclusively for what she called Aldington's 'sad modernity'. He was 'modern' long before he went out to the front:

To be born at the end of the nineteenth century and to be young in the youth of the twentieth must be counted as misfortune to a poet like Richard Aldington. For there is no mistaking his modernity. One half of him is not Greek, and it brings into his poetry an element which is not Greek, a pain, a dissatisfaction, a sadness that the purely Greek soul did not know. . . . And so Richard Aldington brings his sad modernity into the heart of his Greek world. His joy in beauty which was pure joy to the ancient Greek who had to do with beauty unadulterated and unstained, his joy has in it a deep, incurable dissatisfaction. Beauty hurts him as it did not and could not hurt the Greek; because he sees that its position in the modern world is dangerous and impermanent.

Aldington is modern because beauty wounds him with its transience. In his poetry Greek joy and modern sorrow collide: 'Hence the impression of conflict, of profound incompleteness conveyed by these poems of his transition.'[6] Internal contradiction and incompletion defined the modern moment for Sinclair, who like Aldington found herself trying to occupy several worlds at once: the Victorian world of her childhood social values, the world of her early allegiance to German idealist philosophy, and the contemporary world of Pound, H.D., and the others. Her championing of the imagists' immersion in both the classical and the contemporary world was also a defence of her own cultural and psychic predicament.

This simultaneous attraction to the past and to the modernist era found expression in Sinclair's life in the coincidence in the years just before and during the First World War of two very different emotional and aesthetic involvements. At the same time that she was vehemently writing in praise of imagism and 'The Love-Song of J. Alfred Prufrock', she was also promoting the work of a poet one of her few critics has called 'one of the last Vic-

---

[4] Richard Aldington to John Cournos, 14 Aug. 1916, in *Richard Aldington: An Autobiography in Letters*, ed. Norman T. Gates (University Park, Pa.: Pennsylvania State University Press, 1992), 21. F. S. Flint, another of the imagists, did not enlist during the war, but served in the army from 1918.

[5] Holograph draft of 'The Poems of Richard Aldington', 19, UP, Box 24, fo. 469.

[6] Sinclair, 'Poems of Richard Aldington', 401.

torians': Charlotte Mew.[7] Sinclair's relationship with Mew is one of the few intense (and problematic) attachments of her life of which there is some record. Not on Sinclair's side: she destroyed all Mew's letters (unusually, since letters from writers were the only private papers she did take pains to preserve). Mew, however, kept all of her correspondence with Sinclair, and through it we can trace the awkwardness and the discomfort of their mutual attraction. Mew's emotional adventurousness was of a very different quality than that of the younger poets with whom Sinclair was simultaneously developing a relationship: where Pound especially was outspoken and rebellious, Mew was secretive, anguished, and intense. But Mew, more nearly Sinclair's contemporary (she was only six years younger), seems to have touched her more closely. Ironically, it was this 'late Victorian' who confronted Sinclair with the limits of her own modernity by revealing her love to her.

Charlotte Mew and May Sinclair were first introduced at the home of Catherine Dawson Scott, known as 'Sappho', and later founder of the PEN Club. Scott had met Sinclair at Evelyn Underhill's in the spring of 1913 and asked Sinclair to call on her.

She agreed and I then asked Charlotte, who resisted, saying she didn't want to meet clever people. Eventually agreed to come [*sic*]. May arrived first and was annoyed, as she had wanted to talk to me. However, when Charlotte came I persuaded her to read to us *The Farmer's Bride*, and May was so won over that she deserted me and they went away together.[8]

Mew had had a few stories and essays published during the 1890s and in the early years of the century in periodicals like the *Yellow Book* and *Temple Bar*, but she was little known when Sinclair first came across her in Dawson Scott's drawing room. Born in 1869, Mew lived for most of her life with her mother and sister Anne in Gordon Square, where she was, for a time, Virginia Woolf's neighbour. She eked out a meagre living by writing, and her earnings were supplemented by her mother's annuity (which ended upon her mother's death in 1923), and by her sister Anne's work as a restorer of antique furniture. She had a history of falling disastrously in love with

[7] Angela Leighton, *Victorian Women Poets: Writing against the Heart* (Harvester Wheatsheaf: Hemel Hempstead, 1992), 266.

[8] Catherine Dawson Scott's diary, cited in Penelope Fitzgerald, *Charlotte Mew and her Friends* (London: Collins, 1984), 120. For detailed discussion of the Mew–Sinclair relationship, see also Boll, 'The Mystery of Charlotte Mew and May Sinclair: An Inquiry', *Bulletin of the New York Public Library*, 74 (1970), 445–53; Mary C. Davidow, 'The Charlotte Mew–May Sinclair Relationship: A Reply', *Bulletin of the New York Public Library*, 75 (1971), 295–300; Leighton, *Victorian Women Poets*, 275; and Suzanne Raitt, 'Charlotte Mew and May Sinclair: A Love-Song', *Critical Quarterly*, 37 (1995), 3–17.

women.[9] 'The Farmer's Bride', the poem she showed Sinclair, is an extra-ordinarily erotic description of a young farmer's yearning for his new wife who, afraid 'Of love and me and all things human', fled their home and was fetched back and put under lock and key.[10] Sinclair had just published the naturalistic novel *The Combined Maze*, in which sexual impulse leads a usu-ally well-disciplined clerk to marry an opportunist draper's assistant. The 'combined maze' of the title is a dance in which the protagonists participate at the local gymnasium, and it becomes a figure in the novel for the deter-ministic influence of sex and environment: 'it was as if Life itself had caught him and locked him with a woman in the whirling of its Great Wheel.'[11] Sin-clair was attracted to the similarly fatalistic intensity of both Mew's person-ality and her poetry. After their meeting at Catherine Dawson Scott's she presented Mew with a copy of *The Combined Maze*, and was surprised when she liked it, writing to Mew in March 1913: 'I never thought you'd read it!'[12] Sinclair was in Yorkshire for a few weeks in May and June, but Mew called on her on her return to London and Sinclair, who had to send her away since she was about to go out, wrote to reassure Mew: 'I do so want to see you & know you better. I was more grieved than I can say at having to let you go the other evening.'[13] A few days later Mew was reading her poetry aloud to Sinclair in her lodgings and the friendship was firmly established.

The women certainly had many things in common. Close in age, both had spent years caring for difficult, ageing mothers who believed absolutely in the importance of keeping up appearances; both had fathers whose busi-nesses failed (Frederick Mew was an architect whose career faltered and never recovered after the death of his father-in-law and partner in 1885); and both had lost siblings to hereditary disease. When the two women met, Sin-clair's five brothers were all dead of a congenital heart condition. Mew's brother Henry and sister Freda were schizophrenic and died in mental hos-pitals, Henry in 1901 and Freda many years after Mew's own death. It is unclear how much Sinclair and Mew knew of one another's history: both were reserved and Mew was ashamed of her family's 'taint', as she saw it: even her closest friend Alida Monro knew nothing of Freda's existence.[14]

[9] See Fitzgerald, *Charlotte Mew and her Friends*, 84–7.

[10] 'The Farmer's Bride' was first published in the *Nation* in Feb. 1912, and then appeared as the title poem of Mew's collection *The Farmer's Bride* (London: Poetry Bookshop, 1916). The volume was reissued in 1921 with some additional poems, and reprinted again in 1953 in *Collected Poems of Charlotte Mew*, ed. Alida Monro (London: Duckworth, 1953). In 1982 Val Warner edited *Charlotte Mew: Collected Poems and Prose* for Virago. 'The Farmer's Bride' appears on pp. 1–2.

[11] Sinclair, *The Combined Maze* (New York: Harper's, 1913), 88.

[12] Sinclair to Mew, 17 Mar. 1913, HA.   [13] Sinclair to Mew, 4 July 1913, HA.

[14] Fitzgerald, *Charlotte Mew and her Friends*, 153.

But whether or not Mew and Sinclair confided in each other, both had remained unmarried (in Mew's case, deliberately to avoid passing on her family's illness), and both had developed ways of protecting their inner lives from the world.[15] Mew's brusque gaucherie and her capacity for rudeness did not deter Sinclair: after all, she tolerated and even enjoyed the peremptory Ezra Pound.

Sinclair quickly moved to help Mew get more publications—and earn more money. She sent her poems to the *English Review* and to Ezra Pound, who in turn sent them on to Harriet Monroe, editor of *Poetry*.[16] But Mew was reticent. Sinclair had to coax her into sending her short stories out: 'Cd. they not be published anonymously, or under another name, if you don't want to sign them?'[17] Mew was suspicious and easily hurt. When Sinclair returned her manuscripts to her before leaving for two months in Scotland and Yorkshire in August 1913, Mew took this gesture, and the way Sinclair signed her letter ('Good-bye and Good Luck, always and sincerely yours'), as a sign that the friendship was over. Sinclair had to explain:

what I <u>meant</u> was that your duplicate mss. wd. be safer with you than accompanying me in my wanderings. . . . As for 'Good-bye' I never dreamt it wd. be interpreted 'Good-bye for Ever'! But it is my own fault if—going to Yorkshire & Scotland for two months—I write as if I were bound for the North Pole.

In November—I hope, we meet, if you are not too disgusted with my style![18]

But Sinclair continued to disappoint—perhaps to avoid—Mew. She had to apologize for not inviting her up to Yorkshire, explaining that she needed time and solitude to work on the opening chapters of *The Three Sisters*: 'I'm not behaving worse to you than to the other friends I wanted to have here!'[19] When Sinclair returned to London, she was extraordinarily busy with the Medico-Psychological Clinic, which had its inaugural meeting in November 1913. Mew's offer to address circulars for her was met with a determined negative, and even though Sinclair promised in October that when the clinic was 'fairly launched' the two would spend a Sunday together, she seems never to have extended an invitation.[20] Meanwhile *Poetry* refused Mew's

---

[15] See Alida Monro, 'Charlotte Mew—A Memoir', in *Collected Poems of Charlotte Mew*, pp. vii–xx: at p. xiii.

[16] Sinclair and Monroe met in 1910, probably through their mutual friend Alice Meynell. Harriet Monroe describes Sinclair as 'the quiet little spinster novelist whose *Divine Fire* I had admired when it was first published' (*A Poet's Life: Seventy Years in a Changing World*, New York: Macmillan, 1938, 223). Monroe and Sinclair were still in touch in 1924, and met in New York during Sinclair's visit there as a delegate to the second international convention of PEN (see Monroe to Sinclair, 9 June 1924, UP, Box 2, fo. 64).

[17] Sinclair to Mew, 17 July 1913, HA.

[18] Sinclair to Mew, n.d. [Aug. 1913], HA.

[19] Sinclair to Mew, 18 Sept. 1913, HA.

[20] Sinclair to Mew, 17 Oct. 1913, HA.

poems, and Mew, still loyal, embroidered a 'dear little cloth with . . . birds & beasts & fishes' for Sinclair's Christmas present.[21] But even after this gesture, Sinclair's promise to call on Mew in early January 1914 was double-edged: 'Don't stay in. I shall be in yr. neighbourhood anyway.'[22] Sinclair was trying to keep Mew at arms' length, both attracted to and wary of her. It was clear that Mew was falling in love with her, but Sinclair tactfully avoided any reference to her growing attachment. She may well have felt sympathetic to, and responsible for—even occasionally responsive to—Mew's anguished desires.[23]

Mew continued to court Sinclair's approval. When in early March Sinclair wrote to her from Yorkshire telling her that Pound wanted to publish Mew's poem 'The Fête' in the *Egoist*, she added casually that she had managed to find new tenants for her studio flat in Kensington, where she had been disturbed by her neighbours' music practice, and was looking for somewhere quiet to live. Immediately Mew went into action, going round agencies, visiting flats, awkwardly anxious to help, and keen to repay Sinclair for her support and advice. Sinclair was embarrassed: 'How perfectly angelic of you to go & take all that awful bother. . . . all my days I shall be haunted by a vision of you, small, & too fragile by far for the hideous task, going up & down those infernal houses. . . . A thousand thanks for all you've done. I shan't forget it in a hurry'.[24] Mew was rewarded with an invitation to tea, and for a while things proceeded smoothly, with regular teas and dinners. 'The Fête' was finally published in the *Egoist* (which unfortunately did not pay), and Mew seemed to have temporarily recovered some measure of equilibrium.

But in May 1914 Mew's delicate emotional balance was thrown off once more. After an intimate Saturday night dinner at her house, Sinclair offered to walk with Mew to the tube station. Something in her suggestion offended Mew. In response to a letter from Mew that is now lost, Sinclair wrote:

Not by way of 'answer' but as a general statement, may I assure you that I really have not a complicated mind, but in some ways rather a simple one, & when I say 'I want to walk with you to Baker St Station', I mean I want to walk, & I want to walk

---

[21] Sinclair to Mew, 1 Jan. 1914, HA.   [22] Ibid.

[23] Janice H. Harris has argued that, in her fiction at least, Sinclair explored the dynamics of erotic energy between women with some intensity ('Challenging the Script of the Heterosexual Couple'). Harris cites Anne Majendie's identification with Lady Cayley in *The Helpmate* (1907), the relationship between Kitty Tailleur and her companion in *Kitty Tailleur* (1908), and 'the homoeroticism that plays between Jane and Nina, and later between Laura and Nina' (454) in *The Creators* (1910). But Jane's relationships with women are mediated more by a shared passion for writing than for each other.

[24] Sinclair to Mew, 8 Mar. 1914, HA.

with you, & I want to walk to Baker St Station. The act of walking is a pleasure in itself, that has no ulterior purpose or significance.

Better to take these things simply & never go back on them, or analyse them, isn't it?

I, (who am so complicated), took it all quite simply & was glad of it—of yr. being here, of yr. talking to me—well, why can't you do the same?[25]

Boll, relying on a report from Sinclair's friend novelist G. B. Stern that Sinclair regaled a tea party with stories of Mew's indiscretions, maintains that on this May night Mew finally declared her love, and chased Sinclair into her bedroom, where she had to leap the bed five times to escape Mew's amorous advances.[26] Catherine Dawson Scott certainly seems to have believed that Mew was putting sexual pressure on Sinclair, and she dropped Mew around this time.[27]

But was their evening together really as outrageous and farcical as Boll believes? Mary C. Davidow, one of Mew's biographers, dismisses out of hand the idea that Mew tried to force the issue by pursuing Sinclair into her bedroom:

[The May 1914 date] forces one to accept a ludicrously out-of-focus sequence of events: two women, one forty-four years old, the other fifty, quietly enjoy supper one Saturday evening in May 1914. Suddenly, the younger one, seized by a wild fit of passion, gives chase to the older woman who makes a dash for the bedroom, of all places, and, amid moving-crates and cartons and displaced furnishings, leaps the bed five times. Five days later, May 14, the victim of this passionate attack writes to ask the attacker to 'try her luck again on Tuesday, 19th, 4.30' when the Aldingtons and Evelyn Stuart-Moore [Underhill] will be present.[28]

---

[25] Sinclair to Mew, 14 May 1914, HA.

[26] Boll quotes as evidence a letter by novelist G. B. Stern in which Stern recalls a tea party with Sinclair and West at which Sinclair regaled the younger women with a story about 'how a Lesbian poetess named Charlotte M. had once in a wild fit of passion chased her upstairs into her bedroom—"And I assure you, Peter [G. B. Stern], I assure you, Rebecca [Rebecca West], I had to leap the bed five times!" '(Boll, 'Mystery of Charlotte Mew and May Sinclair', 453). This story is supported by an entry in Catherine Dawson Scott's journal in which she recounts how during a teatime discussion of the lesbian union of Radclyffe Hall and Una Troubridge, Sinclair told Scott and the novelist Netta Syrett that ' "You wouldn't like it if it happened to *you*. It did happen to me," but I said, "My good woman, you are simply wasting your perfectly good passion" ' [punctuation in original] (quoted in Fitzgerald, *Charlotte Mew and her Friends*, 134). This anecdote is rendered more convincing by the fact that the final phrase is echoed in a 1921 story by Sinclair, 'Lena Wrace': 'it was preposterous that she should waste so much good passion' ('Lena Wrace', *English Review*, 32, Feb. 1921, 103–15; *Dial*, 71, July 1921, 50–62; repr. in *Tales Told by Simpson*, New York: Macmillan, 1930, 33–46: at 35). There is an ambiguity in the quotation itself, of course: does 'It did happen to me' mean that Sinclair felt that way herself, or that a woman approached her sexually? However, Scott was more than likely careless in the way she recorded the comment (the punctuation is erratic e.g.), and the ambiguity is probably unintentional.

[27] Fitzgerald, *Charlotte Mew and her Friends*, 133–6.

[28] Davidow, 'Charlotte Mew–May Sinclair Relationship', 299.

Put this way, Boll's reconstruction of events does seem exaggerated and incongruous, to say the least. Stern's recollections were recorded several decades after the event, and are not entirely convincing: it is hard to imagine the tight-lipped Sinclair gossiping about such a delicate matter. Even if Mew's feelings did become clear during the course of the evening, it is unlikely that the two women actually engaged in some kind of physical tussle. It may be that Sinclair offered to take Mew home in an attempt to save her from further revelation and embarrassment, and Mew felt dismissed before she was ready to leave. In her state of heightened sensitivity the smallest slight assumed monstrous proportions.

Somehow the two women managed once again to patch things up. For the next two years their letters and meetings continued. Mew helped Sinclair with her poetry; Sinclair continued to assist Mew in finding publishers for her stories and verse. Gradually, as time passed, their letters became more distant and infrequent. Mew became more and more absorbed in seeing *The Farmer's Bride* into print (the volume was published in May 1916 by the Poetry Bookshop). Sinclair for her part was preoccupied from 1914 onwards with the war and her trip to Belgium, and she spent most of 1916 in retreat in Yorkshire working on her book on philosophy, *A Defence of Idealism*. With the publication of *The Farmer's Bride*, her mission to help Mew had been accomplished. As a crowning touch, Sinclair's friend H.D. wrote an enthusiastic review of the volume in the *Egoist*.[29] Sinclair's duties as a patron were over, and she and Mew had no further communication after February 1916. Their relationship may conceivably have ended with a dramatic bedroom scene (although not, as Boll believes, in May 1914); but it is much more likely that it simply fizzled out. In a final twist of the plot, years later Mew's friend Alida Monro blamed not Mew's but Sinclair's indiscretions for the break between them: 'Among people who appreciated [Mew's] work was May Sinclair, now almost forgotten, with whom she had a very complete friendship, until something she heard about Miss Sinclair destroyed it forever.'[30] If it is true, as I suggested in Chapter 3, that Sinclair was involved in some kind of sexual relationship at the time of her mother's death, then it is possible that Mew, who 'had a strict moral code in respect of other's people's . . . sex relationships', got wind of something in Sinclair's past.[31] But it is more likely that Monro was trying to preserve Mew's reputation at the expense of Sinclair's. Mew, with a fatal weakness for women who, for whatever reason, did not respond to her, seems simply to have fallen in love with someone who, in spite of her admiration for Mew, did not return her feelings.

[29] H.D., '*The Farmer's Bride*', *Egoist*, 3 (Sept. 1916), 135.
[30] Monro, 'Charlotte Mew—A Memoir', p. xv.   [31] Ibid., p. xii.

Sinclair *was*, however, fascinated and compelled by Charlotte Mew as a writer. She tolerated Mew's excesses because she saw her—as she saw Ezra Pound—as a remarkably talented poet from whom she could learn a certain kind of artistic and emotional honesty. Mew's macabre themes—the rotting body of the beloved in 'The Forest Road', the lunatic asylum of 'Ken'—coupled with an intensely eroticized sense of colour and smell appealed to the darker side of Sinclair's imagination, the side revealed in the spectral poignancy of 'The Intercessor', and the sinister delusions of the aptly named Aunt Charlotte in *Mary Olivier*. Mew's work and companionship sparked the late Victorian, decadent side of Sinclair's writing persona. Penelope Fitzgerald argues that Sinclair's relationship with Mew lies behind her February 1915 story 'The Pin-Prick', in which a young woman kills herself after being made to feel unwelcome at a friend's house.[32] The elaborately staged death of May Blissett (she dies by burning sulphur candles as she lies in her room) is certainly reminiscent of some of the theatrical deaths in Mew's own fiction, such as 'Passed' (1894) or 'A White Night' (1903), and Sinclair's projection of her own name on to the doomed protagonist suggests that she had some feeling of guilt over her relationship with Mew. Ironically, by the time Mew—overwhelmed by grief at her sister's death—*did* take her own life, in 1928, Sinclair, incapacitated by Parkinson's disease, was almost past understanding what had happened.

Mew's macabre and baroque style (both in her poetry and in her persona) were linked in Sinclair's mind with the emotional intensity with which Mew experienced (and described) the world. Sinclair, so reticent herself, was fascinated by Mew's raw, dramatic performances of her own poetry. In early January 1915 Mew read the first verses of her long verse monologue, 'Madeleine in Church', aloud to Sinclair, who urged her to finish it:

Finish—finish yr. Courtisan. She's magnificent. . . . even as you read that last poem I cd. see how great it was. I sd.n't say 'even', for you read furiously well; I never knew anybody who cd. get out the passion of a thing as you can. But this time I felt that it was there—depths & depths of passion & of sheer beauty that were unassailable by the worst reading. Even a cockney accent or a dreary monotone cd.n't have destroyed them.

But I sd. be afraid to let you read anything of mine aloud—you'd put into it all that it ought to have had & hadn't & oh! how flat it wd. fall afterwards![33]

---

[32] Sinclair, 'The Pin-Prick', *Harper's Magazine*, 130 (Feb. 1915), 392–7; repr. in *Tales Told by Simpson*. See Fitzgerald, *Charlotte Mew and her Friends*, 137–8.

[33] Sinclair to Mew, 6 Jan. 1915, HA.

Mew's body—her voicing of her poetry—was crucial to Sinclair's appreciation of it. She liked 'The Fête' less well when she read it to herself than
when Mew performed it for her, writing to Dawson Scott that on the page
'the versification, wh. she made all right when she delivered it in her broken,
dramatic manner, seemed somehow all wrong. . . . It absolutely needed her
voice, her face, her intonation & vehemence to make it carry.'[34] It was for
what we might call the 'somatics' of her readings, as well as for the poetics of
Mew's work, that Sinclair admired her. But that high Victorian melodrama
also made the shy Sinclair feel inadequate. Even as she valued what was
passé in Mew's style it made her uncomfortable. Where Sinclair had early
learnt to discipline her own desires, and to imagine love itself as a form of
discipline, Mew seemed reluctant to accept such constraints, reproducing
the gaucheries of adolescence right into middle age. Mew's work and presence were disruptive both to Sinclair's composure and to her sense of contemporary poetic evolution. Her writing continues to seem anachronistic
even today: Isobel Armstrong, in her monumental study of Victorian
poetry, sees Mew as an isolated talent in an otherwise unexceptional decade,
and Celeste M. Schenk argues that adequate attention to Mew's work will
force us to 'renounce, salutarily, any hope for a unitary, totalizing theory of
female poetic modernism'.[35] Sinclair's fascination with Mew was also a nostalgic farewell to a poetry, and to an emotional theatre, of which she was
suspicious, even as she responded to it. The waning of her involvement with
Mew coincided with her increasing commitment to the definition and
promotion of a poetics that, unlike Mew's, heralded the arrival of a 'modern'
poetry, and rejected both the Victorianism to which Mew still clung, and the
kind of suburban English values about which Sinclair wrote so satirically in
1913 in *The Combined Maze*. That poetics was imagism, and Sinclair threw
herself into print in its defence with an enthusiasm for contemporary work
that she had never shown before.

   Part of her excitement derived, of course, from her affection for Ezra
Pound. Even though, as we have seen, she was critical of Vorticism in *The
Tree of Heaven*, she was interested enough in it to record and explore her
ambivalence, and his sponsorship of a poetry that deliberately turned its
back on the generic and thematic conventions of the Victorian era moved her
to a much more unequivocal endorsement. It is not clear exactly when she

[34] Sinclair to Catherine Dawson Scott, 18 Feb. 1914, Beinecke Rare Book and Manuscript Library,
Gen. MSS 144, Box 1, fo. 22.
[35] Isobel Armstrong, *Victorian Poetry: Poetry, Poetics, Politics* (London: Routledge, 1993), 483; Celeste
M. Schenk, 'Charlotte Mew (1870–1928)' [Mew's actual birthdate is recorded elsewhere as 1869], in Scott
(ed.), *Gender of Modernism*, 316–21: at 317.

met Pound. He apparently remembered having tea with Sinclair in 1908, shortly after he arrived in London, and the two were certainly corresponding as early as March 1909.[36] Sinclair introduced Pound to Ford Madox Ford, and became a member of Pound's dining club at Bellotti's in Soho, where she mixed with people like T. S. Eliot, Arthur Waley, Violet Hunt, G. B. Stern, Wyndham Lewis, and W. B. Yeats.[37] When H.D. and her companion Frances Gregg were on their way to England in 1911, Pound felt confident enough of Sinclair's interest in younger writers that he asked her to invite the two young women to tea.[38] Gregg responded with a mixture of admiration and resentment, describing Sinclair as 'little and mean-souled and repellent, but she could write, and I envied her'.[39] Virginia Woolf had similarly mixed feelings when she had tea with Sinclair in 1909, describing her as 'a woman of obtrusive, and medicinal morality'.[40] Sinclair's relations with Pound were less problematic, perhaps because he was a man. Although he was much younger than her, and teased her mercilessly, Sinclair felt protective towards him, and even at the very beginning of the imagist movement, she was anxious enough about the fragility of poetic reputation to write, in late 1913, a short story in which a young journalist must choose between writing the life and letters of an exceptional young poet, and of a famous, trite writer to whose daughter he is engaged.[41] The journalist's dilemma is that he will jeopardize his own credibility, and render himself unable to help the young poet develop the reputation he deserves, if he writes a suitably hagiographic biography of the mediocre older poet. Throughout the story the main characters are preoccupied with how best to present and celebrate the work of the younger poet, a challenge Sinclair herself already knew she might have to face if she were to remain loyal to Pound over the years that followed.

By the time she wrote 'The Wrackham Memoirs', Pound, H.D., and Aldington had already gone into print under the banner of imagism. Pound coined the word 'Imagiste' in 1912 as a signature for H.D., and the November 1912 issue of *Poetry*, in which three of Aldington's poems appeared,

---

[36] See Charles Norman, *The Case of Ezra Pound* (New York: Funk and Wagnalls, 1968), 18.

[37] See Ford, *Return to Yesterday*, 357, and Douglas Goldring, *The Last Pre-Raphaelite: A Record of the Life and Writings of Ford Madox Ford* (London: Macdonald, 1948), 203. It was probably through Pound that Sinclair met the striking and notorious writer Mary Butts, to whom she lent £25 in 1920 (see Mary Rodker [Butts] to Sinclair, 8 Jan. 1920, UP, Box 1, fo. 79).

[38] Pound to Sinclair, 29 Sept. 1911, UP, Box 3, fo. 74.

[39] Frances Gregg Wilkinson, unpublished memoirs (Oliver Wilkinson), pp. 1345–7, cited in Gillian Hanscombe and Virginia L. Smyers, *Writing for their Lives: The Modernist Women 1910–1940* (London: Women's Press, 1987), 21.

[40] Woolf to Lady Robert Cecil, 12 Apr. 1909, *The Flight of the Mind*, 390.

[41] Sinclair, 'The Wrackham Memoirs', *Harper's Magazine*, 128 (Dec. 1913), 36–47; repr. in *The Return of the Prodigal* (New York: Macmillan, 1914).

described the 'Imagistes' as 'a group of ardent Hellenists who are pursuing interesting experiments in *vers libre*; trying to attain in English certain subtleties of cadence of the kind which Mallarmé and his followers have studied in French'.[42] Sinclair was, naturally enough, keen to help publicize and defend imagism, as the brainchild of someone whose energy she so much admired.

There was more to her support than personal loyalty, however. Sinclair was preoccupied during the years of the imagist movement (which lasted, to all intents and purposes, until 1917) with her work for the Medico-Psychological Clinic, and as she reflected on imagism she was also thinking about psychoanalytic remappings of culture and consciousness. Both contemporary poetry and psychoanalysis seemed to her to be expressions of a new, modern, spirit of the age. In May 1913 she published an appreciative review of Rabindranath Tagore's volume *Gitanjali*, in which she celebrated him as a 'modern, a very modern poet', 'too various to be bound by one tradition'.[43] In 1916 Sinclair published her 'Clinical Lectures on Symbolism and Sublimation', discussions of the English translation of Jung's volume *Psychology of the Unconscious* (1912). The endnotes to the lectures make it clear that in the preceding months and years much of her reading had been in Freudian and Jungian psychoanalysis (she read German), and a chapter of her 1917 book *A Defence of Idealism* deals with psychology and psychoanalysis. Sinclair's defence of imagism went hand in hand with her embracing of modernity in the psychological sphere. Pound saw imagism as a quintessentially modern poetry, despite—or perhaps because of—its roots in classical Greek and Japanese culture. He wrote to Harriet Monroe when he sent her H.D.'s poems: 'I've had luck again, and am sending you some *modern* stuff by an American. I say modern, for it is in the laconic speech of the Imagistes, even if the subject is classic.'[44] Sinclair felt herself to be watching the emer-

---

[42] H.D. describes Pound's giving her the name 'H.D. Imagiste' in *End to Torment*, 18. The note from the Nov. 1912 issue of *Poetry* is quoted in Peter Jones, 'Introduction' to id. (ed.), *Imagist Poetry* (Harmondsworth: Penguin, 1972), 18. There are many detailed accounts of the imagist movement. See e.g. Stanley K. Coffman, *Imagism: A Chapter for the History of Modern Poetry* (Norman, Okla.: University of Oklahoma Press, 1951); Glenn Hughes, *Imagism and the Imagists: A Study in Modern Poetry* (Stanford, Calif.: Stanford University Press, 1931); John T. Gage, *In the Arresting Eye: The Rhetoric of Imagism* (Baton Rouge, La.: Louisiana State University Press, 1981); J. B. Harmer, *Victory in Limbo: Imagism 1908–1917* (London: Secker and Warburg, 1975).

[43] Sinclair, 'The "Gitanjali": Or Song-Offerings of Rabindranath Tagore', *North American Review*, 197 (May 1913), 659–76: at 674. Most of the article was reprinted in the chapter on 'The New Mysticism' in *Defence of Idealism* (1917). William Rothenstein was responsible for introducing Yeats to both Tagore's poems, and to Tagore himself, who visited London in 1912 (see William Rothenstein, *Men and Memories: Recollections, 1872–1938*, ed. Mary Iago, Columbia, Mo.: University of Missouri Press, 1978, 168–70). Sinclair heard Yeats read Tagore's poems to a small gathering at Rothenstein's house, and Tagore wrote to her on 10 July 1912 thanking her for her letter in praise of his poems, and for 'the evident sign of response that they had awakened in your heart' (UP, Box 3, fo. 87).

[44] Pound to Monroe, Oct. 1912, quoted in Jones (ed.), *Imagist Poetry*, 17.

gence of a new culture and a new understanding of the relations between subject, object, and language.

Imagism was poetry in a quite different style from that of late Victorian poetry such as Mew's. Where Mew wrote dramatic monologue, imagism attempted to displace the texture of the perceiving imagination altogether; where Mew wrote sensationally and erotically about human situations (the deserting lover, the humiliated woman), the imagists wrote about objects and visual images; where Mew's poems were partly written to be read aloud, the imagists wrote very much for the page; where Mew's themes were wasted lives and unfulfilled dreams (as Leighton puts it, her 'characteristic self-signature' was 'the elaboration of a missing purpose, a missing life'), the imagists sought to produce a sensation of immediacy, of 'sudden liberation' and 'sudden growth'.[45] Sinclair's simultaneous involvement with both aesthetics pushed her to evaluate them one against the other, and to decide where the future of poetry lay. She recognized that imagism was generically unsuited to the kind of emotional and psychological intensity that Mew represented (she wrote to Mew after the publication of her 'Two Notes' that the 'precise criticism that I sd. have applied to the Imagists—if I'd been out that day for criticism—is that they lack strong human passion') but she also recognized it as a formulation which was intimately tied to the psychoanalytic concepts with which she was becoming so familiar.[46] Imagism was a poetry of the modern moment, and it seemed to offer a way of thinking across new disciplinary boundaries (even Pound had written that when he described the 'image' as 'that which presents an intellectual and emotional complex in an instant of time', he was using the term 'complex' 'rather in the technical sense employed by the newer psychologists, such as Hart').[47] Sinclair, working in 1916 on Jung, and writing about Jung's use of the word 'complex' in her *Medical Press* articles, must have seen imagism as potentially the aesthetic correlative to psychoanalysis. By 1918 she was writing to Arthur Adcock, editor of the *Bookman*, of her own struggle for 'simplicity & concentration'.[48] Imagist techniques and vocabularies (in 1913 F. S. Flint had described imagism as 'direct treatment of the "thing" ') slowly began to shape Sinclair's own methods and self-descriptions, even as she simultaneously

[45] Leighton, *Victorian Women's Poetry*, 285; Pound, 'A Retrospect', 1918; repr. in *Literary Essays of Ezra Pound*, ed. T. S. Eliot (Westport, Conn.: Greenwood, 1968), 4.

[46] Sinclair to Mew, 9 June 1915, HA.

[47] Pound, 'Retrospect', 4. Bernard Hart, a psychiatrist in an adolescent unit, was the author of 'Freud's Conception of Hysteria', *Brain*, 33 (1911), 338–66, and of *Psychology of Insanity* (1912). Hart footnotes Freud, Abraham, Stekel, Ferenczi, Jones, and Jung. Rapp describes his work as an 'eclectic, diluted account of Freudianism' ('Early Discovery of Freud by the British General Educated Public', 220).

[48] Sinclair to Arthur Adcock, 16 Jan. 1918, UP, Box 1, fo. 1.

began to use psychoanalytic models as the basic structures for her plots and her narrative techniques.[49]

But it was as a poet, not as a novelist or even as a critic, that Sinclair first allied herself with imagism. When, in May 1915, Aldington published a 'Special Imagist Number' of the *Egoist*, he included Sinclair's First World War poem 'After the Retreat', along with work by himself, H.D., John Gould Fletcher, and Marianne Moore. By this time, the imagist movement was well under way: the anthology *Des Imagistes* had been published in March 1914, and Amy Lowell's *Some Imagist Poets* had appeared in April 1915. Sinclair's poem was in no sense part of the defining moment of imagism, but it showed her throwing in her lot with the poets whose practice she defended in the very next number of the *Egoist*.

In publishing as an imagist, Sinclair was identifying herself with an unpopular movement. Many copies of the first anthology, *Des Imagistes*, had been returned to the Poetry Bookshop, which published it, and the anthology had received bad reviews both in England and the USA. When Sinclair followed up her poem with her 'Two Notes. I. On H.D. II. On Imagism' in the next number of the *Egoist*, she found herself defending imagism against Harold Monro himself, proprietor of the Poetry Bookshop and publisher of *Des Imagistes*, who was about to enter into negotiation with Charlotte Mew over the publication of *The Farmer's Bride*. Monro had contributed an essay on imagism to the special number of the *Egoist* in which Sinclair's 'After the Retreat' had appeared, in which he charges it with being 'petty poetry. . . . Such reticence denotes either poverty of imagination or needlessly excessive restraint'.[50] In her response, Sinclair suggests that Monro's judgements are constrained by his reverence for poetic tradition, a desire to 'be supported in his attitude by Ben Jonson, Dryden, Addison, Burke, Samuel Johnson, Coleridge, Wordsworth, and—"even Matthew Arnold"'. Monro, she remarks, has failed to see 'that for sheer emotion, for clean-cut and perfect beauty, [imagist poetry] stands by itself in its own school'.[51] Monro, in other words, has not appreciated the radical innovation of imagist techniques, whose antecedents reach so far back into the classical past that they are virtually unrecognizable.

But, as we saw in her letter to Mew, Sinclair had her own feelings of ambivalence about what the imagists were trying to do, and 'Two Notes' is as much an argument with her own, as with Monro's, critical response. She

---

[49] Quoted in Jones (ed.), *Imagist Poetry*, 129, from the Mar. 1913 number of *Poetry*.
[50] Harold Monro, 'The Imagists Discussed', *Egoist* (1 May 1915), 77–80: at 79.
[51] Sinclair, 'Two Notes. I. On H.D. II. On Imagism', *Egoist*, 2 (1 June 1915), 88–9: at 88.

was caught between her allegiance to the Victorian cadences of Mew's verse, and the Hellenic spareness of imagist aspirations. In a way, she was torn between the values of two generations. She found herself apologizing to Mew for 'Two Notes':

About the Imagists—I'm not so stupid, really, as I seem. Remember, I'm defending H.D. against what I know to be an unfair & rather spiteful attack from a writer who isn't fit to lick her boots. H.D. is the best of the Imagists (You'll observe that I don't say very much about the others) . . .

I am not stupid, & I can feel poetry even if I cannot understand it; but I have a catholic taste, & I see that these young poets are doing something that <u>at its best</u> is beautiful; & it is intolerable that they sd. meet with ridicule and contempt because they are not doing something else. . . .

I know one poet whose heart beats like a dynamo under an iron-grey tailor-made suit (I <u>think</u> one of her suits is iron-grey) & when she publishes her poems she will give me something to say that I cannot & do not say of my Imagists.[52]

Evidently Mew was jealous of Sinclair's public allegiance to a poetry that was so different from her own, and Sinclair, stung by Mew's accusations of 'stupidity', emphasized the extent to which she was going to the defence of the unjustly attacked (an act of which Mew would heartily have approved), rather than her own genuine enthusiasm for imagist work. But Mew had reason to feel offended by some of the comments Sinclair made in 'Two Notes'. Trying to work through her own sense that imagism was a poetry of form rather than of feeling (she wrote to Aldington: 'Some day you will have an emotion that the "image" will not carry: then where are you?'), Sinclair dissected that Victorian 'passion' that she simultaneously so admired in Mew's work, citing all the poets to whose writing Mew's was most similar.[53]

If you are sworn to admire nothing but Swinburne, or Rossetti, or Mrs. Browning or Robert Browning and their imitators for ever and ever, you may reject the 'Hermes' because there is no 'passion' in it.

But why, in Heaven's name, should there be passion in it? Haven't we had enough of passion and of the sentiment that passed for passion all through the nineteenth century? We can't hope to escape the inevitable reaction. And isn't it almost time to remind us that there is a beauty of restraint and stillness and flawless clarity? The special miracle of those Victorian poets was that they contrived to drag their passion through the conventional machinery of their verse, and the heavy decorations that they hung on it.[54]

---

[52] Sinclair to Mew, 9 June 1915, HA.
[53] The sentence is quoted in Sinclair to Mew, 9 June 1915, HA.
[54] Sinclair, 'Two Notes', 88.

Mew's verse was far from conventional: even Sinclair was confused by the form and metre of 'The Fête'.[55] But it was close enough to the style of Rossetti and Browning, and 'heavily decorated' enough, that this paragraph must have seemed like a direct attack on both the form and the content of her work. Sinclair's confusion about the significance, even the definition, of 'passion' in poetry is an indirect comment on her uncertainty about the value of 'passion' in itself, and of Mew's unpredictable admiration. Later in 'Two Notes' she argues for a continuity between the Victorians and the imagists: 'the Imagists are doing for the first time, consciously and deliberately and always what the Victorian poets, at any rate, only did once or twice in a blue moon.'[56] But this backtracking allowed the Victorians only a few random successes at best. By 1920, in a piece on Ezra Pound in the *English Review*, Sinclair was unequivocally celebrating the 'bright impression of modernity' in his early work.[57] Her residual loyalty in 'Two Notes' to the Victorians and their style seemed a thing of the past.

Sinclair's direct challenge to Monro, and her attempt to help explain the aesthetics of imagism, established her reputation both as a conscientious defender of experimental work, and as a mediator between the older and the younger generations. Aldington, then editor of the *Egoist*, was pleased with her account of imagism, writing to Amy Lowell on 21 May 1915 that 'Miss Sinclair has done a charming article on H.D. & the Imagists in general'.[58] A couple of years later it was to Sinclair again that Pound turned when T. S. Eliot needed defending, this time specifically because Sinclair was allied in the public mind with the work of a previous era. As R. Brimley Johnson noted in 1920, Sinclair 'published novels before some, at least, of her contemporaries could use the pen', but nonetheless 'because she has kept alive and remained young . . . she belongs—unmistakeably—to the new movement. Experience only adds strength and clearness of vision to her identity with modern thought.'[59] Pound thought Sinclair would be useful in bridging

---

[55] Sinclair wrote to Mew on 8 Mar. 1914: 'it was something in the <u>form</u>, something that obscured my vision . . . something in what Ezra Pound wd. call "the metric" ' (HA).

[56] Sinclair, 'Two Notes', 89.

[57] Sinclair, 'The Reputation of Ezra Pound', *English Review*, 30 (Apr. 1920), 326–35; repr. in Scott, *Gender of Modernism*, 468–76: at 475.

[58] Quoted in *Richard Aldington*, ed. Gates, 16. Aldington was energetically trying to organize a critical campaign in defence of imagism. He himself had written a piece on Amy Lowell that he held back from the June number of the *Egoist* in order that it should not distract attention from Sinclair's 'Two Notes', but it appeared in the July issue ('The Poetry of Amy Lowell', *Egoist*, 1 July 1915, 109–10). Meanwhile, Amy Lowell was writing about Aldington, and her 'Richard Aldington's Poetry' appeared in Pound's new journal, the *Little Review*, in Sept. 1915. The intensity of Aldington's commitment to imagism and its reputation is revealed in his promise to Lowell that he will try to write his defence on 21 May 1915, even though H.D., then his wife, had given birth to a stillborn daughter the night before.

[59] R. Brimley Johnson, *Some Contemporary Novelists (Women)* (London: Leonard Parsons, 1920), 33–4.

the gap between the new and old, and he wrote to his co-editor at the *Little Review*, Margaret Anderson, that he was going to ask Sinclair to do a short piece on Eliot, remarking that 'M.S. once had a name in America, but I suppose that's a thing of yester-decade.???' He thought that it would 'add sting to slap on Quarterly to have a brief bo[u]quet from the former generation'.[60] Naturally, Sinclair obliged: she was one of Pound's first subscribers when he set up the *Little Review* in May 1917, and only when she was under extreme pressure to complete her own work did she refuse to supply copy for him.[61] Her essay on T. S. Eliot appeared promptly in the December 1917 issue of the *Little Review*.

Once again, then, Pound was decisive in precipitating Sinclair's public endorsement of a bafflingly modern poetry which had, like H.D.'s, already received poor reviews. It was only due to Pound's energy and conviction that Eliot's first volume of poetry, *Prufrock and Other Observations*, had ever appeared at all.[62] Eliot was worried and distracted, both about money and about his wife's health, and it fell to Pound to collect and arrange the poems that made up the collection. Publishers were nervous or sceptical, and in the end Pound promised to raise the money for production costs himself (in fact his wife ended up paying) if Harriet Shaw Weaver of the *Egoist* would allow him to use her imprint. Predictably, the volume sold poorly, and most reviewers disliked it. Pound, whose defence of Eliot appeared several months earlier than Sinclair's, in the June 1917 number of the *Egoist*, aimed his comments directly at Arthur Waugh, whose attack on Eliot in 'The New Poetry' had been published in the *Quarterly Review* of October 1916.[63]

---

[60] Ezra Pound to Margaret Anderson, 6 Aug. 1917, 13 Sept. 1917, in *Pound/The Little Review: The Letters of Ezra Pound to Margaret Anderson: The 'Little Review' Correspondence*, ed. Thomas L. Scott, Melvin J. Friedman, and Jackson R. Bryer (New York: New Directions, 1988), 106, 122. In Feb. 1922 Pound and Sinclair were once more collaborators on a scheme to help Eliot when, along with Richard Aldington, they were 'initial life members' of 'Bel Esprit'. 'Bel Esprit' was a fund intended to provide authors with sufficient funds to devote themselves full time to writing. Aldington, Pound, and Sinclair each pledged £10 a year for life, and Eliot was named as the first beneficiary. Although twenty-two subscribers pledged £300, the plan never got off the ground. See *The Letters of Ezra Pound 1907–1941*, ed. D. D. Paige (New York: Haskell House, 1974), 241.

[61] In late Feb. 1918 Pound wrote to Anderson that Sinclair had agreed to write something on Henry James, but that she couldn't 'be sure of having it ready on time, as she is in the middle of a novel' (*Pound/The Little Review*, 203). In fact the article never materialized, and Sinclair wrote to Violet Hunt sometime early in 1918: 'I want to be in Yorkshire, all alone, writing my novel. But I'm very, very tired, & I don't know how I'm going to do it' [n.d.], HA. The novel she was writing was *Mary Olivier*.

[62] See Peter Ackroyd, *T. S. Eliot: A Life* (New York: Simon and Schuster, 1984), 79–80, for a full account of the preparation and publication of *Prufrock and Other Observations*.

[63] Ezra Pound, 'Drunken Helots and Mr. Eliot', *Egoist*, 4 (June 1917), 72–4; repr. in Michael Grant (ed.), *T. S. Eliot: The Critical Heritage*, i (London: Routledge, 1982), 70–3; Arthur Waugh, 'The New Poetry', *Quarterly Review* (Oct. 1916), 226; repr. in Grant (ed.), *T. S. Eliot: The Critical Heritage*, i. 67–9. *Prufrock and Other Observations* was published in June 1917. Sinclair's review makes it clear that she knows Arthur Waugh's article only through its citations in Pound's piece, and she seems to think it is a review of *Prufrock*.

Waugh was reviewing Pound's 1915 anthology, *The Catholic Anthology
1914–1915*, which included a reprint of 'The Love Song of J. Alfred
Prufrock', and much of his distaste stems from the un-English nature of the
collection: 'only one or two of the contributors [are] of indisputably English
birth'.[64] Eliot's poetry comes in for particular contempt in terms that suggest
that Waugh saw Eliot's work as an attack on his own generation (Waugh was
about Sinclair's age, and father of Alec and Evelyn), and on Englishness
itself. Eliot's work, writes Waugh, proceeds on 'the convenient assumption
that everything which seemed wise and true to the father must inevitably be
false and foolish to the son'.[65] Waugh proposes an especially callous lesson:

It was a classic custom in the family hall, when the feast was at its height, to display
a drunken slave among the sons of the household, to the end that they, being
ashamed at the ignominious folly of his gesticulations, might determine never to be
tempted into such a pitiable condition themselves. The custom had its advantages;
for the wisdom of the younger generation was found to be fostered more surely by
a single example than by a world of homily and precept.[66]

In this case, Eliot, of course, is the drunken example.

It was to counter this kind of paternalistic ridicule that Pound was anxious
to draw Sinclair into the discussion. His own response to 'The New Poetry'
had been as personal as Waugh's: whenever genius manifests himself, he
wrote, 'some elderly gentleman has a flux of bile from his liver'.[67] Sinclair,
while identifying herself firmly with Pound, tried to understand Waugh's
dislike of the work. In her piece she describes Eliot's 'genius' as 'disturbing',
'elusive', and 'difficult'; she notes that Eliot is associated in the public mind
with 'an unpopular movement and with unpopular people' (some of his
work appeared in *Blast*), and—equivocal enough herself about Vorticism,
as we saw in Chapter 5—she is quick to dissociate him from 'the experimental violences' of that context: his poems, she writes, 'stood out . . . with an air
of tranquil and triumphant achievement'.[68] She defends his work in the same
terms that she had already used for the imagists: 'Reality, stripped naked of
all rhetoric, of all ornament, of all confusing and obscuring association, is
what he is after'.[69] Without echoing Pound's satirical tone, she manages both
to celebrate Eliot's originality (he is 'not in any tradition at all') and to recognize the difficulty and the unfamiliarity of his work in a way that gives a

---

[64] Waugh, 'New Poetry', 68.   [65] Ibid. 69.   [66] Ibid.
[67] Pound, 'Drunken Helots and Mr. Eliot', 70.
[68] Sinclair, ' "Prufrock: And Other Observations": A Criticism', 449.
[69] Ibid. 451. In 'Two Notes' she wrote of the imagists that they were ' "out for" direct naked contact with
reality' (88).

sympathetic air to her challenge to Waugh.[70] Elsewhere she savagely indicted provincial attitudes like his: in a story of May 1921, 'The Return', for example, a successful young poet who (like T. S. Eliot) works in a bank (a 'peculiar mixture of profane satirist and exquisite, passionate poet, the master of *vers libre*') returns to his family home in Devon, and finds that his parents ridicule his talents, and promote those of his brother, who writes highly conventional Georgian verse.[71] But in her response to Waugh she made some effort to spare him. Pound thought she had done the article 'very nobly'.[72]

Sinclair's review of Eliot is most significant, however, for what it tells us about the development of Sinclair's own fictional techniques. An anonymous reviewer in the *New Statesman* for 18 August 1917 (the only review of the volume, other than Pound's, that Sinclair had actually read) complained that he could not 'follow the drift of "The Love Song of J. Alfred Prufrock"', and this challenge was central to Sinclair's own response.[73] She was careful, since her review had been commissioned by Pound, to continue her endorsement of imagist techniques, but in this essay she also begins to formulate her own description of the narrative form that, four months later in her review of Dorothy Richardson's *Pilgrimage*, she would christen 'stream of consciousness'.[74] Discussing Eliot's 'obscurity', she writes:

His thoughts move very rapidly and by astounding cuts. They move . . . as live thoughts move in live brains. . . . Observe the method. Instead of writing round and round about Prufrock, explaining that his tragedy is the tragedy of submerged passion, Mr. Eliot simply removes the covering from Prufrock's mind: Prufrock's mind, jumping quickly from actuality to memory and back again, like an animal, hunted, tormented, terribly and poignantly alive. The Love-Song of Prufrock is a song that Balzac might have sung if he had been as great a poet as he was a novelist.[75]

In her account of the poetry, Sinclair ignores formal questions, unlike, for example, Pound, who, in an August 1917 review of Eliot's work in *Poetry*,

---

[70] Sinclair, ' "Prufrock: And Other Observations": A Criticism', 449.

[71] Sinclair, 'The Return', *Harper's Magazine*, 142 (May 1921), 693–703: at 693. Gerald Marriott, the poet, has spent time working in the bank's branch in Paris and, like Proust, his memories of home are all of odours: 'of mildew in the parish church; of camphor in his mother's gown; . . . of a hot patch in the kitchen garden where the black currants [*sic*] had a throbbing, spicy tang like a mulled wine' (693).

[72] Pound to Anderson, 21 Sept. 1917, *Pound/The Little Review*, 126.

[73] Unsigned review of *Prufrock and Other Observations*, *New Statesman*, 9 (18 Aug. 1917), 477; repr. in Grant (ed.), *T. S. Eliot: The Critical Heritage*, i. 75.

[74] Sinclair, 'Novels of Dorothy Richardson', 444. I discuss Sinclair's review of Richardson more fully in the next chapter. See also Diane F. Gillespie, 'May Sinclair (1863–1946)', in Scott (ed.), *Gender of Modernism*, 436–42: at 438.

[75] Sinclair, ' "Prufrock: And Other Observations": A Criticism', 450–1, 453.

devotes at least half his article to a discussion of *vers libre*.[76] Instead, she reads 'Prufrock' as if it were the germ of a novel, as, in fact, it was for her. As she worked on her review, she was simultaneously beginning to write *Mary Olivier*. Pound was anxious to celebrate Eliot's work as a revolution in poetic technique; Sinclair, almost waywardly, took Eliot's experiments as a starting point for herself, and read them against her personal attempts to evolve a modern prose style. As she struggled to define the modernity of the work of others, she was provoked into finding her own peculiar modern form. After the essay on Eliot, she wrote no more reviews of poetry until *Mary Olivier* was finished. The creative and critical energy that had gone into her engagement with the work of others was temporarily diverted into a novelistic statement of her own.

But even after *Mary Olivier* was published in 1919, and Pound and the others had moved on to other kinds of work, Sinclair continued to publish essays on imagism. Articles on Pound in 1920, Flint in 1921, H.D. in 1922, and, as we have seen, on Aldington in 1921, show that imagism and its philosophies continued to preoccupy her even as she developed and refined her own original fictional voice.[77] As Sinclair worked to realize psychoanalytic structures in her novels (they were sufficiently pronounced that *Psychoanalytic Review* published a review of her 1922 novel *Anne Severn and the Fieldings*), she could not leave imagism behind.[78] Her publications on contemporary poetry during the war were part of the same intellectual endeavour as her support of the Medico-Psychological Clinic and its philosophies, and in her 1922 article on H.D. Sinclair continued to develop her own assessment of the psychic and formal significance of the 'image' long after imagism itself had run its course. Indeed, the fact that the 1922 piece 'The Poems of H.D.' is essentially an expanded version of the 1915 'Two Notes' suggests that many of the issues she raised there continued to puzzle her years later, even though by then her activities as a reviewer of contemporary poetry were almost at an end. Imagism was significant not only for its influence on her prose style (its increasing compression, its fragmentary quality, its concentration on the texture of perception), but also for its contribution to her psychoanalytic thinking. As we have seen, Pound himself linked imagism to contemporary psychology and the idea of the 'complex'. Sinclair, already

---

[76] Pound, 'T. S. Eliot', *Poetry*, 10 (Aug. 1917), 264–71; repr. in Grant (ed.), *T. S. Eliot: The Critical Heritage*, i. 75–80.

[77] Sinclair, 'The Poems of F. S. Flint', *English Review*, 32 (Jan. 1921), 6–18; 'The Poems of "H.D." ', *Dial*, 72 (Feb. 1922), 203–7; *Fortnightly Review*, 121 (Mar. 1927), 329–40 (a longer version); repr. in Scott (ed.), *Gender of Modernism*, 453–67.

[78] Sylvia Strangnell, 'Critical Review: A Study in Sublimations', *Psychoanalytic Review*, 10 (Apr. 1923), 209–13.

moving towards the definition of modernity as a form of anachronistic tension that she laid out in the Aldington article in 1921, found both imagism and psychoanalysis, during the war years, offering their own formulations of this kind of dissonance. She wrote to Adcock in September 1916 about a 'book I'm working on now & have nearly finished "Some Ultimate Questions of Psychology & Metaphysics" '.[79] The book, *A Defence of Idealism*, appeared in the autumn of 1917, and its unpublished sequel, a manuscript called 'The Way of Sublimation', was mined to produce the two 1916 articles on symbolism and sublimation. As Sinclair read and thought about imagist poetry, she was simultaneously assessing contemporary shifts in philosophical and psychological thinking. Key to her work on Jung and Freud, in particular, were the concepts of the 'symbol' and the 'complex', and her excitement at the evolution of imagist aesthetics ran parallel to her interest in psychoanalytic terminology and methods.

The 1916 articles started out as review essays of Jung's *Psychology of the Unconscious*, which had been published in German in 1912, and translated into English by Beatrice Hinkle in 1916.[80] The book marked a defining moment in psychoanalysis, since it was in this volume that Jung explicitly stated his differences from Freud. As Douglas A. Davis has pointed out, *Psychology of the Unconscious* 'was the explosion of all those psychic contents that could find no room, no breathing space, in the constricting atmosphere of Freudian psychology and its narrow outlook': Jung argued in favour of the existence of a collective unconscious, declared that the libido was not exclusively sexual, and suggested that fantasies of incest have a symbolic, not a literal meaning.[81] After 1913 the collaboration between Freud and Jung was at an end. Sinclair's essays thus comment on one of the originary events of psychoanalysis: its theory and practice were as yet fairly little known in England, and hers was one of the few assessments to appear in an English journal.

[79] Sinclair to Adcock, 6 Sept. 1916, UP, Box 1, fo. 1.

[80] C. G. Jung, *Psychology of the Unconscious: A Study of the Transformations and Symbolisms of the Libido: A Contribution to the History of the Evolution of Thought*, trans. Beatrice M. Hinkle, 1916 (repr. as *Supplementary Volume B* of *Collected Works of Jung*, Princeton: Princeton University Press, 1991). Sinclair also alludes to Jung, *Collected Papers on Analytical Psychology*, ed. Constance E. Long (London: Baillière, Tindall and Cox, 1916), to Freud's *The Interpretation of Dreams* (1899) in German, and to the work of Adler and Janet. *Psychology of the Unconscious* was originally published in 1912 as *Wandlungen und symbole der Libido*, and Jung continued to return to, and to revise, the text throughout his life.

[81] Douglas A. Davis, 'Freud, Jung and Psychoanalysis', in Polly Young-Eisendrath and Terence Dawson (eds.), *The Cambridge Companion to Jung* (Cambridge: Cambridge University Press, 1997), 35–51: at 49. See also Peter Gay, *Freud: A Life for Our Time* (New York: Norton, 1988) and *The Freud/Jung Letters: The Correspondence between Sigmund Freud and Carl Jung*, ed. W. McGuire, trans. Ralph Manheim and R. F. C. Hall (Princeton: Princeton University Press, 1974), for accounts of the rift between the two.

The central focus of her pieces is the process of sublimation, and I shall discuss Sinclair's exploration of this concept in the next chapter, in relation to *Mary Olivier*. But if, as Jean Radford suggests, *Mary Olivier* was her novel of sublimation, it was imagist poetry that focused her interest in symbolism, the other concern of the 'lectures'.[82] Although Sinclair takes her cue from Jung, in the lectures she also begins to develop her own, idiosyncratic theory of psychic symbolism. The theory of the symbol was of course central to analytic psychology, but Jung makes only passing reference to it in the two texts Sinclair cites in her articles, and it became central to Sinclair's interpretation of Jung partly because she was at the time preoccupied with the idea of the poetic image and with imagism.[83] This is not to say, however, that there is any straightforward correlation between the Jungian symbol, or even the Jungian image, and the image of imagist poetry. Rather, Sinclair's account of the philosophy and practice of imagism often implicitly defines itself against Jungian theory. But, as she remarks resignedly at the end of the second 'clinical lecture', psychoanalysis 'has come to stay, and we must make our peace with it'.[84] Imagism provided her with one vehicle for making that peace.

In the lectures, Sinclair notes that the symbol is defined by, and inextricably bound up with, the libido, which 'chooses its own symbols, saturates them with its own emotions and so fixes them'.[85] Following Jung, she argues that neurosis and psychosis are caused by a regression of the libido into an infantile state (or, as Jung put it, 'the disturbed function of reality' is replaced by 'an archaic surrogate').[86] Symbols become, in Sinclair's schema, a transcendent 'bridge' that holds in tension the 'primitive' past, and the evolving future:

The symbol is a bridge between his [the libido's] past and his future; *for it belongs to both*. It is the oldest, and, therefore, the most familiar thing he knows. It is the most august and poignant thing he knows, therefore the most saturated with memories that are emotions; it trails behind it the whole procession of redemptive mysteries. It is the root of all language, the indissoluble link between primitive emotion and developed concept. It is the golden bridge by which he can come back. If he can

---

[82] Jean Radford, 'Introduction', to Sinclair, *Life and Death of Harriett Frean* (1922; repr. London: Virago, 1980), no page numbers.

[83] Jung does discuss interpretations of particular symbols exhaustively in *Psychology of the Unconscious* (the mother, fish, the sun, serpents, and so on), but he includes very little reflection on the actual function and structure of symbols as a group. Henri F. Ellenberger notes that Jungian symbols serve to transform psychic energy, such that when a symbol is assimilated, psychic energy is liberated and can be used on a conscious level. See Henri F. Ellenberger, *The Discovery of the Unconscious: The History and Evolution of Dynamic Psychiatry* (New York: Basic Books, 1970), 704.

[84] Sinclair, 'Clinical Lectures on Symbolism and Sublimation', II. 144.   [85] Ibid. I. 118.

[86] Jung, *Psychology of the Unconscious*, 137.

respond to anything he will respond to whatever voice from the outside evokes the imperishable symbol within.[87]

The symbol contains the contradiction between the past and the future; between archaism, the world of 'the savage and the child', and modernity, the world of 'steamships, trains and motor cars'.[88] It memorializes and keeps alive the past without altering itself, and it is the psychoanalyst's one means of access to the unconscious and the ill-adapted libido that has been trapped there. Jung described the symbolic process in quasi-Hegelian terms: 'From the activity of the unconscious there now emerges a new content, constellated by thesis and anti-thesis in equal measure and standing in a *compensatory* relation to both. It thus forms the middle ground on which the opposites can be united.'[89] The symbol is a mediator and a facilitator of transitions.

There were many reasons why Sinclair might have made intellectual connections between psychoanalysis and imagism. Both concentrate on the articulation in words of visual and oral images; both are informed by ideas about, and discussion of, translation; both aspire towards finding exactly the right words in which to say something (in psychoanalytic practice the fit between word and memory *is* the cure); and both emphasize the vernacular (psychoanalysts are interested above all in the ordinary speech of their patients, and in her article on F. S. Flint, Sinclair quotes Wordsworth on poetic language—'a selection of the language really used by men'—as a gloss on imagist theory and practice).[90] Jung in particular appealed to Sinclair, drawing as he did on many of the philosophical traditions with which she was most deeply involved: Jung's idea of the play of the opposites derived largely from Hegel, his thought was informed by Vedic philosophy, and he wrote that 'mentally [his] greatest adventure had been the study of Kant and Schopenhauer'.[91] Sinclair commented in 'The Way of Sublimation'

---

[87] Sinclair, 'Clinical Lectures on Symbolism and Sublimation', I. 121.   [88] Ibid. 121, 119.

[89] Jung, *Collected Works*, vi, para. 825. Quoted in Andrew Samuels, Bani Shorter, and Fred Plaut, *A Critical Dictionary of Jungian Analysis* (London: Routledge, 1986), 145.

[90] Sinclair, 'Poems of F. S. Flint', 7. Marie Cardinal's autobiographical novel about a psychoanalytic treatment is called *Les Mots pour le dire* ('the words to say it') (Paris: Grasset, 1975). Freud compared the interpretation of dreams to the translation of Egyptian hieroglyphs: 'the productions of the dream-work . . . present no greater difficulties to their translators than do the ancient hieroglyphic scripts to those who seek to read them'. See *Interpretation of Dreams*, 1899, in *Standard Edition*, v. 341.

[91] Jung, *Collected Works*, xviii. 231. Quoted in Claire Douglas, 'The Historical Context of Analytical Psychology', in Young-Eisendrath and Dawson (eds.), *Cambridge Companion to Jung*, 17–34: at 22. Ellenberger (*Discovery of the Unconscious*, 729) notes that Jung was also influenced by Eduard von Hartmann, whose *The Philosophy of the Unconscious* (1879), was one of Sinclair's early influences (she writes in 'The Way of Sublimation' of her 'youthful enthusiasm over the Philosophy of the Unconscious', holograph version, 3, UP, Box 23, fo. 435).

that psychology's original dependence on philosophy had been reversed by the advances of psychoanalysis, noting that now psychology would be 'calling the tune' and philosophy would simply have to fit in.[92] Jungian psychology must have seemed the perfect example of this. Jung was even anecdotally linked to one of Sinclair's favourite figures: many believed that his grandfather was an illegitimate son of Goethe, a rumour which Jung made no effort to deny.[93] Everything about him was designed to stimulate Sinclair's interest and agreement.

But it was not quite a marriage made in heaven. There were many ways in which Jungian psychology challenged the assumptions of imagism, Sinclair's other intellectual and aesthetic allegiance, and she had to pick her way through a minefield of conflicts and contradictions. Flint had already noted in the March 1913 number of *Poetry* that imagism depended on '[d]irect treatment of the "thing", whether subjective or objective', and Amy Lowell had followed that up in the preface to the 1915 anthology *Some Imagist Poets* with the call to 'produce poetry that is hard and clear, never blurred nor indefinite'.[94] The kind of free association that Jung and Freud espoused, and Freud's idea that any psychic image was 'bound to branch out in every direction into the intricate network of our world of thought', were inimical to the imagist method, which, though often dependent on figure, sought as much as possible to make the object materialize in the texture of the poetry itself.[95] Sinclair's own reflections on imagism occur in the 1915 'Two Notes' and were reprinted in the 1922 article on H.D.:

I am pretty certain which of several old things [imagism] is *not*. It is not Symbolism. It has nothing to do with image-making. It abhors Imagery. Imagery is one of the old worn-out decorations the Imagists have scrapped.

The Image is not a substitute: it does not stand for anything but itself. Presentation, not representation, is the watchword of the school. The Image, I take it, is Form. But it is not pure form. It is form *and* substance. . . . in no case is the Image a symbol of reality (the object); it is reality (the object) itself. You cannot distinguish between the thing and its image.[96]

Sinclair was fascinated by the idea of an image which made no reference beyond itself, which, unlike the Jungian symbol, was remarkable exactly

---

[92] Sinclair, 'The Way of Sublimation', typescript version, 4, UP, Box 23, fos. 436–8.
[93] See Ellenberger, *Discovery of the Unconscious*, 661.
[94] Quoted in Jones (ed.), *Imagist Poetry*, 129, 135.
[95] Freud, *Interpretation of Dreams*, in *Standard Edition*, v. 525.
[96] Sinclair, 'Poems of "H.D." ', 454, and 'Two Notes', 88. Originally Sinclair had drafted the longer article much more as a commentary on H.D.'s translation, including quotations in classical Greek (which she knew). Most of this discussion did not survive in the published version, which thus concentrates much more specifically on H.D. as a poet, and an imagist.

because it was singular and perfectly realized only in the form in which it appeared ('For each imagination its image is ultimate and unique', she wrote in the H.D. article).[97] The image held out no possibilities for allegorical interpretation. When, in her article, Sinclair tried to explain the effect of H.D.'s 'Oread' to Monro, she could only rearrange and repeat its terms: 'Doesn't he see that in this one image . . . there are at least three passions and three agonists, the pine-wood, the wind, and the "Oread" who desires to be covered with the pine-waves, to be splashed, to play with the tumult of the pine-wood and the wind?'[98] Interpretation becomes an exercise in reiteration. The imagist poet has already used the perfect words; the image has reached its articulate limit. Nothing could be farther from the Jungian symbol with its infinitely creative connections to both the individual and the collective unconscious.

In the end, however, it was not the theory of the symbol that entranced Sinclair so briefly in 1916, that stayed with her, but the awareness that psychoanalysis had given her of the intricacies of the conscious mind. It is perhaps no accident that her most explicit and detailed discussions of imagism in the 1920s, in 'The Poems of "H.D." ', were in fact merely reprints of an article of seven years earlier. Her interest was shifting away from the self-contained image of the imagists towards the more fluid and endlessly ramifying psychological textures described in psychoanalytic theory.

In her January 1921 article on F. S. Flint, Sinclair hailed the arrival of a poetic that matched the complexity of 'modern states of mind' in terms that picked up her earlier description of 'The Love Song of J. Alfred Prufrock'. She defended Flint's refusal to rhyme on the grounds that rhymed verse in this period tends to be derivative, 'to be saturated, not with fresh, direct, personal associations, but with an overpowering odour of stale literature'.[99] Flint's 'break with tradition' is symptomatic of his subtle awareness of the modern condition:

The modern poet requires a greater freedom of form and movement, not only because the prescribed metrical forms and movements have been used up, but because he has a larger heritage of emotions and ideas. It is not true that the stock of emotions or ideas is or can be exhausted; on the contrary, every age adds to it something of its own; and so far as these modern states of mind are subtler and more complex, they call for a subtler and more complex medium of expression.[100]

The coarseness of metrical convention cannot hope to convey the fine,

---

[97] Sinclair, 'Poems of "H.D." ', 456; 'Two Notes', 89.
[98] Sinclair, 'The Poems of "H.D." ', 457; 'Two Notes', 88.   [99] Sinclair, 'Poems of F. S. Flint', 9.
[100] Ibid. 11.

shifting texture of the modern mind. It is the task of the modern poet, Sinclair writes, to convey the rhythms of this mind: 'it is in rendering psychological states, in presenting unaltered and unabridged the truth of ordinary reality, that the modern poet most shows his modernity; in sticking, that is to say, close to consciousness.'[101] In this version of modernity, it is no longer the precision of the image that counts, as it was with imagism, that earlier experiment in modern poetry; now Sinclair, with *Mary Olivier* already three years behind her, unequivocally endorses a very different aesthetic as the key not just to a fictional, but to a poetic, form of modernism. In abandoning the idea of the image or the symbol as the key to modernity, she returned all the same to psychoanalytic priorities in this later, less hesitant, definition. In her 1918 review of Dorothy Richardson she wrote that consciousness had no obvious form: '[*Pilgrimage*] is just life going on and on. It is Miriam Henderson's stream of consciousness going on and on. And in neither is there any grossly discernible beginning or middle or end.'[102] But this was not to say that *Pilgrimage* was formless. Jung had taught her that even something as apparently random as the word association test revealed the patterns and the structure of the mind.[103] Consciousness like poetry, Jung suggested, would reveal its own forms if allowed enough latitude. By 1922 Sinclair believed that the mind and its forms were the key to the spirit of modernity. The '*vers librist* . . . is free to follow his thoughts in their own movement', and those thoughts have their own music: in Flint's poetry the 'delicate, subtle waves, the unfinished turn and return of his unrhymed, metreless cadence follow exactly the turns, the delicate, subtle curves of his emotion'; and H.D.'s poems 'have the quick beat of birds' wings, the rise and fall of big waves'.[104] Psychoanalysis taught her both to listen to consciousness, and to discern its patterns.

But even in 1922 Sinclair could not quite shake her nostalgia for Victorian emotional drama, that drama that Mew and her writing had brought so insistently, and so disruptively, into Sinclair's life. In the article on Flint she writes wistfully: 'If we are to compare new things with old, we shall find one

---

[101] Sinclair, 'Poems of F. S. Flint', 16. In a passage in a holograph draft of the article which was omitted from the final version, Sinclair acknowledges that *vers libre* too may become outdated: 'It may be that two generations hence free verse may itself have become captive, subject to borrowed cadences, a thing of stale literature; & the younger poets will then be found clamouring for a renaissance of rhyme and metre', 14, UP, Box 24, fo. 468.

[102] Sinclair, 'Novels of Dorothy Richardson', 444.

[103] See Sinclair's description of the word assocation test, 'Clinical Lectures on Symbolism and Sublimation', I. 121. Jung developed the word association test, first invented by Francis Galton, in the early 1900s while working on schizophrenia (then known as 'dementia praecox') at the Burghölzli hospital in Zurich under the direction of Bleuler. See Ellenberger, *Discovery of the Unconscious*, 162, 668.

[104] 'Poems of F. S. Flint', 16; Sinclair, 'Poems of "H.D." ', 462, 467.

thing gone from the modern world, the power to discharge emotion into bursts of music like Keats's *Ode to a Nightingale*, or Swinburne's choruses in *Erectheus*.'[105] Pound had to discipline her while she was working on her piece on his poetry. In a draft she had written: 'You cannot conceive him taking a great, passionate human theme & treating it greatly, passionately, tenderly.'[106] Pound was scathing:

Wotcher mean by 'great, pash. human theem.'??
            'She was pore butt she wuz honest
            Victim OF !!!
                            uh village crime   ' ???
Passons.[107]

Sinclair, duly chastened, took out the reference. The days when she could celebrate 'the passion of a thing' were long gone.[108] And she herself had by 1920 definitively thrown in her lot with the 'moderns'. In a letter to Pound of 1 November 1919 in which she announces her intention to write a piece on his work she notes that after *Mary Olivier* 'I am a person obnoxious to the persons who might be useful to you'.[109] Sinclair herself was now identified beyond doubt with the literary modernity she had done so much to promote. Her transformation was complete.

---

[105] Sinclair, 'Poems of F. S. Flint', 16.
[106] Sinclair, holograph draft of 'The Reputation of Ezra Pound', 9, UP, Box 24, fo. 467.
[107] Pound to Sinclair, n.d. [early 1920], UP, Box 3, fo. 74.
[108] Sinclair to Mew, 6 Jan. 1915, HA.
[109] Sinclair to Pound, 1 Nov. 1919, Beinecke Rare Book and Manuscript Library, Ezra Pound Papers, Box 48, fo. 2136.

1919–1946

7

Sublimation and *Mary Olivier: A Life*

=

MARY OLIVIER: A Life, published when Sinclair was 56, was the book of which she was the most proud. 'Probably in some ways the only decent thing I've ever done or shall do', she wrote to Ezra Pound on 24 October 1919.[1] Critics have largely agreed that it is her best novel: certainly it is the one that has received the most scholarly attention.[2] It tells the story of a woman, born, like Sinclair, in 1863, who defies the cramped conditions of a mid-Victorian daughter's life to evolve her own sceptical modernist consciousness. In many crucial ways Mary's story was Sinclair's own. The novel dramatizes all the contradictions that ran like fault-lines through its author's thought and experience. Sinclair used a radically modern literary technique—stream of consciousness—to explore such typically Victorian concerns as heredity, the boundaries of the self, and family relationships. One of modernism's central discourses, psychoanalysis, gave her a conceptual framework—the newly emerging and highly contested idea of 'sublimation'—within which to think about her relationship to her own past. Sinclair at 56 had no intimate ties. That vertiginous freedom allowed her to put all her energies into her writing, while still acknowledging that her emotional roots were in the Victorian world on which she had so decisively turned her back. Although *Mary Olivier* was far from Sinclair's last novel, it was in many ways a retrospective of her intellectual career: a retrospective that, paradoxically, also marked her emergence as a quintessentially modern

---

[1] May Sinclair to Ezra Pound, Beinecke Rare Book and Manuscript Library, Ezra Pound Papers, Box 48, fo. 2136.

[2] Critical work on it includes a chapter on May Sinclair, which mainly deals with *Mary Olivier*, in Sydney Janet Kaplan, *Feminine Consciousness in the Modern British Novel* (Chicago: University of Illinois Press, 1975); Diane F. Gillespie, 'May Sinclair and the Stream of Consciousness: Metaphors and Metaphysics', *English Literature in Transition 1880–1920*, 21 (1978), 134–42, and '"Muddle of the Middle"'; and Terry Phillips, 'Battling with the Angel: May Sinclair's Powerful Mothers', in Sarah Sceats and Gail Cunningham (eds.), *Image and Power: Women in Fiction in the Twentieth Century* (London: Longman, 1996), 128–38.

writer, an assured and confident practitioner of the 'stream of consciousness' technique which she herself had named.

Sinclair's April 1918 review of the early volumes of Dorothy Richardson's novel *Pilgrimage*, with its description of the text as 'Miriam Henderson's stream of consciousness going on and on', has set the terms for most subsequent critical analyses of *Mary Olivier*, whose serialization in the *Little Review* began in January 1919, and which, like *Pilgrimage*, is told entirely from the perspective of its female protagonist.[3] The novel was hailed as a radical break with tradition, and compared to the work of Dorothy Richardson.[4] Sinclair's own admission to the editor of the *Yale Review* that she was 'immensely interested in the subject of modern methods' supports critical interpretations of *Mary Olivier* as an experiment in narrative technique.[5] Sinclair was determined to build on her achievement, announcing to Violet Hunt on 16 December 1922 that she 'must keep to the method of "Mary Olivier", even if I must pass from mind to mind'.[6] Even Katherine Mansfield, who disliked the novel, acknowledged that it exemplified 'the new way of writing'.[7] Before *Mary Olivier*, Sinclair wrote for the most part in an under-embellished, fairly conventional style, but *Mary Olivier* seeks to reproduce the fragmented, desultory forms of Mary's private thoughts and impressions, as in the following quasi-imagist description of the Yorkshire landscape: 'Burnt patches. Tongues of heather, twisted and pointed, picked clean by fire, flickering grey over black earth. Towards evening the black and grey ran together like ink and water, stilled into purple, the black purple of grapes' (MO, 178). In *Mary Olivier* Sinclair tried to describe the evolving cultures and beliefs of the modern world in a language which, as she wrote of Richardson, would seize 'reality alive'.[8]

---

[3] Sinclair, 'Novels of Dorothy Richardson', 444. Critics who have read *Mary Olivier* as an experiment in method include Kaplan, *Feminine Consciousness in the Modern British Novel*; Gillespie, 'May Sinclair and the Stream of Consciousness' and '"Muddle of the Middle"'.

[4] See e.g. C. A. Dawson Scott, 'Miss May Sinclair', *Bookman* (London), 59 (Oct. 1920), 7–9: 'when Miss Sinclair published "Mary Olivier", she ranged herself definitely with the pioneers' (8). Babette Deutsch compared *Mary Olivier* with Dorothy Richardson's *The Tunnel* (see 'Freedom and the Grace of God', *Dial*, 6, 15 Nov. 1919, 441–2). See also Swinnerton, *Georgian Literary Scene*, 402.

[5] May Sinclair to Wilbur Cross, 8 Feb. 1921, Beinecke Rare Book and Manuscript Library, Yale Collection of American Literature, Za-Yale Review. As Jane Eldridge Miller has noted, Sinclair was 'one of the few Edwardian novelists who responded to the pressures being exerted upon the novel with formal experimentation' (*Rebel Women*, 165).

[6] Sinclair to Violet Hunt, HA.

[7] Katherine Mansfield, 'The New Infancy', *Athenaeum*, no. 4651 (20 June 1919), 494; repr. in *Novels and Novelists* (London: Constable, 1930), 40–3; 41. Shiv K. Kumar credits Mansfield herself with being one of the earliest writers to experiment with stream of consciousness in her 1908 story 'The Tiredness of Rosabel'. See Kumar, *Bergson and the Stream of Consciousness Novel* (London and Glasgow: Blackie, 1962), 40.

[8] Sinclair, 'Novels of Dorothy Richardson', 446.

As well as an example of a 'new', modernist way of writing, *Mary Olivier* was also a recapitulation of the past. If the form of *Mary Olivier* is typically modernist, the events and characters it describes are mostly Victorian. The book begins with Mary's infancy in the 1860s, and ends well before the outbreak of the First World War, in 1910, just as the Edwardian age gives way to the reign of George V. The action of *Mary Olivier*, like that of Virginia Woolf's 1938 novel *The Years*, spans the turn of the century to investigate the dynamics of historical and cultural change. The novel also exemplifies Sinclair's renewed interest in the philosophical questions which had animated the very beginning of her career as a writer. As Diane F. Gillespie suggests, *Mary Olivier* is an idealist novel, that is, in Sinclair's words, one in which 'the world arises in consciousness'.[9] She defended its technique to Catherine Dawson Scott in philosophical terms, writing in March 1920: 'everything has to come through <u>some</u> recorder. Not even in life do we get <u>direct contact</u> with any object; only with our consciousness of the object (or event).'[10] It was part of the same intellectual project, the rehabilitation of idealism, which had preoccupied her in the 1880s and 1890s, and which she took up again after the First World War in publications such as *A Defence of Idealism* (1917) and *The New Idealism* (1922).[11]

Mary Olivier: A Life was one of a number of semi-autobiographical modernist novels by women to appear during and after the war. Most of these texts are structured around the experience of an unmarried central female character who is in search of new forms of artistic and self-expression. *Pilgrimage* (1915–67), traces the life of its protagonist through thirteen volumes from infancy into middle age. Lily Briscoe, in Virginia Woolf's *To the Lighthouse* (1927), sees the abstract picture she is painting of Mrs Ramsay and her son as both a tribute, and a marker of her resistance, to the aspirations of the older generation. H.D.'s autobiographical novel *HERmione* (published posthumously in 1981) uses the tensions between 'her', 'she', and 'I' to explore its heroine's fragile and shifting subjectivity. Because Sinclair was a

---

[9] Sinclair, *Defence of Idealism*, 112. Diane F. Gillespie e.g. notes that 'Sinclair closely associates aesthetic innovation with the metaphysical position she calls the "new idealism" '. See Gillespie, 'May Sinclair (1863–1946)', 440.

[10] Sinclair to Catherine Dawson Scott, 20 Mar. 1920, Beinecke Rare Book and Manuscript Library, Gen. MSS. 144, Box 1, fo. 22.

[11] In Sinclair's 1926 novel *Far End*, novelist Christopher Vivart first writes a novel about an idealist philosopher who 'converts' to realism just as his defence of idealism is about to appear, and then writes a novel entirely from within the consciousness of its central character. Vivart's account of his own method reproduces verbatim sections of Sinclair's Richardson review. See May Sinclair, *Far End* (New York: Macmillan, 1926), 80–6. Although *Far End* discusses some of the issues which *Mary Olivier* engages, it is an unremarkable love story narrated in an entirely conventional style. See Gillespie, 'May Sinclair and the Stream of Consciousness', 138–9, for further discussion of *Far End*.

generation older than all these writers, *Mary Olivier* necessarily describes a different, more distant world, but it shares with *Pilgrimage*, *To the Lighthouse*, and *HERmione* a sense of the peculiar difficulties of female development and, in particular, of women's sexual choices.

Mary Olivier's predominant psychic drama is with her mother, who exerts a powerful and contradictory influence over her until the day of her death. Mary, the only daughter in a family of brothers, is adventurous both physically and intellectually, developing her own, unorthodox religion at an early age. In spite of her mother's opposition, she teaches herself Greek and reads widely in German and other philosophy. As her brothers one by one leave home, and the family moves to Yorkshire when her father's business fails, Mary becomes her mother's companion, watching her father die in an alcoholic stupor, witnessing the terminal illness of her brother Roddy, and finally having to break to her mother the news of her brother Mark's death in India. When the last brother left alive, Dan, emigrates to Canada, Mary is left in sole charge of the mother whose will has dominated her life. She refuses an offer of marriage from poet Richard Nicholson (although she does become his mistress), because of her mother; and she finds herself continually frustrated by her mother's jealousy and by her own feelings of filial responsibility and love. The novel ends with Mary embracing her solitude after Richard's marriage to someone else, and her mother's death. She discovers that happiness lies in renunciation, and that she can sublimate all her restless energy into the writing of poetry.

Sinclair herself thought of the book as an intellectual autobiography, telling Marc Logé, her translator, that 'all this description of the *inner life* is autobiographically as accurate as I can make it'.[12] Novelist G. B. Stern, one of the women in whom Sinclair is supposed to have confided the nature of Charlotte Mew's feelings for her, was in no doubt that Sinclair had drawn intimately on her own life to write *Mary Olivier*:

I know that Mary isn't autobiography, and yet somehow I feel a sort of shyness in writing to you about her, as though I might at any moment say something clumsy and not even be aware of it. . . . I hated Little Mamma—hated her from the very first mention of her. I remembered you told me once you had a nervous breakdown because you tried to write in the same room with your own mother. . . . I remembered, too, in the brook-jumping part, how you had jumped the patches of rushes at St Merryn, and told me how you had always jumped like that with your brothers.[13]

---

[12] Cited in Boll, *Miss May Sinclair*, 244. See Ch. 1 n. 5, for more discussion of the autobiographical roots of *Mary Olivier*.

[13] G. B. Stern to May Sinclair, 15 June 1919, UP, Box, fo. 89.

Even though *Mary Olivier* is written as a novel, Sinclair drew on vignettes and events from her own history to write the story of a woman who shares her own given name, her religious doubts, many of her intellectual passions (Mary Olivier reads Spinoza, Kant, and Hegel), and the year of her birth.[14]

If *Mary Olivier* was Sinclair's intellectual and spiritual autobiography, it was also the text in which she developed some of her most sophisticated ideas about the origins, constitution, and boundaries of the 'I'. Although the novel is written largely in the third person, all the action is described through Mary's eyes, and the landscapes she sees are as indicative of her inner geographies as of the visible world. As Kaplan notes, the narration oscillates between third, second, and even first person (and in fact opens in the second person):

There is an omniscient narrator for Mary . . ., but it is not an impersonal one; it is Mary herself. Usually this narrator describes the thoughts in Mary's mind through the conventional third-person 'she'. This is where the writer Mary, looking at her own life from a great distance in time or feeling, separates herself from the thoughts of the character Mary. . . . But when the omniscient narrator gets closer and closer to identification with the character Mary, the pronouns change. Thus she speaks to that other self. 'You,' she calls it. And then, almost with a startling-seeming inconsistency, she switches to 'I'. . . . The narrator, then, is also 'you', but the 'you' who looks back.[15]

Kaplan reads the complex interplay of pronouns as a form of chronology which organizes Mary's history, suggesting a relation between present, past, and future. Pronominal disruption implicates Mary as writer with Mary as character and consequently as evolving subject. In this reading Mary could be said to author herself, in true modernist mode. But the 'you' of a passage like 'You knew he was smiling because his cheeks swelled high up his face so that his eyes were squeezed into narrow, shining slits' (MO, 5) has another potential addressee in the reader, whose perceptions are thus subtly harmonized with Mary's. 'Mary', as writer of the text, is the product of a set of textual transactions which draw in subject positions other than her own. This insight is crucial to an understanding of the context out of which both

---

[14] There are significant coincidences between the facts of Sinclair's own life and those of Mary's: Mary's father is called Emilius, and Sinclair's mother was called Amelia; the Olivier family live in Ilford, where Sinclair spent part of her childhood; Mary, like Sinclair, spends a brief period at boarding school; Mary's brother Mark joins the army, serves in India and dies there, like Sinclair's brother Frank (the dates of Mark's home leave, 1884–5, exactly correspond with those of Frank); Mary's brothers Roddy and Dan emigrate to Canada, like Sinclair's brother Joseph; Roddy dies of mitral valve disease, as had Sinclair's brothers; Mary reads books which were in Sinclair's own library (Kant, Hegel, Schopenhauer); and Mary's father, like Sinclair's, fails as a businessman and dies an alcoholic.

[15] Kaplan, *Feminine Consciousness*, 51.

Sinclair's phrase 'stream of consciousness', and her writing practice in *Mary Olivier*, grew.

Critics tend to assume that Sinclair borrowed the phrase 'stream of consciousness' for her review of Dorothy Richardson from William James's *The Principles of Psychology* (1890).[16] Melvin Friedman quotes the following paragraph from James as Sinclair's source:

Consciousness, then, does not appear to itself chopped up in bits. Such words as 'chain' or 'train' do not describe it fitly as it presents itself in the first instance. It is nothing jointed; it flows. A 'river' or a 'stream' are the metaphors by which it is most naturally described. In talking of it hereafter, let us call it the stream of thought, of consciousness, or of subjective life.[17]

Taken out of context, as this paragraph usually is, it looks like a description of the movements of a mind as it idly observes and reflects on the world around it, without logical order or necessary sequence. Indeed this is how Sinclair herself uses it in the Dorothy Richardson review: 'It is just life going on and on. It is Miriam Henderson's stream of consciousness going on and on. And in neither is there any grossly discernible beginning or middle or end.'[18] It has thus usually been taken as a description of the formal properties of novels like *Pilgrimage*. Friedman, for example, says: 'William James must therefore be accepted as one of the initiators of this new *practice* in the novel [my italics]'.[19] However, the broader context of the quotation reveals it to be a comment on the processes of selfhood, rather than on the texture of perception. The passage follows a discussion of our sense of psychological continuity even after a lapse in consciousness such as sleep: 'a present thought, although not ignorant of the time-gap, can still regard itself as continuous with certain chosen portions of the past'.[20] In other words, 'the consciousness remains sensibly continuous and one. What now is the common whole? The natural name for it is *myself*, *I*, or *me*.'[21] If James really was Sinclair's source for the quotation, then she had in her mind a text in which it is not the texture of the perceiving mind that is at issue, but its sense of its own unity, or, in James's word, its 'self-feeling'.[22]

But there is no particular reason to assume that *The Principles of Psychology* was, in fact, the source of the phrase in Sinclair's Richardson review.

---

[16] See e.g. Melvin Friedman, *Stream of Consciousness: A Study in Literary Method* (New Haven: Yale University Press, 1955), 2; Gillespie, 'May Sinclair and the Stream of Consciousness', 134–5.

[17] William James, *The Principles of Psychology* (London: Macmillan, 1890), i. 239. Quoted in Friedman, *Stream of Consciousness*, 2.

[18] Sinclair, 'Novels of Dorothy Richardson', 444.

[19] Friedman, *Stream of Consciousness*, 75.

[20] James, *Principles of Psychology*, i. 239.

[21] Ibid. 238.

[22] Ibid. 305.

Sinclair, like Mary Olivier, read widely in nineteenth-century biology and psychology, including Herbert Spencer, Samuel Butler, William McDougall, Théodule Ribot, and Henry Maudsley, as well as William James, and during the years immediately preceding the composition of *Mary Olivier* she was engaged in writing the two-volume work that eventually appeared in 1916 as the two clinical lectures on Freud and Jung, and in 1917 as *A Defence of Idealism*. Many of the texts she cites in *Mary Olivier* and *A Defence of Idealism* use the phrase 'stream of consciousness' as a matter of course, and she had further come across it in Evelyn Underhill's 1911 best-seller, *Mysticism*, which she read even before it was published.[23] The phrase, then, far from alluding specifically to William James, invokes a range of scientific and popular contexts, none of which are concerned primarily with the nature of perception, but all of which consider at length the question of the limits of individuality. Mary is anxious about how to define and maintain her selfhood not only because she feels trapped by her genetic links to her mother, her brother, and her aunt, but also because she is wrestling, as her curiosity about her own origins implies, with existential questions about self-consciousness, personality, and subjectivity.[24] *Mary Olivier* is as much a popular fictionalization of recent and current scientific debate about personal identity as it is an attempt to, in Woolf's famous words, 'record the atoms as they fall' on the perceiving mind.[25]

Sinclair (and Mary herself) found debate about the definition of an 'individual' in almost every Victorian scientific text they read. Herbert Spencer, for example, in *The Principles of Biology* (1864), notes that

If a strawberry-plant sends out runners carrying buds at their ends, which strike root and grow into independent plants, that separate from the original one by decay of the runners, must we not say that they possess separate individualities; and yet if we do this, are we not at a loss to say when their separate individualities were established?[26]

---

[23] See Evelyn Underhill, *Mysticism: A Study in the Nature and Development of Man's Spiritual Consciousness* (London: Methuen, 1911), 62: the unconscious contains 'all those "uncivilized" instincts and vices, those remains of the ancestral savage which education has forced out of the stream of consciousness'. I discuss this coincidence further in *Vita and Virginia: The Work and Friendship of V. Sackville-West and Virginia Woolf* (Oxford: Oxford University Press, 1993), 138–9.

[24] See Stark, 'Overcoming Butlerian Obstacles', for further discussion of the issue of heredity in *Mary Olivier*.

[25] Virginia Woolf, 'Modern Fiction' (1925), repr. in Scott (ed.), *Gender of Modernism*, 628–33: at 631. Hermione Lee notes that Woolf's 1918 reading notes on James Joyce's *Ulysses*—which were the kernel for 'Modern Fiction'—open with references to Sinclair's review of Richardson. See Lee, *Virginia Woolf* (London: Chatto and Windus, 1996), 391.

[26] Herbert Spencer, *The Principles of Biology* (London and Edinburgh: Williams and Norgate, 1864), i. 202.

This interrogation of the biological limits of individuality is echoed in *Body and Mind* (1911), a book written by William McDougall, a consultant to the Medico-Psychological Clinic, and heavily cited in Sinclair's *A Defence of Idealism*:

My consciousness is a stream of consciousness which has a certain unique unity . . . Now it is perfectly obvious and universally admitted that my stream of consciousness is not self-supporting, is not self-sufficient, is not a closed self-determining system; it is admitted that each phase of the stream does not flow wholly out of the preceding phase, and that its course cannot be explained without the assumption of influences coming upon it from without. What then are these influences? The Psychical Monist must reply—they are other consciousnesses.[27]

Where Spencer has the individual body unfolding continuously out of the bodies of others, McDougall imagines consciousness as a kind of perpetual flowing together of minds, a network of streams constantly joining and separating from one another. Samuel Butler, in 1878, combined the perspective of the biologist with the language of the psychologist to argue that individuality 'depends simply upon the fact that the various phases of existence have been linked together, by links which we agree in considering sufficient to cause identity, and that they have flowed the one out of the other in what we see as a continuous, though it may be at times, a troubled stream'.[28] The metaphor of the 'stream' was thus endlessly adapted throughout late nineteenth-century science to describe the complicated relationship of individuals to both their external and their internal environments. As McDougall remarked in 1911, 'the most urgent problem confronting the philosophic biologist is the construction of a theory of life which will harmonize the facts of individuality with the appearance of the continuity of all life, with the theory of progressive evolution, and with the facts of heredity and bi-parental reproduction'.[29] Or, in the words of Ribot: 'Is the I, the personality, the constituent element of the individual, transmissible by heredity, as are the various modes of mental activity?'[30]

Mary Olivier struggles with both the formal and the familial dimensions of her problematic consciousness of her self. Two scenes from Mary's childhood demonstrate her unease. In the first, Mary ponders the question of selfhood. She wonders about beginnings of all kinds:

[27] William McDougall, *Body and Mind: A History and a Defense of Animism* (London: Methuen, 1911), 162–3.

[28] Samuel Butler, *Life and Habit* (London: Trübner and Co., 1878), 97.

[29] McDougall, *Body and Mind*, 377.

[30] Théodule Ribot, *Heredity: A Psychological Study of its Phenomena, Laws, Causes, and Consequences*, no translator named (London: Henry S. King, 1875), 140.

There was the day you were born, January the twenty-fourth, eighteen sixty-three, at five o'clock in the morning. When you were born you weren't any age at all, not a minute old, not a second, not half a second. But there was eighteen sixty-two and there was January the twenty-third and the minute just before you were born. You couldn't really tell when the twenty-third ended and the twenty-fourth began; because when you counted sixty minutes for the hour and sixty seconds for the minute, there was still the half second and the half of that, and so on for ever and ever.

You couldn't tell when you were really born. (MO, 45–6)

Mary's dilemma is echoed in Arnold Waterlow's puzzlement (in *Arnold Waterlow: A Life*, 1924) over when and where he begins. Horrified by the idea of fractions, and convinced that 'There isn't any one', he decides that 'at this rate there couldn't be any Himself either. He was only *one of the ones*.'[31] For both children the very medium in which they ponder these questions, their self-consciousness, is problematized by the uncertainties which their questions imply. As scientist Herbert Spencer writes in one of the books Mary reads later in *Mary Olivier*: 'No one can be conscious of what he *is*, but only of what he *was* a moment since. That which thinks can never be the object of direct contemplation; seeing that to be this, it must become that which is thought of, not that which thinks.'[32] *Mary Olivier* is a formal exploration of the impossible condition of self-knowledge (in Spencer's words, 'knowledge of [the self] is forbidden by the very nature of thought').[33] The text's continual slippage into the second person registers the continual disintegration of consciousness into unanswerable questions like Mary's and Arnold's, questions which imply that 'you', in fact, have as good a chance of knowing 'I/me' as 'I' have.

In the second scene, the 2-year-old Mary, lying awake in her parents' bedroom, curiously fingers the wrought-iron work of her cot frame.

Tip-fingering backwards that way you got into the grey lane where the prickly stones were and the hedge of little biting trees. When the door in the hedge opened you saw the man in the night-shirt. He had only half a face. From the nose and his cheek-bones downwards his beard hung straight like a dark cloth. You opened your mouth, but before you could scream you were back in the cot; the room was light; the green knob winked and grinned at you from the railing, and behind the curtain Papa and Mamma were lying in the big bed. (MO, 3–4)

Mary's stream of consciousness is characteristically split here between narrator and audience (the implied 'I', the explicit 'you'), and the reader ('you')

[31] Sinclair, *Arnold Waterlow*, 62–3.
[32] Spencer, *The Principles of Psychology* (London: Gougman, Brown, Green, and Longmans, 1855), 40.
[33] Spencer, *First Principles* (London: Williams and Norgate, 1863), 66.

is implicated in what seems to be a habitual and obsessive nightmare. But the shift from careful recording of physical sensation ('By stretching your arm out tight you could reach the curlykew at the end', MO, 3) into a dream in which the railings become a stony lane inhabited by a man in a nightshirt is imperceptible: the world of the body and the world of the mind are fatally fused. Mary, and the reader, never know if this is a dream or a memory or a version of the Freudian primal scene, the sight (or fantasy) of her father in his nightshirt.[34] The latter interpretation is apparently confirmed in the paragraph that follows:

One night she came back out of the lane as the door in the hedge was opening. The man stood in the room by the washstand, scratching his long thigh. He was turned slant-wise from the nightlight on the washstand so that it showed his yellowish skin under the lifted shirt. The white half-face hung by itself on the darkness. When he left off scratching and moved towards the cot she screamed. (MO, 4)

In this incident the pre-Oedipal encounter with the father, unrecognized and merging grotesquely with the fantastic bogeyman of the child's dreams, is immediately followed by the child—also not yet named—being taken into the mother's bed and choking on her own pleasure as she fingers her mother's body: 'You could feel the little ridges of the stiff nipple as your finger pushed it back into the breast. Her sobs shook in her throat and ceased suddenly' (MO, 4). But the reliability of this account is undermined by the ambiguities of the paragraph before in which Mary's consciousness ranges impossibly over space and time without knowing what is substantial and what is not. The staging of this defining ambiguity in her parents' conjugal room suggests that Mary's consciousness is problematic not only because, in true idealist mode, it cannot guarantee the accuracy of its perceptions, but also because it is shaped by her relations with her mother and father—both in terms of heredity, and in Freudian and Jungian terms.

Mary's fight to establish herself as an autonomous subject in her mother's household is fought on a variety of fronts. On the one hand, she experiences a classically Freudian sense of inferiority in the face of her mother's obvious preference for her brothers. Mary's petulant destruction of her brick tower because her mother ignores it in favour of her brother's snowman is obviously a symbolic moment (MO, 9–10).[35] Mary's mother disapproves of any sign of 'masculine' self-assertion in her daughter, showing her affection

---

[34] In the case history of the Wolf-Man Freud notes that the primal scene, in which the child observes the parents copulating, can never be definitively identified as fact. See Freud, 'From the History of an Infantile Neurosis' (1918), in *Standard Edition*, xvii. 3–122: at 56.

[35] For further discussion of this passage, see Jean Radford, 'Introduction' to Sinclair, *Mary Olivier: A Life* (London: Virago, 1980), no page numbers, and Phillips, 'Battling with the Angel'.

only when she devotes herself to feminine tasks such as sewing and serving tea. Mary's struggle with her mother is a feminist drama, the story of a daughter who aspires to more than the quietly domestic life for which her mother has destined her. But Mary is afraid that she will be overwhelmed not only by her mother's attempts at socialization, but also by her own biological history. Her brother's friend Lindley Vickers, to whom she is attracted, recommends that she read Haeckel, Ribot, Spencer, and Maudsley, because, he says, 'I can't think where you came from' (MO, 284). In effect, he asks the same question as the child Mary, but in different terms: he is concerned not with the origins of her consciousness, but with her genetic make-up.

The section of *Mary Olivier* that deals with Mary's learning about theories of heredity is one of those parts of the novel Sinclair told Logé were autobiographical. It is likely, then, that Sinclair herself read the books that Mary reads, and that she felt the same claustrophobia and fear. *Mary Olivier* summarizes and quotes from a range of named texts by Spencer, Haeckel, Maudsley, and Ribot, and describes Mary's horror at the discovery that her mental autonomy may be fatally compromised by her heredity. The novel is in part a commentary on the corrosive effects of evolutionary science on women like Mary who are desperate, in Sinclair's words, to establish '*some personal identity over and above that of [their] progenitors*'.[36] Ernst Haeckel argues that there is no such thing as mental freedom: '*the will is never free*, but is always determined by external or internal influences. These influences are for the most part ideas which have been either formed by Adaptation or Inheritance, and are traceable to one or other of these two physiological functions.'[37] *Mary Olivier* paraphrases sections of Henry Maudsley's *Body and Mind* (1870), which announces: 'No one can escape the tyranny of his organization; no one can elude the destiny that is innate in him, and which unconsciously and irresistibly shapes his ends.'[38] All of Mary's reading tells her that her attempts at shaping her own life are in vain, and that she is caught in the net not only of hereditary disease but also of inherited personality, which, according to Théodule Ribot, is determined irreversibly and organically: 'Nay, even if with the evolutionists we recognize in heredity a force which not only preserves, but which also creates by accumulation, then not only is the character transmitted, but it is the work of fate, made up bit by bit,

[36] Sinclair, *Defence of Idealism*, 22.

[37] Ernst Haeckel, *The History of Creation: Or the Development of the Earth and its Inhabitants by the Action of Natural Causes: A Popular Exposition of the Doctrine of Evolution in General, and of that of Darwin, Goethe, and Lamarck in Particular* (1868; 4th edn., trans. E. Ray Lankester, London: Henry S. King, 1876), i. 237.

[38] Henry Maudsley, *Body and Mind: An Inquiry into their Connection and Mutual Influence, Specially in Reference to Mental Disorders* (London: Macmillan, 1870), 75.

by the slow and unconscious but ever accumulating toil of generations.'[39]
Mary discovers that not only is her behaviour constrained by her mother's
expectations and needs, but also that her mother and father and all their
ancestors have already determined her social, emotional, and physical
future.

You had been wrong all the time.... You had thought of yourself as a somewhat less
powerful, but still independent and separate entity, a sacred, inviolable self, struggling against them for completer freedom and detachment. Crushed down, but
always getting up and going on again; fighting a more and more successful battle for
your own; beating them in the end. But it was not so. There were no independent,
separate entities, no sacred, inviolable selves. They were one immense organism
and you were part of it; you were nothing that they had not been before you. It was
no good struggling. You were caught in the net; you couldn't get out. (MO, 289–90)

For a time Mary ceases to believe in rebellion and self-assertion; she even
manages to feel sympathetic to the rest of her family, who are as unfree as
she is.

   The theories of Ribot, Maudsley, and Spencer are especially horrifying to
Mary because nearly all the conditions Herbert Spencer lists as hereditary
('gout, consumption, and insanity', along with 'dipsomania' (alcoholism)
and 'a bias towards suicide') appear in the Olivier family.[40] Mary's father
and her brother Dan are alcoholics; her brother has a congenital heart defect;
one of her aunts is insane; and one of her uncles commits suicide. Late in the
novel Mary learns that she too has the mitral valve irregularity that killed her
brother Roddy ('Roddy's heart, the net of flesh and blood drawing in a bit of
your body', MO, 353). The 'tyranny of her organization' has a very specific
meaning for Mary, who already sees around her evidence of the woman she
is condemned to become. Mary, then, faces the possibility that her commitment to self-education and self-development might come to nothing in the
face not only of maternal resistance, but also of the dictates of the body
itself.

   Mary's fear crystallizes around the possibility that she will end up like her
father's unmarried sister Charlotte, who becomes increasingly unbalanced
as the book develops, and who returns to Mary in her dreams even after
Charlotte has been committed to an asylum. Nothing is known of Sinclair's
aunts and uncles, although Boll tells us that she had at least three aunts on her
father's side, but she was certainly aware of her father's alcoholism and of
her brothers' hereditary illness, and as early as 1894 she was advocating

[39] Ribot, *Heredity*, 344.   [40] Spencer, *Principles of Biology*, i. 243.

sexual abstinence for families with genetic diseases.[41] Charlotte's illness
consists in sexual over-assertiveness (she flirts with the vicar), and in the
delusional belief that she is about to be married. The disease takes macabre
forms: Charlotte gives the young Mary secret gifts of little white china dolls
packed away in matchboxes, telling her 'That's Aunt Charlotte's little baby.
. . . I'm going to be married and I shan't want it any more' (MO, 37). Charlotte's actions return, grotesquely transformed, in Mary's nightmares. The
first dream involves both Charlotte and the china-doll babies: 'When you
opened the stair cupboard door to catch the opossum, you found a white
china doll lying in it, no bigger than your finger. That was Aunt Charlotte'
(MO, 37). The second is a more obviously sexual image, 'Aunt Charlotte
standing at the foot of the basement stairs, by the cat's cupboard where the
kittens were born, taking her clothes off and hiding them' (MO, 152); and the
third involves Mary returning in her dreams to the house of her childhood
and searching hopelessly for the schoolroom and her brothers but, at 'the
bottom of the kitchen stairs', finding only 'a dead baby lying among the
boots and shoes in the cat's cupboard' (MO, 311).[42] The dreams are symbolic
both of the child Mary's identification with Charlotte's unloved state (she is
confined and ignored even as Charlotte, like her china babies, is kept locked
away), and of the adult Mary's fear of sharing Charlotte's destiny. Charlotte's illness, which Mary as an adult describes as living 'all her life in a
dream of loving and being loved' (MO, 288), represents both the fate that
Mary may bring on herself, through 'the restlessness and the endless idiotic
reverie of desire' (MO, 234), and the fate which her heredity will bring upon
her. Charlotte takes on a symbolic significance for Mary's unconscious,
marking the uncertain limits of Mary's own agency; and her existence also
intensifies the effects of Mary's scientific reading, seeming to warn Mary
of her eventual fate. As Maudsley wrote in one of the books Mary reads:
'Neither in health nor in disease is the mind imprisoned in one corner of the
body; and when a person is lunatic, he is . . . lunatic to his fingers' ends.'[43]
Mary's body is saturated with Charlotte's degeneracy as well as sustained
by Roddy's limping heart.

---

[41] Boll, *Miss May Sinclair*, 25; and see Sinclair, 'Platonic Sociology', 52: 'If "for persons about to marry"
it were as necessary to obtain a medical certificate as a license, it were no unreasonable officiousness on the
part of the government to prevent the propagation of madness or hereditary disease.'

[42] Sinclair returned to the image of a woman suddenly undressing in public in *The Allinghams* (New
York: Macmillan, 1927), in which Margie, with 'glittering eyes', covers her fiancé with 'sweet, violent
kisses' and then begins to take her clothes off in his drawing room (356). The doctor diagnoses 'acute mania'
(361) and Margie is sent to live at his house. Her fiancé breaks off their engagement, telling Margie's mother:
'I should be afraid for—for our children' (360).

[43] Maudsley, *Body and Mind*, 41.

Charlotte's overshadowing presence at the beginning of the book signals sexuality as the main arena in which Mary's battle for independence will be fought. Charlotte, we are to believe, is ill partly out of sexual frustration. Even Mary's mother acknowledges that there is nothing much wrong with her: 'She just fell in love with every man she met. If she'd only seen him for five minutes she was off after him. Ordering her trousseau and dressing herself up. She was no more mad than I am except just on that one point' (MO, 237). Charlotte's story has clear parallels with Mary's, since every romantic encounter Mary has, except one, fails. When Mary does finally become Richard Nicholson's lover, she is obsessed with the fear of being found out. While Mary is away with Richard, her mother becomes catatonic with anxiety, and Mary rushes home to be at her side. 'What had [Mrs Olivier] been thinking of those five days? It was as though she knew' (MO, 363). Just as Charlotte's pleasure spelt death—the dead baby in the dream—to the child Mary, so Mary's pleasure in turn nearly kills her mother. But it is precisely her pleasure—the space of her freedom both to think and to feel—that Mary is most anxious to preserve. Mary and Mark agree that Charlotte is in some ways 'the sanest of the lot' because 'she knew what she wanted' (MO, 250). Pleasure (or, as Mary calls it, 'the flash point of freedom', MO, 377) is associated with self-assertion and with the perversity both of desire and the will. Balancing Aunt Charlotte in the novel is Mary's father's other sister, Lavinia, who is frowned upon for her 'opinions' (MO, 33–4), but who nonetheless asserts her religious nonconformity even at the Oliviers' dinner table. In adulthood Mary discovers that Lavinia wanted to marry a Unitarian, but instead, faced with opposition from her mother and her brothers, she spent her life taking care of her sister Charlotte (MO, 221). Lavinia represents both the restrictions and the limited freedoms of Mary's life: on the one hand, Mary, like Lavinia, drags out her days taking care of a family member, but on the other, like Lavinia, Mary develops 'opinions' that she refuses to give up even in the face of familial opposition. The child Mary's excited misunderstanding of 'opossums' for 'opinions' underscores the subsequent identification of aunt and niece: ' "I've read about [opinions]," she said. "They are dear little animals with long furry tails, much bigger than Sarah's tail, and they climb up trees" ' (MO, 34). From the beginning 'opinions' are associated with laughter and with a form of wildly creative speculation. It is such free pleasure that Mary's mother seeks to contain: Mary and her brothers are sent out of the dining room for giggling uncontrollably at one of Aunt Charlotte's most erratic remarks (MO, 36). It is after this episode that Charlotte ceases to be a source of amusement and wonder, and becomes the dark shadow-self with whom Mary identifies and of whom she is afraid.

Charlotte's legacy, then, is both symbolic and somatic: Mary is afraid that her heredity and her 'restlessness. That was desire' (MO, 228) will lead her inevitably into insanity, and her mother's distress at her absence with Richard seems only to confirm that pleasure is potentially fatal. Lavinia's legacy, on the other hand, is intellectual, and it is through her identification with Lavinia's heretical obstinacy that Mary begins slowly to find a way out of the parental net. Lavinia's Unitarianism, the first challenge to her father's authority that Mary is ever aware of, is an implicit comment on Mary's growing confusion about the boundaries of her individuality, since Unitarianism denies the triune nature of the godhead.[44] Lavinia's dissenting 'opinions' thus set the stage for Mary's subsequent philosophical speculations about the nature of God and of substance. Mary has already wondered where her parents end and she begins. Lavinia simply asks the same question about God and his son.

Mary's irritation with God (as well as the careful recording of her dreams and fantasies near the beginning of the novel) reveal the lasting influence on Sinclair's thought of the psychoanalytic theory she had been reading a couple of years before writing *Mary Olivier* as she worked on the 'Clinical Lectures'. Even as a child Mary, like Lavinia, is suspicious of God: 'you couldn't help thinking of God as a silly person; he was always flying into tempers, and he was jealous' (MO, 43). In this he is exactly like Mary's own father, and the novel makes this point explicitly when, early on, it describes Mary at dinner 'sitting at the right hand of Papa in the glory of the Father' (MO, 62). In the second 'Clinical Lecture' Sinclair noted that Jung's 'quarrel with the Christian religion is that, besides being a first-class engine of repression, it has fostered an infantile dependence on God as the Father to which man is already too much prone through the persistence in him of what Jung and Freud call the "Father-Imago"'.[45] Mary's annoyance at both her

---

[44] The Rachovian catechism, one of the founding documents of Unitarianism, is concerned with the boundaries between persons: 'The essence of God is one not in kind but in number. Wherefore it cannot in any way contain a plurality of persons, since a person is nothing else than an individual intelligent essence. Wherever then there exist three numerical persons, there must necessarily in like manner be reckoned three individual essences, for in the same sense in which it is affirmed that there is one numerical essence, it must be held that there is one numerical person' (Socinus, *Racovian Catechism*, 1605; trans. Thomas Rees, London, 1818; quoted in James Hastings (ed.), *Encyclopaedia of Religion and Ethics*, Edinburgh: T. T. Clark, 1921, xii. 521). In *Mary Olivier* Lavinia is reading James Martineau, *Endeavours after the Christian Life* (1843). Martineau (1805–1900) was one of Unitarianism's main popularizers in the 19th cent., and he tried without success to establish a united Unitarian church in 1888.

[45] Sinclair, 'Clinical Lectures on Symbolism and Sublimation', II. 144. The corresponding passage in *Psychology of the Unconscious* reads: 'The strong and natural love which binds the child to the father, turns away in those years during which the humanity of the father would be all too plainly recognized, to the higher form of the father, to the "Fathers" of the church, and to the Father God, visibly represented by them' (54). Sinclair introduces a note of satire into her paraphrase of the passage. For Sinclair, as for Mary, religious belief is associated with the limited understanding of infancy.

father and God represents even at this early stage a move out of 'infantile dependence' and ways of thinking. Mary is not content to accept her father's authority, and her increasingly atheistic leanings are also an implicit condemnation of the ways of patriarchy itself.

Mary begins her philosophical and religious explorations in disgust after she learns about sex and ceases to believe in the virgin birth. Mary reads about pantheism and Spinoza in the *Encyclopaedia Britannica* and is enthralled. 'So this was the truth about God. In spite of the queer words it was very simple. . . . He was what you had felt and thought him to be as soon as you could think about him at all' (MO, 99–100). But when she tells her mother she cannot be confirmed because she has lost her faith, her mother dismisses her heterodoxy as simple laziness: 'You just want an excuse for not learning those Thirty-Nine Articles' (MO, 114). Mary's first step towards intellectual autonomy is infantilized in a way that sets the stage for all her subsequent encounters with her mother over her mental life. '[Mamma]'d love me now if I stayed little, so that she could do what she liked with me' (MO, 249), Mary tells Mark. Her mother, trying to stop her learning Greek, identifies her own will with that of God: 'I won't let you have your own way in everything. Until your will is resigned to God's will I may well be afraid' (MO, 127). Mary suspects that her mother uses 'God's will' for her own ends, telling herself at the onset of puberty: 'If you didn't take care she would get hold of you and never rest till she had broken you, or turned and twisted you to her own will. She would say it was God's will' (MO, 124). Orthodox Christianity comes to symbolize the oppressive and hypocritical power of fathers *and* mothers. Even Kant is rejected, after initial excitement, because of the constraining nature of the categorical imperative: ' "You can because you ought." Kant, when you got to the bottom of him, was no more exciting than Mamma' (MO, 254). It seems that Mary is condemned to live out the religious as well as the somatic script of her family's past, with her parents, and especially her mother, responsible for both. As Sinclair wrote in the second 'Clinical Lecture', a 'large portion of Professor Jung's book is given up to . . . the conflict with the mother. That conflict begins in childhood and is waged most fiercely on the threshold of adolescence. It must be fought to a finish, and the child must win it or remain for ever immature.'[46] Mary's challenge to God is also her challenge to her mother and to the inheritances of all kinds that her parents have given her. She must find a place for her own consciousness, and her own selfhood, to develop beyond the tyrannies of the past.

---

[46] Sinclair, 'Clinical Lectures on Symbolism and Sublimation', II. 144.

Sinclair found one model for this kind of development in the Jungian psychoanalysis she had been reading with such attention as she worked on *A Defence of Idealism* and the unfinished 'The Way of Sublimation'. She sometimes felt ambivalent about psychoanalysis, in spite of the enthusiasm with which she had supported the Medico-Psychological Clinic in the early years of the war. She worried that it failed to take account of 'the variety of children's interests and activities', and complained that a 'healthy energetic child has not the time or the patience for the special preoccupations he has been credited with'.[47] She objected to the sexualization of psychic life that she found even in Jung, arguing that if it were really true that the libido was such a mobile and protean appetite, then sexual images would be no more significant than any others.[48] In a sense, hers was a classically Victorian revulsion. But there was one aspect of psychoanalytic theory—the aspect which suggested that sexual activity might not always be central to well-being—which she welcomed and wrote widely about: sublimation. As she noted in *A Defence of Idealism*, for her the 'theory of sublimation is the one thing of interest and of value that Professor Freud and Professor Jung have contributed to Psychology'.[49] Although it is not mentioned explicitly in the novel, Mary Olivier's triumphant joy at the end of the text is a clear illustration of the theory of sublimation that Sinclair advanced in the 1916 'Clinical Lectures': Jean Radford even describes *Mary Olivier* as 'a study of sublimation'.[50] The novel is Sinclair's testimony to psychoanalysis as a description of the evolution of the self. As I pointed out in Chapter 6, the fact that Jung's account of sublimation was partly dependent on German idealism, Schopenhauer, Bergson, and evolutionary theory, only made it more attractive to Sinclair, who, like many other contemporary thinkers, read psychoanalysis in the context of late nineteenth-century philosophy.[51] In Sinclair's hands sublimation is not simply a psychic operation, but an evolutionary process for the species as a whole. In sublimating her desire Mary transcends not only her own instincts but those of her ancestors as well. In other words,

---

[47] Sinclair, unpublished typescript, 'The Way of Sublimation', 113, UP, Box 23, fos. 436–8.

[48] See e.g. her criticism of Jung's 'disconcerting literalism' in 'Clinical Lectures on Symbolism and Sublimation', II. 144: 'You might just as well take Kant's celebrated flight of fancy in the "Critique of Pure Reason" about "die leichte Taube," . . . and argue from it that because the Dove is undoubtedly a sexual symbol, and Pure Reason is a Dove, therefore the whole paragraph has a sexual reference'; and see also 'Way of Sublimation', 133, UP, Box 23, fos. 436–8.

[49] Sinclair, *Defence of Idealism*, 5.   [50] Radford, 'Introduction', to *Life and Death of Harriett Frean*.

[51] Sinclair e.g. often refers to the libido as the 'Will-to-live' (see *Defence of Idealism*, 34), and Swinnerton commented that Jung's definition of libido 'gave it kinship with our old friends the Life Force and the Élan Vital' (*Georgian Scene*, 399). Jung himself makes the analogy with Schopenhauer: 'this word [libido] has become the most frequent technical expression of psychoanalysis, for the simple reason that its significance is wide enough to cover all the unknown and countless manifestations of the Will in the sense of Schopenhauer.' See Jung, *Psychology of the Unconscious*, 122.

sublimation is her escape from the genetic trap prepared for her by her family. It offers her a way of imagining a transformed or displaced relation to the past that is reinforced by a Kantian ideal of moral freedom.

Sinclair offers definitions of sublimation in a variety of different texts. Her earliest formulation comes in the 1916 'Clinical Lectures', originally conceived, as we saw in the previous chapter, as the sequel to *A Defence of Idealism* and as a response to Jung's *Psychology of the Unconscious*, which had been translated into English in 1916. In the lectures she was anxious to differentiate between Freud and Jung, noting that the 'tendency is still to mix up Jung's theory more or less with Freud's'.[52] This was especially unfortunate in reviews of *Psychology of the Unconscious*, since it was the text in which Jung elaborated his revised theory of the libido and definitively broke with Freud.[53] Sinclair was clear that she sided with Jung: she told Macmillan on 4 January 1916 that 'The Way of Sublimation' was 'very anti-Freudian'.[54] She especially appreciated the centrality of sublimation to Jungian theory, seeing in it 'the secret of individuality'—exactly the secret which Mary Olivier works so hard to discover.[55] Sublimation also satisfied Sinclair's Darwinist instincts, since she interpreted it as a phenomenon of racial, as well as individual, evolution:

Sublimation itself is the striving of the Libido towards manifestation in higher and higher forms. The history of evolution is its history. You might almost say offhand that the higher organism is the sublimation of the lower, the animal of the plant, the vertebrate of the invertebrate, the placental mammal of the reptile, the ape-man of the anthropoid ape, palaeolithic man of the Neanderthal and Heidelberg connecting link, civilised man of the primitive savage; and that, when we come to the individual, the adult is the sublimation of the child.[56]

In sublimating her desires Mary accomplishes not only the higher evolution of her own consciousness, but also, in miniature, of her family and of her race. Mary's 'stream of consciousness' unfolds in a profoundly Spencerian universe, in which individual psychologies mirror the evolving forms around them. Or, in the words of Ribot, one of the authors Mary reads, evolution is always 'a transition from lesser to greater', from 'the homogeneous to the heterogeneous, from the uniform to the multiform'.[57] Mary's 'modern' epiphany—like psychoanalysis itself—thus grows out of a profoundly Victorian ideology of progressive determinism.

---

[52] Sinclair, 'Clinical Lectures on Symbolism and Sublimation', II. 142.
[53] See Ch. 6, above for further discussion of this.
[54] MS 1089, Macmillan Archive, University of Reading.   [55] Sinclair, *Defence of Idealism*, 5.
[56] Ead., 'Clinical Lectures on Symbolism and Sublimation', I. 119.
[57] Ribot, *Heredity*, 285.

Sublimation, though, was also essential to Sinclair's understanding of the coming of modernity. Her version of it is in some ways very close to Jung's in *Psychology of the Unconscious*. It was from that text, for example, that she derived the account of sublimation quoted above. Jung, for his part, describes it as follows:

The process of transformation of the primal libido into secondary impulses always took place in the form of affluxes of sexual libido, that is to say, sexuality became deflected from its original destination and a portion of it turned, little by little, increasing in amount, into the phylogenetic impulse of the mechanisms of allure-ment and of protection of the young. This diversion of the sexual libido from the sexual territory into associated functions is still taking place. Where this operation succeeds without injury to the adaptation of the individual it is called *sublimation*. Where the attempt does not succeed it is called *repression*.[58]

Jungian sublimation—and, even more so, Jungian repression—is very dif-ferent from the Freudian version, since for Jung sublimation is a generally adaptive mechanism rather than the source specifically of creative and aes-thetic energy.[59] Repression is, concomitantly, a failure of adaptation to the outside world, and a return to atavistic mental habits, rather than, as in Freud's work, an essential component of psychic health.[60] Mary's form of sublimation involves the transformation of sexual desires into, first of all, poetic creativity ('As long as [the poem] lasted she . . . would be free from the restlessness and the endless idiotic reverie of desire', MO, 234), and, finally, into an 'incredible, supernatural happiness and peace' (MO, 367) which comes from her loss of all those who have been dear to her, and her sense of communion with a mystic power that transcends her. In Sinclair's teleology the diversion of Mary's energies away from sex is a creative evolution of her consciousness into 'higher and higher forms', forms which are also the con-tours of her independent and autonomous self: 'Happiness, the happiness that came from writing poems; happiness that other people couldn't have, that you couldn't give to them; happiness that was no good to Mamma, no good to anybody but you, secret and selfish; that was your happiness' (MO, 234).[61] Sublimation allows Mary to escape both the constraints of desire, and the tightening net of heredity. As Sinclair says in the 1916 lectures, 'throughout man's history man's goal has always been one and the same—

---

[58] Jung, *Psychology of the Unconscious*, 133.

[59] Freud writes about sublimation primarily in ' "Civilized" Sexual Morality and Modern Nervous Ill-ness', 1908, in *Standard Edition*, ix. 179–204. See also *The Ego and the Id*, in *Standard Edition*, xix. 45–7.

[60] J. Laplanche and J.-B. Pontalis note that repression 'may be looked upon as a universal mental process in so far as it lies at the root of the constitution of the unconscious as a domain separate from the rest of the psy-che' (*The Language of Psycho-Analysis*, 1967, trans. Donald Nicholson-Smith, New York: Norton, 1973, 390).

[61] Sinclair, 'Clinical Lectures on Symbolism and Sublimation', I. 119.

Sublimation; the freedom of the Self in obedience to a higher law than preceding generations have laid upon him'.[62] Sublimation is, for Mary, a kind
of secret escape, a process of adaptation that is finally perfected at the end of
the novel.

Sinclair's version of sublimation did, however, challenge Jung's in many
ways. Unlike him, she believed that it was a process that could be consciously
willed. In the 'Clinical Lectures' she refers to it as 'the conscious direction of
the libido into higher channels', and 'the conscious creative imagination'.[63]
She describes psychoanalysis itself as an exercise in sublimation.

Every psychosis, every psychoneurosis is an atavism, a reversion to the primitive,
infantile type. Part of the patient's psyche is cut off from the inexorably adult world
it has come into and belongs to.

Within the region thus isolated the unfortunate libido remains penned up. It may
struggle to get out and sublimate itself; its struggles are recorded in all the symbolic
disguises of the phantasy and of the dream; it is as if, in terror of its own nakedness,
it sought a dress that would allow it to make a decent appearance in the upper world.
But before all the paths of sublimation the Angel of Repression, the psychic Censor,
stands and stops the way.

The business of the psycho-analyst is to expose this Censor and his work, and by
exposing, remove him for ever.[64]

The psychoanalyst is imagined as aiding the deliberate process of sublimation and freeing the libido from its confinement in the atavistic past (Sinclair
is referring here to the prison of genetic origins, as well as of regressive
behaviour). 'Sublimation', Sinclair says, is the 'vision' which psychoanalysis offers as the reward for the extraordinary effort that goes into any analysis.[65] But Jung himself never interpreted psychoanalytic practice in this way.
Indeed he explicitly challenged the notion that people could deliberately
choose sublimation as a means of psychic cure. In an essay written just after
Psychology of the Unconscious (and published the year after the 'Clinical Lectures' appeared), he blamed the Freudian theory of the libido for misunderstandings such as this.

Since it was thought that the energy [of the libido] is nothing but the instinctual
power of sex, people talked of 'sublimated' application of it, on the assumption that
the patient could, with the help of analysis, canalize the sexual energy into a 'sublimation', in other words, could apply it non-sexually, in the practice of an art, perhaps,
or in some other good or useful activity. According to this view, it is possible for the
patient, from free choice or inclination, to achieve the sublimation of his instinctual
forces.

[62] Sinclair, 'Clinical Lectures on Symbolism and Sublimation', II. 144.
[63] Ibid. I. 118, 119.   [64] Ibid. 121.   [65] Ibid. 119.

We may allow that this view has a certain justification in so far as man is at all capable of marking out a definite line along which his life has to go. But we know that there is no human foresight or wisdom that can prescribe direction to our life, except for small stretches of the way.... the individual ... must often learn in his life that so-called 'disposable' energies are not his to dispose.[66]

Sinclair clearly picked up on the 'bastardized' psychoanalysis Jung describes—the form that was being practised at the Medico-Psychological Clinic—and embellished on it for both the 'Clinical Lectures' and *Mary Olivier*. Jung's objection, that such a practice ignored the hidden determinism of the unconscious, and overemphasized the extent of conscious control over the psyche, was precisely why Sinclair was so keen on this bowdlerized form of therapeutic sublimation. Since her aim in *Mary Olivier* was to imagine the self-conscious liberation of the individual from all the forces that drew her back into the past, the idea of sublimation as a form of self-discipline allowed her to construct the self as, in the end, its own salvation. At the end of *Mary Olivier* Mary needs no one, not even an analyst. Sinclair's 'modern heroine' was a complex blend of a quintessentially Victorian ideology of individualism, hard work, and self-help, and a characteristically modernist compromise with the past.

Mary does need some sense of a presence beyond her own, however, and in her achievement of such self-transcendence we see the influence of one of modernism's dominant—and, in literary critical circles, most neglected—movements: mysticism.[67] It suited Sinclair to adopt a version of sublimation that stressed the individual's conscious control not only because such a theory emphasized individual agency, but also because this kind of 'willing', which first appears in her fiction in the 1912 story 'The Flaw in the Crystal', harmonized with the descriptions of the 'mystic way' which she found in Rabindranath Tagore and especially in the work of her friend Evelyn Underhill.[68] Such a convergence of mysticism and psychoanalytic terminology

---

[66] Jung, 'On the Psychology of the Unconscious', 1917, rev. 1926 and 1943, from *Two Essays*, in *Collected Works*, vii, paragraphs 56–92; repr. in Anthony Storr (ed.), *The Essential Jung* (Princeton: Princeton University Press, 1983), 153–4, 156.

[67] Excellent work has been done, of course, on the mysticism of such major figures as Yeats and T. S. Eliot (see e.g. Leon Surette, *The Birth of Modernism: Ezra Pound, T. S. Eliot, W. B. Yeats, and the Occult*, Montreal and Kingston: McGill-Queen's University Press, 1993). But no full-length study of the relation between literary modernism and the 'new mysticism' has yet been written. There is a useful discussion of the similarities between Eliot's thought and Sinclair's in Rebeccah Kinnamon Neff, ' "New Mysticism" in the Writings of May Sinclair and T. S. Eliot', *Twentieth-Century Literature*, 26 (1980), 82–108, and in P. S. Padmanabhan, 'The Irritant and the Pearl: "Jones's Karma" and the Poetry and Drama of T. S. Eliot', *Canadian Review of Comparative Literature*, 9 (June 1982), 188–99.

[68] See Sinclair, 'Flaw in the Crystal': 'you shut your eyes and ears, you closed up the sense of touch, you made everything dark around you and withdrew into your innermost self; you burrowed deep into the

was of course quite in accordance with the spirit, if not the letter, of Jungian psychology and, indeed, as I have argued elsewhere, with the spirit of modernism itself.[69]

Mary Olivier's mystic consciousness begins to emerge fairly early in her life. The following passage describes an experience she has while she is still pre-pubescent:

A queer white light everywhere, like water thin and clear. Wide fields, flat and still, like water, flooded with the thin, clear light; grey earth, shot delicately with green blades, shimmering. . . . She saw the queer white light for the first time and drew in her breath with a sharp check. She knew that the fields were beautiful. . . . Suddenly, without any reason, she was so happy that she could hardly bear it. (MO, 48, 49)

Mary's happiness is echoed elsewhere in Sinclair's work: in *Arnold Waterlow*, in which Arnold as a child sees God on the banks of the Mersey, and in Sinclair's novel in verse, *The Dark Night* (1924).[70] In part, of course, it is one of the symptoms of Mary's agnosticism (Arnold enrages his mother by describing his vision as 'God', 20–1), and it precedes her hailing of Spinoza and pantheism as the (temporary, as it turns out) answer to her spiritual quest. But it is also one of the ways in which Mary reorganizes her own consciousness and its relation to the world. As Sinclair wrote in *The New Idealism*, the new idealism 'must somehow contrive to reconcile the universe of things with the universe of thought', or it will become as irrelevant as 'epistemological idealism' '[w]ith its one-sidedness, its blindness to the actual pattern of the universe, its fantastic logic, its failure to correlate the forms and processes of thought with the forms and processes of things'.[71] Mary herself has similar misgivings about her own philosophical perspective after she reads about the determining force of heredity. Impatient with herself, she realizes that she has 'spent most of her time in the passionate pursuit of things under the form of eternity, regardless of their actual behaviour in time' (MO, 289). Mary's mysticism is a merging of the stuff of consciousness with the stuff of the world, an acknowledgement that the 'stream' of

---

darkness there till you got beyond it; you tapped the Power, as it were, underground' ('Flaw in the Crystal', *Uncanny Stories*, 120). 'The New Mysticism' is the title of one of the chapters of *Defence of Idealism*.

[69] See Raitt, *Vita and Virginia*, 139.

[70] Arnold sees 'an enormous mounded wall, of an unstained and shining and unearthly whiteness' which parts 'asunder at the top and, as if it had wings, [is] lifted up and carried over the sky' (20). See also Sinclair, *The Dark Night* (New York: Macmillan, 1924), 8: 'suddenly, in a flash, my garden changed: | The wall and the hot flagged walk were gold, | The larkspurs became a blue light, burning, | The beech-tree a green fire, shining; | And I knew that the light and the fire were the real, secret life of the flowers and the tree, | And that God showed himself in the fire and the light.'

[71] Sinclair, *The New Idealism* (New York: Macmillan, 1922), 14, 13.

consciousness implies both a fundamental unity, as William James had suggested, and, in Herbert Spencer's words, 'incessant change'.[72]

For many years Mary's 'queer happiness' leaves her. When she recalls it she understands that it was an expression of some fundamental spiritual freedom: 'that ecstasy and this happiness had one quality in common; they belonged to some part of you that was free. A you that had no hereditary destiny; that had got out of the net, or had never been caught in it' (MO, 312). The challenge to her parents' authority that began with her refusal to be confirmed develops into a religious heterodoxy that frees her from the 'net of unclean wool' (MO, 113) in which her family's beliefs are inextricably tangled. Mary learns to summon her sense of her own freedom as a way of liberating herself from the despair and frustration of her life:

If you were part of God your will was God's will at the moment when you really willed. There was always a point when you knew it: the flash point of freedom. You couldn't mistake your flash when it came. You couldn't doubt away that certainty of freedom any more than you could doubt away the certainty of necessity and determination. From the outside they were part of the show of existence, the illusion of separation from God. From the inside they were God's will, the way things were willed. Free-will was the reality under the illusion of necessity. The flash point of freedom was your consciousness of God. (MO, 376–7)

In wanting what God wants, and in striving to bring her will into harmony with God's, Mary experiences an existential freedom that teaches her that things in themselves—the ultimate reality—are both absolutely determined and, because they express the essence of God, absolutely free. Paradoxically, Mary comes to full consciousness of herself through attaining consciousness of a will beyond her own, a will both secular and divine: 'Substance, the Thing-in-Itself, Reality, God' (MO, 378). In many ways this is simply a revised statement of the position Sinclair had outlined in 'The Ethical and Religious Import of Idealism' twenty-six years earlier.

The language of passages such as the one I quoted above also signals Sinclair's debt to the work of contemporary mystics and especially to Evelyn Underhill. Underhill was a contemporary of Sinclair's, and the two women formed a close friendship partly based around their mutual love of yachting (Underhill went on her first cruise aged 13).[73] Even though their relationship

---

[72] Spencer, *Principles of Psychology*, 322.
[73] See *The Letters of Evelyn Underhill*, ed. Charles Williams (1943; repr. London: Darton, Longman and Todd, 1991), 7. See also Dana Greene, *Evelyn Underhill: Artist of the Infinite Life* (1990; UK edn. London: Darton, Longman and Todd, 1991), 38, for a very brief discussion of Underhill's friendship with Sinclair. Greene notes that Underhill 'shared little of her inner life' with Sinclair (38). The two women seem to have met sometime in 1909.

revolved around the active, rather than the contemplative, life (they took yachting holidays together, for example), Underhill would have listened sympathetically to Sinclair's accounts of her own mystic experiences— more sympathetically, at any rate, than Virginia Woolf, who wrote acidly when she met Sinclair in 1909 that Sinclair 'talked very seriously of her "work"; and ecstatic moods in which she swings (like a spider again) half way to Heaven, detached from each'.[74] When Woolf's friend Eleanor Cecil adversely reviewed *The Helpmate*, it was Underhill who came to Sinclair's defence, and Sinclair, in her turn, was heavily involved in, and heavily influenced by, Underhill's writing.[75] It was not until after 1911, when Underhill's best-seller *Mysticism* was published, that Sinclair started to include mystic revelations like Mary Olivier's in her fiction. Underhill thanks Sinclair in the preface to *Mysticism* for reading the manuscript, and Sinclair, with her suspicion of orthodox Christianity and her continued nostalgia for the 'melancholy compulsion' of idealism, was evidently attracted to the idea of a religious life that was not defined by Christian truths.[76] As Dana Greene points out, the 'attacks on Absolute Idealism and Positivism, the rise of the "philosophies of life", the power of Modernism, and the failure of religious institutions all allowed for the growth of mysticism, a way of being religious independent of philosophical, institutional, and doctrinal constraints'.[77] Mysticism, like aspects of Jungian psychoanalysis, seemed to represent a way out of the orthodoxies of the past, without denying the need for a spiritual life altogether.

In *Mysticism* Underhill, unsurprisingly for the woman who defended *The Helpmate*, stresses the importance of an instinctive as well as an intellectual spiritual life. Her objection to idealism is similar to Sinclair's, although framed somewhat differently: 'Idealism, though just in its premises, and often daring and honest in their application, is stultified by the exclusive intellectualism of its own methods: by its fatal trust in the squirrel-work of the industrious brain instead of the piercing vision of the desirous heart.'[78] Both women believed that the philosophy of mind should acknowledge our

---

[74] Woolf to Lady Robert Cecil, 12 Apr. 1909, *The Flight of the Mind*, 390.

[75] Evelyn Underhill wrote a response to Cecil, 'The Cant of Unconventionality', in ' "The Cant of Unconventionality": A Rejoinder to Lady Robert Cecil', *Living Age*, 256 (8 Feb. 1908), 323–9. The opening para. of *Mary Olivier*, with the infant Mary exploring the metal knob on her cot, is reminiscent of Underhill's 1904 novel *The Grey World*, which also opens with a child lying in bed and fixing his eyes 'on the bright brass knob which finished one corner of his cot' (5). Other evidence of mutual influence includes the fact that Underhill originally wanted to call *Mysticism*, *The Quest of the Absolute*; and Sinclair's story 'The Finding of the Absolute' was published in 1930 in *Uncanny Stories*. Sinclair went yachting in Scotland in the summer of 1908, and in the summer of 1909 Underhill lent Sinclair her yacht for a few weeks (see Ch. 4, above).

[76] Sinclair, *New Idealism*, p. x.   [77] Greene, *Evelyn Underhill*, 41.

[78] See the discussion of idealism in Underhill, *Mysticism*, 13–15.

psychic, and libidinal, investment in the material world, and even in the world of our own fantasies. Mary Olivier's spiritual life, for example, has to take account of her frenzied desire for someone, anyone, to share her bed: 'she wanted Somebody. Somebody. Somebody'; an unreliable suitor 'had left her with this ungovernable want' (MO, 226). Mary's mystic life must satisfy her sexual cravings if it is to bring her peace.

Underhill describes something very close to Mary's 'queer happiness' in the follow-up publication to *Mysticism* in 1913, *The Mystic Way*.

[T]he emergence into the field of consciousness, of . . . the soul's spark or seed . . . startles [the self] by its suddenness; the gladness, awe and exaltation which it brings: an emotional inflorescence, parallel with that which announces the birth of perfect human love. This moment is the spiritual spring-time. It comes, like the winds of March, full of natural wonder; and gives to all who experience it a participation in the deathless magic of eternal springs. An enhanced vitality, a wonderful sense of power and joyful apprehension towards worlds before ignored and unknown, floods the consciousness.[79]

Mary's first 'queer happiness' actually takes place in the spring (MO, 48), and her consciousness is flooded with a sense of other-worldly joy. Both Underhill and Sinclair acknowledge that this feeling has sexual dimensions by associating it with critical moments in the female life cycle: Underhill says it occurs either at the 'height of normal adolescence, about eighteen years of age, before the crystallizing action of maturity has begun', or at the 'attainment of full maturity' at age 30; Mary Olivier remembers that 'It had come to her when she was a child in brilliant, clear flashes; it had come again and again in her adolescence, with more brilliant and clearer flashes; then, after leaving her for twenty-three years, it had come like this—streaming in and out of her till its ebb and flow were the rhythm of her life' (MO, 377).[80] Underhill and Sinclair were aware that this association of spiritual with sexual feeling opened up such feelings to charges like those levelled by Sir Almroth Wright at the suffragettes, that this kind of mystic joy is simply a manifestation of sexual frustration and displaced, or even misplaced, sexual desire.[81] Sinclair addressed this problem head-on in the 1912 pamphlet *Feminism*: 'Whoever has known and can remember certain moments of heightened vision and sensation . . . will remain unmoved while the

---

[79] Ead. *The Mystic Way: A Psychological Study in Christian Origins* (London: Dent, 1913), 50.

[80] Ibid. 52. Elaine Showalter notes that women were seen to be particularly vulnerable to mental disturbance at crucial moments in their life cycle (see *The Female Malady: Women, Madness and English Culture, 1830–1980*, 1985; London: Virago, 1987, 55–60).

[81] See Ch. 4, above, for a discussion of the debate between Sinclair and Wright over the suffrage movement.

physiologist points out that these moments are most intimately associated with adolescence and the dawn of womanhood; . . . that they are part of the pageant of sexual passion.' She argues that women are especially prone to these experiences because they are transformations into 'still higher and subtler energies' of the 'Life-Force of which Woman is pre-eminently the reservoir'.[82] Although they may have their roots, then, in the special physiology of women, through an operation akin to sublimation such energies can actually take women beyond the limits of their own bodies and draw them in to a field of force defined by something very like Bergson's *élan vital*.[83] In a proto-Lacanian formulation, Sinclair seems almost to suggest that sublimation works on women's sexual energy to make them into mystics.[84] Underhill makes a similar connection: 'both mysticism and hysteria have to do with the domination of consciousness by one fixed and intense idea or intuition, which rules the life and is able to produce amazing physical and psychical results . . . the mono-ideism of the mystic is rational, whilst that of the hysteric patient is invariably irrational'.[85] In Underhill's version it is reason which makes the difference; in Sinclair's, self-discipline.

But the women did agree that mystic experience involved the disciplined release of the consciousness from awareness of the body. Mary succeeds in willing her mother to recover from the stroke that her absence with Richard has brought on: 'Flat on your back with your eyes shut; not tight shut. You mustn't feel your eyelids. You mustn't feel any part of you at all. You think of nothing, absolutely nothing; not even think. . . . Going and coming back; gathered together; incredibly free; disentangled from the net of nerves and veins. . . . Then it willed. Your self willed. It was free to will.' (MO, 351). This deliberate subordination of the body puts Mary in touch with her free self, the part that has nothing to do with her heredity or the cramped conditions of her life. Mary's powerfully meditative state is one that Underhill too recognized as a source of spiritual power, writing in *Mysticism* that 'by a deliberate inattention to the messages of the senses, such as that which is induced by contemplation, the mystic brings the ground of the soul, the seat of "Transcendental Feeling", within the area of consciousness: making it amenable to the activity of the will'.[86] She may even have given Sinclair

---

[82] Sinclair, *Feminism*, 30–1. Olive Schreiner makes a very similar argument in *Woman and Labour* (1911).

[83] In *Defence of Idealism* Sinclair is sharply critical of Bergson, but she does agree with him that 'matter is the vehicle and plastic tool of the *Élan Vital*; that pure remembrance is a spiritual manifestation; and that with memory we are actually in the domain of spirit' (56).

[84] See Jacques Lacan, 'God and the *Jouissance* of The Woman', 1972–3, in Juliet Mitchell and Jacqueline Rose (eds.), *Feminine Sexuality: Jacques Lacan and the Ecole Freudienne*, trans. Jacqueline Rose (London: Macmillan, 1982), 137–48, where Lacan argues that women experience a '*jouissance* which goes beyond' analogous to the *jouissance* of the mystics (147).

[85] Underhill, *Mysticism*, 72.   [86] Ibid. 66.

specific advice like that she offered to an unnamed correspondent in 1908: 'Deliberately, and by an act of will, shut yourself off from your senses. Don't attend to touch or hearing: till the external world seems unreal and far away.'[87] Certainly Mary follows exactly the instructions Underhill gave to her student.

It is only partly true, then, to say, as Jean Radford does, that 'Mary "sublimates" her sexual energies into art and intellectual achievement'.[88] Mary also engages in a quite deliberate quest to experience some form of ultimate reality: her sublimation leads her to consciousness of a world beyond the self. Thus although Radford is right to question the triumphalism of the ending of *Mary Olivier*, noting that to 'a modern feminist', it 'may well appear an elaborate rationalisation of—yet again—self-denial', in her own cultural context Sinclair's evasions seem less unexpected.[89] Underhill was known for her commitment to the spiritual guidance of women; Sinclair published her discussion of the relationship between women's appetites and their mysticism in a pamphlet brought out by the Women Writers' Suffrage League. Mary's self-transcendence may be an unfamiliar and even baffling form of feminist self-realization for readers in the 1990s, but Sinclair clearly did not think of the novel as entirely tragic: for her the consciousness of a life beyond our own was at least a partial consolation for despair like Mary's, who, aged 25, thinks: 'I've lived half my life and done nothing' (MO, 267). Reviewers were not so sure: in spite of the novel's upbeat ending some still found Mary a tragic and pathetic figure, suggesting that at the end of the novel she finds 'not reality but resignation'.[90] Indeed reviews were generally lukewarm or unenthusiastic (Sinclair told Catherine Dawson Scott in July 1919 that they were getting 'wusser and wusser'), perhaps because the novel was such a strange mixture of modern technique and beliefs (stream of consciousness, mysticism) and Victorian ideology (self-discipline, hard work).[91] It was hard to celebrate it either as a definitive example of modernism, or as a convincing retrospective of Victorian culture and thought. No one was quite sure whether Mary was a heroine or not.

Mansfield's objections exactly sum up the public's confusion. As we saw, she hailed the novel as 'new writing', but then went on to write that 'It is too

---

[87] Underhill to 'M. R.', 16 Jan. 1908, *Letters of Evelyn Underhill*, 73.

[88] Radford, 'Introduction', *Mary Olivier*.   [89] Ibid.

[90] See e.g. the anonymous review 'The Tumult of the Soul', *Nation* (NY), 109 (13 Sept. 1919), 379–80: at 379.

[91] Sinclair to Catherine Dawson Scott, 1 July 1919, Beinecke Rare Book and Manuscript Library, Gen. MSS. 144, Box 1, fo. 22. In the same letter Sinclair refers to Mansfield's '[v]irulent sneers & jeers', thanks Scott for her appreciation of *Mary Olivier*, and notes that H. G. Wells and Evelyn Underhill have both written her 'words exquisitely healing to hurt vanity' about the novel: 'I'm feeling much better!'

late in the day for this new form.'[92] Both too early and too late, *Mary Olivier*, in spite of its minute attention to women's struggles to secure the space and the time in which to write, challenges even the sanctity of the novelist's profession:

if . . . no one thing is to be related to another thing, we do not see what is to prevent the whole of mankind turning author. Why should writers exist any longer as a class apart if their task ends with a minute description of a big or a little thing? If this is the be-all and end-all of literature why should not every man, woman and child write an autobiography and so provide reading matter for the ages?[93]

Mary Olivier's method—Mary's stream of consciousness—is too inclusive; the novel records too much without knowing what is important. Paradoxically a novel about the birth of a writer signals the end of writing as a profession: the genre of the novel is both advanced and retarded by the appearance of a text too old and too new for its time. Sinclair had to defend its form even to Ezra Pound, whose own innovations she had herself been championing for so long: 'I deny that the method is more "subjective" than Joyce. Mary's mind is a sufficiently clear mirror of "objects". Mary's mind is "objective" to me. You may hate Mary's mind, you may damn & blast Mary's mind, but that is irrelevant. I've got it, & I've got the objects reflected in it.'[94] The novel was not just about consciousness but, like the 'new idealism', about the world and Mary's temporizing with it. Even sympathizers like Pound could not place it.

Sinclair was exhausted by writing *Mary Olivier*.[95] The effort of recapitulating all the sorrows and difficulties of her own life—her mother's intransigence, her father's inadequacies, her brothers' relentless deaths—made the disappointing reviews even harder to take. She had tried to show how even a life that on first glance looks unpromising can have its own hidden rewards. In a way she was justifying both her own choices and those that were thrust upon her. But, as if in revenge, her next *Bildungsroman*, the extraordinarily disturbing and bleak *Life and Death of Harriett Frean* (1922), abandons all pretence at optimism and, like a companion piece to *Mary Olivier*, tells the story of a woman whose life is entirely defined by the lives of her parents. If her readers were depressed by *Mary Olivier*, *Harriett Frean* was an even bleaker affair. Where Mary's mother coerces her into compliance, Harriett's kills her with kindness. That killing is the subject of my next chapter.

[92] Mansfield, 'New Infancy', 41, 42.   [93] Ibid. 41.

[94] Sinclair to Pound, 24 Oct. 1919, Beinecke Rare Book and Manuscript Library, Ezra Pound Papers, Box 48, fo. 2136.

[95] G. B. Stern mentions Sinclair's despair in autumn 1918 over the writing of the novel. See Stern to Sinclair, 15 June 1919, UP, Box 3, fo. 89.

8

The Twilight Years and
Life and Death of Harriett Frean

=

MAY SINCLAIR's pride at her achievement in *Mary Olivier* did not prevent her from viewing the future with some misgivings. Now in her late fifties, she was beginning to feel the strain of the long working days she had become accustomed to since her teenage years in the cramped little house in Ilford. It may be that, as she worked on *The Romantic* (1920) and on the comic tale *Mr Waddington of Wyck* (1921), she was already noticing the first symptoms of the Parkinson's disease that would consume the last two decades of her life.

Her later novels suggest that her thoughts were turning to the years ahead and to the possibility of a long, slow decline with no immediate family—no children of her own—to take care of her. She was both anticipating the petty humiliations of age and illness, and returning to the stories and the characters of her past. Arnold Waterlow and his mistress, in *Arnold Waterlow: A Life* (1924) holiday in Sidmouth, where Sinclair and her mother lived in the 1890s; Matty in *The Rector of Wyck* (1925) grows up in Ormonde Terrace, Primrose Hill, the street Sinclair and her mother moved to in 1897; Anne Severn in *Anne Severn and the Fieldings* (1922) is sent back from the Belgian front after a few weeks just as Sinclair was; and fathers succumb to alcohol, as Sinclair's had done, in *The Rector of Wyck* and *The Allinghams* (1927). This return to the familiar, coupled with spending less and less time on each novel (Sinclair published almost one a year from 1919 to 1927), meant that much of Sinclair's later work was thin and repetitive.[1] By 1930 she had retreated into near-silence and almost total immobility: her niece Wilda McNeile described her as having the body of a 2-year-old child.[2]

---

[1] See Zegger, *May Sinclair*, 141, 142: 'The novels she wrote after *A Cure of Souls* are increasingly poor because she was evidently casting about for material and was reworking her previous novels. . . . By 1925, it is evident from her novels that her failing health had also affected her creative and critical powers.'

[2] Wilda McNeile to Theophilus E. M. Boll, 7 Oct. 1961, UP, Box 48, fo. 529.

But among the novels of her later years the haunting and evocative *Life and Death of Harriett Frean* stands out for both the power of its writing, and the subtlety of its engagement with the psychoanalytic theory with which Sinclair was becoming more and more familiar. It tells the story of the slow deterioration of a sterile, unhappy woman who cannot separate her own identity from those of her parents, even after they are dead. Harriett Frean is the only child of devoted parents, who bring her up 'to behave beautifully' (HF, 20) and never to take anything that is not hers. When Robin, fiancé of Harriett's friend Prissie, declares his love to her, Harriett is adamant that she cannot allow him to break his engagement to Prissie, even though she knows that she and Robin are in love. The consciousness of her sacrifice sustains her through uneventful decades with her parents, while Prissie and Robin are trapped in a loveless marriage which drives Prissie to psychosomatic illness. When Harriett's father dies, Harriett and her mother continue to defer to one another's wishes, but on her mother's death, Harriett discovers that, in fact, both adopted habits they disliked, in the mistaken belief that the other wanted it that way. Harriett's sterile and dependent middle age is finally halted by an operation for cancer, and the book ends with Harriett coming round from the anaesthetic and whispering joyfully to the friend who is leaning over her bed: 'Mamma—' (HF, 133).

In a review in the *Dial*, journalist and critic Raymond Mortimer described *Harriett Frean* as 'a study of the psycho-pathology of Peter Pan'.[3] As Mortimer noted, the eponymous Harriett, although she dies in her sixties, never really grows up. Sinclair told Willis Steell in 1924 that in *Harriett Frean* 'I wished to see what I could make out of the study of a small, arrogant creature, not selfish entirely, and not wilfully cruel, but incredibly blind and with a wizened soul.'[4] Harriett 'wizens' instead of growing: she never moves beyond her heredity; she remains trapped in her identity as her parents' daughter, socially (when her father is long forgotten she still tells people 'my father . . . was Hilton Frean', HF, 122), emotionally, and somatically (she dies of the same illness as her mother). She thus fails to achieve the sublimation that, as I explained in the last chapter, was so crucial to Mary Olivier's attainment of an autonomous identity. We can speculate that as Sinclair felt herself weakening she started to think differently about the past. As she told Steell, 'I went with [Harriett] over the road I had already gone with "Mary Olivier", and put her to similar tests.'[5] But Harriett fails them, and by the end of the novel, instead of becoming, like her predecessor Mary, an autonomous,

---

[3] Raymond Mortimer, 'Miss Sinclair Again', *Dial*, 72 (May 1922), 531–4: at 531.
[4] Steell, 'May Sinclair Tells Why She Isn't a Poet', 559.   [5] Ibid.

creative thinker, she regresses into a state of ecstatic, and fatal, identification with her dead mother. Told that she has cancer, Harriett 'felt nothing but a strange, solemn excitement and exaltation. She was raised to her mother's eminence in pain. With every stab she would live again in her mother. She had what her mother had' (HF, 129).

At first glance, Harriett's life bears little resemblance to Sinclair's own. In *Mary Olivier* she had figuratively embraced her own isolation and celebrated it as a creative sublimation of her own powers. But the defiant joy of *Mary Olivier*'s final pages does not mean that Sinclair had no regrets about what had happened to her.[6] In *Harriett Frean* Mary's story, of the unmarried daughter who spends her youth caring for an ageing mother, is retold as tragedy. This is the dark version of Sinclair's own life, the version which Sinclair, in *Mary Olivier*, had so proudly and bravely denied. Where *Mary Olivier* is an optimistic reappraisal of the spinster's life, like those in *Pilgrimage* and *To the Lighthouse*, *Harriett Frean* anticipates the mournful, deceptively simple tone of a spinster-novel like F. M. Mayor's *The Rector's Daughter* (1924), or of Katherine Mansfield's short story 'Miss Brill' (1922). Freedom from domestic and sexual responsibilities could as easily lead to intense loneliness, as to an artistic flowering of the kind Mary Olivier experiences.

As if Sinclair was afraid of confronting her own disappointment too directly, she set *Harriett Frean* some twenty years earlier than *Mary Olivier*.[7] Harriett is born in 1845 rather than, like Sinclair and Mary, in 1863. Where Mary's life spans the transition out of Victorianism into modernity, Harriett is already in her mid-fifties at the turn of the century. As one of the book's reviewers noticed: 'The poignancy of Harriett's tragedy appears all the more convincing because of its Victorian background and her subjection to an ideal of womanhood represented by Evangeline. It also becomes more bearable, for nowadays we may look back on that era of intensive respectability as if from a safe distance.'[8] But Sinclair's distance from it was not at all safe. She had spent the first four decades of her life struggling with the values of that Victorian world as they were embodied in her mother, and even if by the time she wrote *Harriett Frean* the Victorian social and sexual landscape was long gone, psychoanalysis confirmed what Sinclair had always suspected: that our parents and our childhoods shape our lives.

---

[6] As Jean Radford points out, where *Mary Olivier* is a 'study in sublimation', the later novel is a study of 'repression without sublimation' ('Introduction' to *Life and Death of Harriett Frean*, no page numbers).

[7] Boll suggests that this was 'a gesture disguising the personal origins of the might-have-been' (*Miss May Sinclair*, 274).

[8] Katharine Anthony, 'The Wickedness of Goodness', *Nation*, 114 (5 Apr. 1922), 400–1: at 401.

Sinclair's indictment of Victorianism is much more vicious in *Harriett Frean* than in *Mary Olivier*.[9] *Harriett Frean* describes her mother's world, the world and the ideals that Sinclair had opposed from the first moment that she took up a volume of Greek grammar.

Sinclair's ironic distance from the world of *Harriett Frean* is signalled through the novel's style, as well as through its tone. *Harriett Frean* was the only one of the novels Sinclair published in the early 1920s to continue both the thematic and formal experimentation of *Mary Olivier*. Although she wrote after the publication of *Anne Severn and the Fieldings* that it was the last novel she would write in a traditional style ('I must keep to the method of "Mary Olivier", even if I must pass from mind to mind'), in fact after *Anne Severn* Sinclair continued to write novels with conventional plots and narrative styles, and never again experimented with narrative form.[10] But *Harriett Frean*, published just before *Anne Severn*, is told, like *Mary Olivier*, through a single central consciousness.[11]

However, *Harriett Frean* was, at least formally, an advance on *Mary Olivier*. In it Sinclair turned her back on the familiar technique of a diffuse, expansive stream of consciousness and tried out a new, and wholly original, style. As early as 1914 she wrote in the introduction to *The Judgment of Eve and Other Stories* that the stories in that volume were 'tales of a transition period, the passing to a more intense and more concentrated form'.[12] In a 1920 letter to Dawson Scott Sinclair mounted a lengthy defence of her latest technique, with its abrupt transitions: 'It's the conscientious filling up of gaps & bridging of transitions that makes so many novels so deadly dull. It is part of the old superstition I'm out against.'[13] But it was not until—and in fact, only in—*Harriett Frean* that Sinclair actually succeeded in writing with the brevity and spareness to which she aspired. She described the novel to writer Sinclair Lewis as 'an experiment in compression. A story of a long life told in the shortest possible space.'[14] *Harriett Frean* used the psychoanalytic principles of condensation and displacement to develop a fictional language that relied on contextual resonance for its effect. As Mortimer asked: 'But is

    [9] Louise Maunsell Field notes that, despite its brevity, the book presents 'an entire social class, a type and kind of social order' ('*The Life and Death of Harriett Frean*', *New York Times Book Review*, 19 Feb. 1922, 15).
    [10] May Sinclair to Violet Hunt, 16 Dec. 1922, HA.
    [11] However, as Zegger notes, in *Harriett Frean* Sinclair also 'comments and narrates to achieve unity and a level of reality outside her subject's consciousness against which the subject can be judged'(*May Sinclair*, 126).
    [12] Sinclair, *The Judgment of Eve and Other Stories* (London: Hutchinson, 1914), p. xii.
    [13] Sinclair to Scott, 11 Mar. 1920, Beinecke Rare Book and Manuscript Library, Gen MSS 144, Box 1, fo. 22.
    [14] Sinclair to Sinclair Lewis, 25 Jan. 1922, Beinecke Rare Book and Manuscript Library, Yale Collection of American Literature, Za-Lewis.

this true economy? Or is it parsimony?'[15] Harriett's ungenerous attitudes and her avaricious hoarding of her own resources are the foundation of an aesthetic which tries, like imagism before it, never to waste words. Published in the year we have come to know as the *annus mirabilis* of high modernism, 1922, the year of publication of T. S. Eliot's *The Waste Land*, James Joyce's *Ulysses* in book form, and Virginia Woolf's *Jacob's Room*, *Harriett Frean* directly challenges the centrality of the mystic beauty of the hyacinth girl and Molly Bloom's free-flowing generosity of spirit and body to the modernist aesthetic.[16] In *Harriett Frean* womanhood is too meagre a thing to ground anything other than a cramped and minimalist aesthetic practice. *Harriett Frean* exemplifies a resistant, laconic form of modernity which uses linguistic sparsity and intensity to install femininity not as a site of enigma and fecundity, but as a state of deprivation and disappointment.

Harriett Frean opens, like *Mary Olivier*, with the infant Harriett in her cot. But where Mary barely recognizes her father as he moves towards her bed, Harriett, in true Freudian and Jungian style, is already involved in a suggestively erotic and secretive relationship with her father.[17] Where her mother simply leans over the bed to give Harriett her goodnight kiss, her father picks her up in his arms: 'That was the kiss-me-awake kiss; it was their secret. Then they played. Papa was the Pussycat and she was the little mouse in her hole under the bedclothes' (HF, 2–3). Her mother's kiss is soothing; her father's arousing. Like the cat in Harriett's nursery rhyme, who goes to London to see the Queen but ends up only seeing a mouse instead, Harriett distracts her father's attention away from his 'Queen' (her mother) towards Harriett, his diversion and his prey.[18] But this Oedipal frisson is contained by

---

[15] Mortimer, 'Miss Sinclair Again', 533.

[16] T. S. Eliot's image of the hyacinth girl occurs in the first section of *The Waste Land*: 'Yet when we came back, late, from the hyacinth garden, | Your arms full, and your hair wet, I could not | Speak, and my eyes failed, . . . I knew nothing, | Looking into the heart of light' (see Eliot, *Collected Poems 1909–1962*, 64). Both *Mary Olivier* and *Harriett Frean* have aspects of their publishing history in common with *Ulysses*: *Mary Olivier* was serialized in the *Little Review* alongside *Ulysses* in 1919. Richard Ellmann suggests that Molly Bloom's soliloquy at the end of *Ulysses* is a profoundly redemptive moment: 'the final monologue offers a personal, lyrical efflorescence. . . . the ruins of time and space and the mansions of eternity here coexist, at least until the very end' (*Ulysses on the Liffey*, 1972, corr. edn. London: Faber and Faber, 1984, 163). Marianne De Koven adds that 'At the turn of the century and in the first half of the twentieth century, woman is simultaneously reduced to the vagina and enlarged to the sea of seas, becoming the utopian site of the absence of lack, deterritorialization of gender-class-race, repository of all desire' (*Rich and Strange: Gender, History, Modernism*, Princeton: Princeton University Press, 1991, 37).

[17] See Ch. 7, above, for a discussion of the opening pages of *Mary Olivier* and Mary's conflation of her father in the bedroom with the faceless man of her nightmares. Jung noted that the child often has an idealizing relationship with the father: 'The strong and natural love which binds the child to the father, turns away in those years during which the humanity of the father would be all too plainly recognized' (see *Psychology of the Unconscious*, 54).

[18] Boll has a somewhat different interpretation of the symbolic significance of the nursery rhyme with which the novel opens: 'Just as the queen was passing, a little mouse came out of its hole and ran under the

Harriett's knowledge that after she is asleep, her parents revisit her room together, and the 'lighted candle' which she dreams she sees 'going out of the room; going, going away' (HF, 7) draws attention to their intimacy, which has survived the furtive excitement of the 'kiss-me-awake' kiss.

The crucial difference between Mary and Harriett, then, is that the stable triangulation of Harriett's family, their 'motionless communion' (HF, 32), means that Harriett can secure her own pleasure even within a tightly constrained domestic space. She and her parents have a fairly uneventful life: they read aloud to one another, go for walks, occasionally go to concerts or the theatre. But the compulsions of the Oedipal drama, which draws Harriett into complicity with her parents' mutual 'secrets' (HF, 32) without entirely concealing them from her, make her life utterly absorbing. Friends and critics noticed the novel's dependence on psychoanalytic theories of the family. T. S. Eliot, in an article in the *Dial*, described *Harriett Frean* as a tale of 'the soul of man under psychoanalysis', and the reviewer in the *Times Literary Supplement* called it a 'study in pathology'.[19] Like a female Wolf-Man, Harriett lives in constant awareness of a primal scene of which she is only ambiguously conscious (it is only in a dream that she sees her parents' lamp receding down the corridor at night).[20] Her knowledge, however partial, means that—like Lily Briscoe with the Ramsays in *To the Lighthouse*—she has a function as the witness to her parents' happy marriage.[21] Her friends' visits are a troubling disruption of the Freans' familial harmony: 'when they were there they broke something, something secret and precious between her and her father and mother, and when they were gone she felt the stir, the happy movement of coming together again, drawing in close, close, after the break' (HF, 38). Unlike Mary Olivier, who must fight constantly with her brothers for her parents' recognition, Harriett knows that she and her parents are structurally essential to one another's lives.

Harriett's only symbolic excursion beyond the sexual parameters of the family scene occurs when she ventures into the lane at the end of the garden—where she is explicitly forbidden to go—to pick red campion. She

chair, and that is what the pussycat saw. Harriett was to be distracted from her will to succeed as an individual by her instinctive child's impulse to love and obey and submit to her parents' (see *Miss May Sinclair*, 274).

[19] T. S. Eliot, 'London Letter: The Novel', *Dial*, 73 (Sept. 1922), 329–31: at 330; unsigned, 'Mother-Complex', *Times Literary Supplement* (2 Feb. 1922), 73.

[20] Freud's Wolf-Man apparently remembers waking unexpectedly as a baby and seeing his parents making love. In the case history, Freud maintains that even if this episode is a fabrication rather than a memory, the analysis would proceed in the same way: 'The analysis would have to run precisely the same course as one which had a *naïf* faith in the truth of the phantasies' ('From the History of an Infantile Neurosis', in *Standard Edition*, xvii. 50).

[21] 'So that is marriage, Lily thought, a man and a woman looking at a girl throwing a ball' (Virginia Woolf, *To the Lighthouse*, 1927, new edn., ed. Margaret Drabble, Oxford: Oxford University Press, 1992, 98).

knows that the lane is an adult space: as she walks she feels 'like a tall lady in a crinoline and a shawl. She swung her hips and made her skirts fly out. That was her grown-up crinoline, swing-swinging as she went' (HF, 16). The lane is *Harriett Frean*'s version of a wasteland, with its 'waste ground covered with old boots and rusted, crumpled tins', inhabited by a man who preys on little girls (HF, 17). Its sterile obscenity is adorned not with the mystic beauty of hyacinths, as in Eliot's version, but by the graphically sexual spires of the red campion: 'At the turn the cow's parsley and rose campion began: on each side a long trail of white froth with the red tops of the campion pricking through' (HF, 17). *Harriett Frean*'s modernist dystopia, unlike that of *The Waste Land* or even of *Mary Olivier*, does not even hint at a mysticism that might offer transcendence of the detritus of city life. Instead the symbol of promise is the coarsely vulgar campion blossoms, saturated with Freudian phallicism. Although Sinclair objected to the sexual emphases of much psychoanalytic theory, she learned from it that even a hat can be a phallic symbol, and in *Harriett Frean* for the first time she experimented with developing her own sexual imagery.[22] The campion offers no possibility of spiritual, or even psychic, release; it remains crudely and relentlessly carnal.

Although Harriett knows that her visit to the lane is a transgression, paradoxically one of its results is to draw her even more closely into her identification with her parents', and especially her mother's, pleasure. As Harriett's mother comes down the walk to find Harriett, her swaying gait exactly reproduces Harriett's fantasies of herself walking like an adult down the lane: her mother's 'wide, hooped skirts swung, brushing the flower borders' (HF, 18). As she smells the perfume of the flowers Harriett has picked, Harriett's mother, like Harriett, is moved by them:

She was holding the flowers up to her face. It was awful, for you could see her mouth thicken and redden over its edges and shake. She hid it behind the flowers. And somehow you knew it wasn't your naughtiness that made her cry. There was something more.

She was saying in a thick, soft voice, 'It was wrong of you, my darling.'

Suddenly she bent her tall straightness. 'Rose campion,' she said, parting the stems with her long, thin fingers. 'Look, Hatty, how *beautiful* they are. Run away and put the poor things in water.' (HF, 18)

---

[22] In *Psychology of the Unconscious* Jung notes that 'Freud has already called our attention to the phallic meaning of the hat in modern phantasies. A further significance is that probably the pointed cap represents the foreskin' (120). Sinclair wrote in irritation in the 'Clinical Lectures' (1916), in which she reviewed *Psychology of the Unconscious*: 'As if he were still obsessed, in spite of himself, with what formulas of Freud he has not swallowed, he handles poetry and metaphysics as if they were nothing but primitive myths' (II. 143). Freud refers to the phallic symbolism of the hat in the 1911 paper 'A Hat as a Symbol of a Man (Or Male Genitals)', which was later incorporated in *The Interpretation of Dreams*, 1899 (see *Standard Edition*, v. 360–2).

The novel never explicitly analyses Harriett's mother's response—the red-
dened lips, the thickness of her voice—but her mother's feeling for the
flowers suggests that she is not just frightened by what Harriett has done, but
also complicit in Harriett's arousal.[23] Harriett's mother cannot bear to contem-
plate the contradictions of her own pleasure. When Harriett says naughtily
that God and Jesus are not listening to her *all* the time, she thinks to herself:
'Saying things like that made you feel good and at the same time naughty,
which was more exciting than only being one or the other. But Mamma's
frightened face spoils it' (HF, 15). Mamma, like the Kleinian child, can only
operate by organizing the world into bad and good objects.[24] Harriett's
attempts to explore the ambiguities of everyday life are met with the kind of
categorical imperatives that Mary Olivier hated so much: 'It's better to go
without than to take from other people' (HF, 14). Harriett shares in her
mother's forbidden arousal without ever being able to identify what it is.

  Although Harriett's infancy includes the 'kiss-me-awake' kiss from her
father, as she gets older her bond with her father gives way to an increasingly
intense attachment to her mother. When Mrs Hancock, her friend's mother,
tells Harriett that she is 'growing like her mother', she is 'silent with emotion' (HF, 22). Freud, as Sinclair knew, believed that girls needed to develop
a hostility towards their mothers as a means of transferring their affection
to their fathers and moving out of a pre-Oedipal identification with their
mothers.[25] But he also acknowledged the immense difficulty of this transition: 'a number of women remain arrested in their original attachment to
their mother and never achieve a true change-over towards men'.[26] In *Harriett Frean*, Sinclair employs this Freudian paradigm to investigate a woman
who never adequately separates herself from her mother.[27] As time goes on,
Harriett relies more and more on her mother to mediate even her once vital
relationship with her father. When he lies on his deathbed, his dependence
on her is inconceivable: 'she could not get her mother's feeling of him as a

---

[23] See Phillips, 'Battling with the Angel', 135, for an alternative reading of this passage: 'Her reaction to
the flowers preserves the Angel's purity and is a re-enactment of Victorian patriarchy's response to women.
The flowers, already cut from their roots by Harriett, are seen as beautiful and decorative, to be placed in a
vase which parallels woman's pedestal.'

[24] See Melanie Klein's discussion of 'splitting' in 'Notes on Some Schizoid Mechanisms', 1946, in *The
Selected Melanie Klein*, ed. Juliet Mitchell (Harmondsworth: Penguin, 1986), 175–200. Klein settled in
England in 1926.

[25] See e.g. Sigmund Freud, 'Some Psychical Consequences of the Anatomical Distinction between the
Sexes', 1925, in *Standard Edition*, xix. 243–58: '[the girl] gives up her wish for a penis and puts in place of it a
wish for a child: and *with that purpose in view* she takes her father as a love-object. Her mother becomes the
object of her jealousy' (256).

[26] Freud, 'Female Sexuality', 1931, in *Standard Edition*, xxi. 223–43: at 226.

[27] See Phillips' description of Harriett as 'a daughter unable to progress beyond the pre-oedipal bond'
('Battling with the Angel', 136).

helpless, dependent thing' (HF, 64). By the time he dies, Harriett has no emotional life of her own and is unable to feel any grief at his death, and, as she was at the beginning of the novel, she is still shut out of her mother's secret exaltation: Harriett 'looked for her mother's secret and couldn't find it' (HF, 68). In exploring what Freud thought of as the buried vestiges of the pre-Oedipal ('grey with age and shadowy and almost impossible to reviv- ify') Sinclair reveals its hidden tragedy—one that even Freud failed fully to anticipate.[28] He noted that an incompletely resolved pre-Oedipal tension can produce sexual disappointment later on: 'Under the influence of a woman's becoming a mother herself, an identification with her own mother may be revived, against which she had striven up till the time of her mar- riage, and this may attract all the available libido to itself, so that the com- pulsion to repeat reproduces an unhappy marriage between her parents.'[29] But Harriett never even reaches the point of marriage, even less maternity. Her story reveals the intense frustration of identifications between mothers and daughters. Far from achieving symbiosis with her mother, Harriett lives in an obsessive and unfulfilled preoccupation with, and longing for, it. Iden- tification is, of course, always simply a fantasy—no one can really *become* another person—but, for Harriett, it is a tragic fantasy. The violence that Diana Fuss has argued is characteristic of identification is, in Harriett's case, visited only on herself: it is she who is annihilated by it.[30]

After her mother's death, Harriett feels as if she does not exist: 'she was not there. Through her absorption in her mother, some large, essential part of herself had gone. It had not been so when her father died; what he had absorbed was given back to her, transferred to her mother. All her memories of her mother were joined to the memory of this now irrecoverable self' (HF, 79). With her mother's death, Harriett has to face the task of building an autonomous identity, of proving, in Sinclair's words, her 'freedom . . . in obedience to a higher law than preceding generations have laid upon' her.[31] This is the freedom that Mary Olivier finds in a mystic consciousness of something beyond herself, something that transcends the limits of space and time. But Harriett takes the opposite path: she tries to find herself by moving backwards into the life she used to have: 'If only she could have remembered.

---

[28] Freud, 'Female Sexuality', 226.
[29] Freud, 'Femininity', 1933, in *New Introductory Lectures on Psychoanalysis*, in *Standard Edition*, xxii. 112–35: at 133.
[30] See Diana Fuss, *Identification Papers* (London: Routledge, 1995), 9: 'read psychoanalytically, *every* identification involves a degree of symbolic violence, a measure of temporary mastery and possession. . . . identification operates on one level as an endless process of violent negation, a process of killing off the other in fantasy in order to usurp the other's place, the place where the subject desires to be'.
[31] Sinclair, 'Clinical Lectures on Symbolism and Sublimation', II. 144.

It was only through memory that she could reinstate herself' (HF, 80). In her old age she restores all the furniture and the ornaments of her early years. But memory only delivers her back into the emptiness of her identification with her mother. Reading *The Ring and the Book*, Harriett remembers how much her mother loved it. 'She thought she loved it too; but what she loved was the dark-green book she had seen in her mother's long, white hands, and the sound of her mother's voice reading. She had followed her mother's mind with strained attention and anxiety, smiling when she smiled, but with no delight and no admiration of her own' (HF, 80). Once again Harriett's identification with her mother brings her no real emotions, merely a mediated sense of her own pleasure, as if she were watching it pass across someone else's face. Her years alone expose the extent to which her mental life, even while her parents were still alive, was, as the novel puts it, 'a semblance' (HF, 109). As Harriett ages she is alienated even from her own body: 'It was as if she had parted with her own light, elastic body, and succeeded to someone else's that was all bone, heavy, stiff, irresponsive to her will' (HF, 123). Even her cancer is not her own, but a symbol of her 'return' (HF, 127) to the world of her childhood. When she comes round from her operation, the traumas of her life resound through her consciousness, and finally she tells the nurse: 'It's sad—sad to go through so much pain and then to have a dead baby' (HF, 133). As Jean Radford notes, the novel is 'a vigorous indictment of a form of the family whose only issue is waste—a tumour, a dead baby'.[32] Harriett herself, of course, like the tumour, is metaphorically a dead baby, one that failed even to begin the process of development.

It is not only Harriett who is killed by her identification with her mother. Her attitude to other love-objects is predatory and destructive, in spite of her renunciation of Robin. Even as a child she cannot share; the Oedipal triangulation she manages to maintain with her parents cannot be reproduced in her other relationships. When her parents force her to allow her friend Connie to caress her favourite doll, her immediate response is to kill the doll off: 'She thought: "If I can't have her to myself I won't have her at all." . . . She pretended Ida was dead; lying in her pasteboard coffin and buried in the wardrobe cemetery' (HF, 9–10). The killing of the doll anticipates her fantasy of a baby that is entirely her own: 'She would be like Mamma, and her little girl would be like herself' (HF, 12). When she feels the stirring of maternal desire in response to objects that belong to other people (her maid's baby, her neighbour's cat) her response is routinely to destroy them,

---

[32] Radford, 'Introduction' to *Life and Death of Harriet Frean*. The last ten words also appear in this order in Zegger, *May Sinclair*, 124.

since they cannot be hers.[33] After her maid Maggie gives birth, Harriett finds herself once more, as she was with her parents, complicit in, but excluded from, a scene of sensuous pleasure. 'Harriett had to see [the baby] every time she came into the kitchen. Sometimes she heard him cry, an intolerable cry, tearing the nerves and heart. And sometimes she saw Maggie unbutton her black gown in a hurry and put out her white, rose-pointed breast to still his cry. Harriett couldn't bear it. She could not bear it' (HF, 100). The preoccu-pation with the erotics of breastfeeding that had already appeared in much earlier novels such as *Mr and Mrs Nevill Tyson* (1898) and *The Helpmate* (1907) resurfaces here in the horrified ambivalence with which Harriett reacts. Unused to articulating—or even to recognizing—her own desire unless it is emptied out by its mediation through her mother, Harriett sud-denly dismisses Maggie on a pretext. When Maggie returns in mourning because the baby, placed with a nurse in the country, has simply wasted away, Harriett feels instantly culpable: 'It was I who did it when I sent him away' (HF, 102). The fact that Maggie, and Harriett's friends Lizzie and Sarah, dismiss Harriett's claim is largely irrelevant, since Harriett's con-fused guilt is a partial recognition of her own psychic reality. Even if the baby's death was not her fault, she is aware of her enviously destructive instincts towards it. The dead baby continues to resonate through her con-sciousness. When she is attracted to her neighbour's cat she knows that her feelings are a displacement: 'A cat was a compromise, a substitute, a sub-terfuge. Her pride couldn't stoop. She was afraid of Mimi, of his enchanting play, and the soft white fur of his stomach. Maggie's baby.' (HF, 116) So, as she did with the baby, she expels the cat from her world, putting up a piece of wire netting to keep him and his young, lively owner out of her garden. Like her mother, she has grown afraid of ambivalence and of her own desire. It is easier simply to banish its objects.

These sub-narratives in the novel—Maggie's baby, the cat—support and complicate what Phillips calls the 'only major incident' in the novel: Har-riett's refusal to marry Prissie's fiancé.[34] *Harriett Frean* reads almost like a case study of one of the effects of repression as Jung outlined it in *Psychology of the Unconscious*, the text Sinclair reviewed in 1916. There he notes that

repression serves, as is well known, for the freeing from a painful complex from which one must escape by all means because its compelling and oppressing power

---

[33] Sinclair wrote in 1912 of Charlotte Brontë's love of children: '[Such love] has even its perversions, when love hardly knows itself from hate. [It] demands before all things possession. It cries out for children of its own blood and flesh. I believe that there were moments when it was pain for Charlotte to see the chil-dren born and possessed by other women' (TB, 63).

[34] Phillips, 'Battling with the Angel', 135.

is feared. The repression can lead to an apparent complete suppression which cor-
responds to a strong self-control. Unfortunately, however, self-control has limits
which are only too narrowly drawn. . . . people who strive for excessive ethics, who
try always to think, feel, and act altruistically and ideally, avenge themselves,
because of the impossibility of carrying out their ideals, by subtle maliciousness,
which naturally does not come into their own consciousness as such, but which
leads to misunderstandings and unhappy situations.[35]

Harriett, schooled by her parents into the belief that it's 'better to go without
than to take from other people' (HF, 15), persuades Robin, who insists that
he will not be happy with Prissie, that he cannot break his engagement to
her. Although Harriett is depressed after the marriage takes place, she is sustained by a narcissistic consciousness of her own goodness in repressing her
attraction to, and need for, Robin. Far from renouncing her own pleasure out
of a desire to protect someone else, as Mary Olivier does in her decision not
to marry Richard so that she can stay with her mother, Harriett abandons
Robin to secure both her own identification with her mother (who happily
gives up her comfortable lifestyle after her husband's foolish investments
fail), and her enjoyment of the idea of her own goodness. Uneasily aware
that, years into his miserable marriage, Robin is angry with her for pushing
him into it, Harriett comforts herself with the notion that she has somehow
made him a better person: 'It was through her renunciation that he had
grown so strong, so pure, so good' (HF, 56). Harriett's maternal identification and her narcissism form a self-sustaining economy from which there is
no escape.[36] As Jung points out in *Psychology of the Unconscious*: 'It is the sexual libido which forces the growing individual slowly away from his family.
If this necessity did not exist, then the family would always remain clustered
together in a solid group. Hence the neurotic always renounces a complete
erotic experience, in order that he may remain a child.'[37] Because Harriett's
only sexual opportunity is one that, because of her family's structure and
beliefs, she cannot take, she is condemned to an endless childhood in the
house that her mother and father chose.

   The irony of the novel is that even Prissie, who was eager to marry Robin,
suffers because of Harriett's apparently altruistic act. Prissie's response is to
develop a 'mysterious paralysis. It had begun with fits of giddiness in the
street; Prissie would turn round and round on the pavement; then falling fits;

---

[35] Jung, *Psychology of the Unconscious*, 63.
[36] Freud in 'On Narcissism: An Introduction' (1914) anticipated this kind of economy when he commented that 'the human being has originally two sexual objects: himself and the woman who nurses him' (in
Standard Edition, xiv. 69–102: at 88). If the 'woman who tends' is the object both of desire and of identification, in identifying with her the child also narcissistically identifies with her love for him or herself.
[37] Jung, *Psychology of the Unconscious*, 394.

and now both legs were paralysed' (HF, 50–1). On hearing this Harriett immediately—and exultantly—concludes that Prissie must be sexually incapacitated, and she even manages to feel some magnanimous pity for her. But on a visit to Robin and Prissie, she is disoriented by Prissie's revelation that she has had a child who died, and that she hopes one day to have another; and Harriett observes that Prissie's illness allows her to derive 'a quivering, deep content' (HF, 53) from Robin's attentions to her. Savagely she tells Robin that Prissie is 'very happy' (HF, 58) wielding power over him. Prissie's illness thus makes her simultaneously enviable and contemptible, and Harriett goes home relieved to escape both Prissie's querulousness and Robin's resentment.

Prissie uses her illness to compensate for the inadequacies of her marriage. Although in 1916 Sinclair had objected to the 'disconcerting literalism' of psychoanalytic theory, in *Harriett Frean* (and, earlier, in *The Three Sisters*), she takes seriously the pronouncement of Freud's collaborator Josef Breuer that 'the great majority of severe neuroses in women have their origin in the marriage bed'.[38] She even told H. G. Wells that it 'isn't honest to leave sex altogether out of a "Life"'.[39] Robin's second wife Beatrice, who was Prissie's nurse during her final illness, explains Prissie's illness to Harriett. Telling Harriett her symptoms were '[p]ure hysteria', she goes on: 'Robin wasn't in love with her, and she knew it. She developed that illness so that she might have a hold on him, get his attention fastened on her somehow. I don't say she could help it. She couldn't. But that's what it was' (HF, 97). When Harriett objects that Prissie died of her paralytic illness, Beatrice responds sharply: 'No. She died of pneumonia after influenza' (HF, 97). In the face of such a diagnosis Harriett can only refuse, 'obstinately, to connect' (HF, 97) her newly acquired knowledge with a nagging feeling of her own implication in Prissie's distress; but Robin's young niece finally accuses her directly of sacrificing Prissie, Robin, and even Beatrice to 'somebody else's' (her parents') idea of what was right (HF, 106). Harriett's infantile absorption in her parents' lives and her failure to assert her own desires are shown to have ruined not just her own life, but those of Prissie and Robin as well.

Sinclair's indictment of the classic Victorian values of Harriett's parents is not without its contradictions, however. Although she is sharply critical of the Freans' inability to prize love over 'beautiful behaviour', Sinclair continues implicitly to endorse the characteristically Victorian values of self-discipline, hard work, and intellectual endeavour that she had already

[38] Sinclair, 'Clinical Lectures on Symbolism and Sublimation', II. 144; Josef Breuer and Sigmund Freud, *Studies on Hysteria*, in Freud, *Standard Edition*, ii. 246.

[39] Sinclair to H. G. Wells, 29 June 1919, University of Illinois Library at Urbana-Champaign.

celebrated in *Mary Olivier*. Like Freud she retained her nostalgia for some aspects of Victorian culture, even as she violently repudiated others.[40] Mary Olivier is saved largely by her intellectual vitality and tenacity: she refuses to give in to her mother's coercions, insisting on educating herself and pursuing philosophical enquiry even at the risk of definitively losing her faith. Not so Harriett Frean. Although Harriett's father reads some of Mary Olivier's favourite authors ('Darwin, and Huxley, and Herbert Spencer', HF, 33), Harriett has no independent interest in them: 'She took down Herbert Spencer and tried to read him. She made a point of finishing every book she had begun, for her pride couldn't bear being beaten. Her head grew hot and heavy: she read the same sentences over and over again; they had no meaning; she couldn't understand a single word of Herbert Spencer' (HF, 33–4). Harriett tries to persuade herself that her failure to read any further is, once again, a form of self-righteous renunciation: 'If I go on, if I get to the interesting part I may lose my faith' (HF, 34). But in fact, of course, Harriett is intellectually lazy and limited as well as conformist. After her parents' deaths she reads only novels from the circulating library: 'She was satisfied with anything that ended happily and had nothing in it that was unpleasant, or difficult, demanding thought' (HF, 83). It is because of this intellectual inertia, the novel suggests, that Harriett, unlike Mary, is at the mercy of her unconscious. Harriett does not work to free herself. The fault is not only in her environment, but also in her lack of intellectual rigour. Harriett's fear of intellectual adventure (her 'horror . . . of change', HF, 80) means that she never develops beyond her own instincts; she never exceeds the personality her parents bestowed on her. The novel indicts Harriett for a kind of mental decadence which means that she cannot move out of the past into the future.

In *Harriett Frean*, then, Sinclair uses psychoanalytic paradigms to expose the Victorian family and domestic ideology for the destructive force they were for women such as Harriett. In the 1916 review of *Psychology of the Unconscious* she had already identified psychoanalytic theory as progressive and anti-Victorian:

At the present moment there is a reaction against all hushing up and stamping down. The younger generation is in revolt against even such a comparatively mild form of repression as Victorian Puritanism. And the New Psychology is with it. . . . Repression has had its chance in all conscience. Puritanism is now on its trial, if it be not already condemned. Wherever religion has aimed at the extermination of the natural instincts, wherever it has exalted repression to a positive virtue, it has

---

[40] Freud's Victorianism has been discussed in texts such as Frank Sulloway, *Freud, Biologist of the Mind: Beyond the Psychoanalytic Legend* (New York: Basic Books, 1979).

failed of its redemptive end. Our clinics, and lunatic asylums and the consulting-rooms of nerve-specialists are full of its failures. . . . You cannot attempt the destruction of the indestructible without some sinister result.[41]

Harriett's wasted life is one of those 'sinister results'. As Sinclair goes on to say, 'what happens mostly in cases of repression is that the libido . . . is arrested and turned back into those ancestral paths from which with such infinite pain and difficulty and conflict the individual has emerged. The adult becomes an infant, the unconscious prey of his own primitive habits, instincts and memories.'[42] Harriett, because she cannot use her libido to move her out of her familial past, ends up being consumed by it, her only issue a tumour, or as she would have it, a 'dead baby' (HF, 133). Her story is a cautionary tale about the dangers of a failure to sublimate and to escape from the somatic and emotional traps laid by one's parents. In Jung's, and Sinclair's, terms, that makes Harriett a 'neurotic'.[43] Both her own life and the lives of others are laid waste by her cowardice and her lack of imagination.

Reviews of *Harriett Frean* were almost all positive. Katherine Anthony in the *Nation* praised the novel's 'austere economy'; 'Affable Hawk' (Desmond MacCarthy) called it an 'admirably concentrated novel'; and Catherine Dawson Scott loyally remarked on its 'singular beauty'.[44] Sinclair too was pleased with the novel. She told Willis Steell that she had 'succeeded technically', and that it was 'one of the best things' she had done.[45] But at the same time, something about its bleakness seems to have bothered her. As if to compensate, in *Anne Severn* she abandoned *Harriett Frean*'s experimental form, and this time she allowed her heroine to steal and keep someone else's husband. Anne embraces the risks that Harriett was too afraid to take, and she is rewarded by being given the husband she has already taken as a lover.

Anne Severn and the Fieldings tells the story of Anne's relationship with the Fielding family, with whom she has grown up. She is in love with Jerrold, but Jerrold, thinking mistakenly that Anne is sexually involved with his brother, Colin, marries Maisie. When Anne and Jerrold realize that they are in love, they become lovers, until Anne's affection for Maisie makes her reluctant to continue deceiving her. Jerrold, meanwhile, is relieved that

---

[41] Sinclair, 'Clinical Lectures on Symbolism and Sublimation', I. 120.   [42] Ibid.

[43] See e.g. ibid. II. 144: 'the conflict with the mother . . . begins in childhood and is waged most fiercely on the threshold of adolescence. It must be fought to a finish, and the child must win it or remain for ever immature. If the parent wins, ten to one the child becomes a neurotic.' Jung describes the life of a woman who 'simply imitates [her] mother' as one of 'these melancholy silent tragedies working themselves out slowly, torturingly, in the sick souls of our neurotics' (*Collected Papers on Analytical Psychology*, 124, 168–9).

[44] Anthony, 'Wickedness of Goodness'; 'Affable Hawk', 'Books in General', *New Statesman*, 18 (11 Feb. 1922), 532; Scott, 'Miss May Sinclair's New Novel', 266.

[45] Steell, 'May Sinclair Tells Why She Isn't a Poet', 559.

Maisie does not want to make love with him, but he does not know that this is because she suffers excruciating attacks of 'false angina' at night (AS, 261). When Jerrold finally tells Maisie of his affair with Anne, Maisie is devastated, but her angina stops. At the end of the novel she releases Jerrold to live with Anne.

Although novelist Netta Syrett declared 'that psycho-analysis plays but a small part in this latest book of yours', in fact hysterical illness—and a psychoanalytic interpretation of it—are central to its plot.[46] *Anne Severn* was even reviewed in the *Psychoanalytic Review*.[47] In spite of the suspicion Sinclair sometimes expressed about psychoanalytic methodology (in 1917 she wrote, for example, that it was 'on its trial'), *Anne Severn* and, earlier, *The Romantic* (1920), betray a naive faith in its ability to reveal, in a phrase Sinclair used about Emily Brontë, the 'sad secrets of the body' (TB, 249).[48] Rebecca West objected to the way in which Sinclair offered up psychoanalytic interpretation as an unmasking of an essential truth. In a review of *Anne Severn* she commented that 'again, as in *The Romantic*, Miss Sinclair introduces a doctor to tell us what the book really is about. This is not cricket.'[49] West's own fictional portrait of hysteria, *The Return of the Soldier* (1918), lodged interpretive authority in the working-class figure of Margaret, but Sinclair's more orthodox presentation demonstrates the extent to which the spread of a bastardized form of psychoanalysis had begun to blur the boundaries between diagnosis, interpretation, and cure.

It is Jerrold's doctor brother Eliot who explains Maisie's illness. Reminding Anne that Jerrold was initially reluctant to marry Maisie, Eliot tells Anne:

She's never got over it, though she isn't conscious of it now. The fact remains that Maisie's marriage is incomplete because Jerry doesn't care for her. Part of Maisie, the adorable part we know, isn't aware of any incompleteness; it lives in a perpetual illusion. But the part we don't know, the hidden, secret part of her, is aware of nothing else.... [*ellipses in original*] Well, her illness is simply camouflage for that. Maisie's mind couldn't bear the reality, so it escaped into a neurosis. Maisie's behaving as though she wasn't married, so that her mind can say to itself that her marriage is incomplete because she's ill, not because Jerry doesn't care for her. (AS, 272)

This is an example of what Freud called the 'flight into illness', where the body and the unconscious conspire to substitute 'a bearable situation for an

<hr/>

[46] Netta Syrett to Sinclair, 19 Nov. 1922, UP, Box 3, fo. 86. See also Una Hunt, '*Harriett Frean*', *New Republic*, 21 (26 June 1922), 260–1; and Dorothy Brewster and Angus Burrell, *Modern Fiction* (New York: Columbia, 1934), who object that *Harriett Frean* reads like 'diagnosis rather than dialogue' (120).

[47] See Strangnell, 'Study in Sublimations'. [48] Sinclair, *Defence of Idealism*, 4.

[49] Rebecca West, 'Notes on Novels', *New Statesman*, 20 (2 Dec. 1922), 270–2.

unbearable one' (AS, 272).[50] Colin, incapacitated by shell-shock until he realizes that his cure is in his own hands, offers a very similar explanation for his illness: 'I was really hanging on to my illness for some sort of protection that it gave me . . . to save myself, I suppose, from a worse fear, the fear of life itself' (AS, 230). Unlike Colin, Maisie cannot achieve this degree of self-awareness alone: she is tricking not only others, but herself. In a sense she is as much at the mercy of her past and her somatic history as Harriett is; but Maisie's symptoms have an identifiable cause, and are banished as soon as she is finally forced to face reality, in what R. D. Townsend, in a review in *Outlook*, called a 'Freudian cure'.[51] As Eliot says, telling her the truth 'might cure her. . . . By making her face reality. By making her see that her illness simply means that she hasn't faced it. All our neuroses come because we daren't live with the truth' (AS, 273). Maisie suffers not so much from her reminiscences, as Freud would have it, as from her inability to adapt to the conditions of her life.[52]

But, as if she did not want simply to dismiss Maisie out of hand, Sinclair allows her to redeem herself at the end of the novel. In a move that is characteristic both of Maisie's 'unique perfection' (AS, 242) and of Sinclair's protagonists generally, Maisie sacrifices her own happiness in order that Anne and Jerrold may realize theirs.[53] This is a narrative mechanism that is typical of a certain kind of Victorian individualist feminism: in order for Jane Eyre to be happy, for example, Bertha Mason must give up her life.[54] But in Sinclair's hands this characteristically nineteenth-century narrative transforms Maisie from a helplessly suffering invalid into an active angel of mercy. This is Harriett's story with a happy ending: the couple Maisie unites, unlike Robin and Prissie, are not resentful of, but grateful for, her intervention. *Anne Severn* is a rehabilitation of the neurotic woman, an insistence that altruism is not always, as it was for Harriett, the manifestation of a narcissistic desire to command attention and to control.

The figure in which Sinclair attempted fully to realize the ideal of the autonomous woman, one who is able both to feel and to discipline desire, was Anne Severn herself. Sinclair felt that her own predilection for Anne damaged the book, writing to Violet Hunt that she liked the novel least of

[50] Freud discusses the 'flight into illness' several times. See e.g. Freud, 'Fragment of an Analysis of a Case of Hysteria ("Dora")', 1905, in *Standard Edition*, vii. 3–112: at 43 n.

[51] R. D. Townsend, 'The Book Table: The Recent Fiction', *Outlook*, 133 (24 Jan. 1923), 186.

[52] Breuer and Freud, *Studies on Hysteria*, 7.

[53] Angus Burrell notes the prevalence of self-sacrifice in Sinclair's novels in 'The Case for Self-Sacrifice', *Nation*, 121 (22 Jan. 1925), 121–2.

[54] Many critics have discussed the way this structure works in *Jane Eyre*. See e.g. Gayatri Chakravorty Spivak, 'Three Women's Texts and a Critique of Imperialism', in Henry Louis Gates, Jun. (ed.), *'Race', Writing, and Difference* (Chicago: University of Chicago Press, 1986), 262–80.

anything that she had done in the past few years, and that 'the thing suffers
from my liking my people so much'.[55] Anne overcomes her grief at the early
loss of her mother to become, like Hardy's Bathsheba Everdene, a farmer.
Not only does she resourcefully learn through experience how to manage a
farm ('she found herself . . . keeping the farm accounts, ordering fertilizers,
. . . riding about on Barker's horse, looking after the ploughing; . . . plodding
through the furrows of the hill slopes to see how the new drillers were working', AS, 135), she also boldly offers herself to Jerrold knowing that she will
be disgraced if the local community finds out. The novel is quite categorical
(if highly romantic) about the extent of the couple's involvement: we know
exactly when, where, and how often they make love. For Sinclair this was
clearly a statement about the modern world: in a 1925 *Bookman* symposium
on 'Unpleasant Fiction' or ' "sex" novels' she wrote that 'the attitude of the
modern novelist towards sex relations is more enlightened and more sane
than that of those Victorian novelists who ignored this fundamental aspect of
human nature'.[56] At the same time, she was anxious about the novel's
unequivocal endorsement of Anne's behaviour, writing to both Marc Logé
and Richard Aldington that its publication frightened her.[57]

The responses of younger feminists such as Rebecca West suggested,
however, that Sinclair's fear was anachronistic and revealed her Victorian
origins. Anne reminded West of the kind of enthusiastic school prefect so
beloved of women like Dorothea Beale:

damaging to the effect of *Anne Severn and the Fieldings* . . . is Miss Sinclair's reaction
against the fluffy feminine ideal . . . Anne Severn is her author's declaration that a
woman can be passionate and sexual and yet a cool and dignified human being. She
is rather more that than she is a person. She has something of the almost priggish
open-airiness and self-reliance that the early pioneers of the higher education of
women strove to inculcate in their pupils. . . . It is this slight disingenuousness in the
conception of the principal character that makes the book distinctly less impressive
than Miss Sinclair's novels usually are. For it is primarily a novel about passion; . . .
but how startling it is that Anne should have felt it. One feels as a headmistress
might if she discovered that the head prefect was engaged in an ardent love affair.[58]

In her anxiety to balance Anne's lack of scruple with her sensitivity to
others—ironically enough, in her portrait of a woman modern enough to put
passion before convention—Sinclair betrays her age. She was convincing
enough when she described the self-realization of a woman who was her

[55] Sinclair to Violet Hunt, 16 Dec. 1922, HA.
[56] Sinclair, in 'Symposium on Unpleasant Fiction', *Bookman* (London), 68 (Apr. 1925), 6.
[57] See Boll, *Miss May Sinclair*, 139, for references to the letters to Logé and Aldington.
[58] West, 'Notes on Novels', 272.

exact contemporary, Mary Olivier; but *Anne Severn*, in spite of its embrace of the modern discourse of psychoanalysis, reveals a Sinclair who was no longer quite in touch with the world about which she was writing. Anne Severn's complexities were beyond her author as Harriett Frean's were not; and the dissatisfaction Sinclair expressed to Violet Hunt about the novel may have been a recognition of just that. 'I <u>do</u> "do better when I hate [my characters]". I'm even fairer to them', she wrote to Hunt in December 1922.[59] Even if *Anne Severn* was, as Boll believes, Sinclair's 'greatest self-fulfilling novel' because her 'soul needed the fulfillment of a passionate love', Sinclair herself knew that Anne was almost a parody of her own days at Cheltenham Ladies' College.[60] And even if the portrait did exploit the transgressive thrill of Sinclair's own quasi-incestuous desires, as Boll suggests, this may, for Sinclair, only have brought her even more uncomfortably, and ineffectually, close to Anne.[61] If Anne was a New Woman in the style of those Sinclair had encountered or read about in the 1880s and 1890s, if she did embody Sinclair's ideas and fantasies about adulterous passion, she was also marked by Sinclair's ambiguous allegiance to the era of her childhood and adolescence.

Symptomatically, Sinclair's relationship with the next generation was markedly cooler by the 1920s than it had been at the height of her involvement with Pound, Aldington, and H.D. in the years before the First World War. Her acquaintance with Dorothy Richardson, for example, whom she finally met in 1920, was, on Richardson's part at least, resentful and uneasy.[62] Richardson was annoyed enough by Sinclair to dream about her death. She told Bryher in 1923: 'I dreamed last night that I saw someone shoot May. S. [*sic*] & heard her last words. They were the explanation of a tremendous drama that had made up the rest of the dream.'[63] Like the doctors in her novels, Sinclair—in Richardson's dream, anyway—always had an answer for everything. A few months after a disastrous dinner party at Sinclair's in the autumn of 1923, when Richardson and her husband said nothing, Richardson,

---

[59] Sinclair to Hunt, 16 Dec. 1922, HA.   [60] Boll, *Miss May Sinclair*, 276.

[61] Jerrold, who goes to India for a number of years, is clearly modelled on Sinclair's favourite brother Frank. See Boll, *Miss May Sinclair*, 278: 'May Sinclair's innocent family love once more became the emotional well for her most powerful love story, the story of Anne's marrying her adoptive brother . . . By studying it here we can begin to understand what a disturbing obsession, because of its very innocence, it must have been to her peace of mind, and what a stimulation to her creative art.'

[62] Richardson and Sinclair met when novelist J. D. Beresford and his wife took Sinclair to see Richardson and her husband in Cornwall. See Richardson to Edward Garnett, 7 Feb. 1920, in *Windows on Modernism*, 39.

[63] Richardson to Bryher, n.d. [autumn 1923?], *Windows on Modernism*, 84. It was Sinclair who was responsible for the meeting of H.D. and Bryher: Bryher, having read H.D.'s poetry, wanted an introduction, and asked Clement Shorter, a friend of Sinclair's and editor of the *Sphere* (owned by Bryher's father) if he could help. Shorter turned to Sinclair, who gave Bryher H.D.'s address and told her the surprising news that H.D. was a woman. See Guest, *Herself Defined*, 105.

claiming that Sinclair 'froze' everything, started to avoid her: 'we snatch at any straws, & are at the moment still choosing to think May is in America'.[64] In 1928, when Sinclair arrived one Saturday afternoon in her chauffeur-driven car, Richardson felt compelled out of politeness to go for a drive with her: 'we went into <u>Hertfordshire</u>. The Herts. that on a sunny summer's day is more than melancholy. We were frozen too. Frozen inside & out.'[65]

West's percipient review of *Anne Severn*, then, identified the ways in which by 1922 Sinclair's writing, and even her company, were no longer valued by those, such as Richardson, whose work Sinclair had defended in the past. In the 1960s Bryher, H.D.'s companion, wrote that after the war she 'sometimes met May Sinclair, I admired her integrity and love of scholarship but again I was a rebel who longed for, admired and swallowed whole the new age that she found wanting in profundity'.[66] Sinclair's withdrawal from public life in the late 1920s was a statement about something more than her fast failing health. Life, literally, began to pass her by, and, like Harriett Frean, she sank gradually into an apparently happy and childlike dependence on the loyal and affectionate Florence Bartrop. Symbolically her illness looks like a final recognition that her world is fading; that the modernity she strove so hard to embody in Anne Severn was already out of date. No one was shocked by *Anne Severn* as they had been, in 1907, by *The Helpmate*.[67] Sinclair's sure sense of her cultural moment was weakening: reviewers from 1924 onwards noted that she seemed to have little left to say.[68] Sinclair was beginning to tire.

In the summer of 1919, she gave up her room in Yorkshire because the journey—an entire day by train—was too fatiguing. Instead, she took a permanent room at the White Hart Hotel in Stow-on-the-Wold, a pretty little village in the Cotswolds which, in those days, was just under three hours away from London. She was ambivalent about leaving her beloved Yorkshire, writing to Catherine Dawson Scott: 'Stow is very beautiful but it doesn't make me forget Reeth & cease to long for it. Still, it will be quite good to work in. . . . the Groves [owners of the White Hart] look after me as

---

[64] See Richardson to Bryher, July 1924, *Windows on Modernism*, 99, and Richardson to Bryher, n.d. [early Aug. 1925]: 'You will be amused to hear that M.S. freezes even H.G. [Wells]', ibid. 118.

[65] Richardson to Peggy Kirkaldy, n.d. [October 1928], ibid. 160.

[66] Bryher, *The Heart to Artemis* (London: Collins, 1963), 199–200.

[67] See Ch. 3, above, for a discussion of Sinclair's difficulties with serial publication of the novel.

[68] See e.g. J. W. Krutch, 'From Wisdom's Mountain Height', *Nation*, 118 (7 May 1924), 535–6, who notes in this review of *The Cure of Souls* that 'When Miss Sinclair decided long ago to watch life rather than to live she imposed upon herself certain limitations not of intellectual but of emotional understanding' (535); see also his comments in 'An Impoverished Art', *Nation*, 125 (2 Nov. 1927), 481, where he remarks that unlike other experimental novelists, Sinclair's texts have become shorter, simpler, and more straightforward, and that in her last novel, *History of Anthony Waring* (1927) she has nothing new to say.

if I were their most cherished personal possession.'[69] In order to secure peace for her writing, Sinclair also rented a little wooden hut in a field just outside Stow, with views over the wolds, the fields, and the woods, where she would retire every day and work. When the noise of rugby players in the field alongside her cottage became too distracting, she rented the corner of a garden, and had the hut fenced in.[70] Her time in Stow was often solitary but very active: she wrote to Hugh Walpole in July 1920 that she was 'in Stow till Monday: very happy, writing short stories, motoring & cycling & walking. But I must come back to London to find somebody to talk with.'[71] Stow— disguised as 'Wyck'—was the setting for many of her later novels, and both the farming scenes in *The Romantic* (1920) and Anne Severn's knowledge of agriculture demonstrate Sinclair's own interest in the country she had adopted as her second home.[72] Her first few years there were productive and busy: as well as *The Romantic, Harriett Frean*, and *Anne Severn*, she wrote a remarkable seven new novels, and her second book of philosophy, *The New Idealism* (1922).

She also returned to the scene of her old triumph, spending seven weeks in the USA in April and May of 1924 as a delegate to the annual meeting of the PEN Club, an international organization of 'Poets, Playwrights, Essayists, Editors, Novelists' founded in 1921 by her friend Catherine Dawson Scott.[73] Scott, saddened by the war, intended the club to foster international friendship: 'it occurred to me that out of social intercourse comes understanding; and that if the great writers of the world met in friendship and exchanged ideas, a nascent kindliness would deepen till it appeared in their books'.[74] Although Sinclair did not join the organization right away, she was invited to the inaugural dinner, presided over by John Galsworthy, and after she became a member she was a faithful attender at the monthly club dinners in London until 1929. From the outset she was anxious to recruit members, telling Marie Belloc Lowndes: 'I think it is a very good idea'.[75] She was concerned, however, that the organization should not become too large and

---

[69] Sinclair to Catherine Dawson Scott, 1 July 1919, Beinecke Rare Book and Manuscript Library, Gen. MSS 144, Box 1, fo. 22.

[70] See Dorothy Hyde, 'May Sinclair', 3, UP, Box 48, fo. 525. Boll says that Sinclair rented the strip of field and paid a local carpenter to build the hut and equip it with a table, a chair, and a reclining chair. On occasion Sinclair spent the night there with Florence Bartrop. See Boll, *Miss May Sinclair*, 135–6.

[71] Sinclair to Hugh Walpole, 14 July 1920, UP, Box 3, fo. 91.

[72] Sinclair's notes on farming are preserved in UP, Box 40, workbook 19.

[73] C. A. D. Scott, 'The First International Club of Writers', *Literary Digest International Book Review*, 1 (Nov. 1923), 47, 54.

[74] Ibid. 47.

[75] Sinclair to Marie Belloc Lowndes, 19 Sept. 1921, HR, MS (Lowndes, MAB) Recip. See also her letter to Scott of 29 Dec. 1919, Beinecke Rare Book and Manuscript Library, Gen. MSS 144, Box 1, fo. 22, in which she advises Scott on people to contact: 'The trouble presently will be to keep people off!'

inclusive, warning Scott: 'The trouble is that your qualification is so very wide; & the success of a Club of this sort depends as much on the people <u>you keep out</u> as on those you let in.'[76]

Her trip to the USA with PEN was very different from her first visit there nearly twenty years earlier. Then, she had been acclaimed wherever she went, and had been introduced to some of the most famous writers of her day. Now many of the people she had met then were dead (Sarah Orne Jewett in 1909, William James in 1910, and Annie Fields in 1915), and Sinclair at 61 was no longer the focus of attention, but simply one among many delegates to the convention. However, she was still a venerated presence, giving a number of interviews to well-connected journalists. Some reporters gently poked fun at her diminutive size and her timidity as a speaker: 'The call of May Sinclair followed John Farrar's announcement that this great novelist, greatest psychological analyist [*sic*] in fiction, was present. What seemed to be a piece of plush upholstery rose from the sixth row. But soon we distinguished a pair of small, keen eyes beneath a fringe of hair.'[77] Sinclair delivered a 'simple, formal little message of good-will' to the ceremonial dinner in 'so eyrie [*sic*] a monotone, without perceptible movements of the lips, that it sounded very much as if she might be acting as the mouthpiece for a ventriloquist'.[78] She always hated public speaking, and, although she must have welcomed being treated as the *grande dame* of the occasion, she was ill-suited to projecting herself in front of a crowd.[79]

The PEN convention was her last major public appearance. After the mid-1920s she seemed to falter. In response to an invitation from Adcock in late 1926, she wrote simply: 'I am very lazy & I am resting between two novels. I'm afraid I can't do the book you want. I'm so sorry'; and in 1928, in answer to a questionnaire, she stated only: 'The author whom I would most like to meet in the flesh is Shelley. But what I wd. find to say to him I do not know.'[80] Her energy and her powers of invention were leaving her, and there

---

[76] Sinclair to Scott, 30 Aug. 1921, Beinecke Rare Book and Manuscript Library, Gen MSS 144, Box 1, fo. 22.

[77] Alice Rohe, 'Anne Nichols makes the World Safe for Literature', *Morning Telegraph* (8 June 1924), 1, 3: at 1. Interviews with Sinclair included Steell, 'May Sinclair Tells Why She Isn't a Poet'; Rascoe, 'Contemporary Reminiscences'; and Tittle, 'Personal Portraits'.

[78] Rascoe, 'Contemporary Reminiscences', 25.

[79] e.g. Sinclair refused even to take a bow at a performance of a play based on *The Combined Maze* (see Florence Bartrop to Boll, 5 Feb. 1961), UP, Box 48, fos. 518–19.

[80] Sinclair to Arthur Adcock, 4 Nov. 1926, UP, Box 1, fo. 1, and to an unnamed correspondent, 9 Feb. 1928, UP, Box 3, fo. 84. The *Bookman* regularly ran 'symposia' in which writers would write a small paragraph in response to a question or topic. Sinclair contributed both to the 'Christmas Symposium on Dreams, Ghosts and Fairies', *Bookman* (Dec. 1923), 142–9; and to the 'Symposium on Unpleasant Fiction', in *Bookman*, 68 (Apr. 1925), along with Frank Swinnerton, Rose Macaulay, W. L. George, J. D. Beresford, and others.

are very few surviving letters after 1929. After that, in her niece's words, 'it was all silence as far as she was concerned'.[81]

There was general consternation and puzzlement amongst her friends about Sinclair's apparent disappearance in the mid-1920s. Aldington, always one of her closest friends, reported to H.D. that after about 1926 or 1927 Sinclair 'disappeared': 'I wrote several times and had no answer.'[82] H.D. also remembered that she did not see Sinclair after 1927: 'I saw her, about 1927. She was ill then, and later moved out of London, I think. I tried to find out where she was but Dorothy Richardson seemed to think she was in a rest-home somewhere.'[83] Even Richardson, mollified by compassion, felt some concern. She wrote to Bryher in 1932: 'I've heard nothing of May Sinclair since Christmas when I saw Mrs. Dawson Scott who lives near her when she, Miss S., is in town, & occasionally calls on her. May, it appears, always answers enquiries in the same way, declaring that she is quite well, very well, & deploring only her inability to write.'[84] But after 1932 even that brief and irregular contact was lost when Sinclair gave up her London house and moved permanently to Buckinghamshire. To all intents and purposes she had vanished: no longer writing, no longer seeing any of her London friends, no longer even in correspondence with them.

But, of course, Sinclair had not disappeared. It may be that these final years of increasing shakiness and dementia—she was suffering from Parkinson's disease—were among some of the happiest she had known. Florence Bartrop had been her housekeeper and companion since 1919, and as Sinclair became more infirm, their intimacy increased. It is possible that Sinclair was already in the very early stages of Parkinson's when she wrote *Harriett Frean*: certainly her niece remembers Bartrop contacting her in the early 1920s to tell her how seriously ill her aunt was.[85] If she was already anticipating incapacitating illness, Harriett's feelings in *Harriett Frean* may be prophetic: 'She gave up even the semblance of her housekeeping, and became permanently dependent on Maggie. She was happy in the surrender of her responsibility, of the grown-up self she had maintained with so much effort, clinging to Maggie, submitting to Maggie, as she had clung and sub-mitted to her mother' (HF, 124). Bartrop's memories of their final years

[81] Wilda McNeile to Boll, 7 Oct. 1961, UP, Box 48, fo. 529.

[82] Richard Aldington to H.D., 26 Apr. 1947, in *Richard Aldington and H.D.: The Later Years in Letters*, ed. Caroline Zilboorg (Manchester: Manchester University Press, 1995), 88.

[83] H.D. to Aldington, 24 Apr. 1947, ibid. 88. In 1932 Sinclair and Florence Bartrop moved out of London to live at Pembroke Cottage, Little Tingewick, in Buckinghamshire; and in 1936 they moved again to the Gables, Burcott Lane, Bierton, near Aylesbury, where Sinclair died.

[84] Richardson to Bryher, 25 Apr. 1932, *Windows on Modernism*, 235.

[85] Wilda McNeile to Boll, 16 June 1959, UP, Box 48, fo. 529.

together, in which Sinclair could barely walk or speak, represent the two
women as idyllically companionable and affectionate. 'As you say Theo',
Bartrop wrote to Boll after Sinclair's death, 'she was a lovely person & like
me never used any make-up. We had so much in common that is why we
were so happy together I suppose [*sic*].'[86] In their seclusion the two women
were free to concentrate on each other: Bartrop had all Sinclair's diminished
attention, and Sinclair had Bartrop's entire devotion. Sinclair, who had
clung so obstinately to her isolation and her solitude (even Bartrop repeatedly comments on her 'reserve'), was finally, even if against her will, in the
kind of intimate relationship that she had previously avoided or feared.

    Some of her friends were suspicious that Bartrop was overprotective of
Sinclair, and kept her shut away too much. Dorothy Hyde, for example,
believed that Sinclair was kept 'virtually a prisoner by her housekeeper'.[87]
Her financial affairs were taken out of her hands after, in her confusion,
Sinclair started giving away all her money.[88] Richardson and Sinclair's niece
Wilda McNeile believed that they had been entrusted to Robert Singleton
Garnett, grandson of Richard Garnett, who had befriended Sinclair when
she first moved to London.[89] But Bartrop told Boll that by the end of Sinclair's life they were in her control, and there was clearly competition
between Bartrop and Sinclair's nephew Harold Sinclair over who should be
responsible for the ageing and passive Sinclair.[90] Some of Sinclair's family
took Bartrop's part: two of Sinclair's nieces, Nora Assinder and Agatha
Ayre, felt that Sinclair had not sufficiently recognized the extent of Bartrop's
devotion or of her debt to her, and after Sinclair's death made her an annuity
out of the legacies they had themselves received from their aunt.[91] Bartrop
felt that she had been amply rewarded for her attendance by the pleasure she
took in Sinclair's company: 'what I did do for May Sinclair was for the affection [I had] for her & for the love she had for me'.[92] There seems no doubt
that whatever possessiveness came with it, Sinclair was cared for with a loyalty and a dedication that were quite remarkable. The two women spent their
days in an apparently unbroken harmony, taking drives in the country and
going to the cinema. Bartrop was a trained nurse and even in Sinclair's last
days, when she apparently had a stroke, seemed in no need of assistance,

[86] Florence Bartrop to Boll, 6 Nov. 1959, UP, Box 48, fos. 518–19.
[87] Hyde, 'May Sinclair', 6, UP, Box 48, fo. 525.
[88] See McNeile to Boll, 16 June 1959, UP, Box 48, fo. 529.
[89] See Richardson to H.D., 4 Nov. 1931: 'we are easier in our minds about [May] since meeting at her
house a cousin, female & very nice, who visits every fortnight, & since knowing that the solicitor—Garnett
calls each week & pays the bills' (*Windows on Modernism*, 226). See also McNeile to Boll, 16 June 1959,
UP, Box 48, fo. 529.
[90] See Bartrop to Boll, 31 Dec. 1961, and 15 Apr. 1962, UP, Box 48, fos. 518–19.
[91] Bartrop to Boll, 6 Mar. 1961, UP, Box 48, fos. 518–19.   [92] Ibid.

although Sinclair's niece, Wilda McNeile, was there when Sinclair died. Bartrop wrote to Boll: 'Of course I often look back over those times & wish I could live them over again with her of course', recalling that 'from the first time we met until her end she would not go anywhere' without me: 'I used to take her to visit a friend & whenever possible May had me with her.'[93] In Bartrop's mind at least their compatibility was flawless. How Sinclair felt we shall never know.

Sinclair's voice was only heard again one more time: in her will. By the time she died, on 14 November 1946, at the age of 83, many of those whom she named as legatees were themselves dead, among them Lizzie Allen Harker, an old friend from Cheltenham days; Evelyn Sharp, the novelist who had introduced Sinclair to the suffrage movement; Netta Syrett, the novelist to whom Sinclair was supposed to have confided Charlotte Mew's passion for her; Evelyn Underhill, whose work on mysticism influenced Sinclair so heavily. By the time it came to be proved, the will, made twenty-eight years earlier on 11 November 1918 when Sinclair had a sudden premonition of death, read like an elegy.[94] Sinclair's first concern—as it had always been—was for her intellectual legacy, her personal library. All her books on philosophy and metaphysics were bequeathed to the London Library, and after that friends (specifically Otto Kyllmann, her former editor at Constable's, and Robert Singleton Garnett, who was also one of her original executors, although he too was dead by the time Sinclair finally died), and her surviving nephews and nieces (Francis, Harold, Wilda, Agatha, and Eleanor, now known as Nora) were allowed to choose their favourites, although her family were restricted to two books each. Mindful of the economic vulnerability even of married women, she also left trust funds to her three younger nieces, including Helen, daughter of her brother Joseph who had emigrated to Canada. Many of the friends she had not seen for twenty years found themselves the recipients of small legacies and specific gifts: as well as leaving money to her nephews, her godchildren and her eldest niece, she left £50 each to Lizzie Allen Harker, Aphra Wilson, Richard Aldington, Ezra Pound, and H.D. To any housekeeper who had been living with her for at least five years at the time of her death she left £20 (although in a codicil added in 1928 she left Florence Bartrop an additional £100 if she was still with her when she died).

The list of specific gifts is a litany of all the friends who had shaped her

---

[93] Bartrop to Boll, 22 Aug. 1961, UP, Box 48, fos. 518–19.

[94] Sinclair wrote to Curtis Brown on 24 June 1918 that she was afraid she might succumb to the influenza epidemic and die: 'ever since I started Mary [Olivier] I've had a funny feeling that I might not finish her' (HR, MS (Croft-Cooke, R) Misc 1).

emotional life: friends from Sidmouth, the Tyrrells, Lizzie Allen Harker, Janet Courtney (née Hogarth), Lucy Gwatkin, Evelyn Underhill, Evelyn Sharp, Katherine Tynan Hinkson, Otto Kyllmann, Robert Singleton Garnett and his wife, Anthony Deane, Maurice Hewlett, Hector Munro, Netta Syrett, Ezra Pound, Dorothy Pound, Richard Aldington, H.D., her agent Curtis Brown, and many others. For almost all of these people their sudden acquisition of a diamond ring, an aquamarine necklet, a green bronze lamp, Indian brass spoons, or books that Sinclair had specifically named as gifts for them, came like bounty from a lost country. Pound, who had just been interned in a psychiatric hospital, received a pewter cigarette box, volumes of Aristophanes and the Greek poets, and unlimited books of his choice; Dorothy Pound got Gaudier-Breszka's drawing of a black cat and six Wyndham Lewis fans; Richard Aldington was given a pewter inkstand, Sinclair's five-volume set of Rabelais, Aeschylus in Greek, and any books he wanted; and H.D. got Euripides in Greek, Aristotle's *De Poetica*, and any other volumes from Sinclair's library. She and Aldington were pleased and a little embarrassed: H.D. told Aldington how 'deeply touched' she was that Sinclair 'should have remembered us all that time'; Aldington wished they 'could have assured her of continuing affection', and selected 28 of her books, telling H.D. that Sinclair had 'quite a bit' of 'early Imagist stuff', 'chiefly you and Ezra and one or two of my bits of things'.[95] But, of course, Sinclair made her will nearly thirty years before she died. If the legacies did, as Aldington imagined, demonstrate Sinclair's affection for old friends, it was an affection that the failing Sinclair herself had forgotten years before her death, although even in 1918 she was careful to omit Charlotte Mew from the list. Pound was—as he had always been in relation to Sinclair—the only one of the group to eschew sentimentality. He even seemed to Aldington to have selected his books maliciously: 'Ezra chose 11—most modestly—but perhaps out of scorn, as he chiefly chose fat Ford, H. James and a work on Genetics.'[96] The well-meaning solicitors, in drawing up the catalogue of her library, also unintentionally mocked Sinclair's earnest plans: Aldington reported that the list was 'frightfully mispelled. Your [H.D.'s] Palimpsest appears as Palmforest (!) and Ez's Quia Pauper Amavi as "I'm a Pauper Marvi" (!)'[97] What began as the tragedy of Sinclair's slow and painful dying ended partly in farce. But she did ride to her funeral in style: always

[95] H.D. to Aldington, 24 Apr. 1947; Aldington to H.D., 26 Apr. 1947, *Richard Aldington and H.D.*, 88; Aldington to H.D., 2 May 1947, *Richard Aldington: An Autobiography in Letters*, 228.

[96] Aldington to H.D., 18 Apr. 1947, *Richard Aldington and H.D.*, 88. In fact, a 'List of books as chosen by Ezra Pound, from the estate of the late Miss May Sinclair', 25 Feb. 1947 (HR, MS file (Norman, C) Misc) includes over 300 titles.

[97] Aldington to H.D., 18 Apr. 1947, *Richard Aldington and H.D.*, 88.

passionately keen on being driven by car, she was insistent that she should go 'by motor car' to her final resting place.[98] She was cremated in Golders Green in a private funeral attended only by her nieces, her nephew Harold, and her solicitor, and her ashes were interred—as, in a final revulsion from her own agnosticism, she had asked—in Hampstead parish church.

Sinclair's long life thus ended in quiet obscurity, with a simple private funeral. *The Times* marked her passing with an obituary that praised her 'keenly analytical intellect' and her 'comprehensive and imaginative grasp of character', but otherwise her death made scarcely a ripple in post-war London, which had long forgotten the shy, formal author of *The Divine Fire*.[99] Had she died at the height of her fame—or even while she was still active in the literary world—she might have been given the kind of public funeral Henry James received in 1916 (which Sinclair herself attended). As it was, the writer who had been one of the best-known novelists of the early decades of the century had been forgotten long before she died. The world had moved on, and Sinclair, snug in her cottage near Aylesbury, had simply watched it leave her behind. Apart from a brief period during the First World War, Sinclair had always been most comfortable as an observer, even believing that silence and seclusion fostered her creative talent. The fact that she had become so central to a literary movement, modernism, which explicitly rejected the values and culture in which she had been raised, is a tribute to her adaptability and her determination not to be left out of those aspects of the modern world in which she truly believed. But all the same she never quite outgrew her Victorianism, and bad health meant that in the end she had to abandon the fight to keep up with the world around her.

It is a sad irony that someone whose intellectual life had been the core of her existence should have been deprived of it for so many years before her weary body finally gave out. While it lived, it was an intellect of rare passion and scepticism and learning, an intellect that propelled Sinclair forward from the cramped world of her childhood into an adulthood remarkable for its dedication to the life of the mind. A lesser woman might have remained content with the beliefs handed down to her by her mother. But Sinclair was born unwilling to compromise. As she said of Anne Brontë, she had 'the habit of unfettered speech'.[100] Shy, defiant, awkward, determined, Sinclair embodied and articulated the contradictions of her age.

---

[98] Bartrop to Boll, 3 Nov. 1959, UP, Box 48, fos. 518–19.   [99] *The Times*, 15 Nov. 1946.
[100] Sinclair, 'Introduction' to *The Tenant of Wildfell Hall*, p. ix.

APPENDIX
Autobiographical Sketch
The Miss-May-Sinclair[1]

=

BUT LITTLE is known of this very curious & interesting animal. It seems to have been met with first at Rock Ferry, in the riparian district of Cheshire. Naturalists are divided as to the precise date of its appearance in these islands. This may, however, be calculated approximately from certain fossilised remains—unmistakeably the print-marks of an extinct animal— preserved in the Higher Tertiary deposits (? top-shelf literature). A migratory animal, it is known to have inhabited parts of Essex, Gloucestershire, Denbighshire, Yorkshire, Devonshire & Middlesex. It has been seen within comparatively recent years in the neighbourhood of Hampstead (generally in the more wild & unfrequented parts of the Heath). But since this portion of Middlesex became civilised through the introduction of the New Tube, it is only to be found in the older & obscurer parts of Kensington. It wd. seem to be fond of retirement. Its habit is to hide itself in its outer burrow, or studio, during the forenoon, when the little creature applies itself, with comic fury, to building up a heap of manuscripts wh. wd. seem to serve it for purposes of protection & indeed nutrition. In the afternoon it frequently disappears into its inner burrow, or bedroom, where it will remain for hours in a comatose state. When recovered from its torpor, it displays an extra-ordinary activity, cycling, walking (it has been known to cover many miles in the counties of Hertfordshire & Bucks) even dancing with abandonment & to excess.

[1] The manuscript of this comic sketch is preserved in the Manuscripts Division, New York Public Library, Astor, Lenox and Tilden Foundations (Literature Boxes/Sinclair), and is reproduced here by kind permission of the New York Public Library. The sketch appears to have been written for Otto Kyllmann, Sinclair's publisher at Constable, in late 1907 or early 1908. I am grateful to Michele Troy for directing me to this manuscript.

If handled properly, this animal is of a most mild & tractable temper, but it is capable under provocation of an indomitable ferocity wh. renders it for the time extremely difficult to deal with. This mood, however, seldom lasts more than from seven to thirty-four minutes, when it will smile & eat out of your hand. Under favourable conditions it will produce one volume in every three years. When young it is capable of absorbing metaphysics in prodigious quantities & giving them forth in the form of blank verse. This is unmistakeably shown in the deposits of the early period, the so-called Juvenilia.

'Nakiketas & Other Poems'   (date 1887)
'Essays in Verse'.   (date 1891)

& the fossilised fragment known as 'The Ethical Import of Idealism' discovered in *The New World* in 1893. Later remains are free from any taint of abstract thought, but lines of blank verse may be found occassionally [*sic*] even in recent deposits. (Notably in *The Helpmate*—'His silence lay between them like a sword')

A few recent remains of this animal are to be found in Messrs William Blackwoods' collection under the headings of 'Audrey Craven' 1897, 'Mr. and Mrs. Nevill Tyson', 1898. But the fresh specimens are contained in the Constable Museum, labelled 'Two Sides of a Question' (1901) 'The Divine Fire' (1904) & 'The Helpmate (1907) This collection is mainly due to the patient investigations of the curator, Mr. Otto Kyllmann, who is willing to supply all students of the subject, at all times, with the fullest information.

The Miss-may-Sinclair [*sic*] found in America wd. seem to be a distinct species. It is certainly more widely known in that country. Relics have been preserved (for demonstration in Natural History) by the Universities of Minneapolis & Nebraska.

BIBLIOGRAPHY

===

MAY SINCLAIR

Novels

Audrey Craven (London: Blackwood, 1897; New York: Henry Holt, 1906).

Mr and Mrs Nevill Tyson (London: Blackwood, 1898; repr. London: Constable, 1908 in Constable's Sixpenny Series; as *The Tysons*: New York: Grossett and Dunlap, 1906; New York: B. W. Dodge, 1906; New York: Holt, 1907; serial publication in *Ainslee's Magazine*, 17, May–June 1906, 136–54, 39–92).

The Divine Fire (London: Constable, 1904; repr. London: Eveleigh Nash, 1911; New York: Holt, 1904, 1906; excerpt in *Current Literature*, 37, Mar. 1905, 254–7).

Superseded (New York: Holt, 1906, 'Author's Edition'). Originally appeared with 'The Cosmopolitan' in *Two Sides of a Question*.

The Helpmate (London: Constable, 1907; New York: Holt, 1907; serial publication in *Atlantic Monthly*, 99–100, Jan.–Sept. 1907, 5–24, 184–202, 355–78, 450–69, 590–613, 745–69, 10–30, 189–204, 356–72).

The Judgment of Eve, *Everybody's Magazine*, 17 (Sept. 1907), 394–413; and in London as a supplement to the *Lady's Realm* (Dec. 1907); (repr. New York and London: Harper, 1908).

Kitty Tailleur (London: Constable, 1908; repr. 1911 in Constable's Sixpenny Series; London: Hutchinson, 1923; as *The Immortal Moment: The Story of Kitty Tailleur*: New York: Doubleday, Page & Co., 1908; trans. into French by Clément Mottet as *L'Immortel Moment*, Paris: J. Tallandier, 1913).

The Creators: A Comedy (London: Constable, 1910; New York: Century, 1910; serial publication in *Century Illustrated Monthly Magazine*, 79–80 (Nov. 1909–Oct. 1910), 100–16, 240–55, 401–17, 520–35, 713–29, 834–48, 53–68, 193–207, 354–69, 529–44, 709–22, 840–53, with illustrations by Arthur I. Keller, also reproduced in American vol. edn.).

The Combined Maze (London: Hutchinson, 1913; New York: Macmillan, 1913; London and New York: Harper, 1913).

The Three Sisters (London: Hutchinson, 1914; New York: Macmillan, 1914;

London: Virago, 1982, with introduction by Jean Radford, in the Modern Classics series; trans. into French by Marc Logé as *Les Trois Sœurs*, Paris: A. Redier, 1932, with introduction by Jean Maxence).

Tasker Jevons: The Real Story (London: Hutchinson, 1916; as *The Belfry*: New York: Macmillan, 1916; New York: Boni and Liveright, 1916, in The Modern Library Series).

The Tree of Heaven (London: Cassell, 1917; New York: Macmillan, 1917).

Mary Olivier: A Life (London: Cassell, 1919; New York: Macmillan, 1919; London: John Lehmann, 1949, in the Holiday Library; London: Virago, 1980, with introduction by Jean Radford, in the Modern Classics series; serial publication of Book 1, 'Infancy', in *Little Review*, 5–6, Jan.–May 1919, 14–19, 10–11, 52–7, 43–55, 40–50).

The Romantic (London: Collins, 1920; New York: Macmillan, 1920; translated into French by Marc Logé as *Un romanesque*, Paris: Plon-Nourrit, 1922).

Mr Waddington of Wyck (London: Cassell, 1921; New York: Macmillan, 1921).

Life and Death of Harriett Frean (London: Collins, 1922; New York: Macmillan, 1922; London: Virago, 1980, with introduction by Jean Radford, in the Modern Classics series; serial publication in *North American Review*, 212–13, Dec. 1920–Mar. 1921, 721–40, 65–80, 247–59, 389–403; and in *Golden Book*, 19, Jan.–Feb. 1934, 68–85, 235–56; trans. into Norwegian by Camilla Wulfsberg as *Rode Valmuer*, Oslo: Dybwad, 1948).

Anne Severn and the Fieldings (London: Hutchinson, 1922; New York: Macmillan, 1922).

A Cure of Souls (London: Hutchinson, 1924; New York: Macmillan, 1924).

Arnold Waterlow: A Life (London: Hutchinson, 1924; New York: Macmillan, 1924; serial publication in *Home Magazine*, Oct. 1923–July 1924).

The Rector of Wyck (London: Hutchinson, 1925; New York: Macmillan, 1925).

Far End (London: Hutchinson, 1926; New York: Macmillan, 1926).

The Allinghams (London: Hutchinson, 1927; New York: Macmillan, 1927).

History of Anthony Waring (London: Hutchinson, 1927; New York: Macmillan, 1927).

Collections of Short Stories

Two Sides of a Question (London: Constable, 1901, 1904; London: Hutchinson, 1923; New York: J. F. Taylor, 1901).

The Return of the Prodigal (New York: Macmillan, 1914).

The Judgment of Eve and Other Stories (London: Hutchinson, 1914).

Uncanny Stories, with illustrations by Jean de Bosschère (London: Hutchinson, 1923; New York: Macmillan, 1923).

Tales Told by Simpson (London: Hutchinson, 1930; New York: Macmillan, 1930).

The Intercessor and Other Stories (London: Hutchinson, 1931; New York: Macmillan, 1932).

Short Stories

'A Study from Life' [by M. A. St C. Sinclair], *Black and White*, 10 (2 Nov. 1895), 570–1.

'A Friendly Critic' [unsigned], *Macmillan's Magazine*, 74 (Oct. 1896), 435–43.

'Not Made in Germany' [unsigned], *Macmillan's Magazine*, 75 (Jan. 1897), 201–9.

'A Hero of Fiction', *Temple Bar*, 115 (Sept. 1898), 135–60.

'A Servant of the Earth', *Woman at Home* (1899); repr. Annie Matheson, *Leaves of Prose with Two Studies by May Sinclair* (London: Humphry Milford at Oxford University Press, 1912), 289–300.

'Superseded', in *Two Sides of a Question*.

'Cosmopolitan', in *Two Sides of a Question* and *Return of the Prodigal*.

'The Return of the Prodigal', *Blackwood's Edinburgh Magazine*, 171 (Jan. 1902), 28–40; repr. in *Return of the Prodigal* and *Judgment of Eve and Other Stories*.

'The Fault', *Century Illustrated Monthly Magazine*, 75 (Jan. 1908), 466–73; repr. in *Return of the Prodigal* and *Judgment of Eve and Other Stories*.

'Wilkinson's Wife', *McClure's Magazine*, 30 (Feb. 1908), 454–8; *Fortnightly Review*, 89 (Apr. 1908), 754–61; repr. in *Return of the Prodigal* and *Judgment of Eve and Other Stories*.

'The Gift', *American Magazine*, 66 (1908), 353–64; *Fortnightly Review*, 90 (Sept. 1908), 517–35.

'The Intercessor', *English Review*, 8 (July 1911), 569–601; repr. as 'The Intercession: A Novel', *Two Worlds* (Sept. 1926), and in *The Intercessor and Other Stories*.

'Appearances', *Good Housekeeping*, 53 (Aug. 1911), 154–64; *Fortnightly Review*, 100 (Dec. 1913), 1178–91; repr. in *Return of the Prodigal* and *Judgment of Eve and Other Stories*.

'Miss Tarrant's Temperament', *Harper's Magazine*, 123 (Aug.–Sept. 1911), 344–54, 509–19; repr. in *Return of the Prodigal*, *Judgment of Eve and Other Stories*, and *Tales Told by Simpson*.

'Between the Lines', *Harper's Magazine*, 124 (Dec. 1911), 28–41; repr. in *Tales Told by Simpson*.

'The Flaw in the Crystal', *English Review*, 11 (May 1912), 189–228; also published as *The Flaw in the Crystal*, New York: Dutton, 1912; repr. in *Uncanny Stories*.

'"Khaki"', *English Review*, 15 (Sept. 1913), 190–201; repr. in *Tales Told by Simpson*.

'Compensation', *Good Housekeeping*, 72 (Oct. 1913), 437–44; repr. in *Tales Told by Simpson*.

'The Wrackham Memoirs', *Harper's Magazine*, 128 (Dec. 1913), 36–47; repr. in *Return of the Prodigal*, *Judgment of Eve and Other Stories*, and *Tales Told by Simpson*.

'The Collector', *Century Illustrated Monthly Magazine*, 87 (Jan. 1914), 321–30; repr. in *Tales Told by Simpson* and in Ernest Rhys and C. A. Dawson Scott (eds.), *Thirty and One Stories by Thirty and One Authors* (London: Thornton Butterworth, 1931).

'Red Tape', *Queen: The Lady's Newspaper* (14 Nov. 1914), 802–3; repr. in Tate (ed.), *Women, Men and the Great War*, 199–209.

'The Pin-Prick', *Harper's Magazine*, 130 (Feb. 1915), 392–7; repr. in *Tales of Simpson*.

'The Frewin Affair', *Woman at Home*, NS 15 (Jan. 1917), 535–43; repr. in *Tales Told by Simpson*.

'Portrait of My Uncle', *Century Illustrated Monthly Magazine*, 93 (Jan. 1917), 439–43; repr. in *Tales Told by Simpson*.

'Fame', *Pictorial Review*, 21 (May 1920), 10; repr. as a limited edn. (London: Elkin Matthews and Marrot, 1929), and in *Tales Told by Simpson*.

'The Bambino', *Athenaeum* (24 Sept. 1920), 398–9; repr. in *Georgian Stories* (London: Chapman and Hall, 1922), and in *Tales Told by Simpson*.

'Lena Wrace', *English Review*, 32 (Feb. 1921), 103–15; *Dial*, 71 (July 1921), 50–62; repr. in Edward J. O'Brien and John Cournos (eds.), *The Best British Short Stories of 1922* (Boston: Small Maynard and Co., 1922), in Edward J. O'Brien (ed.), *Modern English Short Stories* (London: Cape, 1930), and in *Tales Told by Simpson*.

'The Return', *Harper's Magazine*, 142 (May 1921), 693–703.

'Heaven: A Story', *Fortnightly Review*, 112 (Sept. 1922), 507–27; repr. in *Intercessor and Other Stories*.

'The Victim', *Criterion*, 1 (Oct. 1922), 65–88; repr. in *Uncanny Stories*.

'Where Their Fire Is Not Quenched', *English Review*, 35 (Oct. 1922), 299–320; repr. in Dorothy Sayers (ed.), *Great Short Stories of Detection, Mystery, and Horror* (London: Gollancz, 1928, 1929, 1930), and in *Uncanny Stories*.

'The Nature of the Evidence', *Fortnightly Review*, 113 (May 1923), 871–9; repr. in *Uncanny Stories*.

'Jones's Karma', *Criterion*, 2 (Oct. 1923), 43–56; repr. in *Intercessor and Other Stories*.

'The Token', in *Uncanny Stories*.

'If the Dead Knew', in *Uncanny Stories*.

'The Finding of the Absolute', in *Uncanny Stories*.

'The Villa Désirée', in Cynthia Asquith (ed.), *The Ghost Book* (London: Hutchinson, 1926); repr. in *Intercessor and Other Stories*.

'The Pictures', in *Tales Told by Simpson*.

'The Mahatma's Story', in *Intercessor and Other Stories*.

Poetry

Nakiketas and Other Poems [by Julian Sinclair] (London: Kegan Paul, Trench & Co., 1886).

'A Custance of To-day' [by Mary Sinclair], *Cheltenham Ladies' College Magazine*, no. 20 (Autumn 1889), 207–9.

'A Study from the Life of Goethe' [by Mary Sinclair], *Cheltenham Ladies' College Magazine*, no. 24 (Autumn 1891), 188–95; repr. in *Essays in Verse*.

Essays in Verse (London: Kegan Paul, Trench, Trübner & Co., 1891, pub. Jan. 1892).

'Sonnet', *Cambridge Review* (23 Nov. 1893), 116.

'In Memoriam: Professor Jowett', *Temple Bar*, 99 (Dec. 1893), 472; repr. as 'Sonnets—Professor Jowett', *Cheltenham Ladies' College Magazine*, no. 29 (Spring 1894), 48.

'Clytie', *Pall Mall Magazine*, 2 (Jan. 1894), 365–6.

'Decadence', *Academy*, no. 1142 (24 Mar. 1894), 249.

'Three Singers', *Pall Mall Magazine*, 4 (Oct. 1894), 231.

'Sea Whispers', *Pall Mall Magazine*, 5 (Mar. 1895), 436.

'Sonnet', *Cheltenham Ladies' College Magazine*, no. 36 (Autumn 1897), 248.

'A Fable', *Cheltenham Ladies' College Magazine*, no. 38 (Autumn 1898), 257–8.

'Field Ambulance in Retreat: Via Dolorosa, Via Sacra', in Hall Caine (ed.), *King Albert's Book* (London: Hodder and Stoughton, 1914); repr. in Jacqueline Trotter (ed.), *Valour and Vision: Poems of the War 1914–1918* (2nd edn., London: Martin Hopkinson, 1923), 43–4, and in Catherine Reilly (ed.), *Scars upon my Heart: Women's Poetry and Verse of the First World War* (London: Virago, 1981), 98–9.

'After the Retreat', *Egoist*, 2 (1 May 1915), 77.

'Dedication: To a Field Ambulance in Flanders', at opening of *Journal of Impressions in Belgium*.

'The Grandmother', *Criterion*, 2 (Feb. 1924), 167; repr. as part of *The Dark Night*, 11–14.

The Dark Night (London: Jonathan Cape, 1924).

Philosophical Writings

'Descartes' [by 'Mary Sinclair'], *Cheltenham Ladies' College Magazine*, no. 5 (Spring 1882), 95–8.

Studies in Plato. I: 'Was Plato a "Dualist"?', *Cheltenham Ladies' College Magazine*, no. 27 (Spring 1893), 40–8.

'The Ethical and Religious Import of Idealism', *New World*, 2 (Dec. 1893), 694–708.

'The Platonic Sociology', *Cheltenham Ladies' College Magazine*, no. 29 (Spring 1894), 49–53.

'The Philosopher-King', *Cheltenham Ladies' College Magazine*, no. 32 (Autumn 1895), 20–6.

'The Things Which Belong Unto the Truth: A Translation of the Fragment . . . from the poem of Parmenides on *Nature*', *Cheltenham Ladies' College Magazine*, no. 33 (Spring 1896), 1–6.

A Defence of Idealism: Some Questions and Conclusions (London and New York: Macmillan, 1917).

The New Idealism (London and New York: Macmillan, 1922).

Critical, Biographical, and Other Writings

Translation: Rudolf Sohm, *Outlines of Church History* (London: Macmillan, 1895).

Review of Mary Pulling, *The Teacher's Text Book of Practical Psychology*, *Cheltenham Ladies' College Magazine*, no. 33 (Spring 1896), 71–2.

'The Life of "The Other Half " ' [review of Richard Whiteing, *No 5 John Street*], *Bookman* (London), 16 (Apr. 1899), 16.

'Miss Dougall's New Novel' [review of Lily Dougall, *The Mormon Prophet*], *Bookman* (London), 16 (Apr. 1899), 17.

'Miss Harraden's New Novel' [review of Beatrice Harraden, *The Fowler*], *Bookman* (London), 16 (May 1899), 47.

Translation: Theodore von Sosnosky, *England's Danger: The Future of British Army Reform* (London: Chapman and Hall, 1901).

Thoughts from Goethe, ed. May Sinclair (London: Priory Press, 1905).

'Man and Superman: A Symposium', *New York Times* (1 Dec. 1905), 813–14.

'Type-Writing: A Protest', *Author*, 15 (Feb. 1905), 147–8 [protests against paying typists a lower rate].

'The Eternal Child' [review of Elizabeth Allen Harker, *The Romance of the Nursery* and *Paul and Fiammetta*], *Bookman* (London), 23 (July 1906), 488–90.

'Three American Poets of To-Day', *Atlantic Monthly*, 98 (Sept. 1906), 325–35.

'Message', *Votes for Women*, 1 (Mar. 1908), 79.

'How It Strikes a Mere Novelist', *Votes for Women*, 2 (Mar. 1908), 211.

'Introduction' to Charlotte Brontë, *Jane Eyre* (London: Dent, 1908; New York: Dutton, 1908), in Everyman's Library series.

'Introduction' to Elizabeth Gaskell, *The Life of Charlotte Brontë* (London: Dent, 1908; New York: Dutton, 1908), in Everyman's Library series.

'Introduction', to Charlotte Brontë, *Shirley* (London: Dent, 1908; New York: Dutton, 1908), in Everyman's Library series.

'Introduction' to Charlotte Brontë, *Villette* (London: Dent, 1909; New York: Dutton, 1909), in Everyman's Library series.

'George Meredith', *Author* (1 June 1909), repr. *Outlook*, 92 (19 June 1909) and in
 Annie Matheson, *Leaves of Prose with Two Studies by May Sinclair* (London:
 Humphry Milford at Oxford University Press, 1912), 301–15.

'Introduction' to Charlotte Brontë, *The Professor* (London: Dent, 1910; New York:
 Dutton, 1910), in Everyman's Library series.

Letter to the editor, *Spectator* (24 June 1911) [reply to article on *English Review*,
 Spectator, 10 June 1911].

Letter to the editor, *Author* (1 Dec. 1911) [on authors' agents].

Letter to the editor, 'Sir Almroth Wright on Woman Suffrage: Miss May Sinclair's
 Reply', *The Times* (4 Apr. 1912), 7.

Letter to the editor, *New York Times* (4 Nov. 1912) [on 'The Flaw in the Crystal'].

Feminism (London: Women's Suffrage League, 1912).

'A Defence of Men', *English Review*, 11 (July 1912), 556–66; repr. *Forum*, 48 (Oct.
 1912), 409–20.

The Three Brontës (London: Hutchinson, 1912; Boston and New York: Houghton
 Mifflin, 1912; new edn. London: Hutchinson, 1914).

'The "Gitanjali": Or Song-Offerings of Rabindranath Tagore', *North American
 Review*, 197 (May 1913), 659–76.

'The New Brontë Letters', *Dial*, 55 (1 Nov. 1913), 343–6 (repr. as introduction to
 2nd edn. of *The Three Brontës*, 1914).

'Introduction' to Anne Brontë, *The Tenant of Wildfell Hall* (London: Dent, 1914;
 New York: Dutton, 1914), in Everyman's Library series.

'Chauffeurs at the Front', *New Statesman*, 4 (26 Dec. 1914), 295–7.

'Women's Sacrifices for the War', *Woman at Home*, no. 67 (Feb. 1915), 7–11.

'From a Journal', *English Review*, 20 (May–July 1915), 168–83, 303–14, 468–76;
 repr. as *A Journal of Impressions in Belgium* (London: Hutchinson, 1915; New
 York: Macmillan, 1915).

America's Part in the War (New York: Commission for Relief in Belgium, 1915).

'Two Notes. I. On H.D. II. On Imagism', *Egoist*, 2 (1 June 1915), 88–9.

'Clinical Lectures on Symbolism and Sublimation', I, *Medical Press* (9 Aug. 1916),
 118–22; II, *Medical Press* (16 Aug. 1916), 142–5.

'Introduction' to Jean de Bosschère, *The Closed Door* (London: J. Lane, 1917).

'The Spirits, Some Simpletons, and Dr. Charles Mercier' [review of Charles
 A. Mercier, *Spiritualism and Sir Oliver Lodge*], *Medical Press* (25 July 1917). See
 also correspondence from Oliver Lodge and Sinclair in *Medical Press* (8 Aug.
 1917).

' "Prufrock: And Other Observations": A Criticism', *Little Review*, 4 (Dec. 1917),
 8–14; repr. in Scott (ed.), *Gender of Modernism*, 448–53.

'The War in England and Germany', *New York Times Book Review* (27 Jan.
 1918), 29.

'The Novels of Dorothy Richardson', *Egoist*, 5 (Apr. 1918), 57–9; repr. *Little Review*, 4 (April 1918), 3–11, as 'Introduction' to Dorothy Richardson, *Pointed Roofs* (New York: Knopf, 1919), and in Scott (ed.), *Gender of Modernism*, 442–8.

'The Reputation of Ezra Pound', *English Review*, 30 (Apr. 1920), 326–35; repr. in Scott (ed.), *Gender of Modernism*, 468–76.

'Worse than War', *English Review*, 31 (Aug. 1920), 147–53.

'Introduction' to Emily Brontë, *Wuthering Heights* (London: Dent, 1921), in Everyman's Library series.

Interview on 'The Future of the Novel', *Pall Mall Gazette* (10 Jan. 1921), 7; repr. in Meredith Starr (ed.), *The Future of the Novel: Famous Authors and their Methods: A Series of Interviews with Renowned Authors* (Boston: Small, Maynard, 1921), 87–9; and in Scott (ed.), *Gender of Modernism*, 476–8.

'The Poems of F. S. Flint', *English Review*, 32 (Jan. 1921), 6–18.

'The Poems of Richard Aldington', *English Review*, 32 (May 1921), 397–410.

'The Poems of "H.D."', *Dial*, 72 (Feb. 1922), 203–7; *Fortnightly Review*, 121 (Mar. 1927), 329–40 (a longer version); repr. in Scott (ed.), *Gender of Modernism*, 453–67.

'The Novels of Violet Hunt', *English Review*, 34 (Feb. 1922), 106–18.

'The Man from Main Street' [review of Sinclair Lewis, *Babbitt*], *New York Times* (24 Sept. 1922), 1.

'Psychological Types' [review of Jung, *Psychological Types*], *English Review*, 36 (May 1923), 436–9.

'Putting the Desert's Terrors into a Novel' [review of R. L. Grant Watson, *The Desert Horizon*], *Literary Digest International Book Review*, 1 (June 1923), 15.

'Primary and Secondary Consciousness', *Proceedings of the Aristotelian Society*, NS 23 (1923), 11–20.

Contributor to 'Christmas Symposium on Dreams, Ghosts and Fairies', *Bookman* (London) (Dec. 1923), 142–9.

'Who Wrote *Wuthering Heights*?', *Bookman* (London), 66 (May 1924), 97–8.

'What Sudden Wealth Did to Four People' [review of Henry James Forman, *Sudden Wealth*], *Literary Digest International Book Review*, 2 (Nov. 1924), 856.

Contributor to 'Symposium on Unpleasant Fiction', in *Bookman* (London), 68 (Apr. 1925), 6.

'Introduction' to Romer Wilson, *Martin Schüler* (New York: Alfred A. Knopf, 1928).

COMMENTS AND CRITICAL WORK ON MAY SINCLAIR

Selected Contemporary Comments (Book Reviews, Interviews)

'Affable Hawk' [Desmond MacCarthy], 'Books in General' [review of *Harriett Frean*], *New Statesman*, 18 (11 Feb. 1922), 532.

ANTHONY, KATHARINE, 'The Wickedness of Goodness' [review of *Harriett Frean*], *Nation*, 114 (5 Apr. 1922), 400–1.

'As to the Brontë Family' [review of *The Three Brontës*], *Literary Digest*, 45 (2 Nov. 1912), 811.

'The Author of "The Divine Fire" ', *Outlook*, 131 (25 Nov. 1905), 727–9.

AXON, WILLIAM E. A., 'The Three Brontës', *Bookman* (London), 42 (Aug. 1912), 212.

'Books on the War' [review of *Journal of Impressions in Belgium*], *Nation* (NY), 101 (11 Nov. 1915), 576.

'Briefer Mention' [review of *A Cure of Souls*], *Dial*, 76 (June 1924), 560.

BROCK, H. I., 'Fire and Smoke' [review of *Divine Fire* and Evelyn Underhill, *The Grey World*], *New York Times*, 11 Mar. 1905, section 2, 150.

—— '*The Helpmate* a Noteworthy Book', *New York Times Book Review* (24 Aug. 1907), 510.

BURRELL, ANGUS, 'The Case for Self-Sacrifice' [review of *The Rector of Wyck*], *Nation*, 121 (22 Jan. 1925), 121–2.

CECIL, ELEANOR, 'The Cant of Unconventionality' [review of *The Helpmate*], *National Review* (Nov. 1907); repr. *Living Age*, 255 (7 Dec. 1907), 579–89.

CHESTERTON, G. K., 'The Weird Sisters: GKC Reviews May Sinclair's Life of the Brontës', *New York Times Book Review*, 22 Sept. 1912, 515 [repr. from the London *Nation*].

COLBY, F. M., 'Miss Sinclair's *The Divine Fire*', *Bookman* (New York), 21 (Mar. 1905), 66–8.

COOPER, FREDERIC TABER, '*The Divine Fire*', *Bookman* (New York), 20 (Feb. 1905), 553.

—— 'Some Novels of the Month' [review of *The Three Sisters*], *Bookman* (New York), 40 (Jan. 1915), 552–7.

—— 'The Coward' [review of *The Romantic*], *Publishers' Weekly*, 98 (18 Sept. 1920), 657.

'*The Creators*', *Times Literary Supplement* (29 Sept. 1910), 350.

'*The Creators*', *Athenaeum*, no. 4328 (8 Oct. 1910), 415.

'*The Creators*', *Current Literature*, 49 (Dec. 1910), 690–1.

'Current Fiction' [review of *The Helpmate*], *Nation*, 85 (19 Sept. 1907), 259–60.

DEUTSCH, BABETTE, 'Freedom and the Grace of God' [review of *Mary Olivier*], *Dial*, 6 (15 Nov. 1919), 441–2.

'*The Divine Fire*', *Reader*, 5 (Apr. 1905), 622–3.

DUNBAR, OLIVIA HOWARD, 'Books Reviewed: Fact and Fiction' [review of *The Divine Fire*], *Critic*, 46 (Feb. 1905), 183.

ELIOT, T. S., 'London Letter: The Novel' [review of *Harriett Frean*], *Dial*, 73 (Sept. 1922), 329–31.

'Emily Brontë' [review of *The Three Brontës*], *Nation*, 96 (30 Jan. 1913), 104–6.

'*Far End*', *Booklist*, 23 (Nov. 1926), 84.

F.H. [FRANCIS HACKETT], 'The Rendezvous with Death' [review of *The Tree of Heaven*], *New Republic*, 14 (2 Feb. 1918), 28–9.

'Fiction for November' [review of *The Three Sisters*], *New York Times Book Review*, 19 (8 Nov. 1914), 485–6.

'Fiction: *The Helpmate*', *Academy*, 72 (21 Sept. 1907), 929.

'Fiction' [review of *The Three Sisters*], *Spectator*, 113 (12 Dec. 1914), 854.

FIELD, LOUISE MAUNSELL, '*The Life and Death of Harriett Frean*', *New York Times Book Review* (19 Feb. 1922), 15.

GILMAN, LAWRENCE, 'The Book of the Month. May Sinclair's New War Novel' [review of *The Tree of Heaven*], *North American Review*, 207 (Feb. 1918), 284–8.

HEAP, JANE, 'Eat 'em Alive!' [review of *Mary Olivier*], *Little Review*, 6 (Dec. 1919), 30–2.

'*The Helpmate*', *Athenaeum*, no. 4165 (24 Aug. 1907), 204.

'Heroines of the War' [review of *A Journal of Impressions in Belgium*], *Spectator*, 115 (9 Oct. 1915), 477.

HUNT, UNA, '*Harriett Frean*', *New Republic*, 21 (26 June 1922), 260–1.

IRVING, CARTER, 'Miss Sinclair's *Creators*: A Novel from which We Learn Much about the Imaginary Writers of Wonderful Books', *New York Times Book Review* (22 Oct. 1910), 584.

KELLY, FLORENCE FINCH, 'Eye Witnesses of the War' [review of *A Journal of Impressions in Belgium*], *Bookman* (New York), 42 (Dec. 1915), 462–6.

KRUTCH, J. W., 'From Wisdom's Mountain Height' [review of *A Cure of Souls*], *Nation*, 118 (7 May 1924), 535–6.

—— 'An Impoverished Art' [review of *History of Anthony Waring*], *Nation*, 125 (2 Nov. 1927), 481.

MANSFIELD, KATHERINE, 'The New Infancy' [review of *Mary Olivier*], *Athenaeum*, no. 4651 (20 June 1919), 494; repr. in *Novels and Novelists*, ed. John Middleton Murry (London: Constable, 1930), 40–3.

—— 'Ask No Questions' [review of *The Romantic*], *Athenaeum*, no. 4721 (22 Oct. 1920); repr. in *Novels and Novelists*, 274–9.

MARSH, EDWARD CLARK, 'Miss Sinclair's *The Tysons*', *Bookman* (New York), 23 (July 1906), 535–6.

'May Sinclair', in Dilly Tante (ed.), *Living Authors: A Book of Biographies* (New York: The H. W. Wilson Company, 1931), 373–4.

'More Novels' [review of *The Divine Fire*], *Nation*, 79 (24 Nov. 1904), 419–20.

MORTIMER, RAYMOND, 'Miss Sinclair Again' [review of *Harriett Frean*], *Dial*, 72 (May 1922), 531–4.

'Mother-Complex' [review of *Harriett Frean*], *Times Literary Supplement* (2 Feb. 1922), 73.

'New Books Reviewed' [review of *A Journal of Impressions in Belgium*], *North American Review*, 211 (Nov. 1915), 779–81.

'New Novels' [review of *Audrey Craven*], *Athenaeum*, no. 3639 (24 July 1897), 122.

'New Writers: Miss May Sinclair', *Bookman* (London), 14 (Sept. 1898), 151.

'Novels and Tales' [review of *The Helpmate*], *Outlook*, 87 (23 Nov. 1907), 621–2.

Obituary, *Cheltenham Ladies' College Magazine* (Autumn 1946), 36.

PAYNE, WILLIAM MORTON, 'Recent Fiction' [review of *The Divine Fire*], *Dial*, 38 (1 Jan. 1905), 18.

—— 'Recent Fiction' [review of *The Helpmate*], *Dial*, 43 (16 Oct. 1907), 250–1.

—— 'Recent Fiction' [review of *Kitty Tailleur*], *Dial*, 45 (1 Nov. 1908), 296.

—— 'Recent Fiction' [review of *The Creators*], *Dial*, 49 (16 Oct. 1910), 287–8.

'People in the Foreground', *Current Literature*, 38 (Mar. 1905), 223.

PHELPS, WILLIAM LYON, 'The Advance of the English Novel', *Bookman* (New York), 43 (May 1916), 306–7.

RASCOE, BURTON, 'Contemporary Reminiscences: Two Important English Visitors—May Sinclair and Bertrand Russell', *Arts and Decoration*, 21 (July 1924), 25–6.

'Recent Novels' [review of *Audrey Craven*], *Spectator*, 79 (28 Aug. 1897), 284.

'*The Romantic*', *Spectator* (London), 125 (13 Nov. 1920), 641.

ROYDE-SMITH, NAOMI, 'New Novels' [review of *The Allinghams*], *New Statesman*, 24 (23 Apr. 1927), 44.

RUSSELL, BERTRAND, 'Philosophic Idealism at Bay' [review of *The New Idealism*], *Nation and Athenaeum*, 31 (5 Aug. 1922), 625–6.

SCOTT, C. A. DAWSON, 'Miss May Sinclair', *Bookman* (London), 59 (Oct. 1920), 7–9.

—— 'Miss May Sinclair's New Novel' [review of *Harriett Frean*], *Bookman* (London), 61 (Mar. 1922), 265–6.

SEAMAN, OWEN, 'Our Booking Office' [on *The Divine Fire*], *Punch*, 128 (1 Feb. 1905), 90.

'The Season's Books' [review of *The Helpmate*], *Outlook*, 87 (23 Nov. 1907), 621–2.

SELIGMANN, HERBERT J., 'May Sinclair, Sentimentalist' [review of *The Tree of Heaven*], *Dial*, 64 (23 May 1918), 489–90.

'Shall a Genius Marry?' [review of *The Creators*], *Independent*, 69 (1910), 1156–7.

SIMONDS, W. E., 'The House of Brontë' [review of *The Three Brontës*], *Dial*, 53 (1 Nov. 1912), 329–30.

'Some New Novels: *The Divine Fire*', *Sewanee Review*, 13 (Jan. 1905), 119–20.

STEELL, WILLIS, 'Miss Sinclair Tells Why She Isn't a Poet', *Literary Digest International Book Review*, 2 (June 1924), 513, 559.

STRANGNELL, SYLVIA, 'Critical Review: A Study in Sublimations' [review of *Anne Severn*], *Psychoanalytic Review*, 10 (Apr. 1923), 209–13.

SWINNERTON, FRANK, '*The Tree of Heaven*', *Bookman* (London), 53 (Jan. 1918), 137.

'The Three Brontës', *Independent*, 73 (28 Nov. 1912), 1254–5.

'*The Three Sisters*', *Athenaeum*, no. 4539 (24 Oct. 1914), 424.

'*The Three Sisters*', *Saturday Review*, 99 (2 Jan. 1915), 18.

TITTLE, WALTER, 'Personal Portraits—May Sinclair', *Illustrated London News*, 166 (27 June 1925), 1280.

'Topics of the Week' [on *The Divine Fire*], *New York Times*, 18 Feb. 1905, sect. 2, 97.

TOWNSEND, R. D., 'The Book Table: The Recent Fiction' [review of *Anne Severn*], *Outlook*, 133 (24 Jan. 1923), 186.

'*The Tree of Heaven*', *New York Times*, 23 (27 Jan. 1918), 29.

'The Tumult of the Soul' [review of *Mary Olivier*], *Nation* (NY), 109 (13 Sept. 1919), 379–80.

UNDERHILL, EVELYN, ' "The Cant of Unconventionality": A Rejoinder to Lady Robert Cecil' [on *The Helpmate*], *Living Age*, 256 (8 Feb. 1908), 323–9.

WALKER, RYAN, 'May Sinclair Talks of Everything Except Herself', *New York Times Book Review*, 18 May 1924, 2.

WEST, REBECCA, 'Miss Sinclair's Genius' [review of *A Journal of Impressions in Belgium*], *Daily News* (24 Aug. 1915); repr. in *The Young Rebecca: Writings of Rebecca West 1911–1917*, ed. Jane Marcus (London: Macmillan, 1982), 304–7.

—— 'Notes on Novels' [review of *Anne Severn*], *New Statesman*, 20 (2 Dec. 1922), 270, 272.

WOODBRIDGE, BENJAMIN M., 'Belgium's Agony' [review of *A Journal of Impressions in Belgium*], *Dial*, 60 (20 Jan. 1916), 72–4.

Critical and Biographical Work on May Sinclair

BOLL, THEOPHILUS E. M., 'On the May Sinclair Collection', *Library Chronicle of the University of Pennsylvania*, 27 (Winter 1961), 1–15.

—— 'May Sinclair and the Medico-Psychological Clinic of London', *Proceedings of the American Philosophical Society*, 106 (Aug. 1962), 310–26.

—— 'The Mystery of Charlotte Mew and May Sinclair: An Inquiry', *Bulletin of the New York Public Library*, 74 (Sept. 1970), 445–53.

—— 'May Sinclair: A Check List', *Bulletin of the New York Public Library*, 74 (Sept. 1970), 454–67.

—— *Miss May Sinclair: Novelist: A Biographical and Critical Introduction* (Cranbury, NJ: Associated University Presses, 1973).

DAVIDOW, MARY C., 'The Charlotte Mew–May Sinclair Relationship: A Reply', *Bulletin of the New York Public Library*, 75 (1971), 295–300.

GILLESPIE, DIANE F., 'May Sinclair and the Stream of Consciousness: Metaphors and Metaphysics', *English Literature in Transition 1880–1920*, 21 (1978), 134–42.

—— ' "The Muddle of the Middle": May Sinclair on Women', *Tulsa Studies in Women's Literature*, 4 (Fall 1985), 235–51.

—— 'May Sinclair (1863–1946)', in Scott (ed.), *Gender of Modernism*, 436–42.

HARRIS, JANICE H., 'Challenging the Script of the Heterosexual Couple: Three Marriage Novels by May Sinclair', *Papers on Language and Literature*, 29 (Fall 1993), 436–58.

KAPLAN, SYDNEY JANET, ' "Featureless Freedom" or Ironic Submission: Dorothy Richardson and May Sinclair', *College English*, 32 (1971), 914–17.

—— *Feminine Consciousness in the Modern British Novel* (Chicago: University of Illinois Press, 1975) [chapter on May Sinclair].

KEMP, SANDRA, ' "But how describe a world seen without a self?": Feminism, Fiction and Modernism' [on 'Where Their Fire Is Not Quenched'], *Critical Quarterly*, 32 (Spring 1990), 99–118.

KINNAMON, REBECCAH, 'May Sinclair's Fiction of the Supernatural', Ph.D. thesis (Duke University, 1974).

MUMFORD, LAURA STEMPEL, 'May Sinclair's *The Tree of Heaven*: The Vortex of Feminism, the Community of War', in Cooper, Munich, and Squier (eds.), *Arms and the Woman*, 168–83.

NEFF, REBECCAH KINNAMON, ' "New Mysticism" in the Writings of May Sinclair and T. S. Eliot', *Twentieth-Century Literature*, 26 (1980), 82–108.

—— 'May Sinclair's *Uncanny Stories* as Metaphysical Quest', *English Literature in Transition 1880–1920*, 26 (1983), 187–91.

PADMANABHAN, P. S., 'The Irritant and the Pearl: "Jones's Karma" and the Poetry and Drama of T. S. Eliot', *Canadian Review of Comparative Literature*, 9 (June 1982), 188–99.

PHILLIPS, TERRY, 'Battling with the Angel: May Sinclair's Powerful Mothers', in Sarah Sceats and Gail Cunningham (eds.), *Image and Power: Women in Fiction in the Twentieth Century* (London: Longman, 1996), 128–38.

PRATT, ANNIS, 'Women and Nature in Modern Fiction', *Contemporary Literature*, 13 (1972), 476–90.

RADFORD, JEAN, 'Introduction' to Sinclair, *Mary Olivier: A Life* (1919; repr. London: Virago, 1980).

RADFORD, JEAN, 'Introduction' to Sinclair, *Life and Death of Harriett Frean* (1922; repr. London: Virago, 1980).

—— 'Introduction' to Sinclair, *The Three Sisters* (1914; repr. London: Virago, 1982).

RAITT, SUZANNE, 'Charlotte Mew and May Sinclair: A Love-Song', *Critical Quarterly*, 37 (1995), 3–17.

—— ' "Contagious Ecstasy": May Sinclair's War Journals', in Raitt and Tate (eds.), *Women's Fiction and the Great War*, 65–84.

ROBB, KENNETH A., 'May Sinclair: An Annotated Bibliography of Writings about Her', *English Literature in Transition 1880–1920*, 16 (1973), 177–231.

—— 'May Sinclair', *English Literature in Transition 1880–1920*, 18 (1975), 72–3.

STARK, SUSANNE, 'Overcoming Butlerian Obstacles: May Sinclair and the Problem of Biological Determinism', *Women's Studies*, 21 (1992), 265–83.

TAYLOR, CORRINE YVONNE, 'A Study of May Sinclair—Woman and Writer, 1863–1946—with an Annotated Bibliography', Ph.D. thesis (Washington State University, 1969).

ZEGGER, HRISEY D., *May Sinclair* (Boston: Twayne, 1976).

GENERAL

ACKROYD, PETER, *T. S. Eliot: A Life* (New York: Simon and Schuster, 1984).

ALDINGTON, RICHARD, 'The Poetry of Amy Lowell', *Egoist* (1 July 1915), 109–10.

—— *Images of War: A Book of Poems* (London: Beaumont, 1919).

—— *Richard Aldington: An Autobiography in Letters*, ed. Norman T. Gates (University Park, Pa.: Pennsylvania State University Press, 1992).

—— and H. D., *Richard Aldington and H.D.: The Later Years in Letters*, ed. Caroline Zilboorg (Manchester: Manchester University Press, 1995).

ALEXANDER, SALLY, 'Psychoanalysis in Britain in the Early Twentieth Century: An Introductory Note', *History Workshop Journal*, no. 45 (Spring 1998), 135–43.

ARDIS, ANN, *New Women, New Novels: Feminism and Early Modernism* (New Brunswick, NJ: Rutgers University Press, 1990).

ARMSTRONG, ISOBEL, *Victorian Poetry: Poetry, Poetics, Politics* (London: Routledge, 1993).

BATTERSBY, CHRISTINE, *Gender and Genius: Towards a Feminine Aesthetics* (Bloomington, Ind.: Indiana University Press, 1989).

BAUDELAIRE, CHARLES, *The Painter of Modern Life and Other Essays*, trans. and ed. Jonathan Mayne (London: Phaidon, 1964).

BEALE, DOROTHEA, *On the Education of Girls* (1865; repr. London: Bell and Dalby, 1866).

—— *A Few Words to Those Who Are Leaving* (London: George Bell, 1881).

—— *Address to Church Sunday School Teachers* (London: Society for the Propagation of Christian Knowledge, 1888).

—— *Address to Parents* (London: George Bell, 1888).

—— 'Introduction', and 'Philosophy and Religion', in ead., Lucy H. M. Soulsby, and Jane Frances Dove, *Work and Play in Girls' Schools* (New York and Bombay: Longman, Green and Co., 1898).

—— *Literary Studies of Poems, New and Old* (London: George Bell, 1902).

—— *History of the Cheltenham Ladies' College 1853–1904* (Cheltenham: Looker-On Printing Works, 1904).

—— *Addresses to Teachers* (London: Longman, Green and Co., 1909).

BEER, GILLIAN, 'The Dissidence of Vernon Lee: *Satan the Waster* and the Will to Believe', in Raitt and Tate (eds.), *Women's Fiction and the Great War*, 107–31.

BELFORD, BARBARA, *Violet: The Story of the Irrepressible Violet Hunt and her Circle of Lovers and Friends—Ford Madox Ford, H. G. Wells, Somerset Maugham, and Henry James* (New York: Simon and Schuster, 1990).

BENJAMIN, ANDREW (ed.), *The Problems of Modernity: Adorno and Benjamin* (London: Routledge, 1989).

BENJAMIN, WALTER, 'The Work of Art in the Age of Mechanical Reproduction', 1936, in *Illuminations: Essays and Reflections*, 1955, rev. edn. trans. Harry Zohn, ed. Hannah Arendt (New York: Schocken, 1969).

BENNETT, ARNOLD, *The Journal of Arnold Bennett* (Garden City, NY: Doubleday, 1932).

BONHAM-CARTER, VICTOR, *Authors by Profession*, 2 vols. (Los Altos, Calif.: William Kaufmann, 1978).

BOWLBY, RACHEL, *Just Looking: Consumer Culture in Dreiser, Gissing and Zola* (New York and London: Methuen, 1985).

BREUER, JOSEF, and FREUD, SIGMUND, *Studies on Hysteria*, in *The Standard Edition of the Complete Psychological Works of Sigmund Freud*, trans. and ed. James Strachey (London: Hogarth, 1966–74), ii.

BREWSTER, DOROTHY, and BURRELL, ANGUS, *Modern Fiction* (New York: Columbia, 1934).

BROME, VINCENT, *Ernest Jones: Freud's Alter Ego* (New York: Norton, 1983).

BRONTË, CHARLOTTE, 'Biographical Notice of Ellis and Acton Bell', written for the 2nd edn. of *Wuthering Heights* and *Agnes Grey*, 1850; repr. in Emily Brontë, *Wuthering Heights*, ed. William M. Sale, Jr. and Richard R. Dunn (3rd edn. New York: Norton, 1990).

[BRONTË sisters], *The Life and Works of Charlotte Brontë and her Sisters*, ed. Mrs Humphrey Ward (London: Smith, Elder & Co., 1906–10).

BROWN, WILLIAM, *The Essentials of Mental Measurement* (Cambridge: Cambridge University Press, 1911).

BRYHER [WINIFRED ELLERMAN], *The Heart to Artemis* (London: Collins, 1963).

BUTLER, SAMUEL, *Life and Habit* (London: Trübner and Co., 1878).

CAIRD, EDWARD, 'The Problem of Philosophy at the Present Time', Introductory Address to the Philosophical Society of the University of Edinburgh, 1881, in *Essays on Literature and Philosophy*, 2 vols. (Glasgow: James Maclehose and Sons, 1892).

CALINESCU, MATEI, *Faces of Modernity: Avant Garde, Decadence, Kitsch* (Bloomington, Ind.: Indiana University Press, 1977).

CARDINAL, MARIE, *Les Mots pour le dire* (Paris: Grasset, 1975).

CARRIER, JAMES G., *Gifts and Commodities: Exchange and Western Capitalism since 1700* (London: Routledge, 1995).

COFFMAN, STANLEY K., *Imagism: A Chapter for the History of Modern Poetry* (Norman, Okla.: University of Oklahoma Press, 1951).

CONNOR, STEVEN, *Theory and Cultural Value* (Oxford: Blackwell, 1992).

COOPER, HELEN M., MUNICH, ADRIENNE AUSLANDER, and SQUIER, SUSAN MERRILL (eds.), *Arms and the Woman: War, Gender and Literary Representation* (Chapel Hill, NC: University of North Carolina Press, 1989).

CORELLI, MARIE, *The Murder of Delicia* (Philadelphia: J. B. Lippincott, 1896).

[CORNWALLIS, CAROLINE FRANCES], *A Brief View of Greek Philosophy up to the Age of Pericles* (London: William Pickering, 1844), in the series *Small Books on Great Subjects*.

—— *Selections from the Letters of Caroline Frances Cornwallis* (London: Trübner and Co., 1864).

COURTNEY, JANET E., *Recollected in Tranquillity* (London: William Heinemann, 1926).

—— *The Women of My Time* (London: Lovat Dickson, 1934).

COUSTILLAS, PIERRE, and PARTRIDGE, COLIN (eds.), *Gissing: The Critical Heritage* (London: Routledge, 1972).

CRUMP, R. W., *Charlotte and Emily Brontë, 1846–1915: A Reference Guide* (Boston: G. K. Hall, 1982).

CUNNINGHAM, GAIL, *The New Woman and the Victorian Novel* (London: Macmillan, 1978).

DAVIS, DOUGLAS A., 'Freud, Jung and Psychoanalysis', in Young-Eisendrath and Dawson (eds.), *Cambridge Companion to Jung*, 35–51.

DEANE, ANTHONY C., *Holiday Verses* (London: Henry and Co., 1894).

—— *Time Remembered* (London: Faber and Faber, 1945).

DÉJERINE, J., and GAUCKLER, E., *The Psychoneuroses and their Treatment by Psychotherapy*, trans. Smith Ely Jelliffe (1913; 2nd edn. Philadelphia and London: J. B. Lippincott, 1915).

DE KOVEN, MARIANNE, *Rich and Strange: Gender, History, Modernism* (Princeton: Princeton University Press, 1991).

DE T'SERCLAES, *Flanders and Other Fields: Memoirs of the Baroness de T'Serclaes, M.M.* (London: Harrap, 1964).

[—— and CHISHOLM, MAIRI], *The Cellar-House of Pervyse: A Tale of Uncommon Things from the Journals and Letters of the Baroness de T'Serclaes and Mairi Chisholm*, ed. G. E. Mitton (London: A. and C. Black, 1916).

DETTMAR, KEVIN J. H., and WATTS, STEPHEN (eds.), *Marketing Modernisms: Self-Promotion, Canonization, Rereading* (Ann Arbor: University of Michigan Press, 1996).

DIXON, ELLA HEPWORTH, *'As I Knew Them': Sketches of People I Have Met on the Way* (London: Hutchinson, 1930).

DOUGLAS, CLAIRE, 'The Historical Context of Analytical Psychology', in Young-Eisendrath and Dawson (eds.), *Cambridge Companion to Jung*, 17–34.

DOWLING, LINDA, 'The Decadent and the New Woman in the 1890s', *Nineteenth-Century Fiction*, 33 (1979), 434–53.

DOYLE, CHARLES, *Richard Aldington: A Biography* (Carbondale and Edwardsville, Ill.; Southern Illinois University Press, 1989).

DUBOIS, PAUL, *The Psychic Treatment of Nervous Disorders: The Psychoneuroses and their Moral Treatment*, trans. and ed. Smith Ely Jelliffe and William A. White (1905; 6th edn. New York: Funk and Wagnalls, 1909).

—— *The Psychological Origin of Mental Disorders* (New York: Funk and Wagnalls, 1913).

ELIOT, T. S., *Collected Poems 1909–1962* (London: Faber and Faber, 1974).

ELLENBERGER, HENRI F., *The Discovery of the Unconscious: The History and Evolution of Dynamic Psychiatry* (New York: Basic Books, 1970).

ELLMANN, RICHARD, *Ulysses on the Liffey* (1972; corr. edn. London: Faber and Faber, 1984).

ELSHTAIN, JEAN BETHKE, *Women and War* (Brighton: Harvester, 1987).

FAIRBROTHER, W. H., *The Philosophy of Thomas Hill Green* (London: Methuen, 1896).

FELSKI, RITA, *The Gender of Modernity* (Cambridge, Mass.: Harvard University Press, 1995).

FINE, REUBEN, *The History of Psychoanalysis* (1979; rev. edn. Northvale, NJ: Jason Aronson, 1990).

FITZGERALD, PENELOPE, *Charlotte Mew and her Friends* (London: Collins, 1984).

FLINT, F. S., 'The History of Imagism', *Egoist* (1 May 1915), 70–1.

FLINT, KATE, *The Woman Reader, 1837–1914* (Oxford: Clarendon, 1993).

FLINT, ROBERT, *Theism*, Baird Lectures for 1877 (7th edn., Edinburgh and London: Blackwood, 1889).

FORD, FORD MADOX, *Thus to Revisit: Some Reminiscences* (New York: Dutton, 1921).
—— *Return to Yesterday* (New York: Liveright, 1932).
—— *Letters of Ford Madox Ford*, ed. Richard M. Ludwig (Princeton: Princeton University Press, 1965).
FREUD, SIGMUND, *The Interpretation of Dreams*, 1899, in *The Standard Edition of the Complete Psychological Works of Sigmund Freud*, trans. and ed. James Strachey (London: Hogarth, 1966–74), iv–v.
—— 'Fragment of an Analysis of a Case of Hysteria ("Dora")', 1905, in *Standard Edition*, vii. 3–112.
—— ' "Civilized" Sexual Morality and Modern Nervous Illness', 1908, in *Standard Edition*, ix. 179–204.
—— ' "Wild" Psychoanalysis', 1910, in *Standard Edition*, xi. 221–7.
—— 'On Narcissism: An Introduction', 1914, in *Standard Edition*, xiv. 69–102.
—— 'On Transformations of Instinct as Exemplified in Anal Eroticism', 1917, in *Standard Edition*, xvii. 127–33.
—— 'From the History of an Infantile Neurosis', 1918, in *Standard Edition*, xvii. 3–122.
—— 'Group Psychology and the Analysis of the Ego', 1921, in *Standard Edition*, xviii. 67–143.
—— *The Ego and the Id*, 1923, in *Standard Edition*, xix. 3–66.
—— 'Some Psychical Consequences of the Anatomical Distinction between the Sexes', 1925, in *Standard Edition*, xix. 243–58.
—— 'Female Sexuality', 1931, in *On Sexuality*, 1931, in *Standard Edition*, xxi. 223–43.
—— 'Femininity', 1933, in *New Introductory Lectures on Psychoanalysis*, in *Standard Edition*, xxii. 112–35.
[—— and JUNG, C. G.], *The Freud/Jung Letters: The Correspondence between Sigmund Freud and Carl Jung*, ed. W. McGuire, trans. Ralph Manheim and R. F. C. Hall (Princeton: Princeton University Press, 1974).
FRIEDMAN, MELVIN, *Stream of Consciousness: A Study in Literary Method* (New Haven: Yale University Press, 1955).
FRISBY, DAVID, *Fragments of Modernity: Theories of Modernity in the Work of Simmel, Kracauer and Benjamin* (Cambridge, Mass.: MIT Press, 1986).
FUSS, DIANA, *Identification Papers* (London: Routledge, 1995).
FUSSELL, PAUL, *The Great War and Modern Memory* (Oxford: Oxford University Press, 1975).
GAGE, JOHN T., *In the Arresting Eye: The Rhetoric of Imagism* (Baton Rouge, La.: Louisiana State University Press, 1981).
GALTON, FRANCIS, *Hereditary Genius: An Inquiry Into Its Laws and Consequences* (1869; 2nd edn. 1892; repr. London: Macmillan, 1914).

GATES, HENRY LOUIS Jr. (ed.), *'Race', Writing, and Difference* (Chicago: University of Chicago Press, 1986).

GAUDIER-BRZESKA, HENRI, 'Vortex', *Blast*, 1 (20 June 1914), 156.

GAY, PETER, *Freud: A Life for Our Time* (New York: Norton, 1988).

GIBBS, PHILIP, *The Soul of the War* (London: Heinemann, 1915).

—— *Realities of War* (London: Heinemann, 1920).

GILBERT, SANDRA, and GUBAR, SUSAN, *No Man's Land: The Place of the Woman Writer in the Twentieth Century*, ii. *Sexchanges* (New Haven: Yale University Press, 1989).

GISSING, GEORGE, *New Grub Street* (1891; New York: Modern Library Edition, 1926).

—— *The Unclassed* (1896; repr. from 1st US edn. New York: AMS Press, 1968).

—— *The Crown of Life* (London: Methuen, 1899).

[—— and WELLS, H.G.], *George Gissing and H. G. Wells: Their Friendship and Correspondence*, ed. Royal A. Gettmann (Urbana, Ill.: University of Illinois Press, 1961).

[—— and FLEURY, GABRIELLE], *The Letters of George Gissing to Gabrielle Fleury*, ed. Pierre Coustillas (New York: New York Public Library, 1964).

GITTER, ELISABETH G., 'The Power of Women's Hair in the Victorian Imagination', *PMLA* 99 (Oct. 1984), 936–54.

GOETHE, J. W. VON, *The Autobiography of Johann Wolfgang von Goethe*, 2 vols., trans. John Oxenford (Chicago and London: University of Chicago Press, 1974).

GOLDRING, DOUGLAS, *The Last Pre-Raphaelite: A Record of the Life and Writings of Ford Madox Ford* (London: Macdonald, 1948).

GRAND, SARAH, *The Heavenly Twins* (1893; repr. Ann Arbor: University of Michigan Press, 1992).

GRANT, MICHAEL (ed.), *T. S. Eliot: The Critical Heritage*, i (London: Routledge, 1982).

GRAVES, ROBERT, *Goodbye to All That* (1929; repr. New York: Anchor, 1985).

GREEN, T. H., *Prolegomena to Ethics*, ed. A. C. Bradley (Oxford: Clarendon Press, 1883).

—— 'Essay on Christian Dogma' and 'The Witness of God', in *Works of Thomas Hill Green*, iii, ed. R. L. Nettleship (London: Longman, Green & Co., Press, 1888), 161–85, 230–52.

GREENE, DANA, *Evelyn Underhill: Artist of the Infinite Life* (1990; UK edn. London: Darton, Longman and Todd, 1991).

GRIMM, HERMAN, *The Life and Times of Goethe*, trans. Sarah Holland Adams (Boston: Little, Brown and Co., 1880).

GUEST, BARBARA, *Herself Defined: The Poet H.D. and her World* (New York: Doubleday, 1984).

GURSTEIN, ROCHELLE, *The Repeal of Reticence: A History of America's Cultural and*

Legal Struggles over Free Speech, Obscentiy, Sexual Liberation, and Modern Art (New York: Hill and Wang, 1996).

H.D. [HILDA DOOLITTLE], '*The Farmer's Bride*', *Egoist* (1 Sept. 1916), 135.

—— *End to Torment* (New York: New Directions, 1979).

HABERMAS, JÜRGEN, *The Philosophical Discourse of Modernity*, trans. Frederick G. Lawrence (1985; trans. Cambridge, Mass.: MIT Press, 1987).

HAECKEL, ERNST, *The History of Creation: Or the Development of the Earth and its Inhabitants by the Action of Natural Causes: A Popular Exposition of the Doctrine of Evolution in General, and of that of Darwin, Goethe, and Lamarck in Particular*, 2 vols (1868; 4th edn., trans. E. Ray Lankester, London: Henry S. King, 1876).

HAINES, HELEN E., *What's in a Novel* (New York: Columbia University Press, 1942).

HAMILTON, CICELY, 'Man', *English Review*, 11 (Apr. 1912), 115–25.

—— *William: An Englishman* (London: Skeffington, 1919).

HANLEY, LYNNE, *Writing War: Fiction, Gender and Memory* (Amherst, Mass.: University of Massachusetts Press, 1991).

HANSCOMBE, GILLIAN, and SMYERS, VIRGINIA L., *Writing for their Lives: The Modernist Women 1910–1940* (London: Women's Press, 1987).

HARDWICK, JOAN, *An Immodest Violet: The Life of Violet Hunt* (London: André Deutsch, 1990).

[HARDY, EMMA and FLORENCE], *Letters of Emma and Florence Hardy*, ed. Michael Millgate (Oxford: Clarendon Press, 1996).

[HARDY, THOMAS], *The Collected Letters of Thomas Hardy*, ed. Richard Little Purdy and Michael Millgate, 7 vols. (Oxford: Clarendon Press, 1978–88).

HARMER, J. B., *Victory in Limbo: Imagism 1908–1917* (London: Secker and Warburg, 1975).

HART, BERNARD, 'Freud's Conception of Hysteria', *Brain*, 33 (1911), 338–66.

—— *The Psychology of Insanity* (Cambridge: Cambridge Manuals of Science and Literature, 1912).

HASTINGS, JAMES (ed.), *Encyclopaedia of Religion and Ethics* (Edinburgh: T. T. Clark, 1921), xii.

HENRY, MICHEL, *The Genealogy of Psychoanalysis*, trans. Douglas Brick (1985; Stanford, Calif.: Stanford University Press, 1993).

HEPBURN, JAMES, *The Author's Empty Purse and the Rise of the Literary Agent* (Oxford: Oxford University Press, 1968).

HIGONNET, MARGARET, JENSON, JANE, MICHEL, SONYA, and WEITZ, MARGARET COLLINS (eds.), *Behind the Lines: Gender and the Two World Wars* (New Haven: Yale University Press, 1987).

HINSHELWOOD, R. D., 'Psychoanalysis in Britain: Points of Cultural Access, 1893–1918', *International Journal of Psycho-Analysis*, 76 (Feb. 1995), 135–51.

HOGARTH, JANET, 'Literary Degenerates', *Fortnightly Review*, 63 (1895), 586–92.

HOLT, HENRY, 'The Commercialization of Literature: A Summing Up', *Putnam's Monthly* (Feb. 1907), 563–75.

—— *Garrulities of an Octogenarian Editor, with Other Essays Somewhat Biographical and Autobiographical* (Boston: Houghton Mifflin, 1923).

HOLTON, SANDRA STANLEY, *Suffrage Days: Stories from the Women's Suffrage Movement* (London: Routledge, 1996).

HOMER, *The Odyssey*, i, trans. A. T. Murray, Loeb Classical Library, no. 104 (Cambridge, Mass.: Harvard University Press, 1919).

HUGHES, GLENN, *Imagism and the Imagists: A Study in Modern Poetry* (Stanford, Calif.: Stanford University Press, 1931).

HULME, T. E., 'Modern Art and its Philosophy', 1913, in *Speculations: Essays on Humanism and the Philosophy of Art* (New York, Harcourt Brace, 1924).

HUME, LESLIE PARKER, *The National Union of Women's Suffrage Societies 1897–1914* (London: Garland, 1982).

HUNT, VIOLET, *Tales of the Uneasy* (London: Heinemann, 1911).

—— *The Flurried Years* (London: Hurst and Blackett, 1926).

HUNTER, JEFFERSON, *Edwardian Fiction* (Cambridge, Mass.: Harvard University Press, 1982).

HUYSSEN, ANDREAS, *After the Great Divide: Modernism, Mass Culture, Postmodernism* (Bloomington, Ind.: Indiana University Press, 1986).

HYDE, LEWIS, *The Gift: Imagination and the Erotic Life of Property* (New York: Random House, 1979).

HYNES, SAMUEL, *A War Imagined: The First World War and English Culture* (London: Bodley Head, 1990).

INGRAM, ANGELA, 'Un/Reproductions: Estates of Banishment in English Fiction after the Great War', in Mary Lynn Broe and Angela Ingram (eds.), *Women's Writing in Exile* (Chapel Hill, NC: University of North Carolina Press, 1989), 325–48.

ISAAK, JO ANNA, *The Ruin of Representation in Modernist Art and Texts* (Ann Arbor: UMI Research Press, 1986).

JAMES, WILLIAM, *The Principles of Psychology*, 2 vols. (London: Macmillan, 1890).

JEFFREYS, SHEILA, *The Spinster and her Enemies: Feminism and Sexuality 1880–1930* (London: Pandora, 1985).

JOHNSON, R. BRIMLEY, *Some Contemporary Novelists (Women)* (London: Leonard Parsons, 1920).

JONES, ERNEST, 'Reminiscent Notes on the Early History of Psycho-Analysis in English-Speaking Countries', *International Journal of Psycho-Analysis*, 26 (1945), 8–10.

JONES, ERNEST, *Free Associations: Memories of a Psycho-Analyst* (New York: Basic Books, 1959).

JONES, PETER (ed.), *Imagist Poetry* (Harmondsworth: Penguin, 1972).

JUNG, C. G., *Collected Papers on Analytical Psychology*, ed. Constance E. Long (London: Baillière, Tindall and Cox, 1916).

—— *Psychology of the Unconscious: A Study of the Transformations and Symbolisms of the Libido: A Contribution to the History of the Evolution of Thought*, trans. Beatrice M. Hinkle, 1916 (repr. as *Supplementary Volume B* of *Collected Works of Jung*, Princeton: Princeton University Press, 1991).

—— 'On the Psychology of the Unconscious', 1917, rev. 1926 and 1943, from *Two Essays, Collected Works*, vii, paragraphs 56–92, repr. in Storr (ed.), *Essential Jung*.

—— *Psychology and the Occult* (1977; repr. London: Ark, 1987).

—— *The Essential Jung*, ed. Anthony Storr (Princeton: Princeton University Press, 1983).

KAMM, JOSEPHINE, *How Different from Us: A Biography of Miss Buss and Miss Beale* (London: Bodley Head, 1958).

KANT, IMMANUEL, *Critique of Pure Reason*, trans. and ed. Paul Guyer and Allen W. Wood (Cambridge: Cambridge University Press, 1998).

[——] *Kant: Selections*, ed. Lewis White Beek (New York: Macmillan, 1988).

KEMP, SANDRA, MITCHELL, CHARLOTTE, and TROTTER, DAVID, *Edwardian Fiction: An Oxford Companion* (Oxford: Oxford University Press, 1997).

KLEIN, HOLGER (ed.), *The First World War in Fiction: A Collection of Critical Essays* (London: Macmillan, 1976).

KLEIN, MELANIE, 'Notes on Some Schizoid Mechanisms', 1946, in *The Selected Melanie Klein*, ed. Juliet Mitchell (Harmondsworth: Penguin, 1986), 175–200.

KOHON, GREGORY, 'Notes on the History of the Psychoanalytic Movement in Great Britain', in id. (ed.), *The British School of Psychoanalysis: The Independent Tradition* (New Haven: Yale University Press, 1986), 24–50.

KUMAR, SHIV K., *Bergson and the Stream of Consciousness Novel* (London and Glasgow: Blackie, 1962).

LACAN, JACQUES, 'God and the *Jouissance* of ~~The~~ Woman', 1972–3, in Juliet Mitchell and Jacqueline Rose (eds.), *Feminine Sexuality: Jacques Lacan and the Ecole Freudienne*, trans. Jacqueline Rose (London: Macmillan, 1982), 137–48.

LAPLANCHE, J., and PONTALIS, J.-B., *The Language of Psycho-Analysis* (1967; trans. Donald Nicholson-Smith, New York: Norton, 1973).

[LAWRENCE, D. H.], *The Letters of D. H. Lawrence*, ed. Aldous Huxley (New York: Heinemann, 1932).

LE BON, GUSTAVE, *Psychologie des Foules*, 1895; repr. as *The Crowd*, ed. Robert A. Nye (New Brunswick, NJ: Transaction, 1995).

LEE, HERMIONE, *Virginia Woolf* (London: Chatto and Windus, 1996).

LEIGHTON, ANGELA, *Victorian Women Poets: Writing against the Heart* (Harvester Wheatsheaf: Hemel Hempstead, 1992).

LEWES, GEORGE HENRY, *The Life and Works of Goethe*, 2 vols. (London: Daniel Nutt, 1855).

—— *The Story of Goethe's Life* (London: Smith, Elder and Co., 1873).

LOWNDES, MARIE BELLOC, *A Passing World* (London: Macmillan, 1948).

LYON, JANET, 'Militant Discourse, Strange Bedfellows: Suffagettes and Vorticists before the War', *differences*, 4 (Summer 1992), 100–33.

MACAULAY, ROSE, *Non-Combatants and Others* (London: Hodder and Stoughton, 1916).

McDOUGALL, GRACE, *A Nurse at the War: Nursing Adventures in Belgium and France* (New York: McBride, 1917).

McDOUGALL, WILLIAM, *Physiological Psychology* (London: Dent, 1905).

—— *Body and Mind: A History and a Defense of Animism* (London: Methuen, 1911).

—— *The Group Mind, a sketch of the principles of collective psychology with some attempt to apply them to the interpretation of national life and character* (London: G. P. Putnam and Sons, 1920).

—— *An Introduction to Social Psychology* (1908; 15th edn. London: Methuen, 1920).

—— *Outline of Abnormal Psychology* (New York: Charles Scribner, 1926).

MACKAY, ANGUS, *The Brontës: Fact and Fiction* (London: Dodd Mead, 1897).

MALHAM-DEMBLEBY, J., *The Key to the Brontë Works: The Key to Charlotte Brontë's 'Wuthering Heights', 'Jane Eyre', and her Other Works* (London: Walter Scott Publishing Co., 1911).

MARTINEAU, JAMES, *Endeavours after the Christian Life: A Volume of Discourses*, 2 vols. (London: J. Green, 1843).

MARX, KARL, *Capital* (1867; trans. from 3rd German edn. Samuel Moore and Edward Aveling, ed. Friedrich Engels, rev. Marie Sachey and Herbert Lamm, in *Great Books of the Western World*, 50, Chicago, University of Chicago Press, 1952).

MATUS, JILL L., *Unstable Bodies: Victorian Representations of Sexuality and Maternity* (Manchester: Manchester University Press, 1995).

MAUDSLEY, HENRY, *The Physiology and Pathology of the Mind* (London: Macmillan, 1867).

—— *Body and Mind: An Inquiry into their Connection and Mutual Influence, Specially in Reference to Mental Disorders* (London: Macmillan, 1870).

—— *Responsibility in Mental Disease* (London: Henry S. King, 1874).

MEW, CHARLOTTE, *The Farmer's Bride* (London: Poetry Bookshop, 1916; 2nd edn. 1921).

MEW, CHARLOTTE, *Collected Poems of Charlotte Mew*, ed. Alida Monro (London: Duckworth, 1953).

—— *Charlotte Mew: Collected Poems and Prose*, ed. Val Warner (London: Virago, 1982).

MILLER, JANE ELDRIDGE, *Rebel Women: Feminism, Modernism and the Edwardian Novel* (London: Virago, 1994).

MILTON, JOHN, 'Methought I saw my late espousèd saint', in *Complete Shorter Poems*, ed. John Carey (London: Longman, 1968), 413–14.

—— *Paradise Lost*, Book II (1667), ed. Alastair Fowler (London: Longman, 1968).

MITCHELL, DAVID, *Women on the Warpath: The Story of the Women of the First World War* (London: Jonathan Cape, 1966).

MONRO, ALIDA, 'Charlotte Mew—A Memoir', in Mew, *Collected Poems*, ed. Monro, pp. vii–xx.

MONRO, HAROLD, 'The Imagists Discussed', *Egoist* (1 May 1915), 77–80.

MONROE, HARRIET, *A Poet's Life: Seventy Years in a Changing World* (New York: Macmillan, 1938).

MURRAY, JESSIE, 'Introduction', in Marie Carmichael Stopes, *Married Love: A New Contribution to the Solution of Sex Difficulties* (London: Putnam, 1918).

—— and BRAILSFORD, HENRY NOEL, *The Treatment of Women's Deputations by the Police. Copy of Evidence collected by Dr Jessie Murray and Mr H. N. Brailsford, and forwarded to the Home Office by the Conciliation Committee for Women's Suffrage* (London: Woman's Press, 1911).

NORMAN, CHARLES, *The Case of Ezra Pound* (New York: Funk and Wagnalls, 1968).

OLIPHANT, MARGARET, 'The Sisters Brontë', in ead. et al., *Women Novelists of Queen Victoria's Reign: A Book of Appreciations* (London: Hurst and Blackett, 1897).

OUDITT, SHARON, *Fighting Forces, Writing Women: Identity and Ideology in the First World War* (London: Routledge, 1994).

PANKHURST, CHRISTABEL, *Unshackled: The Story of How We Won the Vote* (1959; repr. London: Century Hutchinson, 1987).

PANKHURST, E. SYLVIA, *The Suffragette: The History of the Women's Militant Suffrage Movement 1905–1910* (1911; repr. New York: Sturgis, 1912).

PICK, DANIEL, *Faces of Degeneration: A European Disorder, c.1848–c.1918* (Cambridge: Cambridge University Press, 1989).

POLLITT, KATHA, 'Masterpiece Theatre: Subject to Debate', *Nation*, 267 (24/31 Aug. 1998), 9.

POOLE, ADRIAN, *Gissing in Context* (Totowa, NJ: Rowman and Littlefield, 1975).

POUND, EZRA, 'Drunken Helots and Mr. Eliot', *Egoist*, 4 (June 1917), 72–4; repr. in Grant (ed.), *T. S. Eliot: The Critical Heritage*, i. 70–3.

—— 'T. S. Eliot', *Poetry*, 10 (Aug. 1917), 264–71; repr. in Grant (ed.), *T. S. Eliot: The Critical Heritage*, i. 75–80.

—— 'A Retrospect', 1918, repr. in *Literary Essays of Ezra Pound*, ed. T. S. Eliot (Westport, Conn.: Greenwood, 1968).

[——] *The Letters of Ezra Pound 1907–1941*, ed. D. D. Paige (New York: Haskell House, 1974).

[——] *Pound/The Little Review: The Letters of Ezra Pound to Margaret Anderson: The 'Little Review' Correspondence*, ed. Thomas L. Scott, Melvin J. Friedman, and Jackson R. Bryer (New York: New Directions, 1988).

[—— and FORD, F. M.], *Pound/Ford: The Story of a Literary Friendship: The Correspond-ence between Ezra Pound and Ford Madox Ford and their Writings about Each Other*, ed. Brita Lindberg-Seyersted (New York: New Directions, 1982).

[—— and SHAKESPEAR, DOROTHY], *Ezra Pound and Dorothy Shakespear: Their Letters 1909–1914*, ed. Omar Pound and A. Walton Litz (New York: New Directions, 1984).

PRINCE, MORTON, *The Unconscious: The Fundamentals of Human Personality Normal and Abnormal* (New York: Macmillan, 1914).

Unsigned review of *Prufrock and Other Observations*, *New Statesman*, 9 (18 Aug. 1917), 477; repr. in Grant (ed.), *T. S. Eliot: The Critical Heritage*, i. 75.

PYKETT, LYN, *Engendering Fictions: The English Novel in the Early Twentieth Century* (London: Edward Arnold, 1995).

RAIKES, ELIZABETH, *Dorothea Beale of Cheltenham* (1908; 2nd edn. London: Constable, 1910).

RAITT, SUZANNE, *Vita and Virginia: The Work and Friendship of V. Sackville-West and Virginia Woolf* (Oxford: Oxford University Press, 1993).

—— and TATE, TRUDI (eds.), *Women's Fiction and the Great War* (Oxford: Clarendon Press, 1997).

RAPP, DEAN, 'The Early Discovery of Freud by the British General Educated Public, 1912–1919', *Journal of the Society for the Social History of Medicine*, 3 (Aug. 1990), 217–43.

RAUCH, ANGELIKA, 'The *Trauerspiel* of the Prostituted Body, or Woman as an Allegory of Modernity', *Cultural Critique*, 10 (Fall 1988), 77–8.

RIBOT, THÉODULE, *Heredity: A Psychological Study of its Phenomena, Laws, Causes, and Consequences*, no translator named (London: Henry S. King, 1875).

[RICHARDSON, DOROTHY], *Windows on Modernism: Selected Letters of Dorothy Richardson*, ed. Gloria Fromm (Athens, Ga.: University of Georgia Press, 1995).

RICHTER, MELVIN, *The Politics of Conscience: T. H. Green and his Age* (London: Weidenfeld and Nicolson, 1964).

RIGNALL, JOHN, 'Benjamin's *Flâneur* and the Problem of Realism', in A. Benjamin (ed.), *Problems of Modernity*, 112–21.

RIVIERE, JOAN, 'Womanliness as Masquerade', 1929, in Victor Burgin, James Donald, and Cora Kaplan (eds.), *Formations of Fantasy* (London: Methuen, 1986), 35–44.

ROHE, ALICE, 'Anne Nichols makes the World Safe for Literature', *Morning Telegraph* (8 June 1924), 1, 3.

ROSE, JACQUELINE, *The Haunting of Sylvia Plath* (London: Virago, 1991).

ROTHENSTEIN, WILLIAM, *Men and Memories: Recollections, 1872–1938*, ed. Mary Iago (Columbia, Mo.: University of Missouri Press, 1978).

SAMUELS, ANDREW, SHORTER, BANI, and PLAUT, FRED, *A Critical Dictionary of Jungian Analysis* (London: Routledge, 1986).

SCHENK, CELESTE M., 'Charlotte Mew (1870–1928)', in Scott (ed.), *Gender of Modernism*, 316–21.

SCHREINER, OLIVE, 'Woman and War', *Woman at Home*, 66 (Jan. 1915), 556–9.

—— *Woman and Labour* (1911; repr. London: Virago, 1978).

SCHWEGLER, ALBERT, *Handbook of the History of Philosophy*, trans. James Hutchison Stirling (1847; 7th edn. Edinburgh: Edmonston, 1879).

SCOTT, BONNIE KIME (ed.), *The Gender of Modernism: A Critical Anthology* (Bloomington, Ind.: Indiana University Press, 1990).

SCOTT, C. A. D., 'The First International Club of Writers', *Literary Digest International Book Review*, 1 (Nov. 1923), 47, 54.

—— *From Four who are Dead* (London: Arrowsmith, 1926).

—— *Is This Wilson? Messages Accredited to Woodrow Wilson Received by Mrs C. A. Dawson Scott* (New York: Dutton, 1929).

SHARPE, ELLA FREEMAN, review of Julia Turner, *The Psychology of Self-Consciousness*, *International Journal of Psychoanalysis*, 6 (1925), 78–9.

—— *Collected Papers on Psycho-Analysis*, ed. Marjorie Brierley, introd. Ernest Jones (1950; repr. New York: Brunner/Mazel, 1978).

SHILLITO, ELIZABETH H., *Dorothea Beale* (London: Society for the Propagation of Christian Knowledge, 1920).

SHORTER, CLEMENT, *Charlotte Brontë and her Circle* (1896; 2nd edn. London: Hodder and Stoughton, 1908).

—— *Charlotte Brontë and her Sisters* (London: Hodder and Stoughton, 1905).

—— (ed.), *Complete Works of Emily Brontë*, i. *Poetry* (London: Hodder and Stoughton, 1910).

SHOWALTER, ELAINE, *A Literature of their Own: British Women Novelists from Brontë to Lessing* (1977; rev. edn. London: Virago, 1982).

—— *The Female Malady: Women, Madness and English Culture 1830–1980* (1985; London: Virago, 1987).

—— *Sexual Anarchy: Gender and Culture at the Fin de Siècle* (New York: Viking, 1990).

SIDIS, BORIS, *The Psychology of Suggestion: A Research into the Subconscious Nature of Man and Society* (1898; repr. New York: D. Appleton, 1920).

SIME, JAMES, *Life of Johann Wolfgang Goethe* (London: Walter Scott, 1888).

SLEE, PETER, 'The H. M. Gwatkin Papers', *Transactions of the Cambridge Bibliographical Society*, 8 (1982), 279–83.

SMART, CAROL, *Regulating Womanhood: Historical Essays on Marriage, Motherhood and Sexuality* (London: Routledge, 1992).

SMITH, HELEN ZENNA, *'Not So Quiet . . .'—Stepdaughters of War* (London: Albert E. Marriott, 1930).

SPENCER, HERBERT, *The Principles of Psychology* (London: Gougman, Brown, Green, and Longmans, 1855).

—— *First Principles* (London: Williams and Norgate, 1863).

—— *The Principles of Biology*, 2 vols. (London and Edinburgh: Williams and Norgate, 1864).

SPINOZA, BENEDICT DE, *Ethics*, ed. and trans. Edwin Curley (1994; repr. Harmondsworth: Penguin, 1996).

SPIVAK, GAYATRI CHAKRAVORTY, 'Three Women's Texts and a Critique of Imperialism', in Gates (ed.), *'Race', Writing, and Difference*, 262–80.

STUBBINGS, FRANK, *Forty-Nine Lives: An Anthology of Portraits of Emmanuel Men* (Cambridge: Emmanuel College, 1983).

SULLOWAY, FRANK J., *Freud, Biologist of the Mind: Beyond the Psychoanalytic Legend* (New York: Basic Books, 1979).

SURETTE, LEON, *The Birth of Modernism: Ezra Pound, T. S. Eliot, W. B. Yeats, and the Occult* (Montreal and Kingston: McGill-Queen's University Press, 1993).

SWINBURNE, ALGERNON CHARLES, *A Note on Charlotte Brontë* (1894; new edn. New York: Haskell House, 1970).

SWINNERTON, FRANK, *The Georgian Literary Scene: A Panorama* (London: Hutchinson, 1935).

TATE, TRUDI (ed.), *Women, Men and the Great War* (Manchester: Manchester University Press, 1995).

—— *Modernism, History and the First World War* (Manchester: Manchester University Press, 1998).

TENNYSON, ALFRED, *The Poetical Works of Tennyson, Cambridge Edition*, ed. G. Robert Stange (Boston: Houghton Mifflin, 1974), 27.

The Thirteen Principal Upanishads translated from the Sanskrit, ed. and introd. Robert Ernest Hume (1877; rev. edn. Oxford: Oxford University Press, 1931).

THURSTAN, VIOLETTA, *Field Hospital and Flying Column: Being the Journal of an English Nursing Sister in Belgium and Russia* (London: Putnam, 1915).

TROTTER, DAVID, 'Gold standards: Money in Edwardian Fiction', *Critical Quarterly*, 30 (Spring 1988), 22–35.

TROTTER, DAVID, 'Edwardian Sex Novels', *Critical Quarterly*, 31 (Spring 1989), 92–106.

TROTTER, W. *Instincts of the Herd in Peace and War* (New York: Macmillan, 1915).

TURNER, JULIA, *The Psychology of Self-Consciousness* (London: Kegan Paul, Trench, Trübner and Co., 1923).

—— *The Dream on the Anxiety Hypothesis* (London: Kegan Paul, Trench, Trübner and Co., 1923).

—— *Human Psychology as Seen through the Dream* (London: Kegan Paul, Trench, Trübner and Co., 1924).

TYLEE, CLAIRE M., *The Great War and Women's Consciousness: Images of Militarism and Womanhood in Women's Writings, 1914–1964* (London: Macmillan, 1990).

TYNAN, KATHARINE, *Twenty-Five Years: Reminiscences* (London: John Murray, 1913).

—— *The Middle Years* (London: Constable, 1916).

UNDERHILL, EVELYN, *The Grey World* (London: Heinemann, 1904).

—— *The Column of Dust* (London: Methuen, 1909).

—— *Mysticism: A Study in the Nature and Development of Man's Spiritual Consciousness* (London: Methuen, 1911).

—— *The Mystic Way: A Psychological Study in Christian Origins* (London: Dent, 1913).

—— *The Letters of Evelyn Underhill*, ed. Charles Williams (1943; repr. London: Darton, Longman and Todd, 1991).

WALKER, JANE H., *A Handbook for Mothers* (London: Longman, Green and Co., 1893).

WARD, MARY, 'Introduction' to Charlotte Brontë, *Shirley* (London: Harper's, 1899).

WAUGH, ARTHUR, 'The New Poetry', *Quarterly Review* (Oct. 1916), 226; repr. in Grant (ed.), *T. S. Eliot: The Critical Heritage*, i. 67–9.

WEES, WILLIAM C., *Vorticism and the English Avant-Garde* (Manchester: Manchester University Press, 1972).

WESTCOTT, BROOKE FOSS, *An Introduction to the Study of the Gospels* (1851; 7th edn. London: Macmillan, 1888).

WHARTON, EDITH, *A Son at the Front* (London: Macmillan, 1923).

[——] *The Letters of Edith Wharton*, ed. R. W. B. and Nancy Lewis (New York: Scribner, 1988).

WILDE, OSCAR, 'The Sphinx without a Secret: An Etching', in *Complete Shorter Fiction*, ed. Isobel Murray (Oxford: Oxford University Press, 1980), 53–8.

—— *The Artist as Critic: Critical Writings of Oscar Wilde*, ed. Richard Ellmann (Chicago: Chicago University Press, 1969).

WILHELM, J. J., *Ezra Pound in London and Paris 1908–1925* (University Park, Pa.: Pennsylvania State University Press, 1990).

WILLIAMS, RAYMOND, *Modern Tragedy* (Stanford, Calif.: Stanford University Press, 1966).

WOHL, ROBERT, *The Generation of 1914* (Cambridge, Mass.: Harvard University Press, 1979).

WOLFF, JANET, 'The Invisible *Flâneuse*: Women and the Literature of Modernity', in Benjamin, *Problems of Modernity*, 141–56.

WOOLF, VIRGINIA, 'Modern Fiction' (1925), repr. in Scott (ed.), *Gender of Modernism*, 628–33.

—— *To the Lighthouse* (1927; new edn. ed. Margaret Drabble, Oxford: Oxford University Press, 1992).

—— *The Flight of the Mind: The Letters of Virginia Woolf*, i. *1888–1912*, ed. Nigel Nicolson and Joanne Trautmann (London: Chatto and Windus, 1975).

WORDSWORTH, WILLIAM, 'Three years she grew in sun and shower', 1799, in *Wordsworth: Poetical Works*, ed. Ernest de Selincourt (London: Oxford University Press, 1936), 148.

WYLIE, I. A. R., *My Life with George: An Unconventional Autobiography* (New York: Random House, 1940).

YOUNG-EISENDRATH, POLLY, and DAWSON, TERENCE (eds.), *The Cambridge Companion to Jung* (Cambridge: Cambridge University Press, 1997).

INDEX

—